To a
good friend
Carl

George Stankevich

Stormy Genius

Books by Richard Rashke

The Killing of Karen Silkwood
Escape from Sobibor
Stormy Genius: The Life of Aviation's Maverick, Bill Lear

Stormy Genius

The Life of Aviation's Maverick, Bill Lear

Richard Rashke

Houghton Mifflin Company
Boston

Library of Congress Cataloging in Publication Data

Rashke, Richard L.
  Stormy genius.

  Bibliography: p.
  Includes index.
  1. Lear, William Powell, 1902–1978. 2. Aeronautics—
United States—Biography. I. Title.
TL540.L364R37   1985   629.13′0092′4 [B]   85-8078
ISBN 0-395-35372-6

Printed in the United States of America

P   10   9   8   7   6   5   4

To Don

Special Acknowledgment

Pat Lear collaborated with me in the research of this book, which was suggested by Marilyn Solarz. Without Pat Lear's promised help, I would not have undertaken such a massive project. She shared her extensive file of newspaper and magazine articles about her father as well as her photograph albums and personal notes. She conducted several interviews used in preparing this book and helped me sort through the Lear Archives in Stead, Nevada. She also made arrangements for me to interview several important sources.

Contents

Stormy Genius

Prologue

THEY ALL SAID it was the perfect sendoff, just the way he would have wanted it. Big and serious, but with a touch of Broadway. His ashes rested in an urn next to his picture. Silver hair parted and swept back in a wave, every strand in place. Blue eyes looking into the future, jaw jutting forward ever so slightly, determined but not aggressive. A scar on the chin of his pudgy face. The way he wanted to be remembered.

Moya wore white, as if to prove his funeral was not a sad occasion. But inside she was close to despair. At first she had planned to take her own life. What finally made her decide to live was the airplane he had left on the drawing board and his last request of her. His wife for thirty-six years, she had, more often than not, held him together. Even her friends could not fathom her devotion or how it had survived his constant philandering.

Although she knew him as no one else did, even Moya found it difficult to understand how he could be so brilliant, creative, and self-confident, yet so driven and insecure. In the end, she stopped trying to figure it out and just accepted him. Now, the overflow crowd and the stacks of telegrams, including condolences from President Jimmy Carter and former President Gerald R. Ford, gave her strength.

Sitting in the front row of the church and sobbing almost uncontrollably was his son John. Most who knew the Lears were surprised at John's emotion, for he and his father had fought constantly. Even though Lear had threatened to get even with his son in the end — and he did — it was John he asked for as he lay dying.

Mary Louise sat nearby. The oldest of his seven children from four marriages, she barely knew her father. She had been caught in the middle of a painful divorce, an episode he was so ashamed of once he matured that he successfully hid it from his friends and the media. Close by were his other children — Bill, Pat, Shanda, David, and Tina. Like Moya, they all had paid a price for his fame and success.

Filling the church were those who had known or worked for him as far back as the early 1930s, when he gave up a promising career in radio engineering to chase a dream to build airplanes. In the back dressed in overalls was an old barnstorming pilot from the early days. When he began playing a sad tune on his harmonica, security guards ushered him out.

There were dozens of engineers who had worked with him on radios, aircraft instruments, steam cars and buses, and airplanes. Even though they had hated him sometimes for the unfair way he had treated them, they had long since forgiven him, recognizing that he had given them the chance to help make aviation history. Above all, they respected him. With only a grade school education, he had patented more than 150 inventions and designs in electronics and aerodynamics. His Lear Jet was hanging from the ceiling of the Smithsonian's National Air and Space Museum. He had received a string of awards ranging from Engineer of the Year to the Cresson Medal of the Franklin Institute of Philadelphia, from honorary doctorates to an honorary fellowship in the American Institute of Aeronautics and Astronautics. Soon he would be elected to the Aviation Hall of Fame, a pilot and inventor who had done more in his unorthodox way to make the skies safe than any single man of his era.

The media were there, too, as if it were another Bill Lear event. Beginning with a *Newsweek* story in 1935 and continuing in such publications as *Esquire,* the *Saturday Evening Post, Playboy,* and *Fortune,* reporters had created a legend that he had carefully cultivated. "King Lear," they had dubbed him. "Aviation's Stormy Genius" . . . "Wonderful Wizard" . . . "Inventor of the Impossible" . . . "Living Legend."

Missing was Bob Cummings, who had once agreed to portray

him in a Columbia Pictures production, *The Honor and the Glory.*
As much as he wanted Hollywood to immortalize him, he never
let the movie project get off the ground. He refused to release
his rights because the script called for a plane carrying his autopilot to crash. He would not allow anyone to make his instrument a villain.

Although Lear had observed no formal religion, a Mormon
bishop delivered the eulogy.

As friends and family poured out of church after the service,
three Lear Jets screamed by overhead. Two peeled off while the
one in the middle rolled high in the clear sky above Reno,
breaking every FAA rule in the book just as Lear had done so
often.

"Good-bye, Dad," Tina shouted.

There was hardly a dry eye.

Part One

Learning to Fly

1

WHEN THE "FLAMING COFFINS" began landing at Grant Park along the Chicago lakefront in the summer of 1919, their plywood pouches filled with canvas mailbags, Willy Lear was waiting to meet them.

He was a seventeen-year-old tinkerer and dreamer who had read every Tom Swift adventure story and Horatio Alger rags-to-riches book in the library. With a round face and soft blue eyes that sparkled when he was excited, he was a curious boy, fascinated by airplanes and radios. He had dropped out of Englewood High School after six weeks of classes because he couldn't learn airplane mechanics there and thought he knew more about radios than his teachers.

Self-confident to the point of being cocky, Willy Lear had talked his way into the Grant Park hangar. Soon, he quit his job monitoring electric generators in a tannery powerhouse and became a volunteer grease monkey, wrangling an occasional death-defying ride in a mail plane.

By this time the Aerial Mail Service, which had begun in May 1918, had three routes: Washington–New York, Cleveland–New York, and Chicago–Cleveland. The airmail delivery system was still rather primitive. On the Cleveland–Chicago run, for example, mail from the morning mail train was loaded into a plane and flown to Chicago in time for the last delivery of the day, cutting sixteen hours off the usual delivery time. The mail planes carried no gyro compass to help the pilot keep the plane on course, no turn-and-bank, and no radio. Besides an ignition switch and an air speed indicator, the instrument panel had a water temperature gauge, an altimeter more sensitive to temperature changes inside the open cockpit than to altitude, a tachometer to measure the revolutions of the engine, and a magnetic Boy Scout compass that oscillated all the way from north to south when the air was rough.

Without flight maps, weather stations, or beacons, pilots had to memorize towns, rivers, barns, even outhouses along the route, so they wouldn't get lost. The smart ones flew low enough to read the names of the towns on the train stations they passed. Wearing small round U.S. Aerial Mail Service badges, they were authorized to stop the train in order to pick up their mail if they were forced to land in a field near the tracks. In spite of the obstacles, 96.5 percent of the flights delivered the mail.

There was plenty of work in the Grant Park hangar for a volunteer grease monkey that summer. The Aerial Mail Service used British de Havilland DH-4s, which the Army Air Service had gladly donated to the Post Office Department after the Armistice. With their two wings separated by wooden struts and braced by wires stretched diagonally to form an *X*, the biplanes always needed repair. The wooden longerons that held the fuselage together were as frail as broomsticks. And, wing to tail, the DH-4 was wrapped in linen painted green with a tasty dope. The pilot often returned to a pasture after a forced landing to find a cow munching on the lower wing.

A twelve-cylinder, 400-horsepower Liberty engine powered the DH-4. Its mounts were made of wood, and the constant vibration frequently drove the bolts right through the frame, leaving the engine floating free. The Liberty had twenty-seven pieces of water hose held together by fifty-seven clamps that had a nasty habit of coming loose during flight, allowing water to leak, heating up the engine, and forcing the pilot to land on the nearest open spot.

The DH-4 landing gear was so poorly designed that the axles sheared off on just about any kind of landing but an eggshell, causing the plane to skid on its lower wing. There were so many torn, warped, and broken wings that the Aerial Service ran out of spares; as a result, nearly every DH-4 flew with the top wing only. The wheels were so small that a bumpy landing either tipped the plane onto its nose or caused the struts to pop out. The oil line sat outside the crankcase, exposed to extreme changes in temperature that created condensation on the tube as the pilot sliced through the clouds into subzero weather. The line would freeze, stopping the engine in flight.

As if all that weren't bad enough, the fuel tank sat behind the cockpit. If the plane crashed, gas spurted on the pilot's back, and if he couldn't scramble out before the fuel on the hot Liberty engine ignited, his chance of survival was slim. Pilots, who called the DH-4s flaming coffins, were getting killed almost as fast as the Post Office could hire them. But flying the mail route was exciting and the pay, outstanding. Pilots waited in line to replace those who had died in action.

The excitement Willy Lear felt around those airmail pilots stayed with him for the rest of his life. They were sky soldiers of fortune, World War I veterans and crazy kids who, like the Wright brothers, had built their own planes in barns and taught themselves how to fly. A hard-drinking, womanizing, flamboyant bunch. Their pay increased after every thirty hours in the air, so with pockets full of cash, they got drunk at bars in the Loop, roamed Broadway, or visited burlesque houses in Washington and Baltimore. They were old-fashioned pilots who flew by the seat of their pants because there was no other way. They learned to listen to the sound of the wing wires. If they heard a shrill whistle, they were flying too fast; a whisper, they were close to a stall. They had a camaraderie born of shared dangers and experiences hard to explain to the land lover. And their friendship and warmth extended to the hangar grease monkeys as well.

Flying in the clouds was especially dangerous. Without even an artificial horizon to tell him he was level with the ground, the pilot could easily lose his sense of equilibrium and his plane would soon begin to turn into a graveyard spiral. Many pilots tried crude levels, like bobs on a string or half-full milk bottles, perched on the instrument board near the windshield, but the centrifugal force created by a turn or a spin rendered the gadgets useless. Most simply tried to develop a feel for staying in the clouds longer by reading the rocking and pull of the plane and the wind on their cheeks. And most of the time they failed. Of the first forty pilots hired by the Post Office, thirty-one were killed before the airmail service was briefly turned over to private airlines.

The danger didn't bother Willy Lear. On his first ride in a flaming coffin, he sat in front of the pilot in the plywood mail pouch; the plane made a hard landing and flipped onto its back. Willy landed on his head in the grass, shaken but not hurt, and more determined than ever to fly.

On the morning of July 22, 1919, Willy was puttering in the Grant Park hangar when the Goodyear blimp, *WingFoot Express,* landed on the field. The 186-foot-long dirigible had been built and assembled in the Goodyear plant in Akron, Ohio, and was moored at the White City amusement park. Goodyear was offering exhibition flights that day as a come-on, for it was planning a passenger service from Chicago to White City, just down the lake.

Besides Captain Jack Boettner, who had been a dirigible instructor during World War I, and two mechanics, *WingFoot* had room for two passengers. On its first flight that day, the blimp took up Goodyear brass; on the second, Army brass. On the third and final flight, it picked up Earl Davenport, the public relations director of the amusement park. This left one empty place, and Willy asked to have it. Captain Boettner agreed. But just before liftoff at four o'clock, E. H. Norton, a photographer with the morning *Herald and Examiner,* asked to join the crew. Naturally, Boettner bumped the boy, who slipped off his parachute and gave it to Norton.

The blimp rose to 1,200 feet over the Loop, where it hovered like a giant watermelon ready to burst. Shortly before five o'clock, Captain Boettner began to feel intense heat. He turned to look at the gas bag in the rear and saw flames. "Over the top, everyone!" he shouted.

Boettner waited until the photographer and the mechanics jumped. He called to Davenport to leap, but the PR man clung to the side of the blimp. Boettner left him hanging there and bailed out.

While Willy Lear and thousands of Chicagoans watched from the streets below, the chute of one of the mechanics caught fire.

Flames spurted from the gas bag. *WingFoot* buckled, shivered, and plunged straight down through the skylight of the Illinois Trust and Savings Bank on the corner of La Salle Street and Jackson Boulevard, where two hundred clerks, mostly women, were finishing up for the day. When the blimp hit the rotunda floor, the two tanks exploded, spraying gas over a hundred and fifty workers. It was thirty minutes before firemen could enter the bank. They found eleven persons dead and twenty-seven severely burned.

The mechanic in the flaming chute followed the blimp through the skylight and hit the marble floor. Captain Boettner's parachute landed on a nearby office building, the other mechanic's on the street. Both men were unharmed. Photographer Norton landed on the street in a partially opened chute. He died the next day.

Willy Lear went back to a full-time paying job. But it wasn't the near misses that scared him away from Grant Park. It was his mother.

To Willy Lear, Gertrude Elizabeth Powell was an awesome woman, big-boned, with wild red hair and a sensuous face. She was born in 1884 in Barry, Illinois, thirty miles east of Hannibal, Missouri. Her father, William, owned the Powell Cigar Store on Main Street and the factory above it. His wife Elizabeth died shortly after giving birth to Gertrude, their first child, and he remarried. But Gertrude and her stepmother could not get along. When Gertrude was ready for school, her father sent her to live with her mother's sister in Dubuque. Gertrude grew into such a rebellious teenager that her aunt put her in a special school; it is not clear whether it was a boarding school for girls or a reformatory.

How she met Reuben Lear of Hannibal, Missouri, is also not clear. He was a tall, thin carpenter with a finely chiseled face, a strong jaw, big dreams, but little ambition. After their marriage in Quincy, Illinois, in September 1901, Ruby and Gertrude moved into his parents' home in Hannibal. He was twenty-three years old and she was eighteen. Their son, William Powell Lear, was born on June 26, 1902.

When Willy was still a baby, Gertrude started walking out on

Ruby. She'd leave with the child for a time, then write to Ruby for train fare home. Sometimes she came back. Most of the time she just kept the money. Until 1908, when her son turned six, she lived with a series of men. Then she moved in permanently with Otto Kirmse, a Dubuque lather with a steady job and a good salary. The couple was ill matched in almost every way. She was heavyset and bossy; he, thin and gentle, "the most generous and kindest man you'd ever know," as a friend described him. Although Gertrude constantly picked on him, Otto rarely complained. In 1913, they moved to Chicago and were married the following spring, when Willy was almost eleven.

Gertrude's attitude toward her son was unpredictable. One day she pampered him, told him how proud she was of him, and made him feel special and important. The next day she flew into a rage and beat him until Otto pleaded with her to stop. After such verbal and physical abuse, the boy felt worthless and guilty.

Willy loved to tinker, and by the time he was twelve he had already built a radio set with earphones, mastered Morse code, and pieced together a crude telegraph with a twenty-five-cent Galena crystal and storage batteries made of old Mason jars. Whenever he bought a radio part, Gertrude accused him of wasting money. Then, when he stopped working on his project to please her, she scolded him for not being able to finish anything. "You'll end up a good-for-nothing, just like your father," she said. She told him this so often that he began believing her.

Willy took refuge from his mother in the Hiram Kelly Library, near his home on West Sixty-fourth Street, where he read every book he could find on electricity, and in the basement of a friend whose father worked for a utility company. There he played for hours with electrical odds and ends — Leyden jars, helixes, coils, condensers, batteries, and a spark gap that filled the cellar with the smell of ozone.

There was more to Willy's relationship with his mother than just the emotional and physical abuse. Until he was eighteen, she perched on the rim of the bathtub while he sat on the toilet finishing his bowel movement and brought him fresh underwear while he was bathing. As a reborn Christian, she was so embarrassed over "living in sin" with Otto that she constantly told Willy that girls were evil and that if she ever caught him with one, there'd be trouble. Gertrude meant it. One day, when Willy was in the sixth grade, she spotted him giving a girl a ride on the handlebars of his bicycle. When he came home for supper, she beat him with a broom handle so savagely that Otto had to step between them. Then she took the bike away to punish him for playing with girls. When she thought Willy was old enough to know about life, she warned him that marriage was only a prison of screaming children and unwashed diapers.

Clutching her Bible, Gertrude attended religious revivals all over Chicago and distributed religious pamphlets on the streets. Her fanaticism rubbed off on Willy, who began haunting the Moody Bible Institute, attending church and classes most of Sunday, then returning to meetings on Wednesday, choir on Thursday, and the Friendship Club on Friday nights to please her. Despite such activities, he was a lonely child with few friends.

After he dropped out of high school, Willy's relationship with Gertrude took a new twist. She made him bring his weekly wages to her and gave him pocket money. When he began quitting jobs because he was bored, she became angry. She wanted him to be a hard worker with a steady job who brought his pay envelope home every Friday afternoon, like Otto. But Willy wanted money and fame, like Alger's heroes, and he knew that being pinned to a monotonous but safe job was not the way to get them. When he told his mother his dreams, she scolded, "Why do you have to be so different?"

When Gertrude finally found out Willy was working for nothing at Grant Park, she ordered him to find a paying job. He obeyed. He could have moved in with his father, who was living in Tulsa and would have welcomed him, but he stayed with his mother. He seemed powerless to break her hold on him.

For the next year, as he moved from job to job, Willy continued to visit Grant Park every chance he could without his mother's finding out. When he managed to save $10, he went to Ashburn Field, a forty-acre patch at Eighty-fifth and Cicero, and bought a fifteen-minute lesson in a Jenny from Elmer Partridge, who managed the field.

When he was eighteen years old, Willy finally recognized that if he was ever going to be somebody, he'd have to break from

Gertrude. Away from her, he felt there wasn't a thing he couldn't do. Near her, he felt almost helpless.

Willy saved a few dollars, packed some clothes, and sneaked away early one morning. To punish his mother, he didn't even leave a note. His plan was simple: like the hero of a Horatio Alger story, he'd work his way to Hollywood, where he'd become a rich movie star. And until he did, he would never tell Gertrude where he was.

2

CHASING THE WHEAT harvest west, Willy Lear found himself stranded in Denver in September 1920, broke and out of work. Determined not to ask his mother for help, he joined the Navy. He was sent to the Great Lakes Training Station just north of Chicago, right back home, to study radio as an apprentice seaman. Lonely and frustrated, he phoned Gertrude, who rushed out to Great Lakes on the first visiting Sunday in October with a bag of cookies and cakes. Happy to find her son alive and well, she didn't even scold him for running away.

After Willy completed his basic training in November, the Navy kept him at Great Lakes as a wireless instructor; but he soon grew bored teaching elementary radio and saw no future in the armed services. When the Navy announced it was trimming its rolls, Willy was the first in line to request an early discharge. On March 1, 1921, after only six months in uniform, he left Great Lakes, moved back in with Gertrude and Otto, and took a job as a Western Union teletype operator. He was no longer determined, as he put it, "to charge off by myself just to see whether or not I could fight my [own] battles."

Gertrude's father died suddenly in the spring of 1922, leaving her his hundred-acre wheat and corn farm in Plainville, Illinois, a few miles north of Barry, and a little more than $8,000 in cash, a small fortune at that time. She and Otto moved to Plainville that summer. Willy had already quit his job with Western Union and was hanging around Grant Park again. But the pull of security was stronger than the urge to fly. He followed Gertrude to the farm.

One day as he passed the Reed Motor Supply Company at 705 Maine Street in Quincy, just twenty miles down the road from Plainville, Willy spotted some home radio parts in the window. Sensing an opportunity, he walked into the store and told the owner, Clifford Reed, that he was a radio engineer and wanted to be his radio salesman.

Although Reed was not impressed with the looks of the young man — Willy wore ill-fitting clothes that didn't match and was badly in need of a haircut — he hired him on the strength of his honest, cherubic face and confident enthusiasm. Willy moved from the farm into Quincy.

Nineteen twenty-two was an exciting year in the history of radio. Two years earlier, on November 2, a Westinghouse engineer named Dr. Frank Conrad decided to broadcast the Warren Harding–James Cox election returns with his 50-watt transmitter from a wooden shack on top of Westinghouse's tallest building in Pittsburgh. Conrad had no idea if anyone would be listening on a crystal set, for no one even knew how many home-made sets were out there. Nevertheless, he began at six in the evening and broadcast straight through until noon the following day, playing music from a Victrola between election results. Afterward, letters poured in, and Conrad began the first regularly broadcast radio program in the country on KDKA, every night from eight-thirty to nine-thirty.

Until June 1921, KDKA was alone on the airwaves. Then came nine more stations, the earliest of which were WBZ in Springfield, Massachusetts, and WJZ in Newark. The first microphones were huge, morning-glory-shaped horns up to eight feet long. The broadcaster would shout into the big end, sometimes sticking his head halfway down just to be certain he would be heard. If he wanted to play phonograph music, he'd place the smaller Victrola horn against the microphone horn. Americans went radio crazy. Soon after KDKA began broadcasting regularly, the number of crystal sets doubled, from an estimated 30,000 to 60,000. In response, Westinghouse quickly brought out a cabinet model crystal set, the Aeriola, Jr., which sold for $25.50 with headphones. It was a smashing success.

By the time Willy Lear went to work for Clifford Reed, there were an estimated 1.5 million sets (three out of four homemade) and almost six hundred radio stations. Even Quincy had two. Radio manufacturers couldn't meet the demand for parts and fully assembled crystal sets. "The rate of increase in the number of people who spend at least part of their evening in listening is almost incomprehensible," the editors of *Radio Broadcast* wrote in June 1922. "To those who have recently tried to purchase receiving equipment some idea of this increase has undoubtedly occurred as they stood perhaps in the fourth or fifth row at the radio counter waiting their turn, only to be told when they finally reached the counter that they might place an order and it would be filled when possible . . . The movement is probably not even at its height. It is still growing in some kind of geometrical progression."

When RCA began marketing its new vacuum tubes (UV-199 and UV-201A) in 1922, it was the death knell of the crystal sets. Led by RCA and Westinghouse, radio manufacturers rushed into making one-tube, battery-operated sets with names like Mu-Rad, Ace, Radak, Crosely, Fada, Paragon, Grebe, Federal, Tuska, Kennedy, and Amrad. Most of these companies would go bankrupt during the Depression seven years later. In 1922, their table model sets, like the popular RCA Radiola, sold for between $50 and $100, and their consoles, like the RCA Aeriola Grand, for between $400 and $500 with batteries and headphones. When Lear began his new job, the fully assembled tube sets were just beginning to hit the market, and most stores like Reed Motor Supply Company couldn't get them.

As a radio salesman, Lear had to help customers pick the right parts for their crystal sets or the one-tube radios they wanted to try to build for themselves; he also repaired sets. He designed his own tube radios in the second story of a carriage house owned by A. D. Weis at Twentieth and Maine, where he also lived. The Weises gave Lear the one room rent free on the condition that he'd teach their son, Henry, how to build radios. One of Lear's early customers, for whom he designed and built a set, was Julius Buerkin, a wealthy building contractor in Quincy.

Spotting the potential in Lear and in the infant radio business, Buerkin suggested that he and Lear go into business together. Buerkin would finance the company and be its president; Lear would provide the know-how and run the business.

In November 1922, Willy Lear opened shop with a simple ad in the *Quincy Daily Herald:* "QRL — Quincy Radio Laboratories — 645 Hampshire." He hired Elmer Wavering, a shy, thin lad with a quick mind and nimble fingers, to wire single-tube radios on evenings and weekends. Wavering had just graduated from grade school and had spent the summer with his older sister, the secretary to the director of the Fitzsimmons Veterans Hospital in Denver. Several times a week, Elmer would work with a couple of patients who had radio fever. Besides running their own little radio station, DN4, they had access to a warehouse filled with war surplus radio parts — variometers, condensers, coils, PT-1 Western Electric tubes. The patients taught Elmer how to build a one-tube radio from scratch, and before he left Denver for Quincy High School, they gave him a set as a present.

After reading QRL's ad in the *Daily Herald* for a part-time radio engineer, Wavering stopped by to see Lear in the shop on the corner of Seventh and Hampshire streets. That Wavering was only fourteen years old didn't seem to bother Lear. If a boy fresh out of grade school could wire sets, he'd get the job. Lear hired Wavering for $3.50 a week.

A typical home-built radio set in late 1922 was a box with a tuning dial and an on-off switch. It was powered by two batteries: an A, the size of a car battery, used for storage; and a B, the size of a medium cereal box, used to supply high voltage. Most people listened to the radio through headsets, but if they had a lot of money to spend, they could buy a horn-shaped loudspeaker.

Quincy Radio Laboratories was probably the most unusual radio store in the country. In the bay window — painted with the word RADIO in huge letters sliced by a lightning bolt — and in the long glass counter that lined the west wall of the store, Will Lear (everyone but his mother now called him Will) displayed the sets he had designed and built as well as every kind of part anyone could use. Customers could bring sets in for repair or order custom-built radios to meet their fancy. But what really made QRL different from Reed's store and the other two in Quincy that sold radio supplies was its basement workshop with a dozen six-foot-long benches equipped with work lights, pliers, wirecutters, drills, and soldering irons. Every evening and on weekends, customers could buy radio parts upstairs, rent a bench downstairs, and, under the supervision of Lear or Wavering, build their own radio receivers. The workshop was open from four or five in the afternoon until ten at night, and it took an average customer about a week to assemble a set.

Lear had designed a template out of stiff paper so that customers could trace the radio design, drill the holes for the tuner and the on-off switch in the black bakelite panels that would form the box, then fix the variometer, tube, condenser, and coil in the correct spots on the chassis. The parts were hooked together with size 14 copper wire the thickness of pencil lead. While Wavering was helping the customers or building sets to sell to Clifford Reed or to display in the store, Lear was redesigning and experimenting in an attempt to make his radios simpler and better.

Years later, Bill Lear loved to tell stories about how hard it was to sell a radio in 1922 to someone who had never heard one before. One day he was demonstrating a set when a catchy tune came over the air. The potential customer was delighted. "That's a wonderful song," he said when the vocalist finished. "Play it again."

Another time, he was showing a set to a half-deaf veteran with a new watch just before the ten o'clock time signal. "There'll be a series of short dashes," he explained to the vet. "At the beginning of the long dash, it will be exactly ten o'clock . . . Now listen for the tone . . . R-r-r-right now it's exactly ten."

"By gosh, you're right," the old-timer said. He was so surprised by the accuracy of the new-fangled radio machine that he bought a set then and there. Any machine as exact as his new watch, he figured, had to be a good buy.

To manage QRL, Lear hired Irving Johnson, a Swede whose father was caretaker of the Quincy cemetery. Lear and Johnson tinkered at their radios until late at night, then went to Johnson's home next to the graveyard for homemade bread and elderberry wine. Unlike cold and critical Gertrude, Mrs. Johnson was loving with her son, whom she affectionately called Yente (my little giant). In light of Gertrude's emotional abuse of her son, Irv Johnson was an important influence on Lear. You don't always have to be poor, the Swede would lecture Will. Rich men aren't necessarily smarter than poor ones, and you'll succeed if you're willing to throw the bull by the horns.

Away from Gertrude's nagging, Will began to blossom. His mind was jumping with ideas as he and Elmer were swept into the excitement of a new industry just learning to walk. The potential seemed limitless, and Quincy Radio Laboratories had to run to keep one step ahead of its competitors.

Shortly after QRL opened its doors, a company in Cincinnati came out with a do-it-yourself single-tube kit, the Harmony, with diagrams and instructions, parts, and panels with the holes already drilled into them. But the Harmony, which all but killed Lear's basement workshop and school, did not come with antennas. So QRL began designing and building diamond-shaped loop antennas that looked like kites and could stand on tabletops. The loops weren't as good as roof antennas, but they were cheaper than 100 feet of wire strung up the side of a house or between trees. Some of the innovations and designs Lear and Wavering created were clearly original, but QRL never filed for a single patent. Lear neither had the money nor was aware of how significant some of the QRL designs were.

On the heels of the do-it-yourself sets came the fully assembled one-, two-, then three-tube radios in cabinets with enough amplitude for loudspeakers. With names like Magnavox, Dictaphone, Vocarola, Telmacophone, and Audiola, the speakers were goose-necked or tuba-shaped horns that sat on the floor or on a stand near the radio and cost anywhere from $5 to $50. In 1922–1923 the quality was atrocious. The horns amplified music reasonably well but badly distorted the human voice.

In another attempt to compete, Quincy Radio Laboratories began offering home services long before anyone else, installing and repairing sets, building and hooking up roof antennas. And when radio parts stores began opening in the small towns nearby, Lear developed QRL into a parts distributorship, supplying stores within a fifty-mile radius. By 1924, there were fourteen hundred radio stations in the country, and one third of the money Americans would spend that year on furniture would go for radio receivers.

Right after Atwater-Kent came out with a five-tube radio set in a metal box that looked like a bread tin, Lear and Wavering began experimenting with a car radio. Although the metal of the box shielded the set to some extent from electrical interference, they still faced two serious problems: finding a way to install an antenna, and muffling the constant static caused by the car's motor and spark plugs.

Through trial and error, they solved the antenna problem by ripping out the upholstery in the roof of the car, cutting the chicken wire padding from the wooden frame, tying the wire back to the frame with silken cord, and running the antenna into the car to the radio, fully shielded. As long as the motor wasn't running, the radio worked beautifully, with the car battery serving as the A, or storage, battery and the B battery sitting on the floor behind the driver. But every time they turned the engine on, the ignition system created so much hum and static that they couldn't hear the music. Putting resistors on the spark plugs helped a bit, but not enough to make the radio practical. However, it did work well from lovers' lane in Riverview Park overlooking the Mississippi. On clear nights they could see fifteen miles into Missouri and reception was superb. High on the bluffs, radio shows from Quincy, Davenport, Des Moines, even KDKA Pittsburgh, came in clearly. Turning on the power without starting the engine, Lear and Wavering could treat the couples in the cars all around them to their favorite performer, Harry M. Snodgrass, "King of the Ivories," an inmate of the Missouri State Penitentiary in Jefferson City.

Lear's passion for flying did not cool while he was experimenting with radio. Quincy had a small airstrip in the early twenties, and every time Will heard an airplane, he jumped into the new Ford touring car he had bought and raced out to the hangar. Usually it was a barnstormer in a Jenny, offering rides for two or three dollars. Will would always go up.

It was an itinerant barnstormer who had given him his first plane ride near his grandfather's farm in Plainville when he was eleven. It was another barnstormer, Lincoln Beachey, who had sparked his interest in flying. Willy had seen Beachey perform when the Glenn Curtiss Flying Exhibition came to Dubuque in the summer of 1912. The daredevil pilot — some would argue the best in America — twisted and turned in the sky above the stadium at Nutwood Park, then climbed 7,500 feet, cut the engine of his biplane, and sent it into his famous "death-defying dive," landing on the grass inside the stadium. Willy had made up his mind then and there that he would be a pilot someday.

But that day was still years off as Lear struggled to make a name for himself and to support his new family.

3

WHEN WILL PROPOSED to Ethel Peterson in the fall of 1922 after a two-year courtship, she accepted eagerly. She was nineteen and Will had just turned twenty. He needed parental consent for a marriage license, but he didn't have the courage to ask Gertrude because he knew she'd bully him. She might even try to block the marriage, forcing him to wait until he was twenty-one, a whole year.

Will had met Ethel on a visiting day at the Great Lakes Training Station. A shy teenager with curly blond hair and a broad, warm smile, she weighed barely a hundred pounds. Her father had died of lung disease four years earlier, leaving eight children behind. Unable to hold the family together, her mother had sent the six youngest to an orphanage, keeping Ethel and her older sister Frances at home to work.

Soon after he proposed, Will sent Ethel a message at the Kirmse farm, where she was staying. He had a license, he said, and he had lined up a Presbyterian minister in Quincy for Monday, October 2; he would send a car for her, and she should try not to arouse Gertrude's suspicions. To get the license, he had lied about his age.

A secret wedding came as no surprise to Ethel, for Gertrude had tried to control the courtship from the beginning. She ordered her son to tell her where he was taking Ethel on each date and when he would be home. No matter what their plans, Gertrude wanted to approve them. Only once did Will try to defy her. But he and Ethel got only a few blocks from the house before Will turned around and went home.

Gertrude sulked when Will finally told her that he and Ethel had gotten married, but she adjusted quickly. Soon she was fawning over him again as if nothing had happened.

Will and Ethel rented a four-room flat on Eighteenth and Vermont Avenue, upstairs from Irv Johnson and his wife, La Verne. Ethel turned the apartment into a cozy home and rarely went to the radio store nearby. Will kept the financial details of his business to himself, as he would most of his life, giving her enough money to run the house. In the evenings while she prepared dinner, Will and Elmer puttered with radios or sat around discussing engineering ideas. Will and Ethel were happy together, even though their first child, William Powell Lear, Jr., died in his crib in January 1924, just five and a half months after his birth. He had been born with a malformed heart.

One day in the summer of 1924, Will came home from work and told Ethel that he had had a disagreement with Julius Buerkin and had sold his share of the business to his partner for $600. Even though she was pregnant again, Ethel was not deeply concerned. Will had always provided well for his family.

It is not clear why Lear broke with Buerkin, but it is safe to assume that he wanted to launch a risky financial project, which Buerkin opposed. Rather than back down, Lear sold out, as he would time and again throughout his life. The twenty-two-year-old Lear was soon in business for himself, repairing and designing radios, first in his living room, then in a rented basement shop downtown. A few months later, however, he came home early to tell Ethel they were broke. He hadn't paid his bills, he said, and had lost all his credit.

Will and Ethel packed what they could into their Ford and fled. They went first to Gertrude in Chicago, where Will was hoping to break into radio engineering with a large manufacturing company, then to Kansas City when he and his mother fought constantly, and finally to his widowed grandmother, Mary Lear, in Tulsa, where she and her husband had moved a quarter of a century earlier as homesteaders. Generous and openhearted, Mary Lear was already supporting Will's father, Ruby, who ran a small business hauling pipes to the oil rigs outside town. But he didn't make enough to pay room, board, and gas, and he was always borrowing money from her to fix his trucks.

If Mary Lear had any doubts about two more mouths at the dinner table in her rooming house, one look at Ethel — a tiny thing with a big stomach, clutching a suitcase tied with rope — was enough to dispel them.

"I just know Gertrude's been abusing you," she told Ethel. "Welcome home."

Mary Lear was a deeply religious woman and a long-standing member of the First Christian Church of Tulsa. When the church purchased radio station WLAL early in 1925, the Men's Club asked her grandson to "overhaul" the transmitter, to add "new apparatus" to make it one of the "most powerful in the entire Southwest," and to serve as the broadcast engineer for its Bible lessons, Sunday church services, and special programs. They offered Will $200 to rebuild the station and a small weekly fee to broadcast to an estimated 2,500 listeners. It was a temporary job, but it was far more challenging than selling and repairing radios in the hardware store where he was then working. Will went to work for the First Christian Church.

The idea of being on the air with all those people listening to him intrigued Will so much that he convinced the pastor of the church, Dr. Claude F. Hill, that he had to run test programs at night, just to make sure everything was in working order for the church broadcasts. Before long, and unknown to Dr. Hill, Will was the emcee of an early night show. (No local or federal agency controlled the airwaves then.) Will interviewed friends about current affairs or homespun topics, like how to train show horses, or invited them to play their guitars and sing.

One of his regular performers was Bob Ellis, a bright, skinny young man who played the clarinet, sax, and oboe and who, like Will, was a radio man. He had studied engineering at Washington University in St. Louis but was forced to drop out because of poor health. His father, Moses, was an oilman. Bob used to take Elmer and Will out to the Ellis oil lines, which lay like a ribbon across the fields. Because natural gas tends to condense in low spots along the pipeline, blocking the flow of the oil, pipefitters had built traps to collect the condensate. Bob would open the traps for Will and Elmer, who siphoned the gas into their car. They had the highest octane in town.

Ethel gave birth to her second child, Mary Louise, in January 1925, after twenty-two hours of labor without sedatives or anesthesia. She was so exhausted that she spent twelve days in the hospital and came home in an ambulance. The baby slept on a blanket on the floor because Ethel couldn't afford a crib, and she was sick off and on that winter with a stomach disorder. Although there were doctors' bills to pay and medicine and baby food to buy, Will seldom gave Ethel any money. It was so unlike him. When she pressed him, he became evasive.

"What about that two hundred dollars the church owes you?" she finally asked.

"I got it a long time ago," he told her, "but I spent it."

Ethel became frightened. She had never seen that shiftless, selfish side of Will's character before. Tensions in the Lear home mounted until Mary Lear stepped in. Before long, Will was giving Ethel five dollars a week for the baby; the first thing she bought was a crib on a fifty-cent-a-week installment plan.

Ethel still couldn't figure out what was happening to the rest of Will's income. He seemed to be doing radio work all over town. He wasn't renting a shop (he was using a room at the far end of the garage as his workshop), and he wasn't buying much radio equipment that she knew of. As far as she could tell, there was only one extravagance. Every time Will heard the barnstormers were in town, he'd drag Ethel out to the airstrip and coax her up into a Jenny or a Swallow.

It didn't take Ethel long to discover the culprit. A truck pulled up to the Lear home in the spring of 1925 and unloaded a mail order airplane kit for a one-seater Lincoln Sport, made by the Lincoln Aircraft Company. Building that airplane became Will's obsession. It was the first time in his life that anything had captured his imagination so completely, and the airplane's hold on him became absolute.

The kit came with a set of blueprints, sheets of plywood and tin, linen and wire, wheels, and a three-cylinder, 35-horsepower, air-cooled Anzani engine. Will didn't know how to fly yet; to him the Lincoln Sport was little more than a big, expensive model airplane. He planned to build it and watch someone else fly it. Then, someday, he'd learn to pilot it himself.

Will invited Elmer Wavering to Tulsa for the summer to help him cut, paste, and wire the plane together. They cleaned out a long narrow room in the shed where Ruby parked his trucks. One side became their radio repair shop; the other, their mechanical shop for the airplane. When they weren't fixing radios for pocket money, Will and Elmer worked on the airplane. They began building it in the backyard, cutting the ribs from plywood and the brackets from sheet metal with hacksaws, then welding the pieces in the shop. Sticks of wood, 12 to 20 feet long, became the longerons that formed the fuselage, which they covered with linen, then doped with banana oil to seal and stiffen the structure.

Will had heard that there were a lot of used six-cylinder Anzanis around, almost twice as powerful as the one in the kit, so he took on more radio work until he had saved enough money to buy one. The French had used Anzanis in their World War I trainers, on which hundreds of U.S. pilots had learned to fly before Glenn Curtiss opened his school. When the Anzani arrived, it was in poor condition. Fortunately, a neighbor had a well-equipped machine shop, so Will took the engine apart, cleaned it, and put in new bearings.

Before long, the neighbors began to complain. The noise in the evening they could bear, but not the smell of the dope, which hung in the sultry Tulsa summer air like exhaust and was sucked into homes through window fans. People couldn't sleep. When the police dropped by one evening to order Lear's plane out of town, Will proposed a compromise. He'd dope the airplane only during the day so there'd be no smell hanging around by nightfall. If people still complained, he promised the police, he'd stop working on it. More curious than angry, the neighbors allowed Will to continue. By the end of the summer, with Elmer working as a mailboy in the Empire Refineries by day and with Will by night, the biplane began to take shape. It filled Grandma Lear's backyard, its wings nearly brushing the fences.

The Lincoln had turned Will Lear into a different man. He worked long hours, forgot to eat, and began dreaming of the day when he would have his own airplane manufacturing company. He repaired or built radios only for enough money to pay Ethel her $5 a week and to buy odds and ends for the Lincoln Sport. And he began hanging out at the airport as he had done at Grant Park as a teenager.

Tulsa had two small private airstrips in 1925, and Will did odd jobs around the hangars just to be close to the ships and the pilots. He'd push the planes in and out and gas them, help the mechanics repair engines, and wait for a chance to talk to the airmen. He'd tell them about the Lincoln Sport he was building and try to mooch rides. There was so much oil money in Tulsa in the mid 1920s that the aircraft manufacturers, like Walter Beech, used to fly in at least once a week to demonstrate and sell planes built for short landings and takeoffs on the oilfields. Will introduced himself to Beech, and soon he was riding in Beech's airplane; they became lifelong friends.

One of the pilots Will met at the airfield was Irvin ("Woody") Woodring, who flew for one of the oil tycoons. Will bragged so much about the Lincoln Sport that Woody drove over to see it one day. He was curious about a radio repairman building an airplane in his backyard almost in the middle of town. The puddlejumper fascinated Woody so much that every time he set down in Tulsa, he dropped by to check on its progress. He'd sit in the open cockpit, play with the stick, order some adjustments, and give Will tips on construction and design.

That fall, both Will and Elmer, who had graduated from high school the previous spring, enrolled at Central High, a four-story English Renaissance building second only to New York City's largest school. Elmer, who had taken a commercial course in high school and needed extra credits before he could be accepted at college, finished the semester. Will lasted a month. For the better part of a year he had been trying to meet rich Tulsans in the hopes of finding another business partner like Julius Buerkin. When that plan failed, he went to school to meet the sons and daughters of the rich, who drove to Central High each morning in a different car. When they showed no interest in him, he dropped out.

Elmer found a job at Small's Radio Shop, repairing sets after school, and sent the money home to his mother for a college fund. But Will just couldn't settle down. He finished the Lincoln Sport late in the fall, then took it apart, piece by piece, and hauled it on Ruby's truck down Main Street and out to the airport. It was the first airplane actually built in Tulsa as far as anyone can recall.

By early winter, Will had pieced the Lincoln back together again, ready for Woody Woodring to test-fly it on his next trip into Tulsa. With Woody at the controls, the plane took off and managed to fly a few feet before it bounced back onto the runway like a huge piece of rubber. Unable to keep the machine in the air or to figure out why it wouldn't fly, Will hauled it back to town and stored it in a neighbor's garage, where it hung from the rafters like a giant discarded toy.

A great change had come over Will in the year he had lived in Tulsa. No longer interested in home radios, he became a freeloader at his grandmother's table, just like his father. When his airplane didn't fly the way he wanted it to, he lost interest in it as well. Broadcasting for WLAL had lost its novelty. He wanted fame and fortune, not a steady, boring job, but he couldn't see a way to get them.

More and more Will Lear began looking for a new challenge and he found one in Madeline Murphy.

On hot summer evenings after working on the Lincoln, Will would take Elmer to Doc Shackle's drugstore on South Main, just around the corner, for a malted milk or an ice cream soda. Will had an almost uncontrollable sweet tooth and couldn't resist chocolate.

Madeline Murphy was a cashier at Shackle's. Like Gertrude, she had had problems with her stepmother. A week before she turned fifteen, she ran away from home and married Roy Benson in El Dorado, Arkansas. They were divorced a year and a half later, in September 1924, and Madeline moved in with her sister Louise in Tulsa and took a job as an apprentice beauty technician while working the night shift at the drugstore. Tall, slim, and poised, with high cheekbones and lips that seemed to pout, Madeline had gentle eyes and a girlish giggle. Elmer liked her but was so bashful he didn't have the courage to ask for a date. Turning to Will for advice, he got a challenge instead. "You don't know the first thing about women," Lear told him. "I'll bet you a dollar I can get a date from her before you can."

At twenty-three, Will was a confident, handsome man with a boyish face and ruddy cheeks. He was a radio engineer and broadcaster, he told Madeline. He was building his own airplane and someday would have his own company. Would she like to go out with him?

One fall evening, Madeline let Will walk her home. She knew only that he was living with his grandmother in the big white rooming house at 1010 South Detroit. When he took her to a Halloween party, she had so much fun that she let him take her to a movie. Then she found out he was married and refused to see him again.

By that time, it was no longer a question of winning a bet. Will was smitten, and the thought of having Madeline began to obsess him as much as the airplane had. Will suggested to Ethel that they spend Christmas in Chicago. Mary Louise was almost one year old, and neither Gertrude nor Mrs. Peterson had seen her. Ethel was eager to go. On December 21, Will put his wife and daughter on the train, promising he'd be in Chicago for Christmas.

With Ethel out of the way, Will began pursuing Madeline like a possessed man, telling her that he hadn't meant to hide the fact that he was married. He and Ethel were having serious problems, he said, and she was with her mother in Chicago, filing for divorce. His marriage was only a technicality, and the divorce would come through any day.

Madeline kept putting him off, but Will wouldn't give up. He'd sit on Mary Lear's front porch and wait for Madeline to leave the drugstore with her girlfriends, Noreen and Clara, then dash after her as soon as she turned the corner. Madeline was flattered by the attention but held her ground.

When Christmas and the New Year came and went without a word from Will, Ethel began to panic. Because there was no spare room in her own mother's small flat, Ethel and the baby were living in Gertrude's house. She had no money, Will didn't answer her letters, and Gertrude was fawning over Mary Louise so much that Ethel was afraid to leave the baby with her, convinced there was "nothing she wanted more than to have Mary Louise as hers."

In desperation, Ethel wrote to Grandma Lear, begging to know why Will hadn't come to Chicago for the holidays and why he didn't answer her letters. Mary Lear's advice was simple and practical. "Ethel," she wrote, "get some money somehow and come home."

Ethel had just begun sewing in the alterations department of Sears, Roebuck to earn the train fare back to Tulsa when the strain became too much for her. She was stranded and broke, scared to death of Gertrude, and had no idea what was happening to her marriage. Not having fully recovered from the difficult birth of the year before, she got sick. Nevertheless, between visits to the doctor and days in bed, she managed to work enough to save the train fare home. When she arrived in Tulsa on April 13, 1926, Will was working for the W & E Electric Company, which had just bought WLAL from the First Christian Church. The station was deeply in debt and the church could no longer pay the operating costs. Since Will had installed WLAL for the church, W & E hired him to rebuild it for them.

Will was not pleased to see Ethel and, at first, would not say anything. But Ethel knew there was another woman and she quickly found out who it was.

"We have to talk," Ethel told Will.

"I want it to end," he said bluntly.

"Why didn't you talk it over with me?" Ethel asked. "Why this way?" She was in tears.

"You would cry," Will said. "I didn't want to see you hurt. I can't bear to see you cry."

"Can't you see it hurts worse this way?"

"Yes, but I wouldn't have to *see it*. You'd be in Chicago."

Unable to face Ethel, his father, his grandmother, and Madeline's sister Louise — who wanted the romance to end almost as much as Ethel did — Will took a $30 advance against his $200 monthly salary and ran away with Madeline, promising to marry her as soon as Ethel got a divorce. When Louise discovered her sister was missing, she hired private detectives to find her.

Two weeks later, Will drove Madeline from Muskogee, Oklahoma, where they had been hiding, to Dallas, Texas, where he had business. They registered in the Dallas Hilton as Mr. and Mrs. W. P. Lear. Louise's detectives followed them. In 1926, to transport a woman across a state line for immoral purposes, even if she was eighteen and willing, was trafficking in white slavery, a violation of the Mann Act, and a felony punishable by up to five years in prison and $5,000 in fines.

After completing his business in Dallas, Will took Madeline back to the Baltimore Hotel in Muskogee. Louise reported them to the police for immorality but said nothing about the trip to Texas. The Mann Act would be her trump card.

The Muskogee police arrested Will and Madeline in mid May and fined them each $20. The magistrate suspended Madeline's fine when Louise promised to send her to live with their sister Elizabeth in Kansas City, Missouri. Before leaving Muskogee with Madeline, however, Louise paid Will a visit in jail. If he ever tried to contact Madeline again, she threatened, the family would report him to the FBI for trafficking in white slavery and would see to it that he went to prison, where he belonged.

To shadow Will Lear with detectives and threaten him with the Mann Act was the worst thing Louise could have done. All Lear had to hear, even then, was that he couldn't have something or that it couldn't be done. He would rise to the challenge and risk everything, if only to prove a point.

Almost as if he were daring the FBI to come after him, Lear went straight from jail to Kansas City after a friend paid his fine, got a job with the Jenkins Music Company, and began wooing Madeline again. But Louise intercepted one of his letters and gave it to the FBI, who dropped by the Lear home in Tulsa to arrest Will. Not only wasn't he there, no one knew where to find him. The last letter Ethel had received was from Coffeyville, Kansas.

When he learned from his father that the FBI was hunting for him, Will took a job with the Diamond Vacuum Products Company of Chicago, selling vacuum sweepers in the East. It never really crossed his mind that the FBI could catch him or that if it did, he could actually go to prison.

Meanwhile, Ethel sued Will for divorce. The judge found him guilty of "gross neglect and adultery," granted Ethel custody of

Mary Louise, and awarded her $50 a month in alimony up to $3,000 and $25 a month in child support. If Will ever became delinquent, the judge ordered, he'd have to pay 6 percent interest.

While on the run, Will foolishly wrote three letters to Madeline. In one of them, he said he would be at the Hotel Buffalo in Buffalo, New York, on July 11, and asked Madeline to write to him there. Louise again intercepted the letter and gave it to the FBI. When Will walked into the hotel lobby, he was arrested.

At first Madeline refused to testify against Will, pledging to stand by him "always and forever." Without her testimony, there was no case. But her family finally badgered her until, confused and frightened, she agreed to cooperate with the FBI. Madeline appeared before a Tulsa grand jury on August 7, 1926, and Will was indicted for trafficking in white slavery. The trial was set for February 1927.

After Gertrude paid his $1,000 bail, Will called Madeline at Sears in Kansas City, where she was working as a bookkeeper and modeling hats. He now had a more compelling reason to wed her than love or infatuation. Marriage was his best hope of staying out of prison. Will told Madeline that he was coming and that she should make plans to get married.

"You better not go near my sister," she warned. "Come to Sears. I'll see you on my break."

Will was waiting in his old Ford. "We're not leaving Missouri until we're married," Madeline said, her bag already packed. She had had enough of the Mann Act. They were married in Boonsville, Missouri, on October 4, 1926.

With his new wife, Will headed back to Chicago, the largest radio manufacturing center in the country, to start life over. He had given up a promising business partnership in Quincy to strike out on his own. Within months, he was bankrupt. He had rebuilt a radio station and played at broadcasting. He had built an airplane that didn't fly, had married twice, and had been indicted for a federal crime. With all he owned either on his back or in his Ford, he was still determined to make it big in Chicago on his own terms as an independent radio engineer. He was twenty-four years old.

4

WITH MONEY HE BORROWED from his mother, Bill (as he now called himself) rented a furnished efficiency at the Dornell Hotel Apartments until he and Madeline could afford furniture and a larger flat. He went back to repairing radios, experimenting, looking for the right people who could lead him to the right job, and catching up on the latest developments. The seven months he had spent running from the FBI had put him out of touch. He spread his tools and radio parts — chassis, tubes, earphones, batteries, tabletop cabinets — all over the small apartment.

At $60 a month, the Dornell was more than Bill could afford, so Madeline took a job as a waitress at Henrici's. They were so poor that her shoes had holes, and she ate at the restaurant every chance she got or brought food home to save money. Bill was worrying so much about work and the upcoming trial in Tulsa that he was rail thin despite his natural inclination to chubbiness. He began to talk incessantly about getting ahead, making a name, and how he'd buy Madeline diamonds someday. He spun wild dreams, as Madeline put it, out of Horatio Alger threads tied together by driving ambition.

The trial hung over Bill's head like a guillotine. Madeline kept writing to the U.S. Attorney in Tulsa, begging him to dismiss the charges because she and Bill were happily married and a prison term would do no one any good. But with more important cases piling up on his desk, the U.S Attorney simply filed her letters. On February 15, 1927, the day before the trial, he notified them that the Justice Department had dropped the charges at his recommendation, "because the prosecution would not be successful."

Lear no longer had that worry and with contacts throughout Chicago, his career took off again, this time in fits and starts. He and Madeline moved out of the Dornell into a flat above a pharmacy on Eighty-first and Cottage Grove. Turning one of the two bedrooms into his laboratory, Lear opened shop as a radio repairman, designer, and troubleshooter. Then he invited Elmer Wavering to join him.

After a semester at Quincy High making up credits for college, Elmer leaped at the chance to work again with Bill, who always pushed him to the limit of his abilities. Their first job together in Chicago was a cliffhanger. The first radio manufacturers show was to open at the Stevens Hotel June 13, 1927. The advance registration totaled 8,700 manufacturers, jobbers, dealers, and advertising executives from all over the country. Secretary of Commerce Herbert Hoover was to be the keynote speaker. And, of course, the manufacturers would all be displaying their 1928 models.

In the two and a half years since Lear had fled Quincy, radio had exploded so quickly that the manufacturers could not keep pace with engineering developments and the ravenous market. The number of home sets had jumped from 30,000 in 1922 to 7.5 million in 1927, with a listening audience estimated at 25 million. The first network, NBC, was born at the end of 1926 and soon spawned twenty-four stations. The neutrodyne and superheterodyne circuits, uncanny in their selectivity and sensitivity, had revolutionized the radio industry, making five-, seven-, and nine-tube sets common. B-battery eliminators made it possible to use the "light socket" (house current) for the B power source, though not for the A source. An AC tube, which RCA perfected late in 1926, paved the way for Radiola #8, the first all-electric radio on the market. And, of course, there was a string of gadgets to attract the buyers — illuminated dials, remote controls, push-button receivers, even a radio with a primitive built-in wire recorder so listeners could copy their favorite songs.

The convention's organizers had planned to display their all-electric sets and their battery eliminators on the fourth, fifth, and sixth floors of the Stevens Hotel. But they neglected one important item — the Stevens used its own high-pressure steam boilers to generate its own DC electricity. None of the new AC radio equipment would work.

At the last minute, the organizers hired the Modine Electric Company of Chicago to design and build a series of small generators to convert DC to AC. Lear knew from his work on the car radio in Quincy that, although the generators would convert the electricity, the arcing of their brushes would create so much noise that Rudy Vallee would be merely a whistle and Herbert Hoover a hiss. He also suspected that the electrical interference was a problem that Modine's mechanical engineers would never be able to muffle. In fact, he was betting on it.

Lear waited until panic had gripped the organizers, then confidently announced he could solve the problem for $1,000. In less than a hundred hours, working around the clock between naps and sandwiches, he and Wavering designed and built a series of filters to fit each piece of electrical radio equipment on display. By the time the convention opened, there was hardly a manufacturer's representative who hadn't heard of Bill Lear.

Lear met Howard Sams at the radio show. They knew each other well from Quincy because, as a Universal Battery sales representative, Sams had supplied Quincy Radio Laboratories with batteries for its parts division. In the summer of 1927, Universal realized that the radio industry was rushing toward the all-electric set with abandon. There was still a market for batteries, however — 74 percent of all radios sold in 1927 were battery sets — and there would be for several more years because millions of rural Americans were still without electricity, and millions more with it already had battery radios, which they were unlikely to toss away for an all-electric set that sold for between $125 for a table model and $500 for a console. At most, they would strike a compromise, buying a $50 B-battery eliminator for their old sets. Lear understood the dilemma, saw an opportunity, and asked Sams to introduce him to Universal's president, R. D. Morey.

Even though he had never built one before, Lear told Morey he could design a B-battery eliminator for Universal. There were already slightly more than fifty eliminators on the market, and although all of the major bugs had been caught, most of the power packs created an annoying hum in the sets. Lear promised Morey that he could smother the hum, thereby making Universal's eliminator the best on the market. Morey hired him, and after studying the models at the radio show, Lear went back to the lab to build his own. Universal moved into the B-battery eliminator business.

Lear had no difficulty finding a string of troubleshooting jobs after the convention because engineers had been turning out so many new parts (especially tubes) so fast that manufacturers began using them without properly redesigning their sets. The Apex Radio Company, for example, had a warehouse full of radios built around the neutrodyne circuit and some new tubes. But it couldn't get the tweets and whistles out of its entire inventory. Lear told Apex he could fix the sets. Recalls Wavering: "Bill set the price pretty high. The figure a thousand dollars sticks in my mind. But Apex was in the bucket in a big way and they grabbed the offer."

Lear brought a few Apex sets into his home lab, and within hours he and Wavering had filtered out the squawks with resistors. Lear showed Apex how to rewire the sets to muffle the tweets.

Next, Lear took one of the QRS Music Company's new rectifier tubes, which converted AC into DC — eliminating both the A and B batteries — and built an all-electric radio around it. Lear invited Thomas Fletcher, the president of QRS, to listen to his set. Fletcher was so impressed with the sound that when Bill Grunow of the Grigsby-Grunow Company asked him if he knew an engineer who could eliminate a loud hum that was making thousands of his new B-battery eliminators almost useless, Fletcher said he had just the man.

To avoid conflict between Lear and his own engineers, who couldn't solve the problem, Grunow set up a laboratory for Lear in a basement apartment on Armatage Avenue, five or six blocks from the plant. After Lear and Wavering redesigned the company's radios, ridding them of the interference, Grunow hired Lear as a consultant and idea man.

Wavering was having fun and learning more than he ever had before. He slept on a cot in Bill and Madeline's living room, and he and Bill would spend half the night working to meet a deadline, then sit in a nearby basement nightclub listening to Guy Lombardo, or go dancing at the Trianon and Aragon ballrooms to the music of Ted Weems and Wayne King. Bill would tell Madeline that they were out on house calls, fixing radios, and she would answer the phone for them. Bill hated to be alone, Elmer noticed. Surrounded by a chattering crowd or friends laughing at his stories, Bill felt more at ease and secure.

Before long, Elmer was sick of going out almost every night; yet he didn't like the idea of staying home alone with Madeline. Worrying about what Bill's mother, who lived nearby, and the neighbors would think, they began telling everyone they were brother and sister. It was ironic. Elmer, who had fallen for Madeline in Tulsa (although she never knew it) and lost her to Bill, was now at home with her while Bill was out dancing. As crazy as it seemed to Elmer, it never bothered Bill.

That fall, Wavering left Chicago for George Washington University in Washington, D.C., while Lear continued troubleshooting. The dynamic speaker was the big breakthrough of 1928; but few if any of the radio manufacturers, who had been playing with loudspeaker horns and cones for five years, seemed to know what to do with this new development. Lear took a new dynamic speaker to his Grunow lab and built a radio around it. He asked Bill Grunow to listen to it. If Grigsby-Grunow would start building radios with the new dynamic speakers built into them, Lear argued, it would be months ahead of the competition. Once again, Grigsby-Grunow leaped into the radio market, this time with "the Majestic." Lear was so confident of the company's future that he began buying Grigsby-Grunow stock.

Lear was enjoying the best of both worlds, and that's the way he wanted to keep it. He had a steady salary from Grigsby-Grunow for a consultant relationship that was so loose, he could still work for new clients or hunt for the big break that would make him a million. But in spite of his relative freedom, Lear was trapped and he knew it. He was always working for someone else, not for himself; his designs and product improvements were not original enough to be patented; and he didn't have enough money to go into business for himself or to concentrate, as he later did, on inventing something so revolutionary it would give him the fame and fortune he craved.

Late in 1928, Lear had an argument with Bill Grunow, just as he had had with Julius Buerkin in Quincy, probably over developing a new product that Grunow thought was too risky. Grunow fired him and Lear sold his stock. Within a year, Grigsby-Grunow would be making seven thousand Majestic radios a day and the price of Grigsby-Grunow stock would soar.

* * *

Madeline gave birth to William Lear, Jr., in May 1928, and Bill seemed concerned about the extra mouth to feed, although his business was running smoothly even without the Grigsby-Grunow contract. He never seemed to have any money, for he spent it as fast as he made it on friends or clothes. Or he poured the money back into his radio business, trying one experiment after another while he hunted for the big invention.

When Gertrude moved back to the farm in Plainville late in 1928, Bill, Madeline, and Bill Jr. moved into her home on Sixty-sixth Place, not far from what later became Midway Airport. The move was an important step in Lear's career.

Gertrude's large house had a detached garage and a full basement. Lear pushed the washer and tubs to the far end of the basement, built workbenches and cabinets with individual outlets — something like the old Quincy Radio Laboratories workshop — and went into business with Ernie Tyrman of the Tyrman Electric Company of Chicago. Tyrman would supply the parts, including RCA patented tubes, and Lear would design radios, trying to keep one step ahead of the big manufacturers like RCA. His basement crew of eight to ten would build the sets, which Tyrman would sell in his store. Lear got a fee for each set built and a commission on each one sold.

Of course, what Lear and Tyrman were doing in their mom-and-pop workshop was an infringement on the patents of RCA, which sold licenses to manufacturers (if they were big enough) and collected a royalty on each set built. Grigsby-Grunow, for example, was paying the giant $5.3 million a year before it went bankrupt. But RCA was so busy making sure the big companies paid that it didn't have time to sue the small independents like Lear and Tyrman. Besides, with 2,400 radio patents already existing on every conceivable part, engineers experimenting in radio could never be sure they were not violating somebody's legal rights. Not even RCA, which claimed to own anywhere from 50 to 90 percent of the useful radio patents, was certain who had title to what. The courts were soon choked with suits and countersuits that took years to unravel. Even so, the fear of getting caught and the resulting certain bankruptcy got to Ernie Tyrman, who died of a bleeding ulcer within a year of his partnership with Bill Lear.

Building nine-tube sets (nine in a line) and using the latest in radio technology, Lear recognized the need for more efficient frequency coils. To cover the full AM frequency cycle from 500 to 1,500 kilocycles, the industry was using a large coil two to two and a half inches high and wide with one strand of copper wire wound around it. Lear designed a coil half that size by taking ten strands of enamel-coated Litzendrat wire, thin as a hair, twisting them into a single strand coated with silk, then bank-winding the larger strand in layers around the coil. It worked beautifully.

With money borrowed from a friend, Lear designed a coil-winder and, because Litz wire was so expensive, a wiremaking machine. Melvin King, a mechanic who, like Lear, had little formal education, built both machines. Gertrude's garage became headquarters for the Radio Wire and Coil Company. In charge of production was Don Mitchell, a Santa Fe Railroad engineer and designer.

Lear installed a set of his new coils in a Zenith receiver and invited Zenith's president, Eugene McDonald, to a demonstration. It was a typical Lear maneuver — go right to the top man, hurdling over the middle-level engineers, who would be threatened by a better product.

Commander McDonald was Lear's kind of man — self-made, aggressive, and a gambler. He had started out as a used car salesman but soon was buying his own cars and selling them in a novel way — on time payments. After a stint in World War I as a naval intelligence officer, he began searching for a new business in which he could invest his fortune. One New Year's Eve in the early 1920s, he saw a group of people huddled around a $200 radio in a gas station and decided radio was the business for him. Teaming up with two engineers who already had a license to manufacture sets, McDonald founded the Zenith Radio Corporation of Chicago. Through quality engineering and McDonald's creative marketing, Zenith was soon a leader in the field.

McDonald brought his chief engineer and partner, Carl Hassel, to the meeting at Lear's house. Bill first played a Zenith radio with the standard Zenith coil, then a Zenith with his coil. The difference in quality was striking. "But they can't possibly be as good as ours," Hassel objected, as Lear later recalled. "Buy 'em!" McDonald ordered. "Buy fifty thousand of 'em!"

That sale was the beginning of a hot streak and a relationship with Zenith and McDonald that would last for four years.

The Lear house became a truck stop. Madeline learned how to solder radio sets at the benches in the basement; her muffin tins held the screws. With the garage and house full of people, sometimes working late into the night trying to meet a rush order for coils or sets, and with Bill telling visitors, "Come on up, Madeline will fix you something," there was little privacy. And between soldering, the laundry with Bill Jr. on her hip, and the kitchen almost a restaurant, Madeline still had to do the cleaning and shopping.

In the fall of 1928, Lear moved his enterprise out of the garage into a nearly empty warehouse at 847 Harrison Street, headquarters for the Galvin Manufacturing Company, which was building radios for some twenty stores around town. Galvin bought Lear's coils and hired him as its chief engineer for $100 a week. Typically, the arrangement was loose, leaving Lear free to do other contract work.

Paul Galvin, president of the company, had been a co-owner of the Stewart-Galvin Battery Company in Marshfield, Wisconsin. When it went bankrupt in 1923, Galvin lost everything. His partner, Edward Stewart, organized a new battery company in Chicago, hired Galvin, and launched into making B-battery eliminators. Unfortunately, Stewart's design, like many of the early eliminator designs, was so faulty that dealers began returning them. By the time Galvin solved Stewart's engineering problem (it's not clear if Lear helped him), the business had gone bankrupt a second time.

Impressed with the quality of the improved Stewart eliminator, Sears, Roebuck suggested that Galvin buy out Stewart and start his own company. Sears would give Galvin's eliminator an exclusive listing in its catalogue. Galvin scraped together $1,000 and purchased Stewart's design, tools, and inventory at a public auction and rented half of a floor on Harrison Street, surrounded by small factories and shops, Greek and Italian restaurants, apple vendors and winos.

Until he could find a product that would plant his new company firmly on its feet, Galvin continued to manufacture B-battery eliminators and radio chassis with Lear's coils inside a Lear cabinet, designed with a slight difference for each distributor. Competition with the big names was vicious. To survive, Galvin stayed one step ahead by filling orders immediately, frequently overnight. On payday, Galvin's men would rush out with a carload of radios or B-battery eliminators and try to sell them for cash. Sometimes there wouldn't be enough money to pay everyone, so Galvin would put the cash on the table, and Lear and the other engineers would divide it up as fairly as possible.

Black Thursday, October 24, 1929, almost crushed the Galvin Manufacturing Company — as it would 253 of the 258 companies building radio sets in the mid to late 1920s. Major brand makers began dumping their inventories onto the market at ridiculously low prices. Galvin ended up with radios it couldn't sell, customers who wanted to return sets, and parts it couldn't use. By Christmas 1929, Paul Galvin was almost bankrupt for the third time.

Lear, on the other hand, was floating on a blanket of cash. Still selling coils (his were the best in town), troubleshooting, and doing custom designs as well, he did not feel Galvin's panic. Lear suggested that Galvin move into designing and manufacturing car radios. To Bill Lear, it seemed like a good idea. If the market wasn't there today, it would be tomorrow. But to Paul Galvin, the idea sounded too risky for 1929 and he dismissed it. Many years later, Lear would tell the story like this:

Howard Gates, a Zenith engineer, was toying with one of Lear's midget coils in Lear's office on Harrison Street one day. "They ought to make a nice radio for automobiles," Gates suggested.

"Suppose I design a set and give you drawings to make up the metalwork," Lear said. "Then I'll put in the coils, condensers . . . "

A few days later, Lear put on Galvin's desk a steel container with cords sticking out and a small box with two knobs.

"What is it?" Galvin said.

"An automobile radio," Lear said.

"They'll *never* be allowed in cars," Galvin said. "There'll be laws against them."

Lear disagreed. Music would relax the driver, he argued, making him less nervous, especially in a traffic jam. No one would dare pass a law against them.

Both men were right. Traffic authorities in Washington were predicting bans on car radios all over the country. "It takes no imagination to picture what might happen in traffic along Fifth Avenue or, better still, on Michigan . . . in Chicago where it moves faster, if a hundred or so radios were playing," a traffic spokesman argued. "Music in the car might make [the driver] miss hearing the horn of an approaching automobile or a fire or ambulance siren. Imagine fifty automobiles in a city street broadcasting a football game. Such a thing as this, I am sure, would not be tolerated by city traffic authorities."

Controversies flared up in cities like New York, where use in taxicabs was limited, and in St. Paul, where they were banned. Other cities proposed legislation to limit the radio's volume or to permit their use only when the car wasn't moving.

Lear's idea was not a new one. In mid 1929, the Automotive Radio Corporation of Long Island began equipping cars with a Transitone radio, designed and perfected by William Heina in 1927. The set was an ordinary six-tube, six-volt receiver installed behind the dash. The B battery sat in a metal box under the floorboards, and the speaker could be placed either over the windshield or above the rear seat. But the Automotive Radio Corporation was not a mass marketer. It merely sold radios to car owners and installed them in its Long Island shop.

Chrysler was so impressed with Transitone that it bought part interest in the radio and announced in October 1929 that a Transitone would be an option in its 1930 models. Almost at the same time, the Cadillac Corporation announced that it would equip its 1930 models with a built-in aerial and offer a car radio designed by the Delco-Ray Company (a subsidiary of General Motors) as a $150 option. Finally, the American Bosch Magneto Corporation of Springfield, Massachusetts, was preparing to unveil its model car radio for the January 1930 automobile show in New York City. The race to corner what would become an extremely lucrative market was on.

Paul Galvin heard about Transitone on a business trip to New York not long after Lear suggested the idea to him. What impressed Galvin was that the Automotive Radio Corporation was getting $150 to $200 for each radio it sold and installed (a new car cost only $600). On the way back to Chicago, Galvin began to realize that if his company could develop, mass-produce, and mass-market a practical, affordable car radio, it could make a fortune.

"Did you run a bill of material on that automobile set you made?" Galvin asked Lear when he got back to Chicago.

"Twenty-two dollars," Lear said.

The Galvin Manufacturing Company decided to plunge into the market in 1930. Galvin set a deadline for a prototype car radio to be installed in his Studebaker, Memorial Day weekend, for that was when the Radio Manufacturers Association convention would open on the Boardwalk in Atlantic City. Both Galvin and Lear were excited — Galvin, because he sensed the car radio could be the product around which he could build his company; Lear, because he knew that designing and developing the radio would be challenging. He called Elmer.

Lear had kept in touch with Wavering ever since he had left Chicago two and a half years earlier. Wavering had lasted one year at George Washington University before he bought an old Model A turtleback coupe and chugged over the Alleghenies back to Quincy. He had found the grind of full-time work, installing and repairing radios for Washington's socially elite, and full-time school more than he could handle. And he had missed the excitement of standing in the center of an exploding radio age. Back in Quincy, Wavering opened his own radio store with Lee Wright — they called it Wave-rite — and had dreams of a Wave-rite chain. But when he got the call from Lear, he left his partner in charge of the business.

The race for a slice of the car radio market was getting tighter each month. By the end of February, when Wavering arrived in Chicago, at least five companies were already making sets. The president of the National Federation of Radio Associations predicted that radios would soon become stock equipment on automobiles, just like bumpers and headlights.

Working on the car radio was mad and exciting. "We knew the basics," Wavering explains. "The radio had to be inside a metal case, perfectly grounded so no interference could leak in. The antenna wires had to be completely shielded."

Of course, Lear and Wavering had licked the antenna problem five years before, in Quincy, and since automobile frames were still wooden, cutting through the upholstery in the ceiling and refastening the chicken wire with silken cords still worked perfectly. The problem that plagued them was the interference in the radio caused by the car's electrical system. "You could hear every spark plug fire," Wavering recalls. "It would blot out reception. The brushes of the generator would cause static."

By this time, Lear's engineering leadership style had evolved into a pattern. Wavering and his assistants, Hank Saunders and Herbie Moose, would meet with Lear to evaluate progress and discuss problems. Lear would toss out ideas. "Did you try this?" he'd ask. "Try that," he'd say. They had no books to consult; everything was hit or miss, experience, and intuition. When Wavering or someone else proposed a solution, Lear would chew it over and talk it out, and by the time Wavering was ready to try it in Paul Galvin's Studebaker, there was a piece of Lear woven into it. "Bill's great strength," Wavering recalls, "was that he was an idea man. He had great creativity and liked to brainstorm. Ideas would just flow in numbers. He had the kind of mind that could sort out the technicalities and get to the heart of the problem."

Lear's style worked well because it was clear to everyone that the car radio was his project, and he was number one. If he wasn't, nothing much would get done because he would get bored and move on to something else.

Wavering and Saunders installed radios in several of the staff members' autos because each car model posed slightly different problems and they were seeking a universal solution. Although none of Lear's engineers had a college degree, it didn't seem to bother them. "Six months ago," they'd joke, "I couldn't spell 'inganeer.' Now I are one." Their biggest breakthrough was learning how to put suppressors on the spark plugs; the rest was a matter of identifying and isolating other sources of static, then muffling them one by one. "In the beginning," Wavering explains, "we often had to use so many suppressors that the engine wouldn't start, or if it did, it would die out when it picked up speed."

They worked on Harrison Street in front of the warehouse, two wheels up on the curb so they could crawl under the car, because neither Galvin nor Lear could afford a garage for the project. They'd try something, run up to the fourth-floor lab to design, tool, cut, and weld, then bring the new piece down to the curb to see if it would work. They'd saw, drill, bolt, and resaw, frequently working around the clock, using Red Silvers's service station garage at night. They learned very quickly to bring their tools inside whenever they left the car alone because the bums hanging around Harrison Street would steal them faster than they could weld two pieces of metal.

By late spring the prototype, 5T71, was finished — a metal can with a removable cover for easy access and a five-tube chassis inside. From the can stretched two flexible cables that traveled up the steering column to a small box below the steering wheel. On the box were two knobs, for volume and tuning, and an illuminated window, through which the driver could see the frequency numbers. The B battery was tucked under the floorboards. The box on the steering wheel — a "radio control device," Lear called it — was his first patent. Concerned about driver safety, he felt the controls should be within easy reach.

Next came road testing around the city to make sure that parts wouldn't jar loose and that the volume was strong enough to compete with street noises and the motor. There were so many failures that no one even bothered to keep count. But Lear never seemed to run out of ideas until he had it — a car radio that worked, that could be heard well in noisy traffic, that played on bumpy roads, and that could be installed in any car, not just in Cadillacs or Studebakers or Nashes.

There was one more critical test before the trip to Atlantic City. Hoping to secure a production loan, Paul Galvin brought over a banker with a new Packard to see the car radio. The banker was so impressed that he asked Galvin to put one in his car so that he could test-drive it for a few days and show it to potential backers. Wavering and Saunders installed the radio; Lear checked it out before the banker pulled away. The music was loud and sweet. A few minutes later, Wavering saw a fire engine race down Harrison Street. Sure enough, the Packard was on fire. "Here goes the company," Wavering said to himself. "Here goes Wavering." The insurance company poked through the charred frame and concluded that the fire was caused by a faulty electrical system (there had been fires in other 1930 Packards), not by the radio. Galvin got his loan.

In mid May, Galvin and Lear took off for Atlantic City. Since the Galvin Manufacturing Company couldn't afford exhibit space at the radio manufacturers show, Wavering had hooked up a loudspeaker on the front fender of Galvin's Studebaker. Galvin and Lear parked as close as they could to the Boardwalk, somewhere between Indiana Avenue and Park Place. They began collaring dealers, dragging them over to the Studebaker and giving them rides. Most were skeptical, but there were enough orders for one or two demonstration sets to have made the trip worthwhile. It was a beginning.

With orders for several dozen sets, which his company was selling for $120 installed, Galvin bought enough parts to make a hundred radios. Two weeks after the convention, he had the orders filled and was sending out samples to other dealers he had reached by phone. Lear had already moved on to other projects. He had no interest in production and no enthusiasm for improving the model. Other engineers like Wavering could do that.

One Friday night, soon after he had returned from Atlantic City, Galvin asked each engineer to think up some names for the car radio by Monday morning. Galvin himself suggested Motorola, a name he and Lear had concocted on the way back from Atlantic City — "motor" after the car, and "ola" to mimic the popular brands like Victrola, Audiola, Grafanola, and Radiola.

In the second half of 1930, the Galvin Manufacturing Company made and distributed almost a thousand Motorolas, 3 percent of the car radios sold that year. Wavering went on the road to teach distributors how to install and repair them after Galvin got a call from an angry dealer in Texas, who shouted: "How the hell can we sell them if nobody can install them?" Galvin continued to beat the countryside for more and more distributors, one eye on the assembly line and the other on the bank. And Lear started spending more and more time at the airport.

5

IN 1930, Lear teamed with another creative engineer, Bob Wuerfel, to form Lear-Wuerfel. While Galvin's company was concentrating on the car radio, Lear-Wuerfel was designing radios and chassis for other Chicago manufacturers, collecting a flat fee for the design plus a fifty-cent royalty on each set sold. Naturally, Lear coils were an integral part of the sets' design.

Lear was bursting with ideas. He designed a radio remote control, "the Lazy Boy," that was far ahead of any other on the market. A smart-looking control box with an illuminated dial, it had a special light that flicked on when the station was tuned perfectly. The Lazy Boy got Lear his first newspaper publicity. The Chicago papers ran a photograph of him sitting behind his desk with the caption: "William P. Lear, chief engineer of the Galvin Manufacturing Corporation, whose remote tuning device takes a load off the feet while traveling the country by radio."

Lear also designed another car radio, which could be installed under the floorboards of the car instead of under the dash. He sold the patented design to Grigsby-Grunow. And he patented a coupling device that provided greater volume and better tuning, which he sold to the Meissner Manufacturing Company of Chicago. By most standards, Lear had finally made it. He had come to Chicago in 1927, penniless and determined to become an independent radio engineer. Four years later, he was one of the most sought-after radio designers and inventors in the Chicago area and was making, by his own estimate, the equivalent of $150,000 a year today.

With his pockets full of money, Lear bought a sleek Fleet biplane. He hired F. L. ("Fly Boy") Yeomans, a United Airlines pilot, to teach him how to fly, and they set out for New York. By watching the compass and following the railroad tracks east, they managed to find Roosevelt Field on Long Island without getting lost too often. Before they returned to Chicago, mechanics had to replace the windshield, which had cracked on the flight.

On the way back, Lear thought he was having no problem keeping the Fleet on course until he looked out the window and saw that the Allegheny Mountains were running east-west according to his compass, not north-south, the way they did on the maps. Lear landed in a field and asked a farmer how to get to Chicago. It turned out that the Roosevelt Field mechanics had used magnetic screws by mistake, making the compass dangerously useless. "The first thing I discovered on this cross-country trip," Lear said many years later, "was that . . . Indiana wasn't green and Illinois yellow as they were shown on the map. As a result . . . I was lost all the time. Then, I found upon investigation that many of the other fellows who said they never got lost weren't exactly telling the truth."

Lear sold the Fleet soon after his New York trip, bought a new Monocoupe aircraft powered by a Warner radial engine, and called his friend Warren Knotts to install a radio receiver in it. By late 1931, there was a string of Department of Commerce radio beacons across the country beeping out signals. Pilots with receivers could pick up the beeps and guide their ships in bad weather to approximately 200 of the 1,800 airports and landing strips coast to coast. It was a rather crude system. The signals were sometimes weak, and amid the static and interference, pilots had to interpret a series of long and short tones, like the dots and dashes of the Morse code, to find out if they were too far to the right or the left of the beacon. If the airplane was right on beam, the pilots would hear one long dash. "It was ten percent radio," Knotts recalls, "and ninety percent interpretation. It was awfully easy to fly right over the beacon and get lost. But it was the only show in town."

Knotts had stumbled into the airplane receiver business. Like Lear, he was a radio engineer and entrepreneur, co-owner of the South Shore Radio Laboratories, where he was building radios without an RCA license and without paying royalties. "We were pirates," he admits. "But what the hell, we didn't care. Nobody else did."

Knotts got a call from Reeder Nichols, the operations manager for the new Century Airlines (and the future American

Airlines), asking if South Shore Radio Labs could build and install airplane receivers. Nichols thought the going rate of $1,000 to $1,200 that companies like Clinton Radio charged was outrageously high for the simple sets. Knotts told Nichols he would make and install the radios in Century's fleet of Ford Trimotors (Tin Gooses, they were nicknamed) for less than $300 each. Nichols hired him, and Knotts went to Lear for the special coils he needed. Knotts had been using Lear's coils for several years, and from time to time he'd ask Lear to design special coils for different projects.

Soon after the sets for Nichols were finished, Lear asked Knotts to put a receiver in his Monocoupe, which he was parking at a little airport at Sixty-third and Cicero, the future site of Midway Airport. It took several evenings to install the receiver because the problems were similar to, though more complicated than, those of car radios. Knotts had to shield the receiver from interference and filter out the noise; everything had to be handtooled and specially installed.

When the radio was hooked up, Lear asked Knotts if he wanted to fly to Miami with him to check the thing out. They spent the night at a small hotel near the airport, and at four-thirty the next morning they rolled out the Monocoupe, heading southwest with a new radio, a compass, an altimeter, and a turn-bank. It was so dark and overcast that they lost the horizon soon after takeoff. Luckily, Lear caught the lights of Chicago under him through a break in the clouds, and they landed and waited for daylight before taking off once again. This time, they hit heavy fog over the Illinois-Indiana border near Lawrenceville. Studying the maps, Knotts saw there was an airport in Vincennes, about twenty miles away. Flying as close to the ground as possible, Lear followed the highway to a little grass strip where he landed, "happy as hell to be on the ground." Lear phoned a friend to drive down to get them and paid the airport manager to fly the plane back to Chicago.

The flight to New York and the aborted trip to Miami made a deep impression on Lear, and he began to think about designing and building some kind of direction finder. It was a vague idea in the early 1930s, but the conviction that independent pilots like him needed affordable and reliable navigation instruments was not.

Lear's successes had gone straight to his head, and Madeline began to notice a big change in him. He seemed to be getting more and more pigheaded ("He always knew best") and pompous around Gertrude's house. And although she always had enough money to run the house and take care of Bill Jr. and Patti, who had been born on her father's birthday in 1929, Madeline still never knew how much there was or where it was coming from. But Bill seemed more relaxed and swaggered more, so she knew things must be going well.

Then Bill started to spend more and more nights away from home, saying he was out of town on business. Madeline sensed something was wrong but didn't know quite what it was. The winter of 1930–1931 was especially hard for her, huddled at home at night with two babies. The snow would pile up outside, the furnace would go out, and Bill would be "out of town."

Most of the time he really wasn't. Next to his office on the fourth floor of the Galvin building, Lear had a small, tastefully furnished room for entertaining guests. He hired Piedro, a Filipino boy, to prepare sandwiches and serve drinks; it was easy to get moonshine in Chicago. During the day, Lear entertained customers, especially the more important ones, and engineers who came to check on progress or to discuss ideas. At night, he went to the speakeasies and the Trianon or the Aragon, "the ballroom of a thousand delights." He danced (he was light on his feet and especially good at the rumba), bought drinks, and introduced himself to the performers, toward whom he felt an almost irresistible pull. Then, he'd invite them over to his little place for a drink or a party. There was Wayne King, saxophonist, composer, and band leader; Ole Olsen and Chic Johnson, vaudeville comedians; Paul Ash and his Merry-Mad Musical Gang; Elmer Kaiser with his Melody Masters; the Del Lampe Orchestra; Evelyn Mays and the Bordon Brothers; Lee English and the Hull Sisters.

More and more, Charlene (not her real name) was with him. When he traveled, he took her along if he could. He paid for flying lessons for her, but she hated to be in the left seat even after she had soloed. A twenty-two-year-old secretary for a radio manufacturing executive with whom Lear did business, she had resisted Lear's advances for a long time because she knew he was married. But when he told her one day that he and Madeline were not getting along and that he was suing for a divorce, Charlene believed him, just as Madeline had before her.

It was the wife of Lear's chief machinist, Mel King, who told Madeline about Charlene. Galvin's building was still a small place, and everyone who knew Bill Lear knew about the affair. And Lear wasn't the type to keep his womanizing a secret. Whenever he drank too much, Mel would repeat the office gossip. His wife got so angry at Bill for making fools of both Madeline and Charlene that she told Madeline.

Madeline had no intention of playing musical beds. If Bill wanted Charlene he could have her, and she told him so. Bill promised to stop seeing Charlene, but Madeline told him it was a little late for that. Packing up her clothes, Bill Jr., and Patti, she moved into an apartment on the Near Northside and filed for divorce.

Bill continued to see Charlene, but Madeline had deeply bruised his ego. He couldn't admit to his friends that she was divorcing him, so he said that he had dumped her. Jealous to the point of obsession, he took to spying on her apartment from his car or from the fire escape outside her window, peeking through the curtains to make sure she wasn't entertaining a man.

Soon after Madeline won her divorce, Bill asked her to remarry him. He missed her and the children and, he said, his affair with Charlene was over. Not trusting him, she refused. But when he asked her to move back in with him in the spring of 1931, after she and the children returned from Florida where they had spent the winter because of Bill Jr.'s health, she agreed.

Bill bought Madeline a new wedding ring just for appearances and rented the Sears mansion (of Sears, Roebuck) on the Lake Michigan shore a few miles north of Chicago. It was a huge home with a master bedroom as large as Madeline's Northside apartment. Its elegant dining room, with oil paintings and silver and china, seated up to fifteen people. The backyard was a park of rosebushes and shrubs, swings, slides, and a sandbox, with a gardener to care for it all.

For Madeline, that summer was more or less happy. Her sister Elizabeth and her two children, Margaret and Betty Jean, came up from Kansas City for the whole summer to keep her company. A nurse cared for the four children; a Danish couple cooked and served; and the Sears's servant, Augusta, managed the household. To an Oklahoma farmgirl who had run away from home at the age of fourteen, it was a dream. But hanging over it, like a dark cloud, was Charlene. Madeline would hear a car drive up in the evening and park for a few minutes. The car would drive away and Bill would come in. She knew it was Charlene, but for the sake of the children she put up with it all summer. In the winter, she took the two children back to Florida, wondering what to do next.

It wasn't just Lear's relationship with Madeline that was falling apart. His whole life was unsettled, and he seemed to like it that way. He thrived on tension so much that if his professional life grew too calm, he sought excitement in his personal life.

Now that he had his own airplane, he was losing interest in the radio business so fast that everyone at both Lear-Wuerfel and Galvin noticed it. He was spending more and more time at the airport or on "business trips," flying to air races or to visit friends. One day late in 1931, he invited Warren Knotts to come to work for him at a small airport in Glenview, just north of Chicago, where he would build and install receivers for independent pilots. Lear was enthusiastic. It was a brand-new field. The handful of companies making radios for airplanes were supplying the major airlines who had the big money. No one seemed interested in making flying safer for itinerant or sport pilots.

Like almost every independent radio engineer in Chicago, Knotts was in deep trouble. By March 1931, the home radio business had slid to the bottom of the slump that had begun on Black Thursday. Since he didn't have the capital to hold out until the financial climate improved, Knotts joined Lear in Glenview at the Curtiss-Reynolds Airport, owned by the Curtiss-Wright Aircraft Corporation, which had two runways and two hangars twice as long as a football field.

Attached to the sides of the hangars like barnacles were small workrooms, called lean-tos, for mechanics, pilots, and businessmen. In one of these lean-tos, Lear opened Lear Developments in July 1931. Lear and Wuerfel had split up. Still good friends, they had recognized that they would never be able to work together happily. Both were idea men who wanted to be in charge;

both craved the credit for each project; and both were pulled in different directions at the same time. And Wuerfel wasn't the least interested in airplanes.

Lear, Warren Knotts, Reeder Nichols, and Freddie Schnell began building aircraft receivers, in batches of twenty-five, similar to those used by the commercial airlines. They made a good team. Knotts, Nichols, and Schnell had had more experience than Lear in designing and installing receivers, but Lear had had more time in the cockpit, using them. Before long, the Lear Radioaire, as Bill called it, was getting lighter, smaller, and better. Hoping to attract the private pilots who wanted receivers but couldn't afford Clinton's prices, Lear placed an ad in *Aviation* magazine. He also did a hard sell on every pilot who touched down at Curtiss-Reynolds, taking him or her (Amelia Earhart landed there occasionally) up in his Monocoupe, with LEAR RADIOAIRE painted on the side, for a demonstration of the radio. To be as close to the airport as possible, he rented the manager's house across the road. It was difficult to convince pilots accustomed to looking out the window for the railway tracks that they needed a $250 receiver to listen to electronic clicks that would lead them to a beacon, if they were lucky. It took four to five months just to sell the first twenty-five Radioaires. Fortunately, Lear still had his radio business on Harrison Street and was still chief engineer for Galvin. Recalls Knotts: "Radioaire was just a side venture for Bill. But it was his love."

Shortly after Lear began Lear Developments in Glenview, P. R. Mallory, president of the P. R. Mallory Company of Indianapolis, asked him to perfect a very preliminary design to eliminate the B battery from the car radio. One of his engineers had come up with an idea that looked good on paper, Mallory told Lear, but no one at the company could make it work.

Mallory did not have to explain further. Lear recognized that if he could develop the B-battery eliminator, he could make a fortune, for the instrument would cut the price of a car radio by more than half while improving the sound. And every car radio manufacturer in the country would have to buy one until it could design its own without infringing on the Mallory patent. Lear told Mallory that he'd take the assignment for $100 a week and a 3.5 percent royalty on all eliminators.

Lear hired Raymond Yoder, another engineer who had lost

his job during the Depression, as project director for the B-battery eliminator. An engineer's engineer, Yoder focused on the problem like a laser. He began working with Lear's initial sketches for a vibrator that would convert the low voltage of the storage battery under the hood into high-voltage alternating current for the radio while filtering out noise and static. John Wehner, an expert tool and die man who worked inside a locked cage so no one could touch his tools, crafted the steel reeds that were needed. Since no one had ever built such a vibrator before, the job was a complex, try-this-try-that project filled with variables — choice of steel and temper, thickness, and length. "I'd wager to say, Lear had one hundred designs before the vibrator was perfected," Knotts explains. "You needed a certain intuition to make your way through all that. It seemed uncanny — Lear's intuition." Once he gave Yoder the latest design, drawn on a napkin or used envelope, Lear got bored with the eliminator. His heart was in the Monocoupe and the Radioaire. "Bill was like that," Yoder explains. "He'd get an idea, talk it over with you. You'd agree to give it a try. He'd get you going on it, then lose interest."

Within nine months, Lear and his team had perfected the B-battery eliminator for the car radio and the Galvin Manufacturing Company was Mallory's first customer. In the spring of 1932, Galvin began mass-producing its new Motorola. Light, compact, and without the expensive and cumbersome B battery, it was the first practical car radio on the market, a major engineering breakthrough.

Lear couldn't have cared less. He sold his Radio Wire and Coil Company to Galvin, gave the Sears mansion back, and moved into the airport manager's house with Charlene. It was an inevitable but risky decision. Galvin was on the move, and even though the company was still shaky, it was only a matter of time before it would pull ahead of the pack. The Radio Wire and Coil Company was still profitable, even though the home radio business remained in a deep slump, because Chicago engineers still needed Lear's coils. And everyone knew that the business would bounce back after the economic recovery, for although the national pocketbook was empty, the national appetite for radio was voracious.

Developing and selling instruments for airplanes, on the

other hand, was a new, precarious business. The question Lear faced was: How long would it take independent pilots to recognize how badly they needed navigation instruments? Lear was willing to take the gamble even though it meant leaving the radio business just at the point in his career when he was beginning to show what he could invent if he put his mind to it. The vibrator for the car radio was important and creative. It was designed, tested, and manufactured in an incredibly short time. But Lear tossed it all away without so much as a second thought.

"If Bill had decided to stay in the radio field," Knotts explains, "he certainly would have made a name for himself. But he wouldn't have had his heart in it. Bill couldn't work without a challenge. He saw an opportunity once he got into the aviation business. There's where the tremendous frontier was."

Lear left them all behind. His old business partner Bob Wuerfel went on tinkering and inventing until he had a string of patents to his name; Howard Sams, the Universal Battery salesman, ran his own company, producing service manuals for radios and electronic equipment, until ITT eventually bought him out. Woody Woodring, the pilot who tested Lear's Lincoln Sport in Tulsa, became an Air Force test pilot and a member of the Three Musketeers precision flying team. He was killed in a test flight crash at Wright-Patterson Field in Dayton, Ohio.

Elmer Wavering, Ray Yoder, and Don Mitchell, the engineer supervised the Radio Wire and Coil Company, all stayed with Galvin's company, which changed its name to Motorola, after its car radio. Wavering eventually became president and Mitchell and Yoder, chief engineers. Mitchell later founded Mitchell Industries in Mineral Wells, Texas, where he designed and built instruments for small aircraft. And the P. R. Mallory Company made millions from the vibrator before the transistor made it obsolete and won a dispute with Delco over the patent.

Bill Lear started all over once again.

6

LIFE AT THE AIRPORT house in Glenview with Bill and Charlene was so unpredictable and noisy that Warren Knotts had to move into a rooming house nearby to get some rest. Besides the couples whom Bill would ask to spend the night after a party, there were the customers who flew into Curtiss-Reynolds to have Radioaires installed or repaired and the engineers and itinerant pilots who loved to drink and spin yarns but had nowhere to sleep.

Lear served them bathtub gin, which he and Knotts made from moonshine that bootleggers smuggled from Canada through the Windsor Tunnel and sold through local distributors for $10 a gallon. They would dump five gallons of the hooch into the bathtub, put in a few drops of essence of juniper, and let the batch set for two or three days. Lear had a water cooler in the corner of the kitchen, complete with paper cups. He would fill the upended bottle with gin and wait for a new guest to ask for a drink of water.

Once, two pilots flew in from Winston-Salem in a Waco cabin ship to buy a $350 Radioaire. Knotts ran into a nest of installation problems, and it took him three days to get the static out of the set. The pilots, who were staying at the airport house, kept complaining about the quality of Lear's gin. When the radio was finally ready, they took off for home, only to return twelve hours later. Worried about the radio, Lear and Knotts ran out on the runway to meet them. The pilots climbed out of the Waco holding a gallon of North Carolina corn liquor. "The radio works fine," they said. "Let's have a drink of *real* whiskey."

With pilots flying into Glenview from all parts of the country in different kinds of planes, Lear had an opportunity to learn a great deal about aviation in a short time. He didn't miss a beat. He'd either pilot each plane to test the Radioaire or he'd sit in the right seat, watch the pilot, and ask questions. "It got so he could fly anything," Knotts recalls. "He'd beg the guys to take him up and show him."

While Lear was having fun flying, wrapped in his boyhood dream, the aircraft radio business was barely moving. Pilots were still treating instruments as toys.

"I don't want to be entertained when I'm flying," they'd say.

"This is not for entertainment," Lear would answer. "This is to help you get where you're going without getting lost."

Lear would describe how the receiver tuned into the radio broadcast range that the Department of Commerce was using to guide commercial airlines flying Tin Gooses and Fokkers.

"What's a radio range?" the pilots would ask.

"A beam or a beacon. It's a little like Morse code. There's a left, a right, and a middle. You fly to the left, you get a broken signal. You fly to the right, you get a different kind of broken signal. You fly down the middle, and you get a continuous signal. You're on course."

"Naw, I don't need anything fancy like that," they would say. "I always follow the railroad tracks."

P. R. Mallory royalties for the car radio vibrator kept Lear alive in 1932–1933. The few dozen Radioaires he sold went to independent pilots (there were only 7,500 in the entire United States) and to a few corporations like Western Electric, Bell Telephone Laboratories, Westinghouse, and RCA, which had small fleets of planes for their executives. When his inventory grew too large, Lear traded a hundred radios to Eddie Stinson for a new Stinson Reliant; he then sold the ship, equipped with a Radioaire, to the bandleader Wayne King, who had his own radio show by then and had begun playing outside Chicago. To get publicity for the Radioaire, Lear traded in his old Monocoupe for a sporty new Model 110, with a steel-bladed propeller, and began entering it in national air races with C. L. Claybaugh as his pilot. Lear even sponsored his own Chicago Radioaire air race, open to private pilots flying their own craft.

Madeline returned to Chicago in the spring of 1933. She knew that Bill had been living with Charlene all winter, but he had promised to stop seeing her once Madeline was back home. Madeline decided to give the relationship another try for the sake of the children. Without a great deal of optimism, she moved into the airport house.

After the Sears mansion, the two-story Glenview farmhouse was a letdown, even though it was out in the country, away from the noise of the city, and had Shetland ponies for the children. Elizabeth and her two daughters joined the Lears once again for the summer. And Madeline hired a neighbor to babysit and help with the chores.

Bill Jr. and Patti spent a lot of time at the airport, playing in the hangars or in their father's office. There were always air shows and races to watch. Barnstormers came through, and so did some of the famous pilots of the day, including Charles Lindbergh and Amelia Earhart. Bill took the children up in his Monocoupe and sometimes flew them down to Plainville to see their grandparents, Gertrude and Otto. Lear had painted the Kirmses' barn roof orange so he could spot it easily, and Otto kept the grass cut in the east forty. Bill would buzz the pasture to clear out the cows so he could land.

Madeline wasn't really happy at the airport house, just as she hadn't been at the Sears mansion, and for the same reason. She kept finding traces of Charlene. Determined not to share Bill, Madeline drove into Chicago to face Charlene's mother. She begged the woman to talk to her daughter. Charlene had broken up her marriage once, Madeline complained. Now she wouldn't let Madeline patch it up and make a go of it. There were two small children to think of, she said. The marriage could work if Charlene would just stay away from Bill.

The woman laughed at Madeline. "What do you expect if you go to Florida for six months and leave him alone?"

As they drove home from the office that evening, Bill asked Madeline how her day had been.

"I'll tell you!" She was seething. "Everything that's good and decent has gone rotten. It stinks."

She pulled off her wedding ring and tossed it out the car window. "That's what I think of you," she spat at him. The next day, she moved out of the airport house.

Bill set up Madeline and the two children in the Flamingo, an expensive apartment tower on the lakefront in Hyde Park, and sent her a new Chevrolet, hoping the flash of wealth would change her mind. It didn't. By the end of the summer, Madeline decided to move to Miami permanently. Living farther away from Bill couldn't hurt the children that much since he rarely visited them when he lived only a few miles down the road. His airplanes were too important, she suspected. Besides, the children needed a more permanent home. In the previous six years, they had lived like gypsies — in five different places in Chicago and in a different house in Miami each winter.

While Madeline was settling into the home she had rented for $50 a month, Lear Developments was beginning to fall apart. Warren Knotts and the crew were turning out Radioaires, but no one was buying them. The easy sells had already purchased their receivers months before and Lear was running out of money. Part of his problem was that he couldn't control his personal spending: as long as he had money, he lived as if there were no tomorrow. But another part of the problem was that Glenview was not exactly the flying capital of the world. Too few pilots touched down there. So Lear sent Knotts to Roosevelt Field in Mineola, Long Island — one of the busiest airports for private fliers in the country — to promote, sell, and install Radioaires through Aircraft Accessories, whose owner, Leroy Hill, liked Lear's radios and believed in instruments for independent pilots.

Knotts made a few sales for Lear Developments, the most important of which was to Alexander de Seversky, the most famous Russian Navy pilot of World War I. While visiting the United States when the Bolsheviks seized power in 1917, de Seversky had decided to stay. Soon he was designing and building airplanes. He asked Lear to design a radio for his new amphibian, the Idofloat, a powerful low-wing monoplane with retractable wheels and ingenious floats that could change angles for water landings. Unfortunately for Lear, the Idofloat was never mass-produced. Knotts made a few more sales at Floyd Bennett Field, but he kept running into the same old granite wall: "Who needs radios when we have railroad tracks?" Knotts finally quit Lear Developments and went to work for RCA.

When money got tight in Chicago, Lear traded his Monocoupe for a Waco and flew into Roosevelt Field with Charlene as his secretary, ready to start over again. He set up shop in a one-room storefront at 157 Chambers Street, which was owned by Fred Link, a radio engineer and friend. His $8-a-week room in a Brooklyn hotel, he'd later joke, was so small that he had to hang his toothbrush in the hall.

By April 1934, three months after he had left Chicago, Lear was so deeply in debt that the future seemed hopeless. In Chicago, where he had worked and partied for years, he was somebody. The presidents of all the major radio manufacturing companies there knew and respected him. He had drunk moonshine with every pilot who regularly flew in and out of the Windy City. A whole generation of Chicago radio engineers had watched him design, invent, and wheel and deal. Even the Chicago newspaper reporters had begun to notice him.

In New York, Bill Lear was just one more engineer with a showcase of radios nobody wanted to buy. Though his head was full of ideas, including a preliminary design for a direction finder, he had no capital. At thirty-two, he seemed to be right back where he had been six and a half years earlier, when he moved to Chicago with a new wife and the law nipping at his heels. To make his financial problems seem worse, Galvin was beginning to take off, though not without a few false starts.

Its 1933 Motorola Model 55 had been a disaster. The power supply was underdesigned and the vibrator would stick, causing the transformer to overheat and the car to catch fire if the driver didn't smell something first. One Model 55 owner in Sioux City, Iowa, burned up his car, his garage, and half of his house. Another Motorola installed in a hearse cremated the cadaver it was carrying. Galvin had to recall several thousand sets, salvage the tubes and speakers, and junk the rest.

Sensing the potential, General Electric had also begun moving into the growing car radio market. Only 500,000 of the 20 million cars on the road had radios in January 1934, and slightly more than half of the motorists no longer considered car radios a safety hazard. In mid 1933, GE announced a new set for the 1934 cars — both speaker and receiver in one box that could be attached to the car with a single bolt if the car had a built-in aerial, four superheterodyne tubes delivering the utmost in sound, and the vibrator shielded for noise reduction. GE poured hundreds of thousands of dollars into advertising in slick magazines like the *Saturday Evening Post,* whetting the national appetite for entertainment on wheels. Fortunately for Galvin, GE's 1934 model, which sold for $64.50, was defective, and dealers began returning them. Galvin, which couldn't afford to advertise, picked up the slack with a technically flawless 1934 Motorola offering everything that GE had promised and more, and for only $49.50. Of the 780,000 car radios sold that year, more than half were Motorolas.

For Bill Lear, it was a different story — child support for Mary Louise; alimony and child support for Madeline, who was not working; a staff that hadn't been paid in weeks; creditors pestering Lear's receptionist, Alice Miller, to the point where her only answer was "I haven't been paid either, so what are you complaining about?"; a batch of ideas he couldn't develop because he had no money; and Galvin beginning to grow fat from a product he had engineered.

Lear's future looked so bleak that he seriously thought about suicide. Later, he would joke about how he had gone from riches to rags in one roller-coaster year. "I bought a bottle of Scotch," he'd say, "and spent my last dollar on a room in the tallest hotel I could find. I planned to jump. But when I got to the room, I remembered I was afraid of heights. So I drank the Scotch and went to bed."

Lear threatened suicide many times in his life when his dreams seemed shattered, but he was not the kind of man to give up easily. *The Book of Life* by Robert Collier, which Charlene gave him, offered new hope and ultimately changed the way he viewed life and himself.

Lear found Collier's thesis compelling in its simplicity. The future is entirely in your hands, Collier argued; any *one* thing you want you can have, as long as you know what it is and subordinate everything else to it. To get what you want, fill your conscious mind with all the available facts and let your subconscious work on them. It will seek and find the answer in the Universal Mind, which contains the correct solution to every problem. Then relax, wait, and listen closely. The answer will come. Finally, be successful first in your own mind, never believing you can fail. Look the part. Dress the part. Act the part.

Lear put Collier's principles to work. Forgetting airplanes until he could get his financial bearings, he fell back on what he knew best. He stuffed his mind with all the radio problems and needs he could think of, then told his subconscious to go to work.

Part Two

Creating a Legend

7

FRED LINK HAD an interesting piece of broken equipment in his shop on Chambers Street. "What is it?" Lear asked.

"A signal generator," Link said.

The Ferris signal generator was an important piece of test equipment invented by Dr. Robert Ferris. What made it special was Ferris's drum or turret tuner, which found and tested radio frequencies. Ferris had been selling his invention "from the trunk of his car" because he didn't have the money to hire salesmen, and the De Forest Radio Company, where Link was assistant chief engineer, had bought one. When Lee De Forest, one of America's most creative broadcasting inventors, went bankrupt, the employees who were owed back salary were encouraged to take lab equipment as partial payment. Link grabbed the Ferris signal generator and several of De Forest's U.S. Navy contacts.

As he studied the turret tuner, Lear saw a way to apply it to radios that no one had ever spotted before, even though the instrument had been around for more than a year. Lear told Link he could design a multiband radio around a similar turret tuner, making tuning easier, cheaper, and better. Then he could sell it to the Navy.

Link introduced Lear to a Navy engineer, to whom Lear showed his sketches. After describing his new concept with great confidence, he got a contract big enough to buy a few weeks and to pay back rent. One day Warren Knotts stopped by the shop and saw Lear tooling his multiband tuner. Knotts was impressed with the concept and with Lear's craftsmanship. "The tuner was beautiful," he recalls. "Bill always made beautiful stuff." With nothing specific in mind, Knotts told Lear what a "godsend" that would be for RCA.

The next day, Lear was describing his five-band turret tuner to Russell King, sales manager for RCA Victor. Lear said that in two weeks he could produce a prototype that would fit any RCA home radio. To do that, however, he would need $500 for materials and a box of RCA radio components. If RCA would spring for the development, he'd give the company first option on the tuner. King agreed.

It was not easy to adapt Ferris's concept to a home radio. Lear had to redesign the tuner as well as design and make the tools before he could handcraft each part. Then he had to test and adjust it. When it was finished, after two weeks of almost around-the-clock work with John Wehner and Reeder Nichols, Lear asked to demonstrate the tuner personally to E. T. Cunningham, president of RCA Victor, in Camden, New Jersey.

Lear spent the night before the meeting at the Knotts home. Knotts, of course, had the latest RCA tabletop radio, and Lear pulled out his soldering iron and went to work on it, installing the tuner. It was a dress rehearsal for the show he would put on for Cunningham. Recalls Knotts: "The thing that was so impressive was that Bill put his clean, ordinary-looking package into that RCA rat's nest of wires with so little effort. It cleaned up a mess back there. Bill had the intuition to see how the turret tuner could be used in broadcasting. No one else had the common sense to see that."

Lear's version of his two meetings with Cunningham goes something like this:

When he walked into the president's office, Lear asked for a standard tabletop RCA radio. Then he whipped out his soldering iron and screwdriver. In a matter of minutes, he had the tuner installed and the radio playing. Cunningham listened for a few moments before calling in his production manager and his team of engineers, who weren't impressed. But Cunningham clearly was.

"Can I see you in your office tomorrow to discuss a deal?" he asked.

Lear agreed, but as he left the RCA building, he began to get a little nervous. He didn't have an office to speak of, and he didn't want Cunningham to see how hungry he was. That would give RCA Victor a bargaining edge.

As luck would have it, Cunningham called Lear at eleven the next morning and asked him to come to his New York office instead. In the elevator to Cunningham's fifty-third-floor suite, Lear began to argue out his strategy. If you don't value yourself, no one else will. Don't take a cent less than $10,000 unless you can only get $5,000. Of course, even $2,500 would pay a lot of bills. Better yet, don't quote any price. Force Cunningham to make the offer.

"Bill," Cunningham started, "we looked into your idea, and we believe we have a patent on that thing."

"Well, Mr. Cunningham," Lear said, "I didn't sell you a patent. I just brought you an idea."

"Don't feel badly," Cunningham added hastily. "We're still interested in buying it. What do you want for it?"

"You know more about what it's worth to you," Lear said. "Why don't you suggest something?"

"Well, based on the fact that we don't think it is patentable, we'll give you $50,000 cash," Cunningham offered.

Lear was stunned.

Cunningham misread Lear's silence as rejection. "Also, we'll give you $25,000 a year for five years as a retainer to be our consultant," he added.

Lear was still speechless.

"We'll give you $15,000 worth of work a year besides. That makes a total of $40,000 a year for five years, plus $50,000 for the patent."

"That's very nice of you," Lear managed to say. "I'll take it."

Cunningham wrote out a check then and there for $50,000, and Lear floated the four miles back to his office.

RCA has no record of its financial arrangement with Lear in 1934, so it is not possible to verify Lear's recollection of the specifics of the contract. But both Link and Knotts agree that the deal was substantial and that it was another turning point in Bill Lear's life.

RCA never used Lear's patented design as such. "There were too many empires around the place that the tuner would have put out of business," Knotts explains. "But I think RCA got its money's worth many times over. They used it for ideas. All radios and all TV sets until the mid seventies were based on the turret-type tuner. Had Bill been the originator of that idea, he would have made many, many millions."

With the $50,000 he got from RCA, Lear paid off his creditors and rented an elegant two-bedroom penthouse with a large balcony in the London Terrace Apartment Hotel in Manhattan, living out one of Collier's principles: to be successful, you have to think the part, dress the part, and act the part. Lear became so good at acting out his convictions that he began radiating, even more than in Chicago, a sureness and self-confidence about his work and his future. People began to sense that Lear was a man who knew what he wanted and who had no doubt he would get it.

Properly bankrolled at last, Lear entered into a loose partnership with Fred Link (who already had an engineering staff and a loft full of tools) and hired Norman Wonderlich, the former chief engineer of product design for RCA Victor, to be his executive vice president (Lear hated paperwork); Irv Johnson, who had managed Quincy Radio Laboratories, to be his office manager and treasurer (Lear hated administrative work); and John Wehner, his tool and die man at Galvin, as his chief mechanical engineer. Lear's arrangement with Link was as flexible as his association with Paul Galvin had been. He and Link, who was designing and manufacturing two-way police radios, shared the same 10,000-square-foot loft, tools, and executive office. "The same engineers worked on his projects and mine," Link recalls. "We never had a problem." Irv Johnson kept the books, prorating expenses as best he could. When a customer dropped by Lear Developments or someone from RCA or the Navy came to check on progress, Lear would be perched behind the executive desk, looking very busy. When Link had to meet someone important, the same office became the nerve center for Link Radio.

With a steady flow of capital from RCA for consulting and design work (debts, rent, and furniture had quickly eaten up the $50,000), Lear could turn his attention back to his sketches for a direction finder. Like the Radioaire receiver, the aircraft direction finder, or radio compass, was not a new idea. The Signal Corps, which provided technical assistance to the armed services, had been trying to perfect a direction finder since the late 1920s but hadn't been very successful. The corps' basic problem was human, not technological. There was a vicious power struggle going on between the Signal Corps, whose engineers were supposed to develop the direction finder, and the Army Air Corps, which desperately wanted one in its fighters. Until 1931, when Lear broke into the aviation radio business in Glenview, Signal Corps engineers had been spending so much of their time trying to improve air-to-ground communication that they fell behind in developing navigation instruments. Simply put, Signal Corps engineers were more radio technicians than pilots, and whether fighters ever got to where they were supposed to go was of less importance to them than clearly hearing over their headsets how lost the pilots really were. As one military historian summarized it: "To the Air Corps, the Signal Corps was slow and unimaginative in adapting radio to . . . air navigation. To the Signal Corps, the Air Corps' restiveness . . . appeared grounded upon a desire to take over a province of great prestige."

The smoldering power struggle broke into an open fight in 1934. That year Lieutenant Albert F. Hegenberger, an Air Corps pilot who had made pioneer flights from California to Hawaii in 1927 and who was considered one of the Air Corps' top instrument pilots, organized a navigation instrument section at Wright Field in Dayton, Ohio, in the same building that the Signal Corps' Air Radio Laboratory was located. Under the impression that Hegenberger would only be testing its instruments, ARL loaned him its best civilian engineer, Geoffrey Kruesi, whom the Signal Corps had recently hired to develop the E-1 direction finder under pressure from the Army Air Corps. Kruesi had brought with him to the Signal Corps a direction finder design for which a patent was pending.

Once Hegenberger got the inventor inside his shop, however, he wouldn't give him back to ARL. Instead, Hegenberger and Kruesi began building their own radio compass according to the specifications of a real pilot, not armchair fliers. Soon "a deadly serious fight was going on," with Hegenberger locking his laboratory because Signal Corps engineers were stealing equipment and parts to sabotage his work, and with the Signal Corps' accusing Hegenberger of plagiarizing its radio compass design and kidnapping its inventor. Matters got so bad that Captain Tom C. Rives, the director of ARL, had to ask Washington for an official court of inquiry.

The ramifications of this almost childish power struggle were serious. As the Nazis became more and more strident in Berlin, it was becoming clearer in Washington that war in Europe was inevitable and only a matter of time. A direction finder that was practical, light, and simple would be of paramount importance in a war that, everyone knew, would be won or lost in the air.

Lear had no idea of the climate at Wright Field when he walked into the Air Corps lab to show sketches of his radio compass to Hegenberger and Kruesi. With an antenna like a huge wedding ring attached to the roof of the plane, Lear's direction finder (built around the Radioaire) would allow the pilot to home in on any commercial, marine, or Department of Commerce radio station within a 300-mile radius during the day. For example, pilots flying from New York to Pittsburgh could tune in to Pittsburgh radio station KDKA, lock the direction finder on the beam, and listen to music if they wished. The direction finder had a right-left needle, shaped like an airplane, on the instrument panel. If the plane was on the beam, the needle would be dead center. If the needle wandered to the right, the pilot would turn right to get back on course.

Lear had never dealt with the government before. He figured he could show them what he had in mind, as he had with Russ King at RCA, and they would give him a contract and a pile of development money to make a prototype. Then, after the government saw how well the prototype direction finder worked, it would give him a production contract for a few thousand instruments. With an actor's skill that allowed him to be as smooth as twenty-year-old Scotch or as nasty as bile, depending on what the script called for, Lear misread the cues and chose to be nasty. His own account of what happened at Wright Field went something like this:

Hegenberger showed Lear engineering sketches for the Kruesi radio compass. As he studied the plans, Lear noted a design flaw. "I think I can demonstrate that this equipment will not work," he told Hegenberger.

Hegenberger led him into a black-curtained room where the Kruesi direction finder was hidden. "Take a bearing on any station you want," Lear invited Kruesi. The inventor tuned the receiver.

"Now, where's the station?" Lear asked. Kruesi pointed.

Lear retuned the receiver ever so slightly so that the radio signal would be distorted. "*Now* where is the station?" Kruesi pointed in a different direction.

"How come the station was coming from that corner of the room a minute ago," Lear asked, "and now it's coming from the opposite corner?" Kruesi was so embarrassed, he stomped out of the room without a word.

Hegenberger began to chide Lear. "You know, Bill," he said, "the Air Corps is like a club. If you criticize a member, you criticize the whole club. I think you have made yourself persona non grata with the Air Corps, and I don't think you can do anything for us."

Much of that account smacks of a good "Bill Lear story," but the facts are essentially correct. Lear's design was superior to Kruesi's, as the Air Corps later learned; Lear could have built a direction finder better, faster, and cheaper than the Air Corps; Lear had hoped to sell Hegenberger what *he* wanted, not necessarily what Hegenberger wanted; and Lear's feeling of superiority crushed a lot of toes and sent him back to the loft on West Seventeenth Street empty-handed.

What Lear needed in mid 1934 was a customer who would order a direction finder and who would help bear the development cost. An old friend, Roscoe Turner, gave him the opportunity he had been waiting for.

Turner asked Lear to design and build a radio receiver-transmitter, intercom, and direction finder for the standard Boeing 247 transport he would fly in the MacRobertson International Air Race from London to Melbourne, Australia, which the *New York Times* called "one of the greatest races ever held in the world." Simply having equipment in Turner's airplane, international race or not, meant publicity for Lear. Turner, who called himself Colonel (even though he wasn't one) and who sported a waxed mustache and wore a pale blue uniform with gleaming riding boots and a scarlet scarf as wild as the lion cub who frequently flew with him, was an aviation institution. He had set a string of transcontinental flying records, and his shelves were filled with air race trophies. Although Turner had known Lear from the Glenview airport days, he hired him principally because Reeder Nichols, his radio man for the MacRobertson International, had suggested him. Nick, of course, had built Radioaires for Lear along with Warren Knotts and Freddy Schnell.

With a scant six weeks to design and build the gear, Lear put his and Link's engineering team on the project in shifts around the clock. The radio receiver operated on sixteen different frequencies; the transmitter delivered 160 watts. Whenever he couldn't get out to his Waco at Roosevelt Field on Long Island, Lear tested the direction finder from his Plymouth sedan, driving around Manhattan. As takeoff day approached, Turner and his copilot, Clyde Pangborn, who (with Hugh Herndon) had flown the first nonstop flight between Japan and the continental United States in 1931 in a Wasp-powered Bellanca, were the only fliers with a direction finder in their ship. Laura Ingalls, the U.S. race coordinator, had written to the Army Air Corps to ask if it would equip each U.S. plane with a Kruesi radio compass, but the Air Corps told her it had no spares, thus passing up the opportunity to have its equipment tested under tough flying conditions.

Before he left for London, Nichols promised Lear he'd radio messages to him during the race whenever he had the chance, so it was with great anticipation that Lear waited for the morning of October 20, 1934.

In all, there were twenty planes, from Australia, Britain, Holland, and the United States, competing for the $50,000 purse sponsored by MacPherson Robertson, an Australian businessman who called the race to commemorate Melbourne's centennial. The pilots had to make five control-point stops along their 11,323-mile route: Baghdad, Iraq; Allahabad, India; Singapore; and Darwin and Charlesville, Australia. They could stop or refuel anywhere else they liked.

Early on the morning of October 20, the planes took off into overcast skies from the Mildenhall Aerodrome, just outside London. Each leg of the race was hazardous in its own way. Turner and Pangborn's huge Boeing 247D, which United Airlines was using for its transcontinental flights, bucked a fifty-mile-an-hour headwind all across Europe. "We saw nothing from London to the Alpine peaks," Turner reported. "Then we got a glimpse of the Adriatic." The Boeing touched down in Baghdad in fifth place, well behind the sleek crimson de Havilland Comet piloted by two Englishmen. Before the day was over, five planes had dropped out of the race because of mechanical problems. Turner and Pangborn were the only Americans still in the air.

On the second leg, Turner and Pangborn had to cross mountains at night, and they ran into trouble when they flew 200 miles beyond the airport over dense jungles, where every tree looked like the last. They were lost. "When we saw our gasoline gauge showing zero," Pangborn reported, "we tried to keep up our spirits by joking about whether we would be killed by crashing into the jungle or be eaten by tigers." Although the gauge didn't show it, the Boeing transport still had a hundred gallons of gas. Reeder Nichols put the ship back on course by picking up a radio beam from Allahabad on Lear's radio compass.

The third leg, to Singapore, was smooth. Two pilots in a British Fairey Fox had crashed into the hills near Rome and were dead. Turner and Pangborn were now running third.

The fourth leg of the race led them across shark-infested waters at the southwestern tip of Borneo and across the Java and Timor seas. During the two-hour flight along Borneo, Nick worked a list of radio stations around the world, setting several world transmission records on Lear's radio — KSF and KPH in San Francisco; KUH Manila; LGN in Bergen, Norway; FOAL Marseilles; and the S.S. *President Jackson*, 1,000 miles east of Yokohama, Japan.

One of the Boeing's engines faltered over the Timor Sea because of a broken fuel supply line, and Turner and Pangborn had visions of bobbing in the ocean, waiting for the great whites to come by for breakfast. Instead, after waiting two hours for repairs in Darwin, in northern Australia, they took off across the Australian desert for their last checkpoint at Charlesville. On the final flight, to Melbourne, Nick radioed Lear through San Francisco, 9,000 miles away: "On home stretch . . . arriving Melbourne at daybreak . . . transmitter and receiver working fine."

Turner and Pangborn came in third, behind the two Englishmen (C. Scott and T. Campbell Black) in their de Havilland Comet and two Dutchmen (J. J. Moll and K. D. Parentier) flying an American Douglas DC-2 transport that TWA was using on its transcontinental flights. The Englishmen had streaked to Melbourne in 2 days, 4 hours, and 35 minutes, shattering the old record of 6 days, 17 hours, and 45 minutes.

After eighteen straight hours of sleep, Nichols wrote to Lear from Melbourne: "I want to express my thanks to the boys in the laboratory and the shop for the thorough manner in which they mastered every detail of the design and construction of what I honestly believe to be the best equipment ever installed in an airplane. It was a great source of satisfaction to me to know that among our other worries, I was not bothered by the thought that my radio would let me down . . .

"The direction finder worked beautifully, especially when coming into Charlesville. This country is absolutely featureless and every mile looks just like the last 1,000 miles you have passed, so it was great to pick up bearings 450 miles away and run a chalk line over the jungles until we hit Charlesville right on the nose. Never did the equipment fail me."

Like Commander McDonald, who once advertised Zenith radios as the choice of explorers because he had sent a Zenith short-wave set on a National Geographic expedition to the Arctic, Lear milked the Turner-Pangborn 11,000-mile flight for every drop of publicity he could get, printing their telegrams and letters of congratulations and thanks in his brochures. But the Army Air Corps still clung to Kruesi, and if they followed the rough-and-tumble MacRobertson International, they never told Lear. They merely placed an order for one Lear radio compass.

In January 1935, three months after the air race, Lear publicly unveiled his direction finder, which he called the Learoscope. He had become a master at public relations. *Newsweek* did a major story on him and his radio compass, the first on the market for the independent pilot. Although the technology had been available for several years and inventors in the United States and England had been working on it, Lear was the first person to design a prototype that worked flawlessly and consistently. Elements of the instrument could have been patented, but without the money for a patent attorney to research radio compasses, electrical circuits, and antennas, Lear did not file for any.

Technically, the *Newsweek* feature story "Radio Compass: Fly by It and Listen to Broadcast Music" was sound; but it was filled with Lear hype. Lear had told *Newsweek* that his company had "made a quarter of a million" in Chicago on the Radioaire and that he had come to New York because he was afraid he was getting "in a rut." In fact, he had fled Chicago because he was dancing on the brink of financial disaster. If he had sold $100,000 worth of receivers there, he had been very lucky.

Lear also told *Newsweek* that he had actually worked on the Army Air Corps' radio compass at Wright Field and that he had quit because he had been "completely ostracized by Army pilots for his generous criticism of their radio technique." It is not surprising that Geoffrey Kruesi wrote an angry letter to the editor. "The fact is," he said, "Lear never was employed at Wright Field so he could not have 'left.' Nor did he ever work on the army radio compass. His sole connection with Wright Field was that he built a compass at the order of the government, the exact value of which has not yet been determined."

Around the same time that the *Newsweek* full-page story appeared, the *New York Herald Tribune* ran a piece about two Yale men, Dr. Richard U. Light and Robert F. Wilson, who had just returned from a five-month, 40,000-mile, zigzag trip around the world in a Bellanca Seaplane with a Lear five-band receiver. "We're just a couple of amateurs flying for fun, experience and firsthand information," Dr. Light told the *Herald Tribune*. "And [we were] saved from bother by first-rate equipment. We were never in difficulty, aloft or afloat. We particularly recommend the two-way radio which functioned perfectly."

Soon after these two stories appeared, Lear talked World War I ace Captain Eddie Rickenbacker into putting a Learoscope on an Eastern Airlines flight from Miami to New York. (Rickenbacker was working for Eastern at the time.) In a press conference after the flight, Rickenbacker called Lear's direction finder "the most important air navigation aid developed to date."

Turner, Pangborn, Nichols, Dr. Light, Rickenbacker, an international air race, and a 'round-the-world flight — these were all heady endorsements of Lear's radio and direction finder, but the Army Air Corps still kept Lear at arm's length. So he took the next logical step. He brought his direction finder to the Bureau of Air Commerce, which wanted to improve private flying as well as commercial aviation and which had been working on a radio compass for fifteen years without much success. If Lear could get the bureau to endorse his radio compass, he figured he would have a better shot at reaching the roughly 7,500 private pilots in the country as well as the major airlines. He convinced Director Eugene Vidal to commission the bureau to test his Learoscope to see if it would be of any value to the private pilot. Vidal hired his friend Amelia Earhart, for $1 a year, to fly Lear's direction finder (slightly rebuilt according to bureau specifications) in her bright red Lockheed Vega "primarily to determine its possibilities as an air navigation aid for private owners of aircraft." To draw Earhart as a test pilot was a promotional coup, for the aviatrix — the first woman to cross the Atlantic, in 1928, just one year after Charles E. Lindbergh — was a darling of the media. Vidal asked her "to make notes and observations which will assist [the bureau] to perfect the instrument."

The *Air Commerce Bulletin* described the purpose of the test: "The [Lear] radio direction finder will simplify cross-country air navigation, especially for the private flyer, if it measures up in practice to the results obtained experimentally. Universal application is its main advantage because there is always some type of radio station in operation in almost every section of the country at all hours. Successful application of the radio direction finder would contribute to the safety of flight by helping to eliminate accidents brought about by airmen straying from the plotted course."

At the invitation of the Mexican government, Earhart selected a nonstop flight from Los Angeles to Mexico City as the first test. "I've always wanted to visit Mexico but have never seemed to get around to it," announced Earhart, who had recently soloed from Hawaii to California. "I will . . . put in the Lear radio 'homing' compass that I am supposed to test . . . I intend to use it in this flight, thereby combining business with pleasure, for I always loved Mexican music and all I'll have to do is tune in on a Mexico City station, and use it just as though it were a radio beacon."

Lear couldn't have been more pleased. Earhart drew crowds of tens of thousands wherever she landed around the world, and the press reported her every flight. Besides, no one had ever flown nonstop from Los Angeles to Mexico City. If she succeeded, Earhart would be setting a new world record — with the Learoscope in her sporty little Vega.

8

To PROMOTE the Learoscope and his new two-way radio for small airplanes, the Learophone, Lear scheduled a cross-country tour that would end in Los Angeles, where he'd deliver his radio compass to Amelia Earhart, with a drum roll if possible. At each stop along the way, Lear hoped to demonstrate the Learoscope to airmen and to the local media, and to talk to Bureau of Air Commerce radio operators (the bureau had seventy-eight transmitting stations by then) on his Learophone. He was counting on commercial radio stations in major cities asking for live air-to-ground interviews with him. Although three or four giant companies, like the Bendix Aviation Corporation (which had purchased Kruesi's patent) had radio compasses on their lab benches, they were more interested in the lucrative military and commercial markets than in the private fliers, most of whom could barely afford gas.

Before the official takeoff from Roosevelt Field on April 3, Lear took several Bureau of Air Commerce officials for a demonstration in his Waco cabin biplane. In an airport press conference afterward, they called Lear's direction finder "revolutionary" and of great value for military pilots. It would prove to be a boon for private pilots as well, they said, and might possibly be more powerful than the standard radio equipment required on commercial airlines. After that sendoff, Lear headed for Dayton, Ohio, with Associated Press reporter Wayne Thomis in the right seat.

On the way west, Thomis reported in a widely distributed syndicated story, the needle on the Learoscope began to point to radio station KDKA in Pittsburgh even before they could hear the music. By the time they reached the Alleghenies, the music was clear. Mountain drafts buffeted the plane but, Thomis reported, "the nose of the ship held directly on the radio station."

After flying over Pittsburgh, Lear tuned the direction finder to WOMK in Dayton. The ship held a straight course there. In Dayton, he picked up Howard Ailor, president of the Ailor Sales Corporation and the man Lear hoped would market the instrument for him, and set off for Chicago, homing in on WGN. After press interviews in the Windy City, Lear headed to Wichita to visit Walter Beech, hoping to convince him to offer the Learoscope as an option on all new Beechcrafts. Lear spent an extra day in Wichita to have a live "land-air" interview, the first ever with a private pilot, with radio station KFH. When he landed in Los Angeles a week later, after refuelings and media fun in Amarillo, Texas, Albuquerque, New Mexico, and Kingman, Arizona, Lear was met by Los Angeles reporters. It had cost $43,000 to develop the Learoscope, he told them. And it had once saved the lives of Turner, Pangborn, and Nichols in India. His Learophone was the first practical, affordable, light, two-way communication system on the market for private pilots.

Lear said of the trip several years later: "Howard Ailor used to joke that the only time Bill Lear ever went to church was when he had to listen to a sermon in order to get directional signals on Oklahoma City . . . The thing I remember most on the trip was the large numbers of stations we contacted. It seemed that everybody was eager to talk to a private pilot. These CAA [Civil Aeronautics Administration] radio station operators had heard the airlines, but they had never heard a private airplane.

If they had, it was a very rare occasion. That was really the start of the use of transmitters in private aircraft — after it was discovered that it could be done."

Amelia Earhart took off from Burbank Union Air Terminal at 9:55 P.M. for her historic 1,700-mile nonstop flight to Mexico City on April 19, 1935. She didn't expect to set any speed records in her single-engine snub-nosed Vega, but she did expect to make it there without stopping. Things went well until a bug flew into her eye, forcing her to land in a cow pasture in Napola, a hundred miles from Mexico City. As soon as she touched down, fifty Mexican cowboys "appeared on the run" from nowhere and surrounded the Vega. Their wives and children soon followed. After she cleaned her eye, caught her bearings, and revved her engine, she couldn't take off. Women and children, gauchos and horses, crowded her path. She jumped out of the plane and, with wide sweeping gestures, managed to clear a runway.

Waiting for her and the Learoscope in Mexico City were her husband (the publisher George Putnam), the Mexican Cabinet, and twenty thousand cheering fans. That she had set no new record on her 13-hour, 32-minute flight didn't seem to bother them. Just to have Amelia Earhart visit was enough. The Mexican government feted her, and the Mexican Geographic Society presented her with a medal for her contribution to aviation.

For the 2,135-mile nonstop flight from Mexico City to New York, Earhart had a problem. Taking off in the thin air around Mexico City, 8,000 feet above sea level, with 470 gallons of gas and 22 gallons of oil would be difficult. To give herself plenty of leeway, Earhart hauled the Lockheed Vega to a dried lakebed, four miles long and as flat as a tabletop. It took a mile before the heavy Vega finally lifted off and cleared the mountains around Lake Texoci.

No one had ever attempted a nonstop flight from Mexico City to New York before, although a Mexican pilot had made the reverse flight without a stop in 16 hours and 35 minutes in 1930. Two years later, another Mexican pilot had tried to break that record, but he crashed and was killed shortly after taking off from Roosevelt Field.

Flying an "uneventful" trip in "perfect weather," Earhart

touched down in Newark in 14 hours and 18 minutes, setting three new records: first nonstop flight from Mexico City to New York; nonstop speed record for women in the 2,100-mile category; and a new speed record from Mexico City to Washington, D.C., where she had been clocked as she flew over.

Ten to fifteen thousand fans were waiting in Newark when she touched down, and a cheering mob of three thousand people broke through the cordon of police officers. Before they could reach the Vega, however, she managed to taxi into the Eastern hangar and slip into a waiting limousine. But the car moved barely 200 feet before Earhart's fans surrounded it. Four burly policemen picked her up and carried her to the National Guard terminal, where her husband, Bill Lear, and the press were waiting.

After describing her trip, she told reporters that her Lear radio compass "worked excellently. [It] has persuaded me that this type of equipment will go far toward solving some of transport flying's most vexing problems."

It was another important endorsement for Lear. But two months later Earhart resigned from her $1-a-year job with the Bureau of Air Commerce. "I wish to be free to pursue my commercial aviation activities," she told Vidal. Behind her resignation was a quarrel between Lear and George Putnam. In the years to come, as he told his children about his accomplishments and the people he had known, Lear never mentioned the Earhart episode.

Despite all the promotion and free publicity, Lear was having a hard time selling his receivers, transmitters, and direction finders. Like the good salesman he was, he never missed an opportunity to brag about who was using his Learoscope — movie star and flying buff Wallace Beery, auto tycoon E. L. Cord, Los Angeles talent agent Leland Heyward, jazz pianist and test pilot Roger Wolfe Kahn. There also were curiosity sales to Western, American, and Transcontinental Airlines.

Even Howard Hughes bought a Lear instrument, and Lear gave him a special deal in the hopes of attracting a multimillion-dollar account. But as soon as he had a problem with the set, Hughes started telephoning Lear, collect, three or four times a day. Lear never got the large account. Years later, while Lear was chewing out a salesman, the phone rang. He picked it up and began yelling about an $85 bill. He sputtered, then slammed down the phone.

"My God!" the salesman gasped. "Who was that?"

"Howard Hughes," Lear said. "He borrowed one of my planes. Then the cheap sonofabitch sent me a bill for eighty-five dollars for gas."

The bread-and-butter customers did not come to Lear Developments. The Army Air Corps was sticking with Kruesi; the commercial airlines seemed content with the Bureau of Air Commerce radio beacon system; and private pilots hesitated to spend $600 on a newfangled gadget when they could still follow the railway tracks. It was the same old story.

Lear had dropped RCA because he "didn't want any man or any thing for a boss." Without a market and with limited funds, he did what Marconi had done thirty-five years before. If his own country didn't want his direction finder, he'd take it elsewhere. So, late in the spring of 1935, Bill Lear sailed to Europe on the *Normandie*.

Even though both the Army Air Corps and the Navy had rejected the Learoscope as an alternative to the Kruesi radio compass, the State Department watched with alarm the growing foreign interest in Lear's direction finder. With war in Europe probable, State was not about to allow Lear to export his instrument if it was as good and as important as everyone but the U.S. military was saying. Lear described the government's interest in his trip to Europe this way:

"Every town I would go to, there would be a telephone call as soon as I would arrive. 'This is the military attaché . . . to remind you that any disclosure you make of your direction finder will be considered a violation of the National Espionage Act, and you will be prosecuted accordingly.' Period! Bang!

"This went on. It didn't bother me any because if they didn't want to buy it, I figured it was mine. [But] my people back at the office in New York were getting excited by all of this. Their telephone lines were being tapped and everything. So finally they called me and said, 'Please come home because we can't stand the pressure.' I came home."

Government records support Lear's basic story. Lear had bid

$27,000 to build a direction finder for the Navy according to its specifications, but he lost to RCA, which had never made a direction finder before. Lear also had lost a bid to the Fairchild Aerial Camera Corporation to manufacture 293 Kruesi radio compasses for the Army Air Corps. Both RCA and Fairchild could afford to underbid Lear Developments, which was in debt and could not attract outside financing, because a $200,000 Army Air Corps contract would pull them into the direction finder business without the heavy development costs that Lear had suffered.

When Great Britain, Mexico, Japan, and Canada had all placed orders for the Learoscope, Sidney Mashbir, president of the Washington Institute of Technology, relying on "informed sources," reported Lear to military intelligence. Several months later, after Lear returned from Europe, the Department of State denied him permission to sell any more direction finders to foreign countries, arguing that to do so would be a violation of "military secrecy . . . contrary to the interests of national defense." By the end of September 1935, however, Army Air Corps, Signal Corps, and Navy engineers had all agreed that Lear's direction finder was not the same as the Army's or the Navy's and that his design did not contain Army or Navy secrets.

In the end, the Department of State treated Lear Developments unfairly. It granted export permission first to Fairchild, which had orders from both the Russians and the Japanese, then to RCA. Three months later, State finally notified Lear Developments that it too could export. By that time, both Fairchild and RCA had a slight edge over Lear.

Meanwhile, to keep peace between the Army Air Corps and the Signal Corps, the War Department decided to give back to the Signal Corps the development of all radio and navigation instruments, announcing that it would equip 1,150 warplanes with direction finders by the end of 1936. This decision put the Signal Corps in a politically delicate position. It now had two radio compasses — its own and the one Hegenberger and Kruesi had developed for the Army Air Corps. Which one should it choose?

Even though it believed its own was superior, the Signal Corps could hardly say so without risking the fragile peace. As a compromise, it called for a refereed competition. And to appear open-minded, it invited any reputable company with a direction finder to enter. If a nonmilitary instrument won, its company would be awarded a contract to build approximately five hundred of them.

Lear Developments, Fairchild, and Radio Products of Dayton entered the competition, which was held at Langley Field in Norfolk in late 1935. Lear waited for months for the result. When the Army Air Corps made no announcement, he dismissed the competition as another military farce and went about improving his instrument. Five years later, he asked Colonel George Holloman what had happened in Norfolk. "You won hands down," Holloman said, according to Lear. "There was no comparison of your equipment with the rest."

Who won made no difference, in fact, because the Army changed its mind. Without announcing a winner and with no explanation, it staged a second competition, this time for a direction finder built around a new set of specifications. Any company could submit a model, built at its own expense, and the winner would get a contract for 537.

Lear could not afford to enter this competition, for by the end of 1935 he was in debt once again. In fact, only two manufacturers submitted prototypes — Radio Products and RCA, which won.

Thus Lear, who had contributed more to the development of the direction finder than any other inventor, ended up out in the cold and broke. The only markets open to him were commercial airlines and private pilots (neither of which was convinced it needed direction finders), and the foreign market, which was expensive to find and cultivate. Nevertheless, 1935 was Lear Developments' best year. It had cracked the foreign market, and its net sales had hit $95,240, of which approximately 75 percent was for the Learoscope. Its net loss was only $947. However, by May 1936, Bill Lear was so deeply in debt that his creditors would have forced Lear Developments into bankruptcy if it hadn't been for Gertrude and P. R. Mallory.

Gertrude had died of cancer in December 1935. Bill rarely spoke about her, and when he did, it was only to say how hurt he was that she never understood him. Bill and his stepfather,

Otto, struck a simple deal over her estate. Otto would keep the Plainville farm, Bill, the Chicago house, and they'd divvy up the stock and cash between them. Although Bill's share was substantial, it was not enough to pay off all his creditors.

P. R. Mallory had invited Lear to Indianapolis for what Lear called a "golden sword" award — dinner and his head in a basket. Mallory's executive officers thought they had found a loophole in Lear's 3.5 percent royalty contract on the car radio vibrator and were planning to cut him out. Sensing the ploy, Lear had his attorney draw up a letter stating that he was canceling *his* contract with Mallory and retaining his rights to the vibrator patent.

After the dinner, just as Mallory's chief executive was about to give him the "sword," Lear tossed his letter onto the table and left for his room at the Athletic Club to wait for the hollering. It didn't take long. Would Lear be willing to sell the company his claim on the patent outright? How did $10,000 sound?

Lear told Mallory that he was getting that much each year on royalties alone. How did $25,000 and a stock option at the current price for another $25,000 sound? Mallory accepted the deal. A few months later, its stock quadrupled. Lear exercised his option and made close to $125,000.

With that kind of money to play with, Lear paid off his debts and went back to developing prototype aircraft instruments. He came out with the Learadio R-3 receiver, which weighed just seven pounds and could fit into a five-by-eight-inch panel on the instrument board. Half the weight of most receivers on the market, the R-3 carried all three bands — Department of Commerce beacon (154-400 KC), commercial broadcast (545-1500 KC), and airline (2320-6500 KC). It had simple controls for wave bands, frequency, and volume, and was the most affordable receiver on the market.

Next, Lear redesigned his 15-watt transmitter until it and its battery weighed only fifteen pounds. Hooked into the R-3 receiver, the T-30 became a two-way communications system. To publicize the T-30, Lear flew five miles out over the Atlantic in his Waco to report live, for radio station WOR and the Mutual News Network, the approach of the H.M.S. *Queen Mary* on her maiden voyage to New York.

Next, Lear turned his attention to improving his direction finder. Like the Bendix, Fairchild, and RCA radio compasses, the Learoscope was far from perfect. For one thing, it worked on a 180-degree azimuth. Thus, if the pilot didn't crosscheck his course with a second radio station, he had no way of telling whether he was flying toward or away from the target. Besides this and other engineering defects, there was a much more serious human problem. Pilots simply did not have confidence in the instrument (just as they wouldn't trust autopilots when they first came out many years later).

To see at first hand how pilots were using experimental direction finders, the Army Air Corps put First Lieutenant Roger Williams on a Pan American Airways Clipper flying from Alameda, California, to Manila. Williams reported his observations in May 1936, a year after Lear had begun trying to sell the Learoscope:

"The navigation of the Clipper ships is most effectively done and is accomplished almost entirely by celestial observation. Radio bearings, given every half hour by PA direction finders, were never used when the distance from shore stations exceeded about 200 miles, but were always plotted as a matter of record. In any event, the navigator always regarded the position indicated by radio bearings as subordinate to those indicated by celestial observation and, in a few cases, was well justified in so doing. Without doubt, adverse weather conditions would modify this procedure and the radio direction finder would be of first importance."

The Radio Technical Commission for Aeronautics, which the Bureau of Air Commerce created in 1935, took on the direction finder as one of its first projects. After interviewing commercial pilots, the commission reported that the airlines were reluctant to install direction finders because they cost too much, were too heavy, and slowed the aircraft down too much. Furthermore, the airlines said direction finders were less reliable than the beacon system and that commercial radio stations did not broadcast their call numbers frequently enough.

Rather than discourage engineers like Lear, the commission advised them to improve the instrument by making the loop antenna smaller, to cut down on drag; by shielding the antenna better from rain, snow, and electrical interferences that caused static and finding some way to rotate it for better reception; and by reducing the interference caused by other stations on the band as well as radio wave distortions that led to course error.

Lear took these recommendations seriously and began working on a second-generation direction finder, which he called Aircraft Radio Compass 5. He reduced the size of the loop from 24 inches in diameter to 10; he made the loop moistureproof and invented a reel so that the pilot could turn the antenna toward the transmitting station. And through improved electronic circuitry, he was able to cut down on the static, interference, and distortion.

Lear then concentrated on exporting his equipment, especially the R-3 receivers and T-30 transmitters. He hired independent entrepreneur Lazar Gelin, an MIT graduate who could speak eight languages, to handle his international sales on commission. One of the company's first big export jobs was for the Soviet Union, which had approached it through Gelin to see if Lear could design and build a 100-watt radio transmitter and receiver for its new showpiece flying boat, the *Maxim Gorky,* being built by the Glenn Martin Company of Baltimore. It would be the largest amphibian in the world and the first capable of flying nonstop from New York to London with passengers aboard. Lear bid $25,000 for the job.

"We have a better offer from Western Electric," the Russians told him.

"If you want it ready-made," Lear said, "buy from Western Electric. But if you want custom-made, you have to buy mine." They did.

Foreign markets helped Lear Developments double its net sales in 1937 — Belgium, South Africa, Japan, Lithuania, Java. But despite the improvement in finances, Lear was in worse trouble than ever before. RCA was threatening to shut him down. Lear was using RCA components in his radio equipment without an RCA license. It was a Catch-22. If a manufacturer couldn't guarantee to produce the number of sets per year that RCA required, RCA would deny it a license. If the manufacturer used the patented parts anyway, it faced a possible lawsuit.

He had asked RCA for a license, but it declined to give him

one because he was selling, at most, a total of only two thousand receivers, transmitters, and direction finders a year. (RCA was demanding sales of about fifty thousand sets.) On the other hand, RCA did not seem to care if Lear sold his equipment abroad, so exporting was the one way he could avoid court action.

For Lear, the problem was more serious than living under the constant threat of a lawsuit. Lear Developments desperately needed an infusion of cash to place it on a firm financial footing and to give it time and space to grow. Without an RCA license, however, no bank or professional investor would take the risk.

RCA wasn't Lear's only problem. Vincent Bendix, the president and founder of the Bendix Aviation Corporation, began to see Lear's direction finder as a threat. Compared to the original 1935 Learoscope, the 1938 ARC-5 was a huge improvement; it had a shielded, rotatable, and smaller loop antenna; a 360-degree azimuth, so that pilots could tell whether they were flying toward or away from a radio station; and an antenna reel, which allowed pilots to rotate the loop toward the transmitting station, thus reducing the possibility of navigational error.

Bendix asked to see Lear at the Waldorf-Astoria. Working out of a suite of five rooms, with a deal hatching in each, Bendix was an industrial barracuda who had begun crunching small companies making airplane parts in the mid 1930s — Eclipse Aviation, Scintilla Magneto, Pioneer Instruments, Delco Aviation. Now he had his eye on Lear Developments.

Like Lear, Vince Bendix was a high school dropout with almost 150 patents to his name. He had invented the automobile starter drive just as World War I began, and in 1924 he founded the Bendix Corporation to manufacture an important invention for car brakes. Before long, every car off the assembly line carried at least one Bendix part. When Lindbergh flew the Atlantic in 1927 and single-handedly created an aviation boom, Bendix, ever restless and hungry, seized the opportunity. He changed the company's name to the Bendix Aviation Corporation and began to buy everything in sight. To publicize his name and to focus national attention on aviation, he set up the annual Bendix transcontinental trophy race — in which Bill Lear, Jr., would one day compete.

As Lear recalled, Bendix saw him as fish bait:

"We'll give you $50,000 for a minority interest in your company — 49 percent," Bendix offered. "We want you to control it."

"That seems all right to me," Lear said.

"Bring down all the common stock of your company."

"Not *all*," Lear objected. "You want 49 percent."

"No, bring it all in," Bendix explained. "The way we're going to do it is to issue $100,000 worth of Bendix stock for your company, and we'll give you 51 percent of that."

Lear stared at Vince Bendix for a few minutes, then rose to his feet. "It's one thing to try to cheat me," he said. "It's something else to underestimate my intelligence . . . I wouldn't own 51 percent of my own company. I would have a very minute interest in the Bendix Corporation." And he walked out.

Bendix had completely misunderstood the man. Believing that money was the most important thing, he offered Lear cash for his independence; what Lear really wanted most was recognition and fame. Once he had those, Lear believed, there would be a lot more money than the piddling dollars Bendix was offering. And to get that fame, Lear needed his independence.

Having failed to buy Lear out, Bendix tried a little corporate sabotage by luring away Lear's engineers and designers, paying top dollar and good benefits in the hope that Lear Developments would collapse. Suspecting that Bendix had bought out his chief executive, Norm Wonderlich, Lear fired Wonderlich, considering him a Bendix spy, and held his ground. "I was left completely destitute of talent," Lear would later say.

Bendix asked to see Lear again. "Mr. Bendix would like you to write down exactly what it is you want," the tycoon's assistant said.

Lear sat behind the desk of Bendix's suite and began his list: a dirigible, a fleet of airplanes and cars, an open expense account, no responsibility, and a promise that he'd stay thirty-five years old for the next five hundred years.

Lear waited while the assistant delivered the list. He heard a shout. Bendix burst into the room draped in a barber's apron, his face half covered with shaving cream. "Damn it, Bill," he shouted, "this is what *I* want!"

Lear's accounts of his confrontations with Vince Bendix smack of hyperbole, but the facts are essentially correct. Bendix did try to swallow Lear; Lear swam away; and the two inventors and their companies remained fierce competitors for the next twenty years.

9

IN MID 1938, Bill Lear broke with Fred Link, just as he had with Julius Buerkin in Quincy and Paul Galvin in Chicago. Lear moved first into a hangar in Riverhead, Long Island, then to Roosevelt Field in Mineola, where he converted an old hangar into a factory and painted LEAR RADIO on the roof in huge letters so that every pilot would see it. Within weeks, Building 31, a one-story wooden box on the west edge of the field, was humming. Lear put in rows of worktables and an assembly line, setting aside one room for the laboratory and one for the front office. He hired between thirty and forty men to build R-3 receivers, T-30 and the new UT-6 transmitters, and direction finders. Another small crew installed equipment in customers' airplanes in a nearby hangar. As Lear explained it, the move to Roosevelt Field made great sense: "It was important that I was close to the customer and close to the airplane. And that way I could use some of my engineers and some of my technicians for both the building . . . and the installing of the equipment."

On his own in Mineola, Lear's lifestyle began to freeze into a pattern. Unlike most men, he had no hobbies like hunting or fishing or golf. When fired up by an idea or trying to fill an important order, he worked until he was exhausted, simply snatching a few hours of sleep in his office. He loved to rush into what seemed like impossible projects. Every time he failed, he chalked it up to experience and began hunting for something else to do. As Fred Link observed, "Bill threw away more money than most people will ever know about. Foolish projects." Driven by ideas, he was easily bored; demanding, he got the most from his coworkers. His curiosity and willingness to take risks created an exciting work environment, but his insecurity led him to constantly reinforce his authority. More and more, Lear began to use fear as a way to command respect and to squeeze the most out of his workers; and more and more, he began to take credit for things he never did.

Lear developed the habit of coming up behind workers and shouting at them "What the hell are you doing?" or finding fault with them and dressing them down in front of others. "Some found it difficult to work for him," Joe Lorch, a lab engineer in Mineola, recalls. "If you cringed when he came in, he'd take advantage. If you stood your ground, he'd respect that to a degree."

Lear's stamina became legendary, and he expected everyone else to keep the pace he set. The problem was, he frequently cheated. On the pretext of pressing paperwork, he'd step into his office around ten at night and nap for an hour. "How's it going?" he'd say afterward to his engineers, bent over their workbenches trying to meet an impossible deadline. But Lear wasn't fooling anyone; most of the workers understood the game and played along. It was so exciting to work for Lear that they were willing to put up with his quirks. Standing on the cutting edge of aerial navigation, he brought them drama and history. And with Roscoe Turner, Jackie Cochran, Wallace Beery, bankers, oil tycoons, Wall Street brokers, and corporate presidents walking in and out, they had a taste of fame, too.

Lear's need to be in charge and take credit for all developments — whether his or not — reached almost ridiculous proportions by 1939. The engineers would refine a procedure or a design, noting the improvement in their lab journals. "Bill would come by," Lorch explains, "pick up the log book and enter next to the item, 'Invented by William P. Lear, witnessed by _____.' He'd then ask you to sign as witness. It was never a major invention, just some circuit development. I felt sad but not angry that he'd take the credit. Bill was a genius. Everything else blanches in comparison. People around him would have all the bits and pieces spread out in front of them. Lear would come by and tie them all together when no one else could."

The year 1939 was another turning point in Lear's career for several important reasons. When he first began work on the Learoscope, he was years behind inventors like Kruesi. But once he built, tested, and began improving his direction finder, he jumped so far ahead of the pack that he could file for fifteen patents, all of which centered around two developments: his antenna reeling system for trailing antennas, which hung out of the belly of planes like long, loose wires; and his new automatic direction finder, the first one on the market for independent pilots.

Because trailing antennas were dangerous during both landing and takeoff, pilots would have to reel them in by hand in addition to all their other tasks at those two critical times. Lear, who was sensitive to the needs of pilots, invented an antenna with an automatic remote control. The pilot would set a pointer in the cockpit to the desired antenna length (corresponding to the frequency of the radio transmission) and select the desired speed after takeoff at which the antenna would descend. When the plane reached the correct speed, the antenna would automatically come out of the plane like a big pointer.

Lear's new automatic direction finder (ADF-6) was a breakthrough. Instead of one loop antenna, Lear had two loop coils that rotated, one inside the other, ensuring less static and clearer reception with less course error. The loop coils were kept inside a sealed shell that looked like a football and could be placed on the roof or on the belly of the airplane. The football had a drag of only 3.5 pounds at a speed of 250 miles per hour. The ADF-6 was automatic because Lear had installed a motor to keep the loops constantly facing the radio station at the proper angle. As a result, a needle constantly reported the direction of the ship on a screen, illuminated by one of the new cathode-ray tubes, in degrees of arc rather than right-left, as the Learoscope did. Thus, the pilot not only could see whether the plane was 10 degrees east of the radio tower or 15 degrees west, but, using both the direction finder and a compass, he could chart a straight course to any given destination.

Lear also designed the ADF-6 so that it could be used for blind landings. A decade earlier, the Army Air Corps had introduced a runway localizing beacon that would lead an airplane to the runway if the pilot could pick up and hold on to the signal. The beacon's path, however, was very narrow, and most of the time the pilot would lose it because of drift or wind. In 1934, Captain Hegenberger concocted a system using two beacon signals. So besides trying to fly the airplane and prepare for landing, the pilot also had to fine-tune receivers to two frequencies, make adjustments for drift, read a sensitive altimeter to know how close the ground was, and make several trial approaches to the airstrip just to make sure — all before touching down.

Lear's design used one receiver that simultaneously read both runway beacons on two separate needles. One told the pilot the position of the airport; the other indicated the shortest and most direct approach to the runway. No interpretation or trial approaches were needed. But the Army Air Corps showed little interest in Lear's invention. Instead, at its recommendation, the National Academy of Sciences put together a blue ribbon panel to discuss ways to improve blind landings, which would be vital in the war everyone suspected would soon break out. The panel was to report directly to the President. When Lear heard about the commission, he wrote two letters asking to be appointed. He wasn't, and when the panel finally met, all the members had doctorates of one kind or another.

Hardly had his ADF left the workbench when Lear ran into a puzzling problem that almost cost him his company. Customers began complaining that the new direction finder didn't work. It would function fine for a week or two or even a month; then, without warning, it would stop picking up radio signals for days. As suddenly as it stopped, it would begin working again, hardly a comforting situation. Customers began demanding their money back and the word was traveling like brushfire: "Don't buy Lear's new ADF."

Lear was not totally surprised when the first reports filtered back to him. He had the same problem with the model he had installed in his Beechcraft and it was driving him crazy. He couldn't figure out what was wrong. His circuit designs were sound. He had used the best materials available. There was no reason that it shouldn't work.

One evening, Lear stepped into his dark laboratory. Out of the corner of his eye, he caught sight of a spark leaping from the ADF-6 test model sitting on the workbench with its power switch on. The spark had come from the intermediate frequency transformer. Lear flipped on the lights and took the instrument apart. After hours of study, he found hairlike crystal fibers growing out of the cadmium-plated air trimmers. He had to use a magnifying glass to find the hairs, which were shorting out the system until they broke. Then the instrument would work again until a new fiber grew. Lear changed the coating and the problem disappeared. "It just about ruined me," Lear told Sam Auld many years later.

Even more important to Lear than his move to Mineola, his new automatic direction finder, and his fifteen patent applications (all of which were granted) was RCA's decision to give Lear Developments a license to manufacture receivers, transmitters, and direction finders. But there was a catch. RCA insisted that Lear pay royalties on each piece of equipment he made between 1934 and 1939, when he had been infringing on the corporation's patents.

"How much back royalties do you feel you owe us," RCA asked, according to Lear.

Sensing that RCA was more interested in the principle than in the money, Lear gambled. "Five dollars," he said. RCA accepted the offer.

It didn't take Lear long to find a backer after he had the license. Lazar Gelin introduced him to T. S. Harris, an investor from Lowell, Massachusetts, who was attracted to Lear Developments for its export potential. Lear sold Harris and his two silent partners, Ernest Henderson and Robert Moore (the owners of the Sheraton hotel chain), a 49 percent interest in Lear Developments; then he changed the name of the company to Lear Avia and moved his entire operation to the municipal airport in Dayton, Ohio. The move was smart. It placed Lear Avia close to Wright Field and the Army Air Corps; and it was in the Midwest, easily accessible to customers all over the country.

The municipal airport was in Vandalia, ten miles north of Dayton. Lear rented a one-story brick building there, and before long the factory was running on four shifts, day and night, with three hundred workers. With some of his new stock, Lear set up three irrevocable trust funds for Bill Jr., Patti, and Charlene. The income of each trust would be distributed quarterly; its principal could not be touched for twenty-five to thirty years. Madeline was to be supported from the trusts of her two children.

Lear made no provisions for his daughter Mary Louise, however, who was fourteen years old and whom he had not seen
since she was a baby. He had visited her a few times after Ethel
had returned to Chicago to live with her mother, but he had
found the occasions awkward. Both Ethel and Mrs. Peterson insisted on staying in the front room while he sat with his two-
year-old child, not sure what to say or do and sensing the
women's hostility. One day, he had come unannounced with the
usual armful of gifts, bought and paid for by Gertrude, only to
find that Ethel and her husband, Bob Ellis, Lear's old friend
from radio station WLAL in Tulsa, were out. Mrs. Peterson did
not mince words. He hadn't done a thing for his daughter for
years, she said. Now that she had a daddy who loved and cared
for her, Bill was trying to show him up. Well, Mary Louise did
not want or need his gifts. After the lecture, Bill walked out and
never came back. If the Ellises didn't want him or his help, he
wouldn't force himself on them. And he stopped paying child
support, almost as if he was trying to punish Ethel through his
daughter.

All in all, 1939 was Bill Lear's biggest and best year ever. At
the age of thirty-seven, he finally had a company that was fi-
nanced adequately. His net sales had almost doubled, to
$215,000, and he was becoming well known in aviation circles.
His automatic direction finder was so far ahead of the competition that the Army Air Corps had bought two, promising to test
them thoroughly.

Although he couldn't yet see them, Lear sensed that fame and
fortune were waiting for him around the next corner.

10

IF BILL LEAR'S BUSINESS was unpredictable between 1934, when
he left Chicago, and 1939, when he moved to Dayton, his personal life was hectic. Although he had promised to marry Charlene, he never did. Instead, he took Beth (not her real name), a

New York model, with him when he set sail for Europe on the *Normandie.* Charlene returned to Chicago.

Beth was planning to marry Bill, but when she discovered that he had no intention of remaining faithful to her, she called the marriage off, acknowledging that he couldn't or wouldn't ever belong to one woman.

Six months after he returned from Europe, Bill married Margaret Radell, a doctor's receptionist whom he had met in Miami. The wedding early in 1936 came as a surprise to everyone, especially Charlene, and it was clear to all who knew him, except Margaret, that he did not intend to be faithful. As soon as the couple returned from their honeymoon cruise to the Florida keys, Nassau, and Havana, he set up a mistress in an apartment in the London Terrace, where he still maintained a penthouse. Why he ever married Margaret, even Bill did not seem to know.

She divorced him a year and a half after the wedding. As a settlement, he offered her stock in Lear Developments, but she demanded cash, convinced that he would never amount to anything. She had watched him spend every dollar he made either on high living or on what seemed to her foolish business projects. Since Bill didn't have much cash in 1938, when the divorce became final, Margaret ended up with almost nothing. Had she taken the stock, she would have been a millionaire in less than twenty years.

To his friends and family, Lear would always shrug off his marriage to Margaret Radell as a joke. During the next few years, until Margaret remarried, Lear would send her money through Lazar Gelin, telling him to make sure she didn't know where the money came from. And because of his third failure at marriage, he became convinced that he could never be monogamous. To him, every attractive woman was a potential conquest who momentarily gave him what no man or group of friends ever could. As one of his daughters explains: "He had this immense emotional hunger. Starvation. And he needed to be reaffirmed, reaffirmed."

When he moved to Dayton, Bill invited Madeline to live with him in the Tudor home he rented. She accepted. It was one of the biggest mistakes of her life.

It didn't take Bill Lear long to become the talk of the conservative residential neighborhood that surrounded 59 Maplewood

Avenue. It wasn't just the loud music. (Lear loved the *1812* Overture and used to play it over and over at all hours of the day and night until the house shook with Tchaikovsky's cannon fire.) It was also the women.

By 1940, Lear had the harem he had once told Madeline he always wanted. He was having an affair with Eileen (not her real name), the wife of an employee who knew about it but didn't have the courage to confront Lear. There was also Nina, a dark-haired, dark-skinned dancer whom Lear would ferry back and forth from New York. In addition, there were still Beth and Charlene, whom he visited in Chicago from time to time. He frequently invited Charlene to Dayton, and she would stay at the Maplewood house.

By 1940, Madeline and Charlene had become good friends. They had met in Miami a few years earlier, and Charlene had asked Madeline's forgiveness for breaking up her marriage. Madeline had forgiven her, convinced that if it had not been Charlene, it would have been someone else. The two women found they had much in common. Both had loved the same man, snatching him from his wife, unknowingly at first, then quite deliberately, only to watch yet another woman take him away. Both had suffered pain and humiliation, but neither was bitter toward the man who had hurt her.

To Madeline, what made Charlene's relationship with Bill so bleak was that her love had no strings. Still, afraid that Patti (Bill Jr. was attending a military school in Indiana) would figure out what was going on in the bedrooms in Dayton, Madeline finally asked Charlene to leave. "I felt sorry for [Charlene] because she had been taken in," Madeline explains. "She just worshiped him. But I had to tell her: 'The children are beginning to ask questions. I really think it would be much better if you went down to a hotel.' " Charlene was very understanding and moved out to the Van Cleeve.

To make matters worse, Ole Olsen came down from New York several times. Ole and Chic Johnson, whom Bill had known from his Chicago days, were playing on Broadway in *Hellzapoppin'*, their "masterpiece of mayhem," which would set a new record with 1,404 consecutive performances. Ole and Bill had become such close barroom and bedroom buddies that they had exchanged phone numbers of the women they knew. Bill and

Ole whooped it up in Dayton at the Kitty Hawk Room in the Biltmore Hotel and other night spots. Sometimes Bill invited Madeline and Patti along, then sent Patti home in a cab after dinner.

Madeline stood it for a year, then went to live in Kansas City near her sister Elizabeth. "I just had enough of those goings and comings," she says in summing up Dayton. "I was like one of those madams in a whorehouse."

That was the last time Madeline tried to live with Bill. She eventually settled in Los Angeles, where Lear bought her a house with money from the children's trust funds. She and the children would never want, but neither would they have more than enough to scrape along on until the trusts came due.

As important as Madeline had been in Bill Lear's life, it was Moya Olsen who would give him the stability he needed but didn't seem to know how to find. He had met her in her father's dressing room in the Forty-sixth Street Theatre shortly after *Hellzapoppin'* opened in September 1938. It was an unsettling time for him. He was going through his divorce from Margaret and facing one of his periodic bankruptcies.

Moya's job was to watch the show, take notes, and copy dialogue for Ole and Chic Johnson because they didn't have a script to submit for copyright. The show was so unpredictable that no two performances were alike. The actors would throw rubber snakes and spiders into the laps of the audience. Someone would walk up and down the aisle hawking tickets to a rival show in the middle of a zany scene. Olsen and Johnson would give away live chickens or cakes of ice to people in the front row. Their gags were old, but they tossed them out so fast and with such comic fun that the audiences went wild. Although the critics panned the show, the crowds kept coming.

Bill Lear, who was thirty-six and somewhat pudgy, did not impress Moya the first time they met, and she quickly forgot about him. Then, on Christmas Eve, Bill asked her out for a drink. She accepted, even though at twenty-three she had never had a drink before. Like her mother, she was a strict Christian Scientist.

Bill took Moya to the Stork Club. It was her first time there, and with the waiters nodding "Yes, Mr. Lear. Will there be anything else, Mr. Lear?," the orchestra, and the candlelight, Moya was impressed. There was an intensity and vitality about Bill Lear. He seemed so self-confident that there wasn't even a hint of doubt in his voice. He loved to dance and laugh. And beneath the need to boast she sensed an honest man. In the cab on the way home, Bill held her hand. "I have never taken my hand away," she always told people who asked how they met.

Warm and energetic, Moya Olsen had a voice that seemed too strong for her small frame. Large black eyes, accented by long black hair, dominated her face. They were soft, almost doelike, and when she laughed, they sparkled with mischief.

It seemed as if Moya's whole life had been a dress rehearsal for Bill Lear. She had spent much of her early childhood like a gypsy, following her father and mother from one cheap hotel to another on the vaudeville circuit, eating meals cooked over a can of Sterno. She grew up in dressing rooms and on trains. Backstage was her playground. One time, Ole told Moya and her brother, J.C. (John Charles), to hide in Irene Castle's old trunk on the stage. Irene used to do a takeoff on Pandora's box: she'd open the trunk and pantomime the thoughts flying out. This time, when she opened the trunk, Moya and J.C. popped out like jacks-in-the-box and dashed across the stage. Everyone roared but Miss Castle. Another time, Moya and J.C. were playing backstage, waiting for the show to finish so they could get their dinner. Walter Huston was on, delivering a dramatic soliloquy next to a fireplace. It was dark behind the curtain, so when Moya and J.C. saw a square of light, they crawled through it. The next thing they knew, the audience was in fits. The two children were kneeling at Huston's feet.

In one important way, John Ole Olsen had prepared Moya for William Powell Lear. Like Lear, he loved women and made no attempt to be faithful to his wife; although he did not flaunt his infidelities, his affairs were no secret.

Moya spent the best part of 1939 with and in love with Bill. She liked to fly around the country with him and had such absolute trust in his judgment and skill that she'd relax in the back seat and do needlepoint. If a problem arose, she firmly believed Bill could handle it. Once, in December 1939, he almost didn't.

Moya, Bill, and Bee Edlund, Ole Olson's new secretary, took

off from Santa Monica for New York so they could be home for Christmas. Bill's Beechcraft Staggerwing developed engine problems soon after takeoff. He landed in a newly plowed field nearby. His wheels bit into the soft dirt and the Beechcraft flipped over. Moya and Bee, strapped into their seats, were held upside down, their dresses billowing over their heads. Lear crawled out and stood next to the plane, laughing. "I've never seen so many pretty legs," he said.

Lear called the *Los Angeles Times* and got a nice promotional picture out of the accident. In spite of that near miss, Moya never lost her confidence whenever Bill sat in the pilot's seat.

With Charlene, Nina, Beth, Eileen, and a score of other women around, the competition was tough for Moya. Although she was attractive, she was not stunning in the way many of Bill's actresses and models were. But she never stopped loving Bill. "I kept after him because I was convinced that he would be happy married," she recalls, "and that I was the girl who would make him happy. So finally he said — he was out in California at the time — okay, I'll be there for the weekend and we'll announce our engagement then." It was just before Thanksgiving 1940.

While Moya was arranging the bride-and-groom centerpiece for the engagement party, the phone rang. It was the manager of Lear-Cal, Lear Avia's sales office in Los Angeles. Mr. Lear had asked him to call, the manager said, to say that he wouldn't be coming to the party. Moya asked to speak to Mr. Lear himself, but the manager said he was out of town.

Moya was deeply shaken. Was he ill? Was he away on urgent business? Was the engagement off? What was Bill trying to tell her? "The thing that really blew me away," she says, "was that he didn't call me and say 'I can't make it.' "

It took Moya a week to catch up with Bill by phone. He really didn't want to get married, he said, but he hadn't had the courage to tell her on the day of the party. He needed and wanted his freedom. He wasn't ready to try marriage for the fourth time.

Moya's hurt turned into anger. She cried. She told herself she would never speak to him again. In later years, her feeling about Bill's rejection softened. As she told her son John: "Dad broke up with me at one point in our life because I insisted on getting married. The whole world fell in on me when he backed firmly out. But, John, he was honest. He wouldn't compromise.''

To get Bill out of her system, Ole Olsen talked his daughter into taking a cruise to Brazil for the 1941 Carnival. While Moya was planning her trip, Bill was on his way to the Miami Air Races in a Cessna T-50 he had just bought. For its maiden flight, aboard were John Osborne, a correspondent for *Time,* Robert Moore, one of Lear Avia's silent investors, and Virginia Branton, a New York model. Lear calculated that he'd have just enough fuel to get him to Jacksonville, Florida, where he'd tank up before continuing to Miami. To fly from Roosevelt Field to Jacksonville nonstop was cutting it thin, but Lear liked to see how far he could stretch a full tank, and he enjoyed pulling up to the hangar with the needle pointing to Empty.

Twenty-five miles north of Jacksonville, it became clear to Lear that if he made it, it wouldn't be by much. (He would later say that the fuel indicator on the auxiliary tank was defective and that he thought he had plenty of gas.) He radioed the Jacksonville airport manager, requesting that the field be cleared for an emergency landing, and was told to touch down at a field in St. Mary's, Georgia, just three miles south of his present position.

Lear told Osborne, his copilot, to watch for the airstrip. It was dark, and Lear was hoping to see landing lights before the tank was empty. "I can't see anything," Osborne kept saying. "It's too black. But there's a river."

"Where?"

Lear had to land, and he knew that if he tried to set the Cessna on the treetops, it would be bad news for everyone aboard.

"Right off to your left," Osborne said.

Lear headed for the shallow creek and made a smooth landing at sixty miles an hour. When the Cessna's wings hit the water, the plane decelerated so quickly that everyone pitched forward. Osborne smashed his nose against the instrument panel, and Lear cracked his jawbone and knocked out his lower teeth. Moore and Branton were shaken and bruised.

Lear was so stunned that Osborne had to unfasten his seat belt as the plane began sinking. Within moments, all four were standing on the wings, which were just under the water. "We felt pretty silly sitting out there in the middle of the river shouting 'Help! Help! Help!'" Lear would recall. "So finally Bob Moore swam ashore."

Moore found some hunters in a cabin nearby. They sent for a doctor and rowed the others ashore. After applying some iodine and bandages, the doctor drove them to a hospital in St. Mary's.

Shopping in Manhattan the next day, Moya took a break at the B & B sandwich shop. She glanced at a newspaper and there, on the front page, was a story about her former fiancé in a Georgia swamp. In an absolute panic, she rushed to the nearest phone and called the hospital. Bill's mouth was so swollen, he couldn't talk. He scribbled a note on a pad and asked the nurse to read it to Moya. He was fine, he said, and he loved her so much. When Moya got to her stateroom on the ship, there was a card from Bill and a dozen roses waiting.

Angry at Lear for jilting his daughter, Ole Olsen wrote Lear a tough letter ordering him to leave her alone unless he was willing to marry her. He told the doorman at the Winter Garden, where *Hellzapoppin'* was playing, not to let Bill Lear inside the door.

11

BILL LEAR's next-door neighbor in Dayton was the Army Air Corps. He spent most of 1940 fighting it, yet he never gave up hope of landing a big contract for his automatic direction finder. To Lear, the instrument was like a son, and he paid more attention to it than to his three children. Although he had sold the direction finder to Canada, Nationalist China, France, Japan, Norway, Peru, and Sweden, the Air Corps had only bought two to test. What irked Lear was that the Signal Corps, which developed, tested, and purchased instruments for the Air Corps, was still testing his ADF-6 when he was already building an ADF-8, two generations smarter and better.

Lear kept badgering the Signal Corps engineers to look at his new model. He told them that he could design almost anything if he only knew what the corps actually wanted in an automatic direction finder. He understood that with the government committed to ordering 50,000 new airplanes a year in anticipation of war, the Signal Corps' appetite for direction finders would grow. And there was nothing that Lear wanted more at this point in his life than to see a Lear ADF on every bomber and fighter in the U.S. air fleet. Describing his frustration during 1940, Lear told of inviting Signal Corps engineers to his shop to review his progress on the new ADF-8. When he asked them whether his design was close to what they wanted, they would say, "Oh, yes, it is very nice. It is just about [like] the thing we are thinking about."

"Well, I want to build it so it will meet your requirements," Lear emphasized.

"You're doing just fine," they said.

This went on for about six months until the Signal Corps came out with a new set of specifications for SCR-269. The design was radically different from the ADF-8. "This specification was in preparation for over a year," Lear complained.

"That's right," they said.

"Well, every week I would have you over to my place to see my direction finder. Why didn't you tell me that such a specification was being prepared?" Lear said.

"You never asked us," they told him.

Lear concluded that the whole direction finder contract was wired for the Bendix Aviation Corporation. "That was another indication of a nefarious relationship that Bendix had with the Signal Corps," Lear said, "because Bendix was the one who wrote that specification, and so secretly that it was never made known to the rest of the industry."

The record bears out Lear's allegation of featherbedding. The Signal Corps used the phrase "the Big Five" to refer to the giants to whom it gave most of its contracts, according to one military historian. In 1939, the Big Five — General Electric, Western Electric, Westinghouse, RCA, and Bendix — received $8 million in contracts, the bulk of the money the Signal Corps spent. It became clear to members of Congress with oversight responsibilities for small businesses that the Signal Corps was trying to limit rather than expand the scope of its contracting. Congress viewed that as a dangerous trend in the event of war, when a host of large and small contractors would be needed to feed the military machine. But the Signal Corps paid no heed.

By 1940, the War Department had designated the SCR-269 radio compass a "critical essential item." When it came time to award the first contract ($2.3 million) to build several thousand SCR-269s, Bendix got the plum. Given that the Air Corps was committed to equipping 50,000 airplanes a year, and that whoever nailed the first contract would get the lion's share of future orders, Bendix did well. After Pearl Harbor, it would get a $43 million contract for the SCR-269. Almost as a bone to keep Lear quiet, the Signal Corps tossed Lear Avia a contract for 380 SCR-269s. He was harassed constantly during the construction and testing of the equipment, and after he delivered the completed order, he was not asked for more.

In fact, the Signal Corps had no reason to trust Lear Avia in 1940. Bill Lear did not have a good track record for quality manufacturing. During the late 1930s, everyone admitted, he had produced excellent designs and superior prototypes, but his instruments had suffered from sloppy construction due to the size of his pocketbook and the nature of his personality. Always suffering cash flow problems, he frequently cut corners by using inferior coils or capacitors. Unable to afford a steady staff, he hired extra help when he had a big order, then fired them when the job was completed. It was hard to maintain quality control under those conditions. Finally, Lear was not by inclination a manufacturer. What interested him were inventing, designing, and selling.

The Signal Corps recognized that to give Bill Lear a large production contract for a critical item was to take a huge risk, even though he was a pioneer in the field and his new company, Lear Avia, was doing well. The issue was no longer who had the best radio compass, but who could mass-produce the best according to tight Signal Corps specifications.

Bendix, in contrast, had an excellent record for delivering competent equipment on time. It had the engineers, the floor space, and the capital to grow to meet the demand. The only thing Lear Avia had, as far as the Army Air Corps was concerned, was Bill Lear. Its engineers respected and liked him for the most part; "Bill could really charm them," as one observer put it. But his production quality was suspect, and he couldn't stick to specifications because he always wanted to improve the product even as it was going out the door. Workers and engineers at the plant in Vandalia used to joke that no two ADF-8s were alike because Lear couldn't resist tinkering with everything in sight. Furthermore, the Army Air Corps no longer needed his direction finder, for it had its own that worked well; it didn't need his little brick factory on the edge of a runway at the municipal airport in Vandalia; and it didn't need his engineers to supervise the construction and testing of equipment any competent manufacturer could make.

Yet 1940 was a good period for Lear Avia, and it ended the year with more factory work than it could handle — transmitters for Rumania, SCR-269 direction finders for the Army Air Corps, and direction finders and transmitters for half a dozen foreign countries and for independent pilots. Lear Avia's sales soared from just over $200,000 in 1939 to $912,000, showing a net profit of $179,000. Sixty percent of the sales were exports. But even more important to Lear than the money was the Frank M. Hawks Memorial Award for his new Learomatic navigator.

In the late 1930s, Lear had met Ward Davis, an instrument flying instructor at the Civil Aviation Administration approved school in Wayne County, Michigan. Frustrated with teaching airline pilots and CAA inspectors how to navigate a straight track, Davis was full of ideas about improving instruments and making instrument flying easier. Lear used to fly up to see Davis on weekends to exchange engineering and design ideas.

Davis considered Lear's ADF-8 direction finder the best on the market. When Pan American's pilots threatened to strike if the company didn't install direction finders on its international flights, where they were desperately needed (especially in bad weather), Davis convinced the airline to test-fly a Lear ADF-8. Pan Am agreed and had Lear Avia install one on a Boeing 314 Clipper for a round-trip flight between New York and Lisbon. The instrument worked like a charm. Davis and the navigator homed in on the Azores from 800 miles away and picked out WEAF in New York from 1,200 miles. But unfortunately, as

Davis recalls, "the ADF loop was mounted on a steel rod with one set screw, instead of being drilled and pinned in place. Vibrations shook the loop loose and it wandered around useless. Lear's problem was shop technique. He had good quality, but bad shop engineering." Pan Am eventually installed direction finders, but not Lear's, because companies like Bendix convinced the airline that theirs were better built.

Davis had great respect for Lear and the two inventors complemented each other. Davis was good at gyro compasses, which commercial pilots relied on for straight track navigation; Lear was good with direction finders, which private pilots relied on to find the airports. Both men believed strongly in simple equipment for independent pilots. "When you're on top in a single-engine airplane over strange territory," Davis used to say, "you're chairman of the worrying committee."

One day, Davis phoned Lear with the idea of marrying the two instruments into one indicator. The pilot would tune the direction finder to a radio station, and using that as a fixed bearing, set the directional gyro compass at the precise path desired. The indicator would point to the radio station and at the same time tell the pilot whether the plane was holding the chosen course. If the idea worked, the new instrument would be a great improvement over the complicated calculations pilots were then making, using the gyro and the direction finder separately.

Hardly had Davis finished explaining his concept when Lear jumped into his twin-engine Beechcraft and flew up to Wayne County. Ward roughly sketched out what he had in mind. Lear flew home to Dayton, returning four days later with a prototype Learomatic navigator installed in his ship. Besides charting straight-line navigation, the Learomatic navigator automatically corrected the angle of drift, or "crab," due to crosswinds; it was adapted for a low approach and blind landing on any selected runway; with earphones, it weighed less than sixty pounds; and anyone could learn to use it in thirty minutes. "It worked beautifully," Davis recalls.

Lear filed for a patent (one of seventeen in 1940) in both his and Davis's names. That December, Lear flew to New York to accept the Hawks award, offered by American Legion Post 501, for his "outstanding contribution in aircraft radio," especially the Learomatic navigator. Hawks, a World War I pilot, flight instructor, barnstormer, and speed racer who had set transcontinental records in the 1920s, had died in a plane crash in 1938, and his legion post, a group of World War I pilots, gave the award to honor his memory.

Lear accepted the trophy from Mayor Fiorello La Guardia, who had received it the previous year. In his acceptance speech, Lear stressed that two factors were crucial to the European war — mobility and communication. Aircraft, he said, offered unprecedented mobility and radio, unprecedented communication. "They must be developed to the fullest extent to avoid defensive weakness."

In spite of Lear's continued lack of success with the Signal Corps and Army Air Corps, Lear Avia was doing well. Lazar Gelin was in Latin America, garnering big orders for transceivers and direction finders from Venezuela, Brazil, Peru, Mexico, and the Pan Grace Lines, which flew Sikorsky S-38 amphibians into jungle waterways all over the hemisphere. His biggest sales were in Central America — Panama, Costa Rica, Nicaragua, El Salvador, and Guatemala. But, wherever he went, Gelin found that the airlines and the military generally preferred Bendix equipment because Bendix offered good operation manuals and spare parts along with regular repair and tune-up services. Lear Avia could not compete at that level even though its design was better then Bendix's.

Gelin's biggest catch was Argentina. A handful of Argentinian diplomats and generals had visited Lear's plant in late 1940 for a demonstration of Learadios and direction finders. The diplomats were impressed, the generals, skeptical. "*Our* pilots fly by the seat of their pants," they told Lear with pride.

When the generals sailed for Argentina, Lear sent Gelin along with one direction finder and two cases of Scotch. "That will keep you wet for a month," Lear told Gelin. By the time he reached Argentina, Gelin could speak Spanish and had new friends in high places. But it took him almost six months to convince the generals even to test-fly the direction finder. When they did, they ordered sixty, at $3,000 each, to begin with.

And then there were the Dutch. When the Germans conquered the Netherlands in the spring of 1940, the Dutch set up a government in exile and, like the Norwegians, had their own squadron of pilots, whose missions were coordinated by the British. The Dutch bought their fighters from the Brewster Aircraft Company, their radios and direction finders from Lear Avia.

With business booming, Lear Avia expanded rapidly. It opened a research and development office in New York on Broadway and another in Hollywood at North McCadden Place near Santa Monica Boulevard. It bought an empty match factory in Piqua, Ohio, twenty-five miles north of Dayton, for $46,000 and closed down the Vandalia plant. And it hired an engineer–patent attorney, Richard Marsen, to run its New York laboratory and to develop a patent program for the company. Both Lear and Marsen recognized that the future of Lear Avia, whether the United States got involved in the European war or not, would rest on the company's greatest asset — the ideas of Bill Lear and his engineering staff. Lear and Marsen wanted to protect those ideas both in the United States and abroad, where they anticipated doing a lot of business.

Marsen recommended that in the course of the next several years, the company file for between eight and twelve patents a year. In mid 1941, he reported to Lear's business partner, T. S. Harris, that he was preparing to submit fourteen new inventions (nine of them Lear's) to the Patent Office. Of particular importance in that group, Marsen noted, were Lear's aircraft siren system, which the Air Corps wanted, his gun turret control system, and his northerly-seeking gyro, which Marsen described as "quite significant." Most of the new patents, like many of those filed in 1940, centered around the "fastop" clutch, soon to become the very heart of Lear Avia.

In 1939, Bill Lear had discovered Arling Ryberg, an inventor who was working on electric motors and clutches. Ryberg had found a solution to one of the most perplexing electromechanical problems of the day: how to make the object the motor was moving stop on a dime. Around an electromagnetic clutch, Ryberg designed a simple system to disconnect the motor shaft from the object it was driving the instant the current was cut and the brake applied. In short, Ryberg had made it possible to get split-second cleavage between motor and shaft, paving the way for precision control.

Lear not only appreciated the importance of Ryberg's discovery, but he also saw immediate applications and ways to improve it, as he had with the Ferris drum tuner in 1934. Lear teamed with Ryberg on what Lear would eventually call the fastop clutch and filed for a patent in both their names.

The motors into which Lear would build the fastop clutch would become the second mainstay of Lear Avia. For those, Lear relied on Vaino Hoover, a California engineer who knew more about small electric motors than any man in the country. Hoover and Lear began designing and building electric motors that could drive almost anything. Some weighed less than six ounces.

Lear immediately adapted the fastop clutch and tiny motor to the rotating loop antenna of his ADF. With the fastop, the ADF antenna braked at the precise moment the receiver found the radio station it was seeking, eliminating overshooting and backtracking.

Next, Lear applied the tiny clutch and motor to his automatic reeling system for the wire antenna trailing from the airplane. He had designed and built the prototype reel for the Signal Corps for $499, the most it could spend without competitive bidding. It seemed pleased with the reeling system but did not offer Lear a contract. Figuring that he had just lost another $37,000 in development money, Lear filed for a patent, swallowed his loss, and moved on to other applications of the fastop clutch.

A year later, Lear got a letter from a small company in Racine, Wisconsin, asking for a quotation on parts. As he studied the company's drawings, he realized he was staring at the specs for his own fastop clutch. Lear called the company and asked what the parts were for. "We're building reels for the Signal Corps," it told him, according to Lear, who rushed to Wright Field.

"Are you building motor reels?" he asked.

"Yes," the Signal Corps said.

"Are you buying motor reels against my design?"

"We don't know anything about your design."

Lear tossed the Racine company's drawings onto the desk. "Well, this is *my* design," he said. "This is *my* patent on *my* clutch. I made the first motor reels for you and took a terrible beating on the original order . . . to get into the motor reel business."

"You're not even listed as a motor reel manufacturer," the corps said. "You've got to apply [to get] on the list."

A friend at Wright Field advised Lear privately that he didn't have a chance of winning the bid to manufacture his own reels, that he would simply have to sign over his patent to the government because war was pending.

"We never got an order for a single reel motor," Lear would complain. "And, foolishly, upon Mr. Harris's insistence, we gave the government the rights to use that patent." Once again, Bill Lear was without a product to sell to the military.

Lear's big break finally came in late 1940 at the Consolidated Aircraft Corporation plant in San Diego, where he was trying to sell his ADF-8. Consolidated executives seemed more interested in Lear's opinion about a prickly engineering problem that had them stumped than in his direction finder. Its engineers had designed a hydraulic system to open and close the cowl flaps, which controlled the temperature of the engines, on the prototype bomber it was building for the Air Corps. The cooling system was vital, of course, for if the engines overheated, the pilot could well have a fire on his hands over enemy territory.

Like all other companies building aircraft for the Army Air Corps in 1940, Consolidated was using liquid pressure rather than electricity to move the cowl flaps. Hydraulics was far from safe, for if enemy bullets punctured the system, the liquid inside the pipes would drain out, like brake fluid from power brakes, making the flaps useless. Lear asked to see the Consolidated system in action. "It was horrible," he said later. "A heavy, complex thing."

Asking for a drawing board, Lear quickly sketched an electromechanical system using his motor (to be built with the required horsepower) and his fastop clutch. A specially designed screw jack, powered by the motor through a flexible shaft (like those dentists use on their drills), would mechanically open and close the flaps. It was a clean, simple design, and Consolidated bought it. Though no one realized it that day in December 1940, the decision to go with Lear's design was the death knell for the hydraulic system in all new aircraft.

Once he tested the system (the critical thermostat control was designed by A. L. Klein, a consulting engineer in Lear Avia's Hollywood laboratory), Lear began to sell it all over the country. And he hired Richard M. Mock and Howard McLaughlin to help him develop and market the product.

Richard Mock was working for Fokker Aircraft Company, the Amsterdam agent for the Douglas Aircraft Company, when the Germans invaded the Netherlands in the spring of 1940. Mock lost his job and began sending out résumés, including one to Bill Lear, whom he had met in the mid 1930s when Fokker was seriously thinking about installing the Learoscope in the Douglas flying boats it was selling in Europe. Mock had vetoed the idea because he thought that Lear equipment was not dependable and that Lear Developments could not be trusted for prompt delivery and service.

When he got Mock's résumé, Lear immediately wired the engineer to come to Vandalia for an interview. Mock was late for the meeting because of a snowstorm, and Lear, who was getting ready to fly to New York, was pressed for time. He questioned Mock about actuators and fastop clutches, cowl flaps and screw jacks. Impressed with Mock's quick grasp of his new electromechanical system, Lear explained that he had mistakenly scheduled two meetings at the same time: one in New York City with his engineers to discuss an important project; one in Buffalo with Curtiss-Wright's engineers to discuss his cowl flap system. Would Mock represent Lear Avia and try to get an order from Curtiss-Wright?

Even though he was not on Lear's payroll, Mock agreed to go to Buffalo. When he returned with a large contract, Lear hired him as sales engineer.

Howard McLaughlin, whom everyone called Mac, had read about Lear's award for the Learomatic Navigator and, as a private pilot, was so impressed that he wrote Lear a letter of congratulation before leaving on a business trip. Mac returned home to a stack of telegrams from Bill Lear, asking him to come to Dayton to talk about a job. Although Mac wasn't interested, he decided to stop off at Vandalia during another business trip just to meet the famous Bill Lear.

In the middle of the interview, Lear's secretary, Ruth McIntyre, barged into the office. Lear had just decided to move to

Piqua and McIntyre was excited. "You know what, Bill?" she said. "There are twenty-six churches and only two bars in Piqua."

"Well, we'll correct that," Lear told her.

They all had a good laugh, and Mac decided that working for Lear would be more fun than managing a factory that made machine-gun bullets.

Not too many months after he had signed the Consolidated deal, Lear ran into a problem getting flexible shafting, and he was late on delivery. As a result, Consolidated fell behind on bomber production. The Army Air Corps complained to Consolidated, and Consolidated to Lear. "We can't ship these airplanes without those parts," Consolidated warned.

Lear called Mac into his office when he returned from San Diego. "Mac, I have a special assignment for you," he said. "Get us into the flexible shaft business."

When Mac asked for specifics, Lear cut him off. "Don't ask me how long they are, how big they are, what torque they twist off at, which way the wire is wrapped in them," Lear told him. "I don't give a damn if you have to go to Paris [to buy materials]. Just go down and check out the money and go. Put us in the flexible shaft business."

Within ninety days, Lear Avia was making a thousand pieces of flexible shaft a day.

All in all, 1941 was a good year. With nearly $5 million in back orders, the company reported net sales of $1.6 million (up 60 percent from 1940). And with fastop clutches, actuators, motors, and screw jacks, which Lear and his engineers could design to move, push, or turn anything on an airplane, Lear Avia now had at least one product every aircraft manufacturer needed. Bill Lear had found his niche.

Nineteen forty-one was a good year in another important way. Moya Olsen came back from Brazil.

12

MOYA RETURNED to New York in April 1941, not quite convinced that she had baked Bill Lear out of her life. She had kept in contact with him from the Copacabana through telegrams. When she was angry at him, she paid for the messages. When she was feeling good about their relationship, she sent them collect. That way, Bill always knew where he stood.

Throughout the summer of 1941, while he was digging in at Piqua, Bill wrote to Moya in care of Stan Brown, an actor friend in *Hellzapoppin'*, because John and Lillian Olsen were still so mad that they would have burned his letters. One day in the fall, Bill sent the doorman at the Winter Garden Theatre a coded telegram for Moya. They met at La Guardia because they didn't want anyone who knew the Olsens to see them together, and they talked about marriage once again. Moya felt Bill wavering and knew it was just a matter of time before he'd give in. She was right.

Bill called Moya on Thanksgiving, a year after he had broken off their engagement, and proposed. They both wept over the phone. He had to go to Chicago to tell Charlene, he said, and it was going to be rough. As soon as he hung up, doubts began nagging him. He was afraid of failing for the fourth time; he sensed that if he married Moya, he would hurt her; and he felt guilty about passing Charlene by once again.

After watching him straddle the fence for a month, Moya finally gave Bill an ultimatum. "You don't want to marry her," she said in a tender, angry letter just before Christmas. "You feel indebted to her — I don't blame you — you should. But darling, please be careful how you work it out now, because I will be miserable and ultimately leave you if you insist on keeping her as a mistress.

"If I were aging and getting fretful and losing my grip on life, and forcing you to find contentment somewhere else, I wouldn't blame you one damn bit for keeping a little character around to insure your happiness. But I'm young, angel, and full to the brim with love for you, eager and excited and confident of the future. . . . So what's the score? Should I go on selling myself to you until I start that long walk down the aisle? Hell no! Sweetheart, if you haven't got brains enough to know I'm for you, I give up."

Bill and Moya were married in the Second Congregational Church in Greenwich, Connecticut, on January 5, 1942. Afterward, Bill took Moya back to Piqua.

Bill's house was the tiniest place Moya had ever seen. It had one little bedroom, a dollhouse-sized living room, a dinky kitchen, and a porch. But she loved it. It was there, to the little house, with a mint-lined stream running through the backyard, that she brought her son John, born in December 1942. (They nicknamed him Littlejohn, and his grandfather, John Ole Olsen, after whom he was named, became Big John.) Because there was no basement, Moya hung Littlejohn's diapers on the clothesline outside, where they froze in the midwestern winter. She had never kept house before and didn't know how to cook. Bill taught her, and it was a happy time.

In the spring of 1943, Moya took Littlejohn to New York for two weeks to visit her parents. Bill told her that while she was gone, he'd be in Seattle, working at the Boeing plant. Instead, he stayed home and hired a contractor to work on the house with him as a surprise for Moya. They dug out a basement and added a big living room and a new kitchen. They put in large windows and refurnished the whole house. To keep Moya off his scent, Bill would have a secretary phone her and say, "Mrs. Lear, this is Mr. Lear calling from Seattle." Then he'd get on the line for a chat.

Moya was stunned when she came home. "It was so beautiful," she recalls. "This little house had suddenly grown, and had blue and white awnings. I loved it. I cried when we had to move [the following year]. I just sat there and wept with Littlejohn in the basket and the bags packed."

Bill Jr., who was sixteen years old, came to live with his father and Moya for the 1944–1945 school year. He and Moya got along like mother and son, and he would never forget how kind she had been to him when he was at Howe Military Academy, where he was miserable and lonely. Although he liked the school, he had resented being shuffled away from home and he had felt forsaken. Madeline couldn't come to see him often because she was living in Kansas City, and Howe, Indiana, near the Michigan border, was just too far; his father wouldn't make the time.

Moya had felt so sorry for the boy that she used to visit him on weekends whenever she could, and he would cry bitterly when she had to leave. She'd pick him up for the holidays and let him drive her car back to Piqua, even though he was too young to have a license. When the holidays were over, she'd get him back to Howe a day early so that he could cry himself out before the other boys returned.

While Bill Jr. lived with Bill and Moya, he attended Piqua Central High School and worked for Lear Avia during the summer, doing quality-control tests on actuators. Although he was getting paid much less than the other men doing the same job and it irked him, he feared his father so much that he didn't even think of asking him for a raise. But he found other ways to get even. If an actuator missed specifications by just a hair — one pound less tension or compression than required — he rejected it with a sense of glee. And there was the Scotch.

Bill Lear had several cases of prized Haig Pinch Scotch stashed in the attic. It was wartime, and good whisky was hard to come by. The Pinch "was gold," and Bill Jr. began raffling it off at the plant, a bottle at a time. At 50 cents a ticket, he'd sell a hundred or so, making $50 to compensate for his low wages. The Lear workers, who knew exactly where the whisky was coming from, enjoyed the game. It was worth 50 cents just to see what "the old man" — as most of the workers called Bill Lear, even though he had just turned forty — would do when he caught his son.

Catch him he did, but he didn't fly into a rage or chase his son with a razor strop. He had a dilemma. He didn't want to continue losing his Scotch, but he didn't want to punish his son for being such a good hustler. So he just put a sturdy lock on the attic door and didn't say a word. Bill Jr. got the message.

Bill Lear made no attempt to hide his philandering from his teenage son. Lear workers in Piqua used to joke that the old man would take girls up for a ride in his airplane, and if they didn't put out, he'd push a button, and the girl, bed and all, would drop through the floor. He frequently took Bill Jr. to

New York with him and showed him off at the Stork Club or the Copacabana, as he did his daughter Patti. Xavier Cugat was playing in one of the clubs and Bill's girlfriend Nina was dancing in the floor show. If Nina wasn't around, there were always other chorus girls to take back to the Lexington Hotel for the night. Even *Time* joked about Bill Lear and his women. After a meeting with engineers at the Massachusetts Institute of Technology that left them unable to believe that Lear had quit school at fifteen, the magazine reported, Lear returned to New York and repaired to the Stork Club with a blonde. "Near his table sat Walter Winchell. The moony young man's eyes bulged with appeal to Winchell for a word or even a look of recognition. Ignored, William P. Lear forgot his triumph of the morning, snarled at the blonde, slunk sadly from the Stork Club, and astonished his companions by going home alone."

In Chicago, there was still Charlene. When Bill decided to marry Moya, he softened the news to her as best he could. He told her that he was in love with her, but that he was going to marry Moya. He went on to explain that Moya's father had contacts that were important to his career. He hoped she understood, he had said, and that they would still be lovers. Charlene told him that he had to do what he thought best, but that she would not be his mistress. After he and Moya were married, Bill wrote Charlene letter after letter, telling her how much he missed her and how he couldn't live without her. Couldn't things be as they used to? "She fell for it," a friend of Charlene's recalls. "She was crazy about Bill and forgave him. He had convinced her how important she was for him and that he couldn't accomplish anything unless he had her backing."

And in Piqua there was "Scarlet A," as Lear called her after the adulteress in *The Scarlet Letter*. She was so crazy about Bill that she eventually bore him a daughter. She wanted to be an actress, and he promised to introduce her to the nightclub owners he knew in New York. When he took her out, they usually went to Dayton, twenty-five miles south of Moya's vision. If he was going on a trip, Bill would ask his son to take Scarlet to their favorite haunt in Dayton, the Kitty Hawk Room at the Biltmore Hotel, for dinner and dancing. "She was a young, beautiful, blossoming creature," Bill Jr. recalls. "Incredibly nice. And I would take her down there and would sign the check. The old man would pay.''

Before long, Bill Jr. had become a chip right off the old Lear block. He found a chorus girl to keep him company whenever he went to New York with his father — she danced at the Roxy — and he was the high school Casanova of Piqua. When his son began cutting work for afternoon trysts and his grades began to slip, Bill Lear threatened to send him back to the military academy.

Bill Jr. was still too frightened of his father to plead with him. Instead, he took two $20 bills from his father's money clip one morning and bought a train ticket for New York, planning to live with his chorus girl. But Piqua was a small town, and half the people there worked for Lear Avia. Within hours, Lear learned that his son was trying to skip town. He sent one of his men to the train station with a piece of paper and a message: If you run away, you have to sign an agreement cutting yourself off from your inheritance. With typical teenage abandon and defiance, the boy signed the paper and boarded the train, disappointed that his father wouldn't take the time to deliver his own message.

Because it was wartime the train was jammed, and Bill Jr. stood up all the way from Dayton to New York. When his girlfriend wasn't home, he walked the streets for a few days, sleeping on park benches and in flophouses. Then he called his father. But the old man still had Howe on his mind and his son wouldn't return.

Unable to land a job because he was underage and didn't have a work permit, Bill Jr. hid until he was broke and almost crazy from hunger. In desperation, he went to the Copacabana and asked to see Jack Entratter, the manager and a good friend of his father's. Jack took the boy to his apartment around the corner and gave him $50, a good meal, and a bed for the night. But when Jack threatened to call his father, Bill Jr. fled to the streets.

The $50 gave him a breather. He doled it out carefully, and when he had less than a dollar left, he played his last card. He loved Ole Olsen, who was fabulous with kids, mostly because in many ways he was still one himself, and Bill Jr. had fond memories of the Olsen home in Malvern. Ole loved fireworks and used to buy boxes of all the things boys dreamed about. On the Fourth of July, he and his son, J.C., used to light ladyfingers and cherry bombs and Roman rockets. One Fourth, when Bill Jr. was visiting, a police car came rolling down the Olsen driveway. The neighbors had complained, so Ole took the cops inside the house for some profuse apologies. While the police were lecturing the comedian about safety and keeping the peace, J.C. stuck a bombcracker on the squad car. Assured that the Olsens would behave themselves, the officers jumped into their car and hit the starter. The bombcracker went off with an ear-piercing scream, a big bang, and a cloud of smoke.

Bill Jr. believed that if anyone could convince his father not to send him back to Howe, it would be Big John. He begged for part of the fare to Long Island, since he was short a few cents, and the Olsens took him in. The next day Bill Lear flew into Roosevelt Field to bargain. If his son would come back to Piqua with him, he said, he wouldn't send him to military school. They had a deal.

Bill Jr. left Piqua in the fall of 1945 to take his last year of high school in Hollywood, where his mother and Patti were living.

Moya knew about Scarlet, whose husband had come to the Lear house one day when he was drunk, threatening to rape her because Bill was carrying on with his wife. And when Scarlet and Bill's daughter was born, she sent him a Thanksgiving card, saying that since she had sent one to "the fathers of all her children, you had to be included." Moya got so angry, she grabbed a pair of scissors and began chasing Bill around the house, threatening to castrate him. When he ran into a bedroom and locked the door, Moya stood outside screaming, pounding so hard that her wedding ring pockmarked the wood, demanding that he open the door like a man. She was determined to stand guard until he came out, no matter how long it took, but she left her post in the evening when guests dropped in. Later, concerned that Bill might have escaped, she checked the bedroom only to find one of her guests' children slipping him cookies under the door. "Don't feed him!" she yelled at the kid.

Moya learned in Piqua that if she wanted Bill, she would have to accept his women. Although she didn't want to share him, she refused to allow his mistresses to destroy what they felt for each other. Why he needed all those women, she didn't know, but to save the marriage, she decided to tolerate them as long as he came home to her.

Dick Mock went to Consolidated in December 1941, shortly after the Japanese attacked Pearl Harbor. Consolidated was working on the prototype of the B-24 Liberator bomber, and Lear was hoping for a million-dollar contract to complement his small orders for direction finders and the development work he was doing, which was fun but never seemed to pay off.

When he returned from San Diego, Mock found Lear in a restaurant having lunch with Big John and half a dozen other people. Lear, of course, didn't want to show how anxious he was about a possible Consolidated sale, so he ignored Mock, who played along.

"By the way, Dick," Lear finally asked, "did you get an order?"

Mock pulled out a contract for $1.5 million. Lear was impressed and they all made toasts. Then Mock tossed another contract onto the table, for $3.5 million. Lear Avia was in the war business, and Consolidated was just the beginning.

The war years were very good to Bill Lear and Lear Avia. The company's sales zoomed from $1.6 million in 1941 to $36.8 million in 1944. Under the War Profits Control Act, Lear Avia had to refund to the government $1.4 million in excessive profits for 1942, $3 million for 1943. By then, Lear Avia was no longer making transmitters, receivers, and direction finders. As part of the U.S. war machine, it turned out remote and automatic controls, actuators, screw jacks, motors with fastop clutches, and gearboxes for every major aircraft company in the country. Every bomber, transport, and fighter — B-24s, B-29s, Thunderbolts, Kingcobras, Hellcats — carried at least one piece of Lear equipment that moved or turned cowl and wing flaps, trim tabs and rudders, bomb bay doors and cargo hoists, landing gears, gun turrets, and ammunition boosters. Lear Avia equipment sat so close to the top of the Army Air Force's list of critical materiel that Major J. S. McNally and Captain Al Handschumacher were assigned to coordinate the production and delivery of Lear equipment. And Bill Lear himself had a chance to hone his sell-ing skills to stiletto sharpness.

Howard McLaughlin traveled as Lear's special assistant on sales and troubleshooting trips during 1942 and 1943. Two trips in particular made a deep impression on him.

Lear and Mac flew down to St. Louis in the company's single-engine Cessna Airmaster for a meeting at Curtiss-Wright's headquarters. The company was in the last stages of designing an unusual airplane, called the Ascender, for the Army Air Forces, and its engineers were having problems with landing gears, cowl flaps, and cooling systems, among other things.

The chief engineer ushered Lear and Mac into an empty of-fice. Lear had studied the engineering specs for the Ascender on his previous trip, and, with the propeller mounted in the rear, he thought the ship was laughably stupid and had dubbed it the Ass-ender.

"Now when I'm making a sale," Lear warned Mac, "don't say anything. I'm leading them down a certain path, and I don't want to deviate."

Mac sat near Lear and listened as the Curtiss-Wright engi-neers paraded in, one after the other, to explain their problems. The Army Air Forces was insisting that all new airplanes use electromechanical systems instead of hydraulic ones, and most aeronautical engineers had had little experience with electri-cally run actuators and screw jacks. Lear asked them questions such as how much the landing gear weighed and how fast they wanted it pulled up, Mac recalls. "The wheels were going around in Bill's head, and he would say: 'On that application we would put in model number so-and-so, which runs at so many rpms and puts out so many inch-pounds. And if you want to pull the gear up in so many seconds, it will take fifteen amps on twenty-four volts.'

"And they would say, 'How much do you think it will cost?' And Bill would give them a figure like $482.50. Some damn thing like that right off the top of his head on the first go-round. And in two days down there, he had sold them a total of over two and half million dollars' worth of stuff."

Mac especially remembers the Curtiss-Wright engineer who had a problem mounting an antitank gun under the wings. The gun was supposed to swivel so it could fire continuously as it approached the tank, flew directly over it, and passed by. The engineer couldn't come up with an indicator to show the pilot the angle of his wing canon.

"Very simple," Lear told him. "How far is the cannon from the instrument panel?"

The engineer measured it out on his blueprints.

"We'll put a flexible shaft in there." Lear pointed to the drawings. "The shaft will take a reading off the cannon and make it show on an indicator in front of the pilot up here. For that, we would use one-eighth-inch flexible shafting. It weighs one ounce per foot."

Mac, who was in charge of Lear Avia's flexible shafting operation, gulped. The company didn't even make one-eighth-inch flexible shafting, and he doubted that, if it did make some, it would be so light. But he kept his misgivings to himself.

"Don't spend any time on those parts," Lear told Mac after the sales spree. "The Air Forces will cancel that Ass-Ender before it ever gets off the ground."

"Then why did you spend all that time working on it if you didn't have any faith in it?" Mac asked.

"It's good mental exercise."

The Army Air Forces did scrap the Ascender before it ever got off the Curtiss-Wright drawing boards; Mac eventually made one-eighth-inch flexible shafting for another project, and it weighed just one ounce per foot. "Bill had an uncanny ability for remembering figures and numbers such as that," Mac explains. "He never looked up statistics. He had a memory that stored all the facts like a computer, and he could recall them at any time. He'd interview ten or twelve people, one right after another. Just like that, he'd know them all by name. And he could recall them six months later, every damn one of them."

The other sales trip that stuck in McLaughlin's memory was the one to New York to meet the chief engineers from Bell Laboratories, Western Electric, and AT&T and their assistants, twenty-six engineers in all. Lear sat with them around the oval mahogany table in the Board of Directors conference room at Bell, whose chief engineer chaired the meeting.

"This is a very hush-hush project called radar," Bell's engineer began. He went on to explain how the Germans were sending buzz bombs across the English Channel into London. Radar can see the rockets coming, he said, and British fighters then try to shoot them down before they hit the city. The problem is, the British don't have enough radars for the job. "We want to know if you can make some of the radar parts for us," he said.

"I'd like to look at a schematic," Lear said. He had never heard of radar before. "Then I can tell very quickly if I can make them."

The engineer pulled out blueprints one yard square, and Lear moved into a corner of the conference room. Fifteen minutes later, he rejoined the engineers at the oval table.

"We can make every part of this," he said.

"How much?" Bell's chief engineer asked.

"I'd rather not make it the way it's designed here," Lear said.

"What's wrong with the design?"

"Nothing. But I can show you a circuit that will do the same thing, and it's much simpler to make." Lear drew his circuit on a sketching pad. "This has only a third of the parts. You can count them."

The radar engineers adopted Lear's circuit, but Lear Avia never got the contract to manufacture it. At this point in his life, Lear didn't seem to mind, he was having so much fun. "He'd make a safari around the country," Mac recalls, "and bring back so damn much business that you couldn't help but get behind in deliveries."

And Lear *was* behind. Under the tight supervision of chief engineer Dick Mock, Lear Avia had long since solved its quality-control problem to the point where it had a reputation for excellence. But no matter what its quality, Lear Avia could never catch up on production, and the War Department was worried. The problem was complex.

To begin with, although Lear Avia employed about 4,000 people at its peak, it could never find enough engineers who were willing to live in Piqua, Ohio. "One top engineer came for an interview," recalls Dick Mock, whom Lear had promoted to vice president. "He looked around and said if we had a job anywhere else, he'd work for Lear Avia. But he would not stay in Piqua. I had between one and two hundred in the engineering department. Only eighteen or twenty were real engineers. The rest I took off the street and taught them what they knew."

To compensate, Lear expanded his research and development laboratories in New York and in Los Angeles, where he could find, hire, and hold engineers. Most of the development work was done in this diaspora and all the production in Piqua. Since Lear loved both Los Angeles and New York, the schizophrenia appealed to him. He gathered his engineers around him at the Stork Club, which he called his night office and where he loved to rumba with gusto, and discuss Lear Avia projects late into the night. He had a habit of sketching plans on the tablecloth, and Sherman Billingsly, the manager of the Stork Club, allowed the engineers to take the cloths home with them.

Lear Avia's problem was more than just finding and holding engineers. Piqua had a population of less than 15,000, and the company couldn't find enough workers. It began importing country people, who would sit outside the personnel office bare-footed, shoes tied together and hanging over their shoulders. When called for an interview, they'd put them on.

Even drawing workers from outside Piqua, the company was still understaffed. When Howard McLaughlin returned from Chicago and toured the plant after several months' absence, he was shocked. The place was a morgue, with $600,000 of the finest machinery in the world collecting dust.

"What the hell happened?" he asked Lear.

"The military conscripted all the men."

"That doesn't have to stop you. Train women to run the machines."

"Can you train a woman to run a six-spindle automatic?" Lear asked.

"Why sure. It will take a little time to teach them how to read measuring instruments and things like that."

"Well then, train them!" Lear ordered.

McLaughlin opened a school not far from the plant and trained 3,800 women.

But even women doing "men's work" was not enough to stay ahead of the demand. So Lear rented the Irwin Seating Company plant in Grand Rapids, Michigan. Left by the war effort with little wood and fewer nails, the furniture capital of America was suffering from unemployment. Drawing from that experienced pool of laborers, Lear soon had 1,200 workers there cranking out screw jacks and actuators.

With all these efforts, Lear Avia still couldn't meet its production orders, which only proved that the Army Air Forces and Signal Corps had been right all along. Lear Avia was too small and had too few resources to rely on for massive production contracts. So the Air Technical Service Command licensed three other companies to make the critical items based on Lear Avia's patented designs. "Bill didn't like the idea," recalls Handschumacher, who helped draw up the contracts with the other companies. "But in terms of practical reality, he had no choice."

The problem was more serious, however, than Lear's being too small to deliver critical equipment. Army Air Force Intelligence had uncovered a scam at the Piqua plant, which it and the Air Forces believed was the root of Lear's failure to meet its production promises. Army Air Force Intelligence asked the FBI to investigate ten of the company's subcontractors for paying kickbacks to Lear employees for lucrative contracts, which the subcontractors were in no hurry to fulfill. The FBI emphasized the seriousness of Lear Avia's failure to meet the Army Air Forces' needs:

"Production at Lear was so far behind the anticipated schedule that the most vital aircraft now being produced for the AAF were grounded through lack of parts from Lear, and that production of these vital planes was actually limited . . . The AAF is extremely anxious to have the matter straightened out so that the Lear company could go into production as it should. [It] is one of the most vital war plants in the country today. The entire P-80 [fighter jet] program is being delayed because of failure of production at Lear."

Money and winning the war aside, screw jacks and gearboxes were not Bill Lear's style, no matter how important they were for opening bomb bay doors. Lear appreciated the milk and honey that these "gadgets," as he once called them, brought after ten years of fiscal grits, and he loved solving graduate school problems with his grade school diploma. But he needed something more challenging, something closer to flying than moving cowl flaps with precision.

13

LEAR APPROACHED the Signal Corps with an idea for what he called a northerly-seeking directional gyro. He noted that the standard Boy Scout magnetic compasses, which military pilots, copilots, navigators, and bombadiers depended on for quick bearings, were unreliable. Metal objects nearby set the needle spinning, and the twists and turns of dogfighting made them swing like a pendulum. Pilots had to watch the fluctuations and take an average reading to find out where they were while German Stukas were on their tails. The directional gyroscopes, which pilots also used for bearings, presented a similar problem.

For years, inventors had been toying with ways to point the pilot to true north under all flying conditions, but the best they could do was to design something that would work for an hour or two before drifting. Lear showed the Signal Corps a design that was typically simple and practical. He proposed to link electronically an ordinary gyroscope to an ordinary magnetic compass in such a way that each would correct the other's errors. With Lear's system, the Signal Corps could put all the magnetic compasses it wanted in the airplane, anywhere, and they would all be synchronized. The corps loved the idea and gave Lear Avia a $15,000 development contract. Lear promised to deliver the prototype in ninety days.

One month went by, and Lear hadn't even begun working on it. Then another month passed, and Lear's partner, T. S. Harris, started to fidget. Although $15,000 wasn't a lot of money when the government was awarding million-dollar deals all over the country, Harris didn't want to lose the contract. Lear Avia needed to earn a solid reputation with the military as a company that could deliver.

"There is *no* problem making this thing," Lear told Harris every time he asked for a progress report. "I know two or three ways to do it, and I just haven't decided which is the best yet."

Two more weeks passed, and as far as anyone knew, Lear hadn't even made a mark on a piece of paper. Harris approached Lear again. "There's no use in both of us worrying about it," Lear told him. "It'll be on time."

Two weeks before the deadline, Lear called in twelve to fourteen engineers, outlined what he wanted each one to do, and told them to have their jobs finished by two o'clock the next afternoon.

"When you got out of a Lear meeting," recalls McLaughlin, who was present, "you knew where you were going and what your assignment was and when you were supposed to have it done. Of course, they worked all night and all morning to get it ready. They tested it on the bench, then put it in Bill's airplane so he could fly it around and see how it worked. He flew it up to Chicago and over to Detroit and back, and he said, 'The thing is all right now. You can take it out and put it in a pretty box and I'll deliver it over to Wright Field.'

"When he delivered it, we still had three days to go. Of course, after I got to know Bill, I found out that this was pretty much par for the course."

Even the Signal Corps was becoming more and more impressed with Lear's creative mind, although it didn't award him the contract to build his northerly-seeking directional gyro. When it recovered a wire voice recorder from the cockpit of a German reconnaissance plane, it asked Lear to study the machine and to build one for the United States.

Capturing sound on a band of magnetic steel similar to that in a carpenter's tapemeasure, only thinner, the wire recorder had been around for almost twenty years, but it was unreliable and expensive. When the war broke out, development on wire recorders stopped because the War Department couldn't find a military application, and it didn't want to waste materials on civilian projects. But as soon as the Army Air Forces learned that German pilots were using the device to record what they saw as soon as they saw it, the AAF wanted one too.

Lear approached the project with typical practicality. He told his engineers to collect every kind and style of wire recorder they could. Then, he took the machines apart and studied their similarities and differences, strengths and weaknesses. By the time he delivered his model, using a quarter-inch wire with perforated edges so it wouldn't slip, it was almost a new invention. Explains Dick Mock: "Bill didn't mind using other products. He'd learn the shortcomings of the others and design away from them and make something lighter, smaller, better."

The wartime project that really caught Lear's fancy was the autopilot, a natural but difficult engineering progression from the direction finder. Lear had been thinking of turning his ADF into a primitive autopilot as early as 1939, but he had never gotten around to test the idea seriously.

Autopilots weren't new, either. Ships had been using them for more than twenty years, and they were standard wartime equipment on most bombers. It had been a simple engineering feat to design one for a bomber that lumbered along and needed something just to keep the airplane stable for the bombadier. Although the Big Five had production of the bomber autopilot all tied up, no one was thinking about designing one for fighters. Recalls Al Handschumacher: "The problem intrigued Bill. He was fed up with [screw jacks and actuators] and he wanted to get back into automatic flight controls. But he didn't even understand the fundamentals of gyroscopes and autopilots, and I told him so."

That made no difference to Bill Lear. Designing an instrument so sensitive that it could guide a fighter flying at 250 miles an hour fascinated him. AAF officers at Wright Field had told him that B-24 and B-17 bomber pilots who were flying deep into Germany on raids returned to England reasonably well rested because they had autopilots and back-up crews, whereas the fighter pilots who protected them came home exhausted.

In April 1945, just a few months before the Japanese surrendered, Lear signed a $175,000 deal to design and build two prototype fatigue-relief autopilots that would guide a fighter for ten or fifteen minutes while the pilot rested his eyes or checked a map. Even though the development money was a pittance compared to the production dollars Lear Avia was making, Lear couldn't have been happier. He was doing what he loved best.

Mock recalls how, as chief engineer, he got the news that the company would be making the instruments: "Bill wrote me a one-line note: 'Dick, we're going to make autopilots. Proceed.' "

While Lear Avia began gearing up for autopilot experiments, T. S. Harris sold his shares of the company and retired under pressure from Lear. The two men had been bickering for some time, and no one was sorry to see Harris go. Although he knew little about management, he had wanted to make every decision. Important matters piled up on his desk while he hunted for ways to save pennies. Workers in the mailroom had to guess the weight of a letter because a requisition slip for a postage scale was buried in the bottom drawer of Harris's desk.

As soon as Harris left, Lear changed the name of the company to Lear Incorporated and offered Harris's stock to ten or twelve Lear Avia employees. Then, with the help of the Army Air Forces' procurement office, he asked the Reconstruction Finance Corporation for a $14 million loan so he could expand Lear Incorporated. Congress had established the RFC early in the war, authorizing the government to arrange for and back such loans as it saw fit. (Ironically, the first RFC loan went to Bendix, to produce direction finders.) The RFC gave Lear the loan at 4 percent interest on the condition that the company go public to raise capital.

In May 1945, Lear Incorporated offered 450,000 shares at $5 each underwritten by Kobbe, Gearhart and Company. It told its prospective shareholders that it had $23 million in orders, but it wisely made no promises about the future of the company. "Nor can any forecast be made with respect to the possible effects of the termination of the war," it reported. That was about as close as it could come to saying that Lear Incorporated would be approaching the postwar era with a sense of uneasiness.

Personally, Bill Lear did very well when his company became Lear Incorporated. He now owned 30 percent of the common stock, which, at $5 a share, amounted to $2.5 million on paper; the trust funds for Bill Jr., Patti, and Charlene owned another 13 percent, worth $1.4 million on paper. And the Board of Directors voted to pay him an annual salary of $60,000 for ten years as well as 2.5 percent of the company's annual net profit.

Since both Bill and Moya loved California, they bought a mansion in North Hollywood, a white two-story colonial with a swimming pool and a large guest house. There were servants and parties and an occasional movie or television star, such as Bob Cummings and Art Linkletter, for dinner.

Bill also profferred an olive branch to Mary Louise, who was in her second year at Hanover College. He called Ethel to say he wanted to set up a trust fund for their daughter. Ethel immediately phoned Mary Louise in Hanover, Indiana. "Your father wants to give you some money," Ethel said. "I don't know what strings are attached. I told him it's up to you."

Mary Louise had mixed feelings about her father. He had written her his first letter in 1937, when she was twelve years old, saying that he wanted her to get to know him better, personally, not through the eyes of others. He was convinced that Ethel had been poisoning her against him. Mary Louise, who knew about the nasty divorce and how Ethel had to threaten him with jail in the early 1930s in order to get him to pay child support, had not accepted his offer of friendship. He had sent a few checks, then stopped.

A few months after her father had first written, Mary Louise fell off her bicycle and broke her arm. Ethel had to send her to an orthopedic surgeon at a time when the family was recovering from the Depression. The Ellises had moved to Indianapolis, and Bob was working as a technical writer for Lear's old friend Howard Sams, at the P. R. Mallory Company. Ethel had written to Bill for help.

After he received Ethel's letter, Bill had dropped in to see Mary Louise. The visit shocked and upset Ethel. She didn't trust Bill and couldn't figure out why he had decided to visit just then; he had been in and out of Indianapolis many times in his dealings with P. R. Mallory and had never asked to see Mary Louise. But she invited him inside as graciously as she could and left him and Mary Louise alone in the front room.

The visit between father and daughter had been awkward. He asked how her arm was, wrapped in a cast and all, and before he left he put his arm around her and gave her a squeeze.

Two years later, when Mary Louise, a straight-A student, wanted to go to college, Ethel had written to Bill, asking for $4,832 in unpaid child support. She had kept scrupulous records since her divorce in 1926, and the money he owed his daughter, not to speak of the interest, was more than enough to cover four years of college tuition.

When Bill didn't pay up, Ethel sued. After evading a U.S. marshal, who chased him all over Dayton with a subpoena, Bill proposed a compromise. He would give Ethel $4,000 in back child support if she would burn a stack of his Tulsa letters about him, her, Madeline, and the FBI. Now that he was getting famous, he didn't want the media to find out about his indictment for white slavery. Ethel agreed reluctantly, for the letters were her "insurance policy" in case Bill ever tried to hurt her or their daughter again. Mary Louise went to college, but the victory had been more bitter than sweet.

"I'm not interested, Mother," Mary Louise said after Ethel told her about her father's proposed trust fund. "I don't need his money. We're a happy family."

Even before hanging up, Mary Louise felt pangs of guilt. She sensed she was refusing her father's offer out of loyalty to her mother and stepfather, and she knew that the rejection would hurt him deeply.

It did. Bill Lear did not ask Mary Louise for an explanation. Although she sent him an invitation, he did not attend her graduation two years later nor did he send her a gift. He eventually set up trust funds for John and Shanda and for David and Tina, who were born much later. But never for Mary Louise.

When peace came on August 15, 1945, it didn't catch Lear Incorporated by surprise. As early as January 1944, the company had begun an aggressive advertising campaign to change its image of a cog in the war machine to that of an outfit with a bright postwar future. And Lear had hired R. A. Lasley, Inc., a New York consulting firm, to help it decide what to manufacture after the war, given its machinery, patents, and personnel. After conducting a thorough product survey, Lasley had reported that the company's greatest potential lay in making ship telegraph systems, electric outboard motors, sound recording turntables, motor-driven movie cameras, time-delay devices, electric counters and sorters, remote valve position indicators, pressure recorder indicators, wind velocity and direction devices, and damper controllers.

128

But Lasley made one serious mistake in its product forecast. It forgot to take Bill Lear into account. None of the products on its list remotely interested him. He was not in business primarily to make money but to create and design, and to have fun doing it. Since he still ran the company as if he were the sole owner, even though he held less than a third of the stock, Lear picked his own list of postwar products; it came as no surprise to anyone that his choices were financially risky. Besides continuing to make electromechanical equipment for airplanes — the market was expected to shrink rapidly after the war — Lear Incorporated planned to get back into making receivers, transmitters, and direction finders for light aircraft, to break into the home radio business, and to create a national appetite for wire voice recorders.

The challenges were staggering. Lear would have to wrestle a piece of the aviation market from the Big Five, who had grown fat and respectable during the war. And it would have to convince consumers that Lear home radios were better than RCA, Philco, and Zenith — household words for fifteen years — and that they needed wire voice recorders for their homes and offices instead of Dictaphones, which used disks.

Bill Lear personally demonstrated his new wire recorder, for which he held three patents, at a press conference in the Waldorf-Astoria just weeks before Lear Incorporated went public. The Lear recorder was a vast improvement over any other machine of its kind. Lear told reporters that the hair-thin magnetized wire could be erased or replayed up to fifty thousand times without wearing out. He also demonstrated a tiny wire recorder designed to be plugged into a radio. "By sliding a switch, a news broadcast was recorded," described one New York reporter, "and it came forth when the broadcast was turned off as clearly as the original."

Lear may have been able to fool the *New York Times* and the majority of the stockholders with his confidence in Lear Incorporated, for he was a superb actor. But he couldn't, nor did he try to, hide the harsh, lean reality from his staff. Admits Dick Mock: "We really didn't have much in mind. We used to joke about what we were going to do after the war."

Bill's two favorite postwar "projects" were the Lear good-bye machine and the Lear bullshit machine. The good-bye machine would be designed for people who did a lot of entertaining. It was a simple contraption with mikes all over the room. As soon as anyone said "It's getting late . . . time to go," a trapdoor would open and the person would end up outside on the sidewalk. The Lear bullshit machine, for people who wanted to hear the truth, was even simpler. It was a box worn over the head like big earmuffs. Whenever anyone talked, the machine would automatically separate the facts from the bullshit.

In fact, by the end of the war, Bill Lear was prospering. For the first time in his life, at the age of forty-three, he had more money than he could spend. Between January 1942 and December 1945, he had filed for and eventually received forty-three new patents, all but a handful in his name only. Every major aircraft company in the country knew and respected his special brand of genius. Newspapers and national magazines recognized him both as an electronic wizard with a grade school education and as a playboy pilot. He had developed Lear Avia from a marginal forty-man operation to a publicly owned company with plants in two cities and 4,000 workers. He had learned how to win military contracts and how to charm generals. The Army Air Forces was counting on him to develop an autopilot for fighters for the next war, whenever that would be. And in Moya he had a wife who brought as much stability to his life as anyone could.

But unlike other companies in the war machine, peace found Lear without a product. Early in the war, the Army Air Corps had taken from him the very things he had pioneered and was especially good at and had given them to the larger competitors — transmitters, receivers, direction finders. Choking with war money, the Big Five had further developed these products to the point where they now had a competitive edge over Lear, forcing him to gamble with his own money to catch up. In effect, the military had condemned Bill Lear to starting all over again after the war.

In the spring of 1945, Lear moved his company from Piqua to Grand Rapids, where he thought it could expand more easily and there would be a large pool of skilled laborers, especially cabinetmakers, for his new line of home radios and wire recorders. When the Japanese surrendered, Lear Incorporated was ready to make a fresh start.

Part Three

Making It Fly

14

MOYA AND BILL SOLD their home in North Hollywood and moved to Grand Rapids, to a white frame mansion with a ballroom on the third floor. The moving trucks were days late, and when they finally arrived from California on New Year's Eve, Moya and Bill were across the lake in Chicago, celebrating with Big John. The movers stuffed fifteen rooms of furniture, dishes, and linen into two rooms, then left.

It took Moya months to organize her new home. Littlejohn was five years old and Shanda, four. Moya was pregnant and not feeling well. Her doctor couldn't find a problem, but one day she began hemorrhaging while visiting friends. They rushed her to a hospital just in time to save her life, though not the baby's.

Thoroughly shaken, Bill stood at Moya's bed, weeping. Almost losing her made him realize how much he needed her. So deeply did her brush with death frighten him that he became, as Moya put it, "afraid of everything for a while."

In 1946, the Lears decided to live in Santa Monica and spend a few months each year in Grand Rapids. They bought a three-story home at 222 Fourteenth Street. In Grand Rapids, their home became a virtual hotel, with engineers dropping in for dinner, spending the night, even staying on for weeks. It was not unusual to have three or four in guest rooms, tables cluttered with engineering designs, discussions going on into the small hours. Bill frequently would wake up in the middle of the night with an idea needling him. He'd yank an engineer out of bed, then pad down to the kitchen in his pajamas to brainstorm over a chocolate sundae. (Lear was quite pudgy by 1946 and spent the rest of his life fighting his sweet tooth.) For Christmas, Big John sent Moya a handsomely bound hotel registry, which she kept inside the front door so her guests could sign in. Although she longed for a home instead of a "boarding house," as she called it, she didn't complain.

Instead, she did her best to keep close to Bill under the circumstances. She played poker with the boys at night. She put together a barbershop quartet and on warm evenings they would sit on the front steps and serenade the cicadas. She danced with Bill and their engineer guests around Forest Lawn, their solarium with a fountain. And when Bill and his engineer Nils Eklund would come home from the airport at midnight, discouraged and cold, after test-flying the autopilot, she put a candle, a bottle of Scotch, and a copy of the *Rubaiyat* on the table. Bill and Nils would take turns reading Omar Khayyám aloud while Moya spoon-fed Bill from a casserole.

Bill loved to surprise Moya. One day, he told her he wanted to fly down to St. Louis to calibrate the autopilot and asked her to go along.

"Oh, honey, I don't want to go to St. Louis," she complained. She hated to fly with him when he had the autopilot in pieces, spread out on the floor. Screwdriver in hand, he never seemed to be watching what was going on outside the plane.

"Come on," he coaxed.

Sensing that the trip was important to Bill, Moya packed her needlepoint, settled in the back of the Twin Beech, and went to sleep. She awakened after a couple of hours and looked out the port window. What she saw below didn't look like Missouri. When she walked into the cockpit, stretched out ahead and aglow against the dark sky was New York City. Bill had two tickets for *South Pacific* and reservations for dinner afterward.

Throughout their life together, Bill never lost his love for surprises. A few years later, after Lear Incorporated was on its feet, he walked into the house with a mink coat over his arm. Another time, the bartender at the Ritz in Paris brought Moya what appeared to be a small box of chocolates. When she opened it, she found the most beautiful string of pearls she had ever seen lying on a cushion of velvet.

"His gifts were always impulsive," Moya explains. "He never gave them when he was supposed to. Christmas was depressing for him. He just never knew what to buy."

Even though she knew they were walking the tightrope of bankruptcy in Grand Rapids in 1945 and 1946, Moya was happy because Bill was happy, and Bill Lear had become her whole life.

For Moya, loving Bill was exhausting and dizzying. Besides being lover, wife, friend, and supporter, she became everything that his mother hadn't been, and he called her "Mommie" without shame. She understood Bill's darkest fears — not being loved, being thought of as worthless, being abandoned. She chased those fears away, accepting the mother role as an essential part of being Bill Lear's wife.

When Bill was away for weeks at a time, Moya would send him long, newsy love letters — she knew that Bill would have girlfriends in Grand Rapids to keep him from getting lonely. And she was right. Patti, who was visiting her father in Grand Rapids one summer, walked into the master bedroom to look for something. A teenager at the time, she was shocked to see her father in bed with Scarlet.

Scarlet and Kathy (not her real name), his new girlfriend in New York, weren't the only ones. When he took up the Twin Beech to test his autopilot, he liked to bring a woman along. As the plane flew on auto at 5,000 feet over Lake Michigan, they'd be in bed in the back. She would then become a charter member of Lear's "Mile-High Club."

Moya adjusted to Bill's girlfriends. She gave him the freedom she said she would, and he kept his promise not to bring up "his flirts" with her. She developed several ways to cope. Sometimes she would shrug them off with a joke. "Bill just likes pretty girls," she told *Esquire.* "My father was the same way." And to let Bill know how she felt at any given time without risking a nasty argument, she made a needlepoint that she hung close to the front door. On one side it said, "Welcome home, darling"; on the other, "Get out of town."

To keep her sanity and to remind her that she was still number one in Bill's life, Moya kept another needlepoint on which she stitched the names of the girlfriends she knew about. The incomplete list was a constant reminder that all those women had failed to do what she alone had been able to accomplish — hold and keep Bill Lear. There was Casidy, Margaret, Ethel, Madeline, Nina, Kathy, Deede, Scarlet, Jill, Eileen, Jackie, Beth. The center of the needlepoint was reserved for Moya's biggest threat, the woman who had caused more hurt than anyone or anything in her life — Charlene. After many tearful nights, Moya had come to recognize that Charlene was different from Bill's other take-'em-or-leave-'em girlfriends. Bill really loved her.

No sooner did Moya leave Grand Rapids for Santa Monica than Charlene moved in with Bill. When he learned that Moya was coming back, Bill flew Charlene home to Chicago and waited for Moya at the Kent County Airport like a solicitous husband.

Although he tried to hide Charlene from Moya, Bill was open with his friends and business associates. He took her everywhere — New York, Miami, New Orleans, nightclubs, theaters, restaurants, on pleasure trips, to conventions, to business meetings.

When Moya found out that Bill had not given up Charlene, as he had promised before their marriage, she began a struggle for what she then believed was her survival as the wife of Bill Lear. "I cried, and I fought, and I left him, and I called an attorney, and I did all those things," she explains. "But eventually you get right down to the bottom line and you say: 'Okay, I've had enough of it. One more time and we get divorced!' Then what? Then, I don't have Bill anymore."

Once she recognized that she couldn't get rid of Charlene, Moya tried to understand her, as Madeline had tried before her, in the hope that insight would ease the pain. Eventually Moya came to realize, as Madeline had, that "there was only one thing wrong with [Charlene] — she loved Bill. And, I finally grew to respect her. She lasted the longest and she meant more to him than anybody else."

In spite of the suffering that Charlene caused her, Moya stitched her name on the needlepoint in purple, for "royalty."

Like Moya, Lear Incorporated faced postwar problems in Grand Rapids. But making quality products wasn't one of them.

Lear home radios were beauties. They ranged from a radio-phonograph that sold for $600 to a five-tube plastic table model for $23. In the furniture factory that Lear leased, cabinetmakers worked overtime making consoles that were stunning in both quality and finish.

But the company ran into severe postwar shortages. With no plywood for veneers, Lear bought hardwood logs and hired a mill to make them. Once he had the veneers, he couldn't buy tubes, speakers, capacitors, and condensers. Trying an old trick that had served him well in the 1930s, Lear complained to reporters that the major radio manufacturers, like RCA, Westinghouse, and Philco, were forcing new companies like Lear out of business by creating a monopoly for component parts. He was right — not that he wouldn't have done the same thing given the chance — but reporters were not as sympathetic as they had been when he was an unlicensed David fighting the Goliath of the radio industry.

By mid 1948, the Lear home radio division was such a financial disaster that the Board of Directors decided to phase it out for cash, which the company desperately needed. Dick Mock sold most of the assembled radios and consoles to the May Company, in Los Angeles.

Another new product was the Learecorder, "the most versatile home musical reproduction machine ever built," as the *New York Times* phrased it. But in spite of its quality and an extensive advertising campaign, the recorder had a troublesome design bug — the wire would frequently lock around the spool or break — and while Lear was straightening out his wire, the first magnetic tape recorders were reaching the market. The Learecorder couldn't compete.

Another product that didn't make it was the Learophone, an air-to-ground communication system that made it possible for pilots or passengers to conduct in-flight telephone conversations with anyone on the ground.

What Lear did have were his aircraft instruments for private pilots. By 1948, he had developed a new, low-priced automatic direction finder, the Lear Orienter, and he had introduced a line of VHF (very high frequency) items — transmitters, receivers, and a VHF version of the Learomatic navigator. And of course, there was the Learavian portable receiver and transmitter, which Lear had pioneered in the 1930s and had kept improving over the years.

The problem Lear Incorporated faced with its new line of aircraft instruments was familiar and predictable. On the one hand private flying, so drastically curtailed during the war, was just beginning to revive, but the pool of independent pilots with enough money to buy communication and navigation instruments was small. On the other hand the major airlines, which had the money and the need, were already hooked on the products of companies like Bendix, Collins, and Sperry. The only way Lear could crack that market was to develop something totally unique. That day would come, but in the first few years after the war, Lear's aircraft radio division, which represented only 5 to 10 percent of the company's total sales, walked a thin line between loss and modest profit.

It was the electromechanical division of Lear Incorporated, managed by Dick Mock, that kept the company afloat. As it had during the war, the Air Force still bought 90 percent of Lear's screw jacks, motors, actuators, and automatic controls. By the end of 1947 (and well into 1949), Lear electromechanical systems were still standard for new airplanes. But because the military had cut back production so severely, sales were a mere fraction of what they had been.

Given the personality of its founder and president, Lear Incorporated faced another predictable problem. Bill Lear was trying to control the company as if it were the same one-man shop he had run at the airport in Mineola. But with electromechanical parts, aircraft instruments, home radios, and wire recorders, with a string of Air Force development contracts, and with research laboratories in Grand Rapids, Los Angeles, and New York, Lear simply could not run every aspect of every project.

To complicate the problem, Lear Incorporated acquired the Romec Pump Company of Elyria, Ohio, in an attempt to become less dependent on military contracts. Romec made air, water, fuel, and oil pumps as well as special valves, tractor hoists, and drink dispensers. Complementing Lear's electromechanical division, Romec was soon making submerged water injection pumps for North American, Boeing, and Consolidated Vultee as well as for Pan American Airways, American Airlines, Sabena, and British Overseas Airways, among others.

At first, Bill Lear tried to maintain the appearance of total control by remaining president, chairman of the Board, and director of research and development. But he was spending so much time away from Grand Rapids that company projects began to mire in indecision. To keep things flowing, Lear finally set up a decision-making team of department heads, figuring that a group would pose less of a threat to his power than an individual. But the team approach merely eased tensions, and Bill Lear knew it. When the team recommended that Lear put Dick Mock in charge of the day-to-day running of the company, Lear promoted Mock to executive vice president.

Although Lear was happy to dump all the administrative detail on Mock so he could be free to create and play, that decision only emphasized Lear Incorporated's basic flaw. Bankers and investors had long viewed it as a one-man company. What would become of it, they wondered, if something happened to Bill Lear? Wasn't there anyone with enough skill and vision to be president besides Bill Lear? In the fall of 1948, the Board elected Mock president. Lear remained chairman of the Board as well as director of research and development.

Even with Mock as president, Bill Lear still considered Lear Incorporated his company. In an effort to keep it that way, he made sure that he was the only member of the Board of Directors who actually worked for Lear Incorporated. Given his powers of persuasion, Lear knew he could easily hide from or get from the Board almost anything he wanted.

Caught in a traumatic postwar transition aggravated by Bill Lear's personal business style, Lear Incorporated barely hung together from 1946 to 1949. Its annual sales ran between $5 and $6 million (down from $30 million in 1945), and it showed annual net losses of between $250,000 and $1 million. Things got so bad that Edward Adams, an officer of the National Bank of Detroit, which administered Lear Incorporated's RFC loan, used to come to Grand Rapids every Friday morning to see how much cash the company had taken in that week and what it expected to sell the following week.

The financial uncertainty hit Moya much harder than it did

Bill, who had been dodging creditors most of his life. She remembers those postwar fears vividly: "Our controller came in
one day and said, 'Well, you might as well lock up. We're going
bankrupt.' And of course Bill refused. But I worried about this.
Bankruptcy! The very sound of it worried me.

"But Bill took me in his arms one day and said, 'Honey, you
don't have to worry because they can't bankrupt my mind.
There's an infinite supply of ideas there, and all I have to do is
dip into it.' Bill had that special ability to cope with just about
anything."

15

IT DIDN'T TAKE Lear long to recognize that more was needed
than a simple fatigue-relief autopilot that would give fighter
pilots a ten-minute rest on the way to a mission. What military
and commercial pilots really needed was an instrument that
would actually fly the airplane once the pilot told it where to go.

Lear liked to explain the need for a more sophisticated autopilot by describing the eight basic moves pilots had to make just
to keep their ships in the sky: (1) watch the directional gyroscope
for the heading and if off course, change direction by working
the rudder pedals; (2) scan the vertical gyroscope to make sure
the ship is level and if not, turn the wheel right or left; (3) watch
the horizon bar for pitch and if climbing or diving, push or pull
the wheel; (4) roll the trim tab wheel to relieve the load on their
arm muscles; (5) keep an eye on the altimeter to maintain proper
altitude; (6) regulate the speed; (7) tune and watch the direction
finder to see where the plane actually is; and (8) communicate
with the ground.

"A pilot's busier than a bubble dancer working with Ping-
Pong balls," Lear used to say. "Thinking gets him into trouble.
If you could dig up the ones who crashed and ask them what
happened, the first thing they'd say is, 'Well, I thought.' "

Lear described the risk of flying as an "N plus one" factor. Each pilot can do N number of things at a given time. But each pilot has a limit, and one more factor — a plus one — will force him to make a mistake. Lear saw the autopilot as a way to reduce the N so that flying would be safer; and, for military pilots, fighting would be more effective.

The basic components of the autopilot were well known in the mid 1940s: a control, which the pilot set to chart the course; two reference gyroscopes — a directional gyro to determine whether the ship was flying east or south and at what degree, and a vertical gyro to determine whether the ship was level with the horizon; electrical sensors to compare the information the gyros collected to the course set by the pilot; and electromechanical parts, controlled by the sensors, to move the rudders (which controlled yaw, right or left), the ailerons (which controlled roll, or banking), and the elevators (which controlled pitch, up and down).

The problems in designing an autopilot for fighters with piston engines were quite simple to understand, but the solutions were something else. Given the size of a fighter, its autopilot had to be lighter and smaller than the ones used for bombers; it had to respond instantaneously to the movement of the plane or the ship would soon be out of control; and it had to be extremely accurate, for even a small error in moving the rudder or ailerons or elevators on a fighter at 450 miles an hour could spell disaster.

To build such an autopilot, Lear needed to design special gyroscopes, a new clutch that could stop the shaft on the point of a pin (not on a dime, as the fastop clutch did), and new electronic circuits to guide the system. The whole package had to weigh less than forty pounds. It was the biggest challenge Lear had taken on, and to meet it, he began to assemble a team. His method would be called cruel and ruthless by some, by others, fair and brilliant.

Lear hired engineers from all over the country. He found them in a bar or in an airport or saw them at another company, or they called him with an idea. He went anywhere to meet them. If he liked their thinking, he hired them on the spot.

If the engineer had only one idea, Lear used it, then got Dick

Mock to fire him. He wanted no deadwood. If the engineer couldn't keep up with Lear's own thinking and that of the rest of the team, he'd tell Mock, "Fire the sonofabitch!" And if the engineer couldn't stand the heat of working for Bill Lear — long hours and weekends, accepting Lear as the one who made all the decisions — then he would probably quit of his own accord. In this way, Lear soon had a team of creative, dedicated, enthusiastic engineers who followed and complemented his lead. At the center of the team stood Nils Eklund.

Lear had met Eklund in 1943 and recognized in the Swedish engineer a quick mind and a theoretical originality that balanced his own practical originality. In spite of his impressive academic credentials, Eklund had not lost what Lear had always had, a skepticism for books that said it couldn't be done. As Al Handschumacher put it: "Bill didn't have all the limitations of an education. He didn't know what couldn't be done. He'd start from scratch and find a little twist somewhere, like Edison did. He had an ability to instinctively work his mind around to the right place at the right time and come up with the right answer to make it happen."

Otherwise, Lear and Eklund differed greatly. Tall, lean, and debonair with a pencil-thin blond mustache, Eklund held engineering degrees from Swedish and West German schools. After settling in the United States in 1926, he continued his postgraduate studies at New York University, Brooklyn Polytechnic Institute, Newark College of Engineering, UCLA, and MIT. Mathematics applied to automatic controls was his specialty. He rarely touched a screwdriver and didn't know what to do with a soldering iron, but he loved to breathe the ether of theoretical and applied math.

In 1943, Eklund had seen a Lear Avia ad for engineers in the *New York Times* and applied. Richard Marsen, director of Lear's New York laboratory, had hired him, assigning him to work on synchronizers and controls for a counterrotating propeller that Hamilton Standard needed for a new Chance Vought fighter. The idea was to get two propellers to rotate at the same speed on the same shaft but in opposite directions, so that fighters could accelerate faster. In 1943, Army Air Force pilots had to nurse their throttles because the props then in use couldn't adjust to quick acceleration. Under contract to develop the new props for its parent company, the United Aircraft Corporation, Hamilton Standard had come to Lear Avia for a prototype; Lear was hoping to patent its developments and make a killing once the props went into production.

Eklund met Bill Lear two weeks after he had joined the organization. Lear had stormed into the lab on Broadway one morning to review the progress on the duplex propeller. He listened to the engineering staff explain its problems, gave orders to try such-and-such, and said that he'd expect a progress report when he next returned. After Lear left for Piqua, Eklund told Marsen that he was surprised that no one had pointed out to Lear that his idea wouldn't work. Marsen told Eklund to table the idea.

"Well, what about Mr. Lear?" Eklund had asked.

"Don't worry. Leave him to me."

Eklund scrapped Lear's idea, and Marsen, who was afraid of Lear's temper, conveniently forgot to tell the boss. When Lear returned a few weeks later and asked how his idea had worked, Marsen ducked. "It didn't" was all he could manage to say. Sulking, Lear called Eklund into Marsen's office for an explanation. "It seems that whenever I suggest anything around here, it doesn't work," he told Eklund. Marsen cowered in a corner. "Now, what's wrong with my suggestion?"

"Let me explain," Eklund said in his soft, polite, and precise manner. He went to the blackboard and sketched out the problem.

"I guess you're right," Lear said.

"If we do it this way, it *will* work," Eklund explained. The problem was a complex mathematical one, and at that point in his development Lear was extremely weak in that area. "But it will take time."

"Well, go ahead," Lear ordered.

Without coaching, Eklund had approached Bill Lear in the best possible way. He showed no fear (Lear frequently took advantage of men who feared him); he did not confront him in front of the other engineers (something Lear could not tolerate); he explained clearly, quickly, and without disrespect why it wouldn't work (Lear had no patience with rambling lectures);

and he presented an alternative (Lear didn't mind letting go of one idea if someone could demonstrate a better one). From that day on, Lear and Eklund worked in an atmosphere of mutual respect and honesty and remained friends until Lear died, almost thirty-five years later.

Eklund's idea did work, and when Hamilton saw the prototype prop, it wanted to buy the research outright for $250,000, then do the flight testing and refining itself. But Lear smelled big bucks and refused to sell. Before Eklund and his small staff could perfect the counterrotating prop, however, Lear pulled them off the project for several months to work on the initial plans for the fatigue-relief autopilot. As a result, Lear Avia finished the Hamilton Standard propeller system two weeks after V-J Day, when Hamilton was no longer interested. It paid Lear Avia $50,000 for materials and labor and buried the project in the postwar junk heap of discarded ideas.

Given their compatibility, it was only natural that Lear wanted Eklund to be his chief consultant on the new autopilot. Although Eklund was attracted to the challenge, he wouldn't leave New York City for Grand Rapids. To Lear, the problem was minor.

"You can stay in New York," Lear told him. "You can have my office and my secretary. You just come to Grand Rapids whenever we need you."

A few months after the war was over, Lear was ready to pitch his idea for an advanced autopilot to Army Air Forces officers and civil engineers at Wright Field. He took along Nils Eklund and Nicola Minorsky, a former Russian naval officer and the inventor of an autopilot for ships. Lear was at his best when he could sell an idea, and at Wright Field in the fall of 1945 he gave a command performance. The AAF's acceptance or rejection of the autopilot idea literally meant life or death to Lear Incorporated.

"How long will it take?" the military asked when Lear had finished his pitch.

"A year," Lear said with absolute confidence. Eklund gulped, knowing that it could never be done.

The AAF awarded Lear a development contract for $128,000, and it was almost two years before Lear had anything to show. The development money wouldn't pay for a tenth of the total development cost, but Lear didn't mind. He knew he was standing at the threshold of a new era in aircraft instrumentation. It was where he had stood before, with the car radio and the direction finder. This time, however, he was determined not only to be the first and the best but to savor the payoff as well. He was certain that Sperry and Bendix would soon get around to autopilots for fighters and light aircraft, and he wanted to make sure that he, not they, would spear the fat production contracts.

At first, Lear designed the autopilot with standard gyroscopes made by the leaders in the field — Minneapolis-Honeywell and Sperry, whose founder, Elmer A. Sperry, had first applied the gyroscope to aviation; but it didn't take him long to recognize that the gyroscopes on the market were too heavy and insensitive for his quick-response instrument. "Every time we'd go into a turn," Lear later recalled, "the airplane would start into the turn, but we'd go into the awfulest dive you ever saw in your life."

So Lear began looking for someone to design the kind of gyroscope he needed. After hiring and firing a few "dreamboat" engineers, as one Lear colleague called them, and getting considerable help from John Adkins, the AAF civilian engineer in charge of the gyro laboratory at Wright Field, Lear found John Schoeppel, a gyroscope expert at Minneapolis-Honeywell. Lear called Schoeppel one Friday morning, interrupting an engineering meeting.

"I understand you made Honeywell's gyros," Lear said.

"That's right," Schoeppel said.

"I'd like to talk to you."

"I'm pretty busy, Bill, and Grand Rapids is pretty far away."

"No problem," Lear said. "I'll have an airplane there at eight o'clock tomorrow morning."

Schoeppel was curious. He spent most of Saturday with Lear and Jim Wood, who was in charge of the model shop, where all the parts were tooled. Before the end of the day, Schoeppel left Minneapolis-Honeywell. As he explains: "Bill had done a couple of things that Honeywell said couldn't be done. I saw a lot of imagination at work in Lear's shop. If someone was going to do something, this looked to me like the place to be. It was obvious that Bill was going to build the next-generation autopilot."

Schoeppel set up a "clean room" — a dust-free, air-conditioned, and moisture-controlled laboratory in which to build the prototype gyros, which had to be hermetically sealed inside containers. He found it easy to work with Lear.

"No question that Bill was a genius," Schoeppel says. "I say that advisedly. You didn't have to sit down and draw him pictures. He could visualize what I was saying instantly. In addition to being a damn good engineer, he was a superb marketing man, and that's quite a combination."

While Schoeppel was working on gyros, Eklund was developing electronic circuits in New York. He badly needed an instrument that would simulate rolls, pitches, and yaws electronically so that he could test the response time of the new circuits. The best gyros in the world would be useless if the electronic system did not react quickly enough to the information the gyros fed it. But Lear wouldn't buy the machine.

"He couldn't understand why I needed it," Eklund recalls. "He was very hard to deal with in things he didn't understand. He was a very good mechanical engineer, but he didn't understand theory very well."

Eklund appreciated how Lear's mind worked. Around a pendulum, he rigged up a simple device that would send out a few frequencies so Lear could see for himself the importance of the instrument. "Bill thought it was great," Eklund says. "He wanted to buy the frequency generator immediately." With the new instrument and months of trial and error, Eklund was able to develop the fast-response circuits needed in the autopilot.

Accurate gyros and fast electronic response were still not enough. Lear needed a special lightweight clutch to stop the servomotors that moved the rudder, ailerons, and elevators. He assigned another Swedish engineer, Gunnar Wennerberg, to solve that problem.

An electrical engineer by training, Wennerberg began as Eklund's assistant on electrical circuits, but Lear soon assigned him to work on clutches. The state of the art in 1945 and 1946 was to use electromagnetic disks, which were supposed to stop driving the shaft the instant electrical current reached them. Wennerberg tried everything he could think of, but nothing worked well until Lear brought in a wet powder clutch invented by Jacob Rabinow, a scientist at the National Bureau of Standards. The magnetic material was a fluid made of powdered iron and oil. "It worked beautifully under one condition," Wennerberg recalls. "You had to start it up and never stop it. As soon as you did, it would cake up and lock and never work again."

One day, Wennerberg saw an ad for a new dry powder magnetic clutch, developed by the Eaton Corporation of Cleveland. Lear sent him down to check it out. Impressed, Wennerberg brought a couple back to Grand Rapids for extensive lab tests. The clutch held up, so Lear asked Eaton to make a few according to his specifications, but the company never responded.

Lear told Wennerberg to take the wet powder clutch they had designed specifically for the autopilot and fill it with Eaton's dry iron powder. The idea worked, and the dry powder clutch became the heart of the Lear servosystem for the autopilot.

Lear had the time of his life testing the autopilot. First, he put it in his Twin Beech, then he told the Air Force (it had changed its name from Army Air Forces in September 1947) he needed something larger so he could take a copilot and a few engineers up with him. The Air Force first gave him a 51-foot twin-engine C-56 Lockheed Lodestar, which could carry a crew of two and up to fourteen passengers.

Each night he was in Grand Rapids, Nils Eklund flew with Lear; the routine rarely changed. Between ten o'clock and midnight, they drove out to the plant to pick up the autopilot, which the team had been working on all day, and installed it in the Twin Beech — or Greenie Weenie, as Lear called the Lodestar. After an hour or two of rolling, pitching, and yawing over Lake Michigan, they took the autopilot back to the plant, where Lear wrote a squawk sheet for the crew, telling them what was wrong and what they should try next. Then Lear and Eklund went back to the house or the Pantlind Hotel, where Eklund sometimes stayed, pulled out a bottle of Scotch, and discussed the autopilot. They'd sleep for a few hours and then return to the plant to supervise the day's work. When Nils couldn't take Bill any longer, he'd return to New York.

There was plenty of excitement. While testing the autopilot over Lake Michigan or on a coast-to-coast trip, Lear frequently went back in the cabin to lie down. "You watch the instruments," he'd tell Eklund, who hated heights and who knew even less about flying than he did about soldering. Although he had confidence in the autopilot, Eklund didn't trust it *that* much, and he got Gunnar Wennerberg to make as many of the long flights with Lear as possible.

There were some close calls, too. One night, just after midnight, they were flying the Twin Beech toward the lake when Eklund saw a small airplane in front of them. Lear was up and down, puttering with the autopilot, screwdriver in hand. Not wanting to be a backseat pilot and certain that Lear had seen it as well, Eklund didn't say anything. All of a sudden, Lear threw himself on the wheel and the Beechcraft ducked under the other plane, just feet from disaster. When they landed at Kent County Airport, the other pilot was waiting for them, still shaking. "My God," he said. "I thought I was done for."

The fun really began when Lear started flying the Greenie Weenie from coast to coast. He prepared his trips meticulously. "Bill had a girl in each town," Eklund recalls. "After working all night, he'd call them all over the country. Each one was like she was the *only* one. Whenever we came into an airport, there would be a woman in a limousine to pick us up."

And then there were the progress reports. Lear always insisted on taking Eklund with him to Wright Field and to the Pentagon. Standing at the blackboard, Lear would explain what his team was doing, how the autopilot was performing, and what changes he expected to make. Most of the time, Lear overstated the performance and incorrectly explained the theory behind the design, but he had a special ability to sense when he was getting in over his head. "Nils, would you please show how we're doing it?" he'd ask Eklund, adding, "If it wasn't for Nils Eklund, I wouldn't be able to do this work." Eklund would go to the blackboard and explain the new approach in such a way as not to embarrass Lear in front of the Air Force generals and engineers.

Eklund is quick to point out, however, that Lear's contribution to the autopilot as visionary and leader was significant even if he didn't, at least in the beginning, understand every aspect of every part of the development. He drove himself and everyone else to the limit, demanding perfection from both himself and his team. "I would tell him: 'That's fine, Bill. Leave it that way. It's too much trouble to change.' But Bill would tear the whole damn thing apart and start over just to get it right."

Driven by his vision and totally preoccupied with the autopilot, Lear was not easy to work with on a day-to-day basis. "He had no set pattern," recalls Vern Benfer, one of Lear's autopilot engineers. "He was mercurial, depressive, enticing, alluring, masochistic, and the guys, for the most part, would just take it." But Dick Mock couldn't find a chief engineer who made the grade or wanted to stay. At times, Lear seemed to resent Mock for being president and, as if to show everyone who was boss, he'd dress him down in front of others.

Lear expected his team to work long hours, six days a week, and sometimes on Sundays, which he hated. (When Moya went to church on Sunday mornings to pray and teach Sunday school, he would ask friends like the Mocks to have coffee with him until she returned because he didn't want to be alone.) Recalls Benfer: "No one walked. Everyone ran, mostly out of fear of Bill, I expect. After working twenty-four or thirty-six straight hours, he'd throw up his hands. 'Everybody's too tired,' he'd say. 'Get the hell out of here' . . . There were candy machines in the lobby, and he'd punch a handful of nickels and get Hershey bars out and stuff them in his pockets. We'd all go back to the Lear house and fall into bed. He'd feed us a candy bar. Four hours later we were up and back again."

One Friday afternoon, Lear called Mock from Santa Monica with a list of modifications for the autopilot, telling him to make sure the work was done by Sunday night, when he'd return. He wanted to test it as soon as he flew into Kent County Airport. Mock told Bill Schall to make the changes. Schall, who had been working every single Saturday for a year and many Sundays as well, said he couldn't because close friends, whom he hadn't seen for five years, were coming for the weekend.

"This is important work," Mock told him.

"I don't care. My wife would never forgive me."

Mock called Lear and explained the problem.

"Fire the sonofabitch," Lear yelled. "I don't want to see him when I get back."

Eklund picked Lear up at the airport on Sunday night. When Bill asked about the modifications, Eklund told him they weren't ready because Bill Schall took off on Saturday. "That sonofabitch!" was all Lear could say.

"Bill Schall is probably the most loyal worker you have," Eklund told Lear. Schall had been with Lear in both Vandalia and Piqua. Lear had sent him to Little Norway in Toronto during part of the war to service the Lear Avia direction finders and radios installed in Norwegian fighters. "He's been working day and night. Now you want to fire him because he has friends visiting him. That's not like you, Bill."

Lear went straight to bed without saying goodnight and the next morning at breakfast he didn't even mention Bill Schall. When he and Eklund walked into the lab, Schall was bent over a bench working on the autopilot. Lear put his hand on the engineer's shoulder. "How's it going, Bill?" he asked as if nothing had happened.

Like the others, Eklund also found it hard to work for Lear because of his moods. One day, Lear was called to the phone while he was soldering a circuit. While he was gone, Eklund told the technician working with them to change a few connections to see if that would make a difference in the circuit they were testing. (Eklund was proud that he didn't know how to solder, which peeved Lear.) When Lear saw the changes he blew up. "For Christ's sake," he shouted at Eklund. "Can't I have things my own way? If I'm getting into your hair, tell me!"

Eklund did. He put on his jacket and left. When Lear returned to the hotel, Eklund was sitting in the lobby reading the paper. Lear saw that the Swede was still mad. "Come on up and have a drink," he said. "I'm sorry, Nils. We're all getting tired."

Eklund had one more run-in with his boss early in the development of the autopilot. During an engineering meeting, Lear proposed a change in the design of the clutch. "Bill, you can't do that!" Eklund objected. "You'll lose most of the efficiency."

"Don't worry about that, Nils," Lear said. "It will be all right."

"It won't work that way," Nils insisted.

"It will work all right."

When the conference was over and everyone had left, Eklund told Lear, "Bill, you know just as well as I do that the goddamned thing won't work that way. Why do you insist on it?"

"Okay, do it your way," Lear said in a childish way.

Eklund caught on. "I never did that again," he recalls. "We were really good friends. He never chewed me out. I basically found him a warm, kind, and generous man."

And so it went for a year and a half. Testing, modifying, testing, screaming, testing — always trying something new. As most observers admit, next to Lear, Eklund was the most important engineer on the autopilot. Besides bringing theory and fresh ideas to the project, he was Lear's filter, for Bill had no patience with matters he couldn't understand, and he wouldn't allow anyone to try a solution he hadn't figured out. Lear would send the engineers to Eklund and let them explain what they wanted and why. Sometimes that took hours. Then Eklund would summarize the discussion for Lear in five minutes. The system worked well.

By early 1947, after almost two years of development and testing, the prototype C-2 autopilot was ready. But before Lear could deliver it to Wright Field, he got word that the Air Force now wanted an autopilot for the jet fighter fleet it was building. The C-2, of course, was designed for the conventional fighter, driven by a piston engine, and wouldn't work in a jet, which had a different control system.

The United States began testing a jet (the XP-59-A) late in the war. But the plane was so poorly designed that the Air Force had put all thirty-four of them in mothballs after V-J Day and begun developing the F-80. By the end of 1945, the Air Force was test-flying 236 F-80s. It bought another 400 during 1946 and was so pleased with the performance of the plane that it decided to build the air fleet around the jet if it could get enough money from Congress.

Still hanging on by a thread in early 1947, Lear Incorporated was counting on a production contract for the C-2 autopilot to hold the company together. As Benfer explains: "There were pay periods when people took a few shares of Lear stock in lieu of cash . . . The [office] would complete paperwork against the military contracts, fly to the Air Force to get it signed, then fly to the bank in Detroit for a loan against the contract to meet the payroll."

The Board of Directors was so glum that it didn't want Lear to tell Wright Field that the C-2 wouldn't work in a jet until he had a production contract signed and sealed. Lear refused. His version of the episode goes like this:

"I'm not going to tell them it *can* fly a jet when I know it won't," Lear warned the Board.

"That will embarrass us at Wright Field," the Board said. "You've got to. We'll go broke if we don't get this order."

"We'll get the order, don't worry," Lear promised.

Lear brought the C-2 prototype to Wright Field. Air Force pilots and engineers took it on a test flight and were delighted. Afterward, Lear sat around the conference table with seventeen people — technicians, purchasing agents, production personnel, and staff from the adjutant general's office.

"We're prepared to give you an order now for your C-2 autopilot for our new jets," they told him.

"Well, I would love to have an order," Lear said. "But the autopilot won't fly the jets."

The room was hushed.

"But if you give me a month, I'll redesign it so it will."

To do that, Lear insisted, the Wright Field flight instructors would have to teach him how to fly the F-80 so he could make the initial tests himself. But the Air Force told Lear that, at forty-five, he was too old. And there were no commercial or privately owned jets in the country in 1947.

Lear wouldn't back down. All his life, he had flight-tested whatever he had developed, he argued, and he wasn't going to change just because jets were taking over the skies. Either he flew jets or there would be no autopilot.

Lear learned to fly the F-80, and when the new autopilot, the F-5, was finished after four months of intensive design and testing, it was an engineering marvel. Without telling Lear, however, the Air Force was about to let out a huge autopilot contract to another company because there was one design facet in the F-5 it didn't like.

To cut down on weight, Lear had used a triple servo — one motor with three sets of clutches — to drive the ailerons, rudder, and elevators. That was fine for piston engine fighters, where the cables connecting the autopilot to parts were easily accessible. In the F-80, however, there was less space in which to work with the cables and the Air Force engineers wanted three single servos. They were certain Lear could make the change, but they figured it would mean more long delays, and they were under pressure from the Pentagon to outfit the F-80 before Korea exploded into a war. But they couldn't bring themselves to tell Lear because, as one observer put it, "they liked Bill and didn't want to hurt his feelings. They were going to let him down easy."

Lear heard through the grapevine on a Friday morning that Wright Field was going to put him on hold after all the work he had put into the F-5 and all the money he had spent. He asked the Air Force for a conference on Monday morning and called his team together. "We're going to make a single servo and I'm going to take it down to Wright on Monday morning," he announced. Then he passed out assignments. As the parts were being drawn in the engineering office, they were being machined in the model shop. On Monday morning, Lear and Schoeppel flew into Wright Field.

"It was the slickest sales job I've ever seen," Schoeppel recalls.

"We like your autopilot, Bill," the Air Force told him. "But we'll probably have to get someone else into the act. You don't have a single servo, and the Air Force has decided it has to go single servo."

"Gee, fellas," Lear said, "you should have told me about this sooner."

"We know, Bill. We know you can react fast, but we just can't wait . . . We have a deadline. Maybe yours can get done in another year or so."

"Hell," Lear said, "we have a single servo now."

"You're dreaming."

"No, I have it right with me." Lear dipped into his traveling bag, pulled out the beautifully machined single servo, and set it on the table. The conference stopped in midsentence.

"Well, it probably won't work in the autopilot," the Air Force said.

"Then let's take it to the lab and hook it up," Lear offered.

They did, and of course it worked. The Air Force got a superior instrument. And Lear won a production contract worth close to a billion dollars over the next twelve years.

16

"IT IS THE BASIS of our capability to fend off enemy attack, no matter what the weather," said Air Force General Sory Smith of the F-5 autopilot. "It is the guts and core of the air defense of America."

"It is a miracle of engineering," said Bernard Levine, one of the Air Force engineers responsible for the autopilot program.

"It is a triumph of miniaturization and packaging," said Levine's associate H. F. Kneckt. "There isn't a cubic inch of wasted space."

But there was much more to the F-5 than a simple autopilot. There was the specially designed vertical gyro indicator and the automatic approach coupler, which made blind landings practical and safe.

The vertical gyro indicator was almost an afterthought. Hardly had John Schoeppel settled into his dust-free shop in Grand Rapids when Lear mentioned casually that Al Handschumacher, who had been released from the Army Air Corps to work for Lear, had picked up a development contract for a new gyroscopic indicator that showed the pilot through bars and a miniature airplane whether the ship was level with the horizon and if it was turning, at what angle. The Air Force needed a new vertical gyro indicator because the one used in piston engine fighters had two problems. Like a mirror, the image on the indicator was backward, and the indicator had a turn error for which the pilot had to compensate mentally on long, leisurely banks.

Although the World War II fighter pilots had learned to live with the turn-error problem, jet pilots couldn't. F-80s depended on long turns, which made the turn error so critical that jet pilots were slipping into dives before they realized what was happening. The situation became so dangerous that the Air Force would allow the F-80 in the air only when the weather was clear, something like the early days of the DH-4 "flaming coffins." It was the same old problem: airplanes had developed faster than the instruments needed to fly them safely.

Lear told Wright Field he could design and build a new vertical gyro indicator that would automatically correct the turn error. Wright gave him a development contract. Stuck with two full-time projects, Schoeppel decided to design a gyro and indicator that would work in the autopilot and, at the same time, satisfy the terms of the second contract. While he was at it, he reversed the image on the indicator so that when the airplane appeared to be banking left on the screen, it really was.

The Lear sales force had contacts at all the major aircraft companies. When Schoeppel had the vertical gyro indicator (VGI) ready for testing, Lear sent a batch of the instruments to companies like Lockheed and Republic, which were building and testing F-80s and F-84s. That way, he would get free flight-testing hours and build up support for the VGI among the pilots who actually flew the airplanes. Even though there was some controversy among the armchair colonels about whether the true image would confuse pilots who were used to reading reverse images, the reports filtering back to Grand Rapids from the pilots themselves were superb. Dick Mock remembers how Bill Lear convinced Colonel Carl ("Smokey") Caldera, chief of the Safety Command, that the Lear VGI was natural to use and safer than the standard model.

Lear put two VGIs in his Twin Beech, a standard model and Schoeppel's new version. He covered the new one and told Smokey to close his eyes until he tapped him on the shoulder, then to straighten out the airplane. Lear put the ship into a turn and nudged Smokey, who opened his eyes, read the standard indicator, and turned the wheel — the wrong way until he had a chance to think. Then he quickly reversed the motion and leveled the ship.

Lear repeated the test with the new indicator. Smokey turned the wheel the correct way the first time; Lear had an important convert. But in spite of the obvious need for the new VGI and its wide acceptance among jet pilots, the generals at the Pentagon who held the purse strings didn't see the need for another instrument. Not until the fly-over fiasco, that is.

To demonstrate to President Harry S. Truman and Congress

the might of the new jet airplane in the hope of fattening the postwar military budget, the Pentagon planned to send over the Capitol a flying armada such as the world had never seen. Since no single military airport had enough jets to impress Washington, the Pentagon had to draw them from all over the country. They were to rendezvous and take off from one airport.

Luckily for Lear, the weather was so bad around the country that most of the jets in the fly-over had to be grounded, even though the sky was clear in Washington. Embarrassed, the Pentagon descended on Wright Field in a fury when it learned that the multimillion-dollar jets couldn't take off because they didn't have a $2,000 gyro that corrected the turn error. Lear Incorporated was the only company in the country that had developed the instrument. It became such a hot item that by 1951, when the Korean War was in full swing, every jet fighter and bomber flew by a Lear VGI.

To leap from the autopilot to a blind landing system was logical, for once engineers had developed an instrument that could guide the airplane by the electronic signals it received from its gyros, it was then possible to add a second electronic system to read and transmit to the autopilot the radio beams that airports used for instrument landings when visibility was low. Bill Lear started to design the approach coupler that would make the blind landings work. "Bill said he would have it done in ninety days," Handschumacher recalls. "Everybody was just aghast that he would make a promise like that, including me."

Within three months, however, Lear was ready to demonstrate the blind landing system to the All-Weather Flying Command. He installed the autopilot and the new approach coupler in a C-24 that the Air Force had given him and took off for Columbus, Ohio, where a group of skeptical Air Force pilots, purchasing agents, and engineers were waiting to see the promised miracle. When Lear and Gunnar Wennerberg neared the airport, Lear turned on the approach system. It worked momentarily, but then a one-dollar part in the receiver stuck. Wennerberg tried to free it but couldn't. Lear landed the plane manually and told the Air Force crowd that the instrument didn't work. If Lear was embarrassed or angry, he didn't show it. He just turned the plane around and went back to Grand Rapids to remove the bug.

About a month later, Lear asked to demonstrate the approach coupler once again. This time, he put the F-5 in a Lodestar and landed at Wright Field, where, once again, a group of generals, purchasing agents, and engineers were waiting. "They were expecting a big riot," recalls Al Handschumacher, who flew down with Lear. "They thought it was a joke. What happened next was unbelievable."

Lear flew the Lodestar filled with military spectators a few miles away from Wright Field. The interior of the ship was a "rat's nest of wires and equipment, like an experimental laboratory." Lear put the ship on autopilot, pushed a button on the F-5's control box, and took his hands off the wheel. As if drawn by a huge magnet, the Lodestar's nose swung around until it pointed toward the airport's runway, guided by the instrument landing beam from the ground. The ship swerved and swayed until it found the exact center of the runway without losing any altitude. It felt as if the Lodestar was being towed liked a glider.

Next, a needle on the control box began to quiver, indicating to Lear that the ship was now picking up the glide-slope beam from the ground. Lear leaned over and pushed a second button. The Lodestar bounced for a moment until the approach coupler found the exact center of the beam and the autopilot locked onto it like a dog on a bone. Then the ship began a gentle slope down toward the runway. "Bill just sat there," Handschumacher recalls. "He absolutely did not touch the controls. Everyone was just watching him."

The Lodestar approached the end of the runway at seventy-five feet, bisecting it perfectly. At twenty-five feet, the autopilot was still flying the plane. At five feet above the runway, Lear pushed a third button to disengage the autopilot and took over the controls himself, easing the Lodestar onto the runway. "By God, it worked," Handschumacher remembers. "It took all the wind out of the disbelievers' sails."

That was the first complete blind landing the Air Force had ever seen. Lear hid his pride and excitement as if to say "Of course it worked. What did you expect?"

After the Air Force had tested the F-5 and approach coupler for a full year, William Powell Lear, the high school dropout, was awarded the Collier Trophy. Established in 1911 by Robert J. Collier (the former editor of and son of the founder of *Collier's* magazine) and awarded by the National Aeronautic Association "for the greatest achievement in aviation in America, the value of which has been demonstrated by actual use during the preceding year," the Collier Trophy is the Pulitzer Prize of aeronautics. It put Lear, at the age of forty-eight, in the company of such men as Glenn H. Curtiss, who won the trophy for the flying boat (1911); Orville Wright, for the automatic stabilizer (1913); Elmer Sperry, for the gyroscope (1914); Sylvanus Reed, for the metal propeller (1925); Major E. L. Hoffman, for the parachute (1927); Glenn Martin, for the first modern bomber (1932); Captain Albert Hegenberger, for pioneer work on blind landings (1934); Donald Douglas, for the twin-engine commercial transport plane (1935); Howard Hughes, for his historic around-the-world flight in ninety-one hours (1938); General H. H. Arnold, for his leadership in developing the Army Air Forces (1942); Luis Alvarez, for work on the Instrument Landing System (1945); and Captain Charles E. Yeager, for breaking the sound barrier (1947).

The autopilot team was delighted when Lear received the trophy and to a man agreed that he, not the team, deserved it. The autopilot had been molded from Lear's vision. It was his determination that had pushed the project to completion; his salesmanship that got the Air Force to accept it; and his flight testing, troubleshooting, and demanding perfectionism that made it the technical wonder it was.

As they stood outside the Oval Office, where President Truman was waiting to receive them before the formal White House dinner, after which he would present the trophy to Lear, it was Moya who was nervous. "I know that Bill was thrilled and happy," she recalls. "But he was very poised, very much under control. I put my hand in his to squeeze it, and he leaned down to me and said, 'Don't worry, honey. I'll put him right at his ease.' "

After shaking hands with Bill, Truman turned to Moya. "Mrs. Lear, do you ever help your husband in the business?" he asked. "Do you ever tell him what to do?"

"No, Mr. President," Moya said. "I sometimes tell him where to go — but I never tell him what to do!"

As pleased and proud as he was, Bill Lear didn't forget Nils Eklund, who had worked with him on the autopilot for almost five years. "Nils," he said in the telegram he sent just hours before receiving the trophy, "without you I couldn't have done it. Thank you . . . Bill."

Nils Eklund once joked with Lear: "If it weren't for the autopilot, you'd still be making screw jacks."

Lear agreed. But it wasn't the autopilot itself that ultimately saved Lear Incorporated from financial disaster, no matter how important and excellent the instrument. It was the Korean War, which created the huge demand for the F-5. From June 1950, when the United States entered the war, to its end in July 1953, sales at Lear leaped from $7.3 to $21 million, then climbed steadily up to $54 million by 1954. Ninety percent of its sales were to the military, mostly for autopilots and vertical gyro indicators for F-82 Twin Mustangs, F-84 Thunderjets, and F-86 Sabres. As in World War II, there was at least one piece of Lear equipment on every fighter, bomber, and cargo plane in the Korean War — an autopilot, VGI, electromechanical items, or pumps made by the Romec division.

By 1951, Lear Incorporated was showing a net profit of approximately $1 million a year. And in 1953, for the first time since the company went public in 1945, it started paying annual dividends, 15 cents per common share. Because it was wartime and the military considered its products vital, the Air Force helped Lear get V-loans with up to $10 million credit; it also licensed another company to manufacture the F-5 because Lear couldn't make them fast enough and the Air Force didn't want to depend on a company that was struggling to stay solvent.

Although Bill Lear was upset that he had to share the production money with another company, he had few other complaints. His salary, dividends, and profit for the period 1950–1954 alone amounted to a conservative $1.5 million; his stock was worth an estimated $7 million on paper. Lear's financial success was so impressive that the Horatio Alger Association of Distinguished Americans granted him its award in 1954. Created in 1947, the Horatio Alger Award is given annually "to individuals from humble backgrounds whose own initiative and effort has led to significant career success, as well as a sense of purpose and participation in assisting those less fortunate."

The Horatio Alger Association recognized one aspect of

Lear's success story; the University of Michigan, another. In 1951, it awarded William Powell Lear an honorary doctorate in engineering. In many ways, the degree meant more to Lear than the Collier Trophy. Although he was proud of what he had accomplished with no formal education, he recognized the limitations its omission placed on his career. Recalls Moya: "That degree was his first, and he didn't feel he deserved it." Nevertheless, for months afterward, he expected everyone in the office to call him "Dr. Lear," and the next Lear Incorporated annual report printed "D.E. (Hon)" after his name. There would be other honorary degrees in the years to come — from the University of Nevada, University of Notre Dame, Art Center College of Design, Northrop University, and Carnegie-Mellon University — but none would taste as sweet as the first.

After finishing the autopilot and accepting the Collier Trophy, Lear went through "a big downer." For five years, he had devoted most of his time, drive, and creativity to the autopilot. Without a new challenge, he felt empty and alone. He became restless, insecure, and meddling, and everyone suffered, especially the Air Force and Dick Mock.

Mock went into action as soon as the ink dried on the development contracts for the F-5 and the VGIs. He set up a dust-free, temperature- and humidity-controlled section in the plant for precision mass production. Gyro specifications were rigid: measurements of up to ten thousandths of an inch and dynamic balancing of motors to five millionths of an inch. Mock also instituted quality-control procedures to ensure the highest performance of the gyros, autopilots, and approach couplers. Mindful of Lear's reputation before World War II for uneven quality and uncertain delivery, Mock was determined that Lear instruments would be the best on the market. His biggest problem was Bill Lear. It began with his catching a design error in the approach coupler specifications that the Air Force had approved; it was compounded by his constant tinkering with the autopilot.

Lear continued to test the approach coupler on his Twin Beech, in which he had installed two different coupler circuits, one timed at eight seconds, the other at twenty-three. Discovering that the twenty-three-second time constant rode the ILS (instrument landing system) beam much better on the Beech (it kept the plane more stable), Lear realized that on a jet the eight-second constant required by the Air Force specifications wouldn't work at all. He took the problem to Wright Field. According to Lear:

"I made a mistake," he told the Air Force engineers. "With an eight-second time constant, the plane will be unstable. It's very easy for me to change it now, before it goes into production. I've got an airplane sitting outside. If you'll go for a ride with me, I'll show you that twenty-three will fly the beam perfectly."

The engineers wouldn't go for a ride. Instead, Lear complained, they covered the blackboard with mathematical formulas proving that "infinity times poop over zero" equals eight.

"If you want eight seconds, I'll give it to you," Lear finally told them. "But I'll also give you a written guarantee it won't fly the airplane on the beam."

Against the objections of just about everyone at the shop, Lear added to the approach coupler an extra set of resistors wired for a twenty-three-second time constant. Many months later, after the couplers were rolling off the assembly line, Lear got a call from Earl Rice, the chief engineer at North American, who was installing the autopilot and approach coupler in the F-86D Sabre. "Bill," Rice said, "your autopilot won't fly the plane on the beam. What are we going to do?"

"I put in an extra pair of resistors," Lear said. "Cut R-134 and R-136 and it'll fly fine."

"But that would be modifying the autopilot," Rice objected. "They'll never allow us to do that."

"I'm sorry for your problem. You asked me the answer. I've given it to you. Now, if you don't want to cut them out, why, just don't deliver the airplanes."

Rice explained his problem and Lear's solution to the engineers at Wright Field. "We argued with Lear for two whole days and showed him conclusively on the blackboard that the eight-second time constant was the only thing that will work," they said. "We're sick and tired of arguing."

"Well, could I just cut out these two resistors and make one flight trial?" Rice asked.

With the Air Force's permission, Rice had his test pilot, Bob Hoover, try out the twenty-three-second time constant. The F-86 latched right onto the beam and took the jet in perfectly. Hoover tried it a few more times. There was no problem.

"We took out the R-134 and the R-136," Rice told Wright Field. "It works perfectly now."

"Well, we'll give you a deviation order," the engineers said. "Theoretically, it shouldn't work, but we'll let you cut the two resistors."

Lear was never satisfied with his autopilot, just as he had never been satisfied with the automatic direction finder in the late 1930s and early 1940s. It made no difference to him that under the terms of its production contract, Lear Incorporated was required to follow exactly the autopilot specifications that the company and the Air Force had worked out after long hours of debate and heated discussion. As far as he was concerned, the F-5 was *his* autopilot, unfinished and imperfect.

Lear began to tinker late at night or on weekends with models already on the assembly line, resoldering this or that. He'd call up Wright Field, insisting that something would work better if they would only switch such-and-such. And he gave orders to workers in the dust-free assembly area that they were to put the instruments together this way, not that. Benfer remembers those days vividly: "I have seen him come in from out of town, walk into the plant, stop the production line, and order changes to be made when the Air Force was screaming for products. Bill had no legal right to stop that production without getting Air Force approval. This kind of thing created havoc."

It got to the point that the Air Force told Handschumacher that it would cancel its production contract with Lear Incorporated if they couldn't keep Lear out of autopilot production. It wanted no changes, it said, no matter how good. The F-5 worked well, and the autopilots were needed for the war. Improvements could come later, under a new development contract. If they had to lock Lear out of the lab, then lock him out they must.

First, Dick Mock issued orders to the assembly line that no changes could be made unless they came directly from the supervisor. He told the supervisors they could not authorize changes in design or procedure unless he, Dick Mock, personally approved. "Bill went off and sulked," Handschumacher recalls. "There were times when he was absolutely raving and ranting."

Handschumacher had worked with Lear long enough both to understand and to appreciate what drove the man. If Handschumacher could just find another project that would capture Lear's imagination, he knew Lear would leave the autopilot alone. Handschumacher talked to the purchasing people at Wright Field and got Lear a development contract for an advanced blind landing system. "He was happy," Handschumacher remembers. "That's how we were able to freeze the design of the autopilot — by redirecting and treating him like a child. I say that in a loving way. We gave him another lollipop to suck on. A bigger one with more challenge. We conned him."

With a great sigh of relief, Mock and the Air Force learned in 1950 that Lear was moving his research and development work to Santa Monica. (The decision to move the corporate headquarters to a new building adjacent to the Santa Monica airport soon would follow.) Lear's first project in California was a piece of unfinished business.

Even in 1947, almost three years before the jet autopilot production contracts, Lear had wanted to adapt and market the earlier C-2 autopilot for light aircraft like the Twin Beech, in which he had first flight-tested the instrument for the Air Force. But the Board of Directors had blocked him — and with good reason. Board member Edward Adams, an officer of the National Bank of Detroit, the company's major creditor, had argued that no investor would dare lend money for a risky project aimed at a small and uncertain market. Furthermore, the success of the commercial autopilot would depend completely on the creativity, salesmanship, and drive of one man — Bill Lear. As another board member put it: "If you're screwing someone's wife, what happens if he comes in and shoots you in the back?" It was not a facetious question. (The Board had also blocked the production of the patented Learepeater tape, which stores could use to announce their bargains to shoppers over and over again, automatically. The Learepeater was the first of its kind in the country, but Lear Incorporated had no production money to push it.)

By the time Lear Incorporated had enough money and bank

credit to indulge its stubborn founder, other companies like Bendix and Sperry already had commercial autopilots on the market. But none could really compete with Lear's, called the L-2, for reliability, weight, and price. The L-2 was an instant, if financially modest, success.

After the L-2, Lear was still restless, searching for that all-consuming aircraft project that would satisfy his two drives — creativity and salesmanship. Bill Schall was working with Lockheed to install the F-5 autopilot, with modifications, in the top-secret U-2 spy plane; and John Schoeppel and Nils Eklund were designing gyro platforms for the new Bomarc missile. But Lear couldn't get excited about pilotless aircraft, even if they were the future. Quite simply, he was a pilot and he loved airplanes. He couldn't fly a missile, feel the controls in his hands, be up there, alone and free.

Then Lear stumbled onto the Learstar. Although he didn't recognize it at the time, it paved the way for a whole new career.

17

MOYA AND BILL REMODELED their home in Santa Monica, adding guest quarters and a big bar area for entertaining. They hired Connie Hazlett as maid, cook, and nanny for John, Shanda, and David, who was two years old; and Bill hired both Patti and Bill Jr. to work for him at the plant.

In the early 1940s, Bill had convinced Madeline that she and the children should move from Kansas City to California. Patti shuttled between two different lifestyles in the Los Angeles area. During the week, she lived with her mother in a one-bedroom apartment in Hollywood; on weekends, with her father at his Toluca Lake mansion, where Bill Jr. was staying. She went to Hollywood High. Then she lived with her father during the week and with her mother on weekends and attended North Hollywood High. Next, Bill rented a home for Madeline and the two children from a Japanese family who was interned in a wartime camp, and Patti went to John Marshall High. Finally, Bill bought Madeline a house in the San Fernando Valley with money from the children's trust funds. It was Patti's twentieth home in sixteen years. She enrolled in the Hollywood Professional School — her twelfth school in twelve years — on a scholarship because Madeline could not afford the $20 monthly tuition. A straight-A student, she graduated at the age of sixteen.

After six weeks at UCLA, where she paid her own tuition by working as a cashier in a movie theater, she quit. A few months later she enrolled in Scripps College, an expensive private women's college. Her trust fund paid the tuition, room, and board. After graduating in 1950, Patti's first job with her father was as "flying secretary," mostly on long trips from Los Angeles to Grand Rapids, where she got to know Charlene well (she would later take a Latin American cruise with Charlene).

Bill Jr. loved flying as much as his father did, and, like his father, he was determined to have his own plane someday. When he was fifteen, he and his friends pooled their gas coupons (it was 1944, wartime) and drove from Los Angeles to Quartsite, Arizona, for flying lessons; the Coast was part of the Western Defense Zone and private flying was prohibited. When he was sixteen, he soloed in a Piper Cub without brakes. After he landed and taxied downwind, he had to jump out, grab the tail, and drag the plane to a stop.

Bill Jr. saved his birthday money, sold his camera, and conned his mother into cosigning a bank loan so he could buy a war surplus Fairchild PT-19 trainer. After he earned his private pilot's license with it, he sold it and bought a faster Vultee BT-13. Then he sold that and bought a still faster AT-6, but what he really wanted was a sleek Lockheed P-38 fighter. He used to watch them take off on runway 15 at the Lockheed plant in North Hollywood during the war and he had promised himself that "someday, somehow, I'm going to fly one of those magnificent machines."

In the summer of 1946, Lear called his son from Grand Rapids and asked if he'd like to fly in the Bendix Race. Bill Jr. was eighteen and oh boy, would he — in a surplus P-38 fighter. Howard Johnson, a Lockheed test pilot, had told the boy that he could buy a new P-38 at the war surplus depot in Kingman, Arizona, for $1,250, including full tanks of gas. With a check from his father for the exact amount in his pocket, the boy and a friend flew the AT-6 to Kingman. "Sorry, son," the salesman said. "You're a day too late. We've just had orders to stop selling them."

When the boy began to cry out of disappointment, the salesman was touched. A gutsy kid had flown in from Los Angeles, his heart set on buying one of the fastest fighters made, only to find out he was just one day too late. The salesman studied the check, which Lear had made out two days earlier to the War Assets Administration. "Well, I guess we can take that date and sell you one," the salesman said. "Pick it out and get it out of here right now."

Bill Jr. chose the shiniest P-38 in the line. Since he had never been inside the fighter before, a Kingman mechanic sat on the wing, gave him a quick cockpit check, showed him how to start the engines, and waved him off.

Bill Jr. didn't have any money to buy gas for a test run over the Bendix route, from Los Angeles to Cleveland, and it was only by selling the Bendix radio compass, which came with the plane, for $500 that he could afford to race the ship at all.

He came in fourteenth. Bill Lear was waiting at the finish line, but when his son didn't come in among the top seven purse winners, he seemed disappointed. He asked Jackie Cochran, a friend who came in second, to look after the boy (who was half frozen and starving after six hours and fifteen minutes in the air) and flew back to Grand Rapids. In the same race the following year, Bill Jr. came in eighth.

After graduating from the Hollywood Professional School, Bill Jr. barnstormed in the All-American Air Show as "Billy, the Flying Kid," looping his P-38 around the country. In 1948, he joined the Air Force as an aviation cadet. After he was honorably discharged as a first lieutenant, his father hired him as a test pilot for Lear Incorporated.

Bill Lear now had five of his six children from three marriages (Valentina, his last child, wasn't born yet) either living with him or working for him. Mary Louise was the exception.

After graduating from college, Mary Louise had done graduate studies at the Presbyterian College of Christian Education in

Chicago and was serving in a Presbyterian church in Oak Park, a suburb. Although Lear approved of her decision to devote her life to the ministry, he was too proud to try to make up for all the hurt and misunderstanding that had always been part of their lives. It turned out to be Mary Louise who offered a small olive branch.

Mary Louise had received a letter from her grandfather, Ruby Lear, whom she had not seen since she was a small child and who was dying. He begged her to make up with her father. She wrote Lear an icebreaking letter, which he answered promptly.

Refusing to accept full responsibility for the wall that stood between them, Lear blamed himself for being selfish and harsh, Ethel for keeping father and daughter apart, and Mary Louise for not being enough of a Christian to forgive. "I hardly know how to address you," he wrote, "much less how to approach you after all these years . . . Why did you never once try to contact me to help *me* be what you are working so hard to help others to be? Take a little time and think that over. Does Christianity seal your mind and force you to believe only one side of a story — or does it 'seek diligently after the Truth.'

"My dear child, I pray God will use you and bless you in your work and that you and your good husband will be *real* Christians — that you will seek after the truth in all things and that you will be steadfast in your faith and energetic in your chosen work — so that I can point to *someone* who not only preaches but follows the precepts of the teaching. Perhaps, the thing I have always half-expected towards my being useful to God will come to pass through your life and efforts.

"I don't expect you will ever *want* to visit your father. However, if at any time you do, I will send my private ship for you and yours to come for as long as you wish."

Lear then offered Mary Louise $10,000, half enclosed in the letter and half to be paid the following year. (He never sent the second half.)

Still wary, Mary Louise wrote her father, thanking him for the gift, which she accepted after much thought and prayer as "a symbol of his concern." Her caution hurt him almost as much as the two previous rejections. "I feel that even when I try to do something nice for you that you suspect some ulterior motive," he wrote her later. "I am what I am — not a very good guy, not too bad — just real selfish but with a desire to be unselfish . . . So if I give you a little something, it's just my selfish way of trying to get even for all the wonderful things I've received from whoever is the disperser of good gifts in this world."

Over the years, Lear helped Mary Louise from time to time with small amounts of money. He sent her a new car when she needed one and visited her in Chicago, trying hard to impress her with dinner at the best table in an expensive restaurant. She visited him once or twice, and was saddened at how insecure she found him, despite all his talent and all his success. One time, on her way to Lebanon, she stopped off in Geneva to see him. But in spite of the letters and telegrams she had sent in advance, he was gone, on the way back to the United States without a word of explanation. She sat down and cried. They never became close. But many years later, when Merv Griffin asked Lear how many children he had and he answered seven, she cried again. For years, he had frequently said he had only six.

Lear loved playing in the 91 Fox Lockheed Lodestar the Air Force had given him so that he could keep testing his autopilot and blind landing system for them. A faithful performer, the two-engine transport was almost twenty years old; most models were in mothballs or rusting on runways. In its day, the Lodestar had been a reliable "barge," and Lear was intrigued with it.

One day the Lodestar's engines began running hot. Rather than send the plane back to the Air Force for a replacement, Lear told his engineers and mechanics in Grand Rapids to overhaul them. They streamlined whatever they could and when Lear took the Greenie Weenie up again, it was a little faster. Intrigued, Lear bought the airplane and began to look for more ways to lessen the drag, going so far as to change the door handles and file down the rivets. Little by little, the Lodestar began to perform better. Now Lear was really having fun. He redesigned the interior, ripping out the seats for fourteen passengers. He put in a toilet and a bar, paneled the walls, and carpeted the floor. After he added new furniture, he had one of the nicest corporate airplanes in the country.

One afternoon, Lear flew the Greenie Weenie over Lake Michigan to pick up the president of the Fairchild Corporation in Chicago. It was love at first flight. Fairchild bought the ship for $200,000. Lear picked up two more Lodestars for $30,000 to $40,000 apiece. One he modified for himself, the other he fixed up and sold to the Butelle Corporation. With each new Lodestar, Lear and his team made more and more minor improvements that made the plane faster, quieter, and more comfortable.

Lear had found a new project. He moved the fledgling Lodestar program from Grand Rapids to a hangar that the company rented from Twentieth Century–Fox at the airport in Santa Monica, where the weather was always good and where there were plenty of aerodynamic engineers. Although the Board of Directors wasn't sure where Lear was taking his new Aircraft Engineering Division, it gave him plenty of rope. If Lear was fiddling with the Lodestar, he couldn't be meddling with autopilot production. And who could tell. While he was playing with his latest toy, he might even come up with a new product or two. The Board didn't realize at the time that the Aircraft Engineering Division was, in Lear's mind, just what it was called: a program to build airplanes.

Lear went hunting for an aerodynamic engineer who could redesign the Lodestar into a Learstar. The aviation community was still small in the early 1950s, and Lear could count the really good engineers on his fingers. One of the best was Gordon Israel.

Like Lear, Israel was self-taught. After graduating from high school, he went to work for Benny Howard, designing and building *Pete,* a little four-cylinder racing plane. In its first competition, *Pete* won five first places and two third places out of seven starts at the 1930 Chicago Air Races. Then Israel designed his own racer, *Redhead,* which made headlines, set speed records, and crashed doing a cartwheel in the dust. Broke and without an airplane, Israel went back to work with Benny Howard, designing, building, and flying *Mister Mulligan,* one of the most famous racing planes of all time. *Mister Mulligan* won the 1935 Bendix Race, finishing just seconds ahead of Roscoe Turner. Israel then took a job with Stinson Aircraft, where he designed the Stinson O-49, the slowest observation plane in the Army Air Corps. When World War II began, he moved to Grumman Aircraft, where he designed jet fighters until the company fired him because of his drinking problem.

Lear found Israel in New York and flew him back to Santa Monica in the Greenie Weenie to take a look at the Learstar operation, with no strings attached. Lear figured he'd have ten hours in the air to talk the engineer into signing up. When they piled out of the plane after flying all night, Israel, who was half smashed, began wandering around the hangar and cross-examining Lear. The more he studied the Learstar in progress, the more excited he became. Lear had a new chief engineer.

Next, Lear roped Ed Swearengen, another maverick designer whom many considered one of the brightest in the field, and he hired Benny Howard as a consultant. Dick Mock appointed Vern Benfer the general manager of the Aircraft Division, and Lear was ready to move.

The idea was to gut and strip the Lodestar down to its skin and ribs and totally rebuild it, adding new engines, Lear electromechanical, navigation, and communication equipment, and a luxury interior for executives. Lear wanted the Learstar to be faster, safer, and quieter than the Lodestar, and to fly a longer distance without refueling.

Lear threw himself into the Learstar project just as he had with the autopilot. He moved his office into the hangar, next to Gordon Israel's, so he could stay on top of the work. "Bill became chief engineer, chief test pilot, chief of production, chief of maintenance," recalls Landis Carr, the Learstar hangar boss. "He was the *chief*. He was out on the hangar floor all day, every day. He had one speed — one hundred percent straight forward. He didn't have a slow, a pause, a stop, rest, a reverse."

Lear managed to exact fierce loyalty from most of his Learstar team, just as he had from his autopilot team. He had hired some of the best mechanics, woodworkers, sheet metal artisans, and plastics men in Southern California and he knew them all by their first names. He loved to be with them, gawking, marveling at their skills, and demanding the highest quality from them. The craftsmen ate it up.

Lear also had a special but different kind of relationship with his engineers. He'd breeze through the engineering department and study their drawings. Within five minutes, and with just a few words, he'd tell the engineers what was good and what was wrong. Sometimes he would explode, especially if he spotted what he thought was a foolish mistake. "One more degree," he'd tell the red-faced engineer in front of his peers, "and you'd be a fucking idiot." Carr explains his volatile boss this way: "I don't care what it was in — engineering, production, trim shop, paint shop — he had a very short fuse when it came to incompetence. He expected everyone to work sixty hours a week and enjoy every minute and do a *perfect* job all sixty hours. There was a saying around the place that you were allowed one mistake per year."

Lear was the first person to recognize his own weakness in developing the Learstar. Although he had great intuition and was superb on anything that "twisted, squirmed, wiggled, and rotated," the technical aspects of overall airplane design were beyond him. That was why he hired Gordon Israel, with whom he fought constantly. The two men were very much alike — intelligent, inquisitive, quick studies, and pigheaded. They rarely had conversation, just confrontations, which usually ended up with Lear shouting at Israel, "Get your ass out of here," and Israel shouting back, "You're goddamned right I will."

The next day Lear would come to work screaming, "Where the hell is Gordon?"

"Well, Bill," someone would say, "you fired him yesterday."

"Get him back here," Lear would order.

Israel would either say "What the hell" and come back to work or sulk and drink for two or three days. After he sobered up, he'd walk back into the hangar as if nothing had happened. After one violent argument over Israel's new tail design, Lear reached into his pocket and fished out a felt bag that he gave to Israel. Inside was a pair of silver cufflinks with sailboats engraved on them. Recalls Israel: "He knew I loved sailboats. He went in one instant from this raging maniac to a grateful person."

Even though Lear and Israel reached a compromise — Lear would teach Israel radio and Israel would teach Lear aerodynamics — sparks between the two men continued to fly for almost two years as the Learstar took shape.

Most of the major innovations on the ship, like the critical redesign of the wing, were Israel's. Lear made all the decisions after listening to everyone's ideas, and he made them quickly even though there was no consensus. He was at his best brainstorming, challenging ideas, stimulating his engineers, troubleshooting, and coming up with design ideas of his own. He'd leave it up to the engineers to figure out how to do it, then challenge their solutions. The cowl rings were a perfect example.

The old cowlings on the Lodestar bugged Lear. The rings slipped off the engines easily but were a bear to put back on. Most mechanics used a rubber mallet to pound them in place, and just about every Lodestar that found its way to the Santa Monica airport had dents all around the cowls. One day Lear walked into the hangar and saw three or four mechanics on a scaffold hammering the cowl rings back on. "Goddamn it," he shouted at them, "I want a cowling designed so that a little old lady could put it back on by herself." Then he stormed out of the hangar.

Lear returned after dinner that night to check on the new cowling. Up on the scaffold were eight men pounding away with rubber mallets. "What the hell are you doing?" he shouted.

The mechanics had been fighting the new design for hours and were frustrated by the time Lear poked his nose in. "Damn it, Bill," one of them said, "unfortunately that little old lady you wanted to put this cowling on isn't here tonight." Lear sent the cowling back to the drawing board, and his designers eventually solved the problem.

Lear hired Clyde Pangborn, the pilot who had raced from London to Sydney with Roscoe Turner on Lear equipment in the fall of 1935, as chief test pilot for the Learstar. (There were other test pilots as well — Ed Swearengen, Bill Jr., Les Coan, and Hal Herman, who taught Littlejohn to fly.) Sometimes Lear went up with Pangborn; sometimes he sat in his office with his ear to the ground-to-air portable transceiver. Test flights usually took place at odd times — Saturday afternoon, Sunday, Christmas morning — rarely during the working day. Lear would tell Pangborn what kind of maneuver to make and then report back on how the ship responded. He'd shout so many questions at Pangborn and ask him to do so many things that the pilot would finally turn the receiver off and run his own tests.

When Pangborn taxied in, Lear would be waiting for him, his chin scar all pink. Clyde would jump out of the plane, turn his back on Lear, and walk away. Lear's rantings never seemed to bother him.

Word flew back to Kelly Johnson, who had built the Lodestar at Lockheed, that that smart-ass Bill Lear was going to rebuild the airplane to fly 80 miles an hour faster. Taking Lear's challenge as a personal insult, Johnson circulated a white paper at Lockheed, proving that what Lear proposed to do was impossible. Lear and Johnson had been rather close friends at one time. It was Johnson who had asked Lear if the F-5 autopilot would work on the U-2 spy plane Lockheed was building for the Air Force under a tight security cloak. Lear had sent him Bill Schall, and the F-5 became standard equipment on the U-2. But once Lear decided to remake the Lodestar, the friendship froze. (The entire time the spy plane was being built, a U-2 model sat in the display window of the Institute of Aeronautical Sciences in Beverly Hills. The Russians eventually got the Lear autopilot in Francis Gary Powers's U-2, which they shot down over the Soviet Union.)

Shortly before the Learstar made its official maiden flight for the benefit of the media, Bill and Moya attended an Air Force party. Moya was in the ladies' room putting on lipstick when she noticed a woman who looked familiar but whom she couldn't place. "Does the name Mrs. Bill Lear mean anything to you?" Moya finally asked.

"Hell, yes," the woman said. "I'm Mrs. Kelly Johnson."

The two women went back to the party and brought their husbands face to face for the first time since Lear had begun tinkering with the Lodestar. The ice thawed, and Lear and Johnson became lifelong friends.

When it was finished, the Learstar was a small wonder. The Lear team had increased the cruising speed of the aircraft from 200 to 300 miles an hour with a nonstop range of 3,800 miles, making it the fastest twin-engine transport with the longest range then under production. "I have flown a good many other 'bullets,'" test pilot Les Coan told the press, "but I never before felt such tremendous acceleration as when I gave this one the gun."

The engineers had squared the wingtips and stabilizers, reduced the size of the landing gear, made the windows flush, and added a huge windshield. Not only had they reduced drag, they had increased the structural strength, made it easier to repair the ship, decreased vibration and noise, and made it safer as well. The plane was designed to make use of airports too small for commercial airliners. By adding a galley for its executive passengers, hot and cold running water, a disappearing bar and television set, divan beds and picture windows, Lear had converted the Lodestar into the Cadillac of executive airplanes. It bore a luxury price tag of $650,000, making it the most expensive executive airplane on the market.

The Learstar made its first flight on May 10, 1954, and was certified as an airline transport plane by the Civil Aviation Administration nine months later, becoming the first reconditioned aircraft to be so certified. Lear delivered his first Learstar to the British American Oil Company Limited of Toronto in February 1955. He told the press that he'd be delivering two a month until he had exhausted the supply of two to three hundred Lodestars still around.

As soon as he had taken the Learstar, "his pride and joy," as far as he could, Lear became restless once again. Redesigning a whole airplane with Gordon Israel, Benny Howard, and Ed Swearengen had been a two-year high. How could he ever go back to just plain transmitters and receivers, direction finders and autopilots?

18

ONE SUMMER NIGHT in 1955, Bill and Moya were going out to dinner with friends when Bill said, "Fasten your safety belt. We're moving to Switzerland."

In three weeks, Moya packed twenty-three trunks and thirty-five pieces of luggage, got shots and passports for Littlejohn,

Shanda, David, and Tina (who had been born the previous year) and leased their house to Grace Kelly.

It wasn't a spur-of-the-moment decision, even though it appeared that way to Moya and her friends. Sylvan Ginsbury, Lear's European adviser whom he had met in London in 1935, had told him that if he was serious about selling Lear products internationally, he should set up a European-based subsidiary just as all the important companies did; Al Handschumacher, among others, had been urging him to open a plant in Munich to make gyros and autopilots. Furthermore, the Board of Directors was growing very cold toward the Learstar, which was not moving well because it was too expensive, and was beginning to question the future of the Aircraft Engineering Division.

Lear had heard so much about Swiss engineers that he wanted to see for himself if they were as good as everyone said, and if so, why. Far from the prying eyes of his Board, maybe Switzerland would be a good place to build his new airplane someday. Besides, Lear wanted a little vacation and a chance to explore Europe like all the international playboys he had read about.

It was Edward Koessler, who worked in the control tower at the Geneva airport and whom Lear had met in a bar, who convinced Lear to settle in Geneva; it was centrally located and multilingual. Lear asked Koessler to help him find and staff a factory, introduce him to the right people, and find a place for him and his family to live. Koessler rented Prevorsier, an old château not far from Geneva, to serve as his home. The five-story stone villa with nearly thirty acres of gardens on the western shore of Lake Geneva was generally rented by diplomats accredited to the United Nations. Koessler also hired a staff of gardeners, cooks, chauffeurs, and butlers and found an office for Lear in downtown Geneva, near the Grand Theatre.

Moya loved Prevorsier, the children feared it, and Bill hated it. Prevorsier especially frightened Littlejohn, who was twelve years old. The villa had forty rooms and more than a hundred and twenty doors, and the staff did not speak English. The first few months, Littlejohn would come home from school, and if Moya wasn't there, he would wait in the foyer for her to drive up. He would not go into the main part of the house alone.

Fortunately for the children, there was Mademoiselle Germaine Stoll, an unmarried independent businesswoman in her forties who had helped political refugees escape from the Nazis during World War II. Having no family of her own, she adopted the Lears. Shanda, in particular, loved Germaine from the day she arrived in a big Lear limousine. Bustling out of the long black car, Germaine came over to Shanda, a chubby eleven-year-old, and said, "Little girl, would you like to come to the store with me and we'll buy some chocolates?"

The first thing Germaine did as unofficial family manager was to fire the cook and butler. The servants had figured that since the Americans were rich, they ought to be extravagant. Germaine hired a more economical cook and took over the shopping herself. She enrolled David in a nearby nursery school and John and Shanda in the International School in Geneva. When they found the French curriculum too demanding, she eventually placed Shanda in a private day school in Nyon, a few miles out of town, and Littlejohn in a boarding school that he didn't like (though he was happy to get out of Prevorsier), then in another, Le Rosey, also a few miles from the house. The baby, Tina, stayed home with her pediatric nurse, Elisabette.

Alberto, the chauffeur, picked Germaine up in Geneva at six o'clock each morning and drove her to Prevorsier, where she organized the house and the meals, the gardeners, and the children. Sometimes she would go to the château in the middle of the night to solve a problem with the staff. She became Moya's traveling companion, the Lears' interpreter, and their lifeline to the village.

Moya loved the château and the excitement of life with Bill Lear in Geneva. "We've never had so much fun in our whole round lives," she wrote in a "Dear Gang" letter to the workers in Santa Monica a few months after they had settled in. "The most fun was when we wheeled over Germany in the little Cessna together. Heidelberg, Stuttgart, Nuremberg, Munich . . . you name it and we've been there. On instruments. And it's such a thrill to sit there beside Bill and watch that little old airplane find its place in the sky, come down through solid murky glurky overcast, right smack onto the runway. I'm impressed. And by golly, so are the Europeans . . .

"Some army boys up at Frankfurt said, 'Is Mr. Lear flying

that airplane?' I said, 'Sure is.' The boys said, 'Gee, we thought with all those instruments he could just send it on over here, no hands.'

"Anyway gang . . . we're all healthy and happy (Tina's walking incidentally) and we hope you are too. With affectionate regards for you all . . . Moya 'n Bill."

And Bill *was* having fun racing all over Europe. He enjoyed shocking the control tower by landing blind under impossible weather conditions, something no private pilot in Europe could do at the time. He was soon dubbed "B. L." (Blind Landing) Lear, and he loved all the attention.

Once Lear had a business meeting in Nuremberg at ten o'clock in the morning. Since nearly all European private airplanes in the mid 1950s were used for sport, not business, Lear was trying to prove that with his autopilot and automatic approach coupler, private air travel was reliable. He took off from Geneva and as he approached Nuremberg, asked for clearance. "Weather is ceiling obscuration," the tower reported. "Visibility less than one-sixteenth mile."

"Roger," Lear said. "Requesting landing and approach clearance."

Lear persuaded the tower to clear him for a beacon approach. The Cessna latched onto the ILS beam and the approach coupler pulled the ship toward the runway. At fifty feet, he finally saw lights breaking through the mist. A call from the aviation authorities in Munich was waiting for him when he taxied in and parked. "You just landed in Nuremberg?" an aviation official asked. "Mr. Lear, I wonder if you'd be so kind as to come to Munich and show us how you did that?"

The next morning, Lear took off in fog and landed in Munich in fog. He spent half the day giving rides to air authorities and pilots, demonstrating his instruments with great pride.

But it wasn't all fun. Lear set up two subsidiaries — Lear, S.A., in Geneva and Lear Electronic GmbH in Munich. The Geneva company won a design contract from the U.S. Army in Europe for a new receiver to be used in blind landings; the Munich factory, which Handschumacher set up, began building automatic direction finders and fuel pumps. Hiring Ed Koessler as his sales manager and Fernand Matile as his chief executive of-

ficer, Lear opened shop in a rented building at the Geneva airport. He was rarely there, preferring to make blind landings
with his Cessna all over Europe, trying to sell his automatic
flight control system to foreign airlines and to the NATO forces.
He was quite successful with sales to the Swedes (with the help of
Nils Eklund) for the SAAB J-35 supersonic fighter; to the Dutch
for the Fokker F-27; to the Italians for the FIAT G-91 ground
support fighter; and to the French for the Caravelle jetliner,
which would be used by Air France, Air Algérie, Swissair, Varig,
and United Airlines.

There were so many power struggles going on in the Geneva
shop that Lear asked his son Bill Jr. to take over its day-to-day
operations. Still raw from the treatment he had received in
Santa Monica, Bill Jr. was hesitant. After the Learstar had been
certified in early 1955, Lear had promoted his oldest son to assistant factory service manager of the Aircraft Radio Division. In
the plant, Bill Jr. had suffered nothing but humiliation from his
father, who either ignored him so completely that even the staff
was embarrassed or chewed him out in front of everyone, calling him a good-for-nothing. To make matters worse, Bill Jr. had
been spending a lot of time at the Van Nuys airport, flying F-86
jet fighters for the Air National Guard, and that galled the old
man. Almost as if he was jealous, Bill had called his son at home
one morning and asked why he wasn't doing such-and-such. Bill
Jr. said that he thought he was doing all he should.

"I don't like your attitude," the old man said. "I think we
ought to give you two weeks' pay and let you go."

"Well, Dad, I've been seriously thinking of quitting," Bill Jr.
answered. "Now that you've made the offer so attractive, I can't
afford to refuse. I accept."

Bill Jr. called Ed Swearengen, who had joined up with Dee
Howard, president of Howard Aero Service in San Antonio,
which was developing the Super Ventura, another rebuilt Lockheed airplane in direct competition with the Learstar. Swearengen hired Bill Jr. as an aircraft radio salesman and test pilot, and
soon he was making three times what his father had paid him.

Naturally wary when his father asked him to come to Geneva,
Bill Jr. pressed for specifics. Precisely what would he be doing
and how much would he be paid? The old man was vague, so Bill

Jr. said no. A few months later, Bill called his son again, this time from Santa Monica, asking for another chat about a job. Bill Jr. jumped into an Air National Guard P-51 and flew to meet with him. The old man asked him to run the Geneva operation.

Bill Jr. had always nursed the hope of working side by side with his father, but he accepted the job offer with a pocketful of doubts. It wasn't that he was still afraid of the old man. That fear had disappeared suddenly one day when he went back to visit the Santa Monica plant. His father sneaked up behind him and said, as he usually did, "Hi, Bill, what are you doing?" Instead of his usual stuttering or sputtering, Bill Jr. had said, "Not a fucking thing, Dad. What are *you* doing?" Stunned that his twenty-seven-year-old son had the guts to stand up to him, the old man smiled his little half smile and walked away. Bill Jr. felt free from that time on.

The young man found the Geneva operation a Tower of Babel. There were 120 Swiss workers in the airport building, most of whom could not speak English. Most of the engineers were qualified university graduates who had worked for reputable firms, but few had ever worked with UHF electronic designs; some were "culls" — engineers whom other companies were delighted to give to Lear International. Communication between Lear and his engineers was so bad, despite interpreters, that the company couldn't even finish the design of the new receiver for the Army, much less get production under way. Recalls Bill Jr.: "We missed so many deadlines it wasn't even funny. It was a mess. Now I'm not knocking the old man. He really thought he could convert these people overnight and show them how we do things back home."

Things were not going well at Prevorsier, either. After nine months, Lear got into a fight with the landlord over a rent increase and used it as an excuse to move. "Bill hated the château," Moya recalls. The plumbing wasn't up to U.S. standards, the silk drapes had holes in them, extension cords hung from the ceiling, and there were no wall plugs. If there were anything Bill Lear couldn't stand in a house, it was too few electric outlets.

With Germaine's help, Lear bought a piece of property near a forest in Onex, a ten-minute drive from Geneva, and hired the architect Clifford May, who was well known in California for his ranch-style homes, to design a house. Lear didn't appreciate the Swiss standard of living and wasn't about to adjust. Unlike Moya, he made no attempt to learn French.

While the house was being built, Lear moved the entire family into the Richemond, a hotel in Geneva where royalty and the superrich stayed. It was not much of a home for the children, who hated eating in the elegant dining room where they had to dress up, lower their voices, and watch their manners. Even eating scrambled eggs in their suite involved so many knives and forks, they didn't know what to do with them. Fortunately, there was Germaine, who found new schools for Shanda and David and cooked marvelous meals on a hot plate in her office. She took them for long walks in the Park of the Bastions in the Old Town and to operas and concerts at Victoria Hall and the Conservatory of Music. Germaine loved music and opera so much that she knew all the famous arias by heart and used to hum and sing them to the children, determined to introduce them to culture.

Surrounded by history and art and living a luxurious life, Bill Lear was trapped in that unhappy limbo between projects. He enjoyed bouncing around Europe as "B. L." Lear, selling his autopilot to the Europeans and basking in the notoriety that his inventions, lifestyle, and money had given him. But he was also restless. To have some fun and to stir things up a bit in Geneva, he decided to fly his Cessna across the Iron Curtain into Moscow for the 1956 Soviet Aviation Day Air Show.

One day in the spring of 1956, when he was back in Santa Monica for a visit, Lear stepped into Dick Mock's office. A U.S. intelligence agent was showing Mock photographs of the new Soviet turbojet airliner, the Tupolev 104, which the Russians had displayed in London and Zürich earlier in the year. Running under the windows of the airplane were what appeared to be handrails, and the agent was asking Mock if he knew what they were and what they did. It was during the height of the Cold War, and U.S. intelligence on Soviet air power was weak. Bill's ear pricked up like a bird dog's, and he ushered the agent into his own office.

Young Willy Lear, Chicago, 1909 or 1910

Unless noted otherwise, all photographs are courtesy of the Lear Archives.

Bill Lear with his first airplane radio, the Lear Radio-Aire *(Courtesy of Fred Link)*

With his second airplane, a Warner Monocoupe Model 110

Demonstrating his direction finder, the Learoscope

The loft in New York City which Lear shared with Fred Link

Lear flew from New York to Los Angeles in this plane, fitted out with his direction finder and telephone transmitter and receiver, to promote his equipment.

With Moya Olsen after their plane flipped over while landing

Testing his F-5 autopilot in Dayton, around 1950

President Truman with Moya and Bill the night he received the Collier Trophy

Building the Lear Jet, Wichita, 1966

Bill Lear demonstrates the strength of the glass in his Lear Jet windshield.

Bill and Moya greet the around-the-world flight crew — Rick King, John Lear, Hank Beaird, and John Zimmerman.

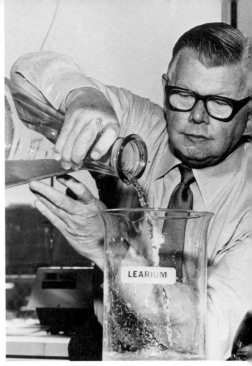

With his friends Danny Kaye and
Art Linkletter

Lear even put his name on the "mystery
fluid" he claimed would make the steam
car practical.

Lear Motors unveils its steam bus in Reno, in 1974.

The intelligence agent (Bill later told Moya he was from the CIA) offered to arrange protection for Lear if he'd try to find out what the handrail was all about. Lear said he'd take the assignment but declined special protection, arguing that the more people who knew about the undercover job, the greater the risk of a leak.

Attracted to James Bond stuff like a kid, Lear enjoyed his undercover role. "I have a mission," he said to tease Al Handschumacher. "I have a mission." But he wouldn't say more, just smiled his impish half smile.

On June 20, 1956, Bill and Moya flew from Hamburg to West Berlin in their twin-engine Cessna 310 equipped with a Lear ADF, autopilot, automatic approach coupler, transmitter, and receiver. Intelligence agents began to track the Lears' every step, reporting to the State Department and the CIA (among others) through Priority and Classified cables sent from Paris, Berlin, and Moscow.

The next day, Bill and Moya took a cab to East Berlin, where they met Soviet Vice Consul Vladimir Vasilievich Krivoshei, who spoke fluent English. Bill told him that he and Moya wanted permission to fly their Cessna into Moscow for the upcoming air show.

"Why don't you want to fly *our* airline?" Krivoshei asked.

"I want to be the first private pilot to fly an airplane into the Soviet Union," Lear said, assuring the Russian that he already had a visa.

The next day, Krivoshei told Lear that permission had been granted but that a Soviet navigator would have to fly with him because the ground radio operators spoke only Russian. When Lear landed at Schoenefeld Airport in East Berlin, a delegation of twenty-five Soviet military officers quickly surrounded the Cessna. The Soviet consul general himself, Sergei Mikhailovich Sergeev, met the Lears at the airport. When Bill asked where he could exchange dollars for rubles to spend in Moscow, Sergeev told him that as guests of the Soviet Union, he and Moya wouldn't need any money.

Unfortunately, while taxiing the Cessna before taking off for the Soviet Union, Lear discovered that his brakes weren't working. Since it was late Friday afternoon, he doubted that he'd find anyone to fix them over the weekend, so he told the Russians that he'd have to postpone the flight until the following Tuesday.

Lear milked the delay for more publicity. "The Russians broke themselves apart to help us," he told the Associated Press, which had been following his story. "They were really discouraged about this brake thing. They were afraid someone in the State Department would change his mind about letting us go. I told them I was sure no one . . . would do that."

The Lears spent the weekend in Stockholm with Bob Cummings and his wife, and when they flew the Cessna back to East Berlin on Tuesday morning, June 26, a Russian navigator was waiting. With a good tailwind, they touched down in Vilna two and a half hours later. Lear took good mental notes. "[It] was just a little strip twenty-nine hundred feet long," he reported later. "And this was one of the major airports in Russia! It had an administration building that was a rather dilapidated structure outside, but in a pretty good state of repair inside. The control tower (they let me into it) was really antiquated . . . It had radio equipment that might have come out about 1935 or 1940 at the latest."

The Lears landed at Vnukovo Airport in Moscow, 1,100 miles from Berlin, after five and a half hours in the air. The Associated Press had already sent its "trail blazing flight" story around the world, and waiting for the Lears was a crowd of twenty-five reporters and television cameras already in Moscow to cover the controversial and historic visit of the U.S. Air Force chief of staff, General Nathan Twining. The Soviets had invited delegations from twenty-eight nations to their air show, to be staged at Tushino Airfield. Over the objections of the Pentagon, which saw the Soviet invitation as a ploy to get a reciprocal visit to the United States, President Dwight D. Eisenhower had sent General Twining and nine other military experts to the show.

Alexander Vladimlov, the Soviet minister of foreign trade, wined and dined the Lears at the National Hotel in a suite of rooms that included a canopied bed. The next day, all hell broke loose. The AP had filed a story saying that Lear had come to Moscow "with a plane load of equipment to show Soviet air and trade experts. The equipment is among the things NATO bars from sale to Soviet bloc countries. Lear . . . said the Soviet Union is interested in buying automatic pilots and flight control machinery such as his company manufactures."

The FBI's Washington Field Office read the AP story in the *Evening Star* and began to investigate William Powell Lear for espionage. Dick Mock spent the day on the telephone, issuing denials to the press, customers, and workers as fast as he could talk. Lear's workers threatened to quit if their company was planning to do business with the Commies. General Twining ordered his staff to investigate Lear's trip. And the U.S. ambassador to the Soviet Union, Charles E. Bohlen, was upset. The last thing he wanted was a complication during General Twining's delicate mission.

The next day, Lear tried to explain to CBS News and other reporters that he had never stated he intended to sell equipment to the Soviet Union, "none whatsoever." Furthermore, he pointed out, his airplane carried no classified instruments.

Lear loved the confusion he caused, and his explanation was accurate — to a point. Although his autopilot and approach coupler were not classified, they were at least ten years ahead of the Soviet instruments. The Pentagon was most anxious that the Soviets not get their hands on Lear's equipment, which was similar to that of the U.S. Air Force. In fact, Lear *was* interested in exploring sales to the Soviets, not necessarily of his autopilot, but of instrument landing equipment that the Soviets would need if they intended to open a Soviet Union–United States passenger route, as they had said.

After the press conference, Lear took Trade Minister Vladimlov and three other Russians for a ride above the city to demonstrate the autopilot. The Soviets were fascinated. "Can it turn?" they asked. "Can it climb? Dive?" While showing off, Lear drifted out of his assigned altitude. The tower immediately radioed him for his position. Given the primitive state of the rest of the communications equipment he had seen so far, Lear was surprised to find the Soviet radar so accurate.

The Lears were invited to a cocktail party that night at the Soviet Star Hotel. When they arrived, General Twining, whom they both knew well, was holding a press conference in the corridor, explaining what little the Soviets had allowed him to see.

Hungry for a story and miffed because Twining wouldn't allow them to tour Moscow with him, the reporters began needling him about Lear's airplane crammed with classified equipment. Twining was angry for a lot of reasons. Lear had upstaged him, stealing most of the press and making all the wires. The embassy had neglected to tell him that Lear was flying his own plane into Moscow even though everyone, it seemed, had known about the trip a week in advance. And while Lear was looping his own Cessna above Moscow, the Soviets were denying the general permission to fly his DC-6 to Stalingrad for a tour.

Recognizing that they weren't welcome, Bill and Moya slipped away, drawing a pack of reporters shouting questions. Yes, he took four Russians for a ride, Lear explained. But all his instruments were sealed and they really couldn't see anything. His Cessna was locked and parked next to Twining's DC-6, which was under twenty-four-hour guard, so why all the excitement?

The next morning, Ambassador Bohlen called the Lears on the carpet. He later filed a confidential memo to the secretary of state in Washington: "While Lear disavows commercial interest brought him here, he has discussed with Soviet officials airport equipment that he says would be needed here to permit eventual operation by U.S. carriers to Moscow. [Embassy] warned him not to underestimate Soviet knowledgeability and expertise in intelligence operations . . . and set him straight on Soviet motive in obliging him to carry Russian navigator (he assumed this solely for reason of language).

"In sum, Embassy appraises Lear as person keenly interested [in] personal and company publicity, sharp business man, apparently highly qualified professional in electronics, and perhaps somewhat gullible about Soviet protestions [sic] of innocent curiosity and good will."

Naturally, the AP picked up the story. "The United States Embassy in Moscow is reported to be investigating the flight into the Soviet Union of William P. Lear," it noted.

The Soviets had asked Lear if there was anything he wished to see in Moscow. Come to think of it, he said quite casually, there was. The TU-104, designed by Andrei Nikolavich Tupolev. The director of the Soviet Central Aerodynamics and Hydrodynamics Institute, Tupolev was the leading Soviet aircraft designer since the Bolshevik revolution. During World War II, he designed the TU-2 bomber, among others, and now, the TU-104. Naturally, the intelligence community was curious. General Twining had wanted to see it too, but the Soviets had allowed him merely to poke his head inside.

A *Life* photographer had been asking the Lears to pose in front of their Cessna, and Lear asked Vladimlov whether the photographer couldn't also take their photograph around the TU-104. The Soviet minister agreed.

Tupolev himself gave Lear a tour of his plane. Lear crawled over every inch of it to the click of the camera.

"What's that?" Lear pointed to the handrail under the windows.

"That's an antenna," the Russian explained.

"Transmitting or receiving?'

"Both."

"That's a very interesting design."

The Russian beamed with pride. And Lear had accomplished his mission. Lear arranged for a Pan American pilot to smuggle the *Life* film out of the Soviet Union and pass it to a U.S. intelligence contact. Neither Lear nor *Life* got back all the negatives, just some frames with Bill and Moya.

On June 29, the Lears pointed their Moscow Mule, as they dubbed the Cessna 310, back to West Berlin, where Lear gave intelligence officers a perceptive analysis of what he had seen. The TU-104 carries a World War II autopilot (the C-1), which anyone can buy in a junkyard for $6, he said. The aircraft's transmitter and receiver are old and work on a medium to high frequency range. The altimeter is also of World War II vintage but good enough for high-level work. The Russians seem to be hiding from the eyes of the West what technology they do *not* have. Most impressive is the TU-104's radar. It looks like an advanced U.S. prototype and shows the Soviet thinking: "Here we need the best." The runway altimeter, which tells the pilot and the tower how high a low-flying plane is, is also very advanced. In sum, although the Soviets are behind the United States in engineering, they are ahead in another way — they are putting their money into important developments like radar and landing devices, not into gadgets, like the U.S. Air Force.

After all the smoke settled, the FBI cleared Lear of espionage;

the intelligence community got what it wanted and much more; and the Lears "had a ball," as Moya put it.

Back in Washington, General Twining wrote a secret report about his visit in which he stressed how little he was permitted to see and how little he had learned about Soviet air power. "The visiting delegations," he wrote, "were not invited to enter any of these aircraft nor to inspect them at close hand. Neither were they permitted to use their cameras. Instead, they were driven past the aircraft at a distance of about twenty-five yards, and at a speed of about five miles per hour."

If General Twining had misgivings about the strategic value of his visit, he had no mixed feelings about Lear. "Bill antagonized him," explains Handschumacher, who was company liaison with the Air Force at the time. "Bill gave a great performance. But it hurt our contracts."

19

WHEN THE HUNGARIANS revolted in October 1956 and the Soviets moved to quash them, Geneva became tense. Almost as if they were expecting World War III, the Swiss began hoarding food and fuel. Demonstrators took to the streets, pressing for the United States to intervene.

Lear decided to go home, leaving Bill Jr. stranded on a sinking ship with their Swiss engineers, craftsmen, and secretaries. By that time, Bill Jr. had reached three conclusions: given the language problem and his father's management style, the factory would never work; the products on the drawing board would never be manufactured; and if they were, they'd never make a profit. Al Handschumacher, who had inspected the shop at the Geneva airport, agreed completely.

Not long after his father was settled back in Santa Monica, Bill Jr. received an overnight telex on a machine that sat in an open corridor. It ordered him to fire everyone and close the plant. By the time he arrived at the office and read the message, there was "absolute pandemonium." Swiss companies practically adopt their employees, and to change jobs is as traumatic as getting married or becoming a parent. Lear had managed to hire a staff only by promising an exciting future.

Bill Jr. called each employee into his office for a chat. "The reactions ranged from sheer disbelief to total depression to violent threats," he explains. "For at least one year after that, I would get phone calls at three or four in the morning, and there would be no one on the line. Someone put sugar in my gas tank. All kinds of crazy things."

He opened a small Lear International sales office in Geneva under a cloud of suspicion. The press had been critical of the shutdown, and the business community began to view Lear Incorporated as an unstable company.

The bad publicity in Geneva didn't seem to bother Bill Lear back in Santa Monica, where he faced another major problem. Although he had told the media and his Board of Directors that he intended to sell two to three hundred Learstars for $650,000 each, he had managed to sell just sixty in more than a year and a half. The Board insisted that he get rid of the Aircraft Engineering Division, hangar and all. The Learstar was losing money, and its potential, as Handschumacher put it, "was penny ante" for a company the size of Lear Incorporated.

The problem with the Learstar was simple enough. Even with Vern Benfer managing the program tightly, the plane could never make a profit because Lear himself spent money lavishly on it. The company was making so much money from the Korean War that Lear wanted to "plow some of it into fun" instead of paying taxes. And plow he did.

Lear's personal Learstar expense account was somewhere between $50,000 and $100,000 a year, and he managed to spend it all on trips, girlfriends, and gifts. With his own money, he would buy the old Lodestars, then sell them to the Learstar program at a tidy profit. The hulks would stack up at the Santa Monica airport because he couldn't rebuild and sell them fast enough, and the rent for the space came out of the Learstar budget. Because Lear viewed the Learstar as the first step toward designing and building his own airplane, he didn't spare the development expense. He'd order new equipment that he didn't need for the Learstar but that he thought he might need later and charged it to the Learstar budget. He hired more consultants than he needed because he wanted to learn as much as he could as fast as he could, and charged it to the Learstar. He and his engineers did preliminary sketches of what would become the Lear Jet, and charged it to the Learstar. Through all this "wheeling and dealing," as Handschumacher called it, Lear tried to keep the Board of Directors off his scent, but it didn't work. The Board simply did not like the direction in which he was pushing the company.

In November 1956, Dick Mock sold the Aircraft Engineering Division, and Vern Benfer with it, to the Pacific Airmotive Corporation, which specialized in redesigning older airplanes. The sale hurt Lear's image. According to one report: "To some on Wall Street, this plane is still Lear Incorporated's best known endeavor. They know it was unsuccessful, therefore the company is still considered unsuccessful."

There was another problem. Before he went to Geneva, Lear had a new set of VHF navigation instruments for private pilots on the drawing board. He'd fly into Santa Monica from time to time to check on their progress, then leave again, to the immense relief of most of his engineers. Lear's general aviation products had been moderately successful since the end of World War II, but their sales represented less than 5 percent of the total sales of Lear Incorporated, even though the company had sold thousands of L-2 autopilots for $4,000 each as well as 13,000 relatively cheap automatic direction finders. Under the direction of Ken Miller, the usual line of transmitters, receivers, indicators, autopilots, and direction finders continued to improve, incorporating the latest developments in electronics. But the Lear product line had taken no radical twists of the kind Bill Lear was famous for, nor did it dent the commercial aviation market, on which companies like Bendix, Sperry, and Collins had strangleholds.

The biggest problem, however, was Lear's habit of starting one thing, then dropping it for another that fascinated him more. He got swept up with the Learstar, neglecting almost everything else, then he folded his tent for Geneva. And throughout that period between 1951 and 1956, he never encouraged his aircraft instrument engineers to be independent. On the contrary, he frequently punished them if they tried something new without his explicit approval. As he used to say, "Damn it, when you own 75 percent of the company, you can make 75 percent of the decisions. This is *my* design. You do it *my* way."

Ken Miller and Sam Arn could not have sprung their surprise on Lear at a worse time. After the financial failure of the Learstar (which Lear would never admit publicly) and after his $1 million loss in Switzerland, Lear was in a mood for ass-chewing, not surprises.

The Aircraft Instrument Division had developed a unique two-way VHF radio and, based on the prototype, had already sold a hundred. All without Bill Lear's approval. Engineers Miller and Arn had approached Lear with the design on one of his visits to Santa Monica, but Lear had scoffed at it. Convinced that it was a good idea, they "bootlegged" it in his absence.

When Sam Arn took Lear up in a company plane to demonstrate the instrument, which worked extremely well, Lear was so mad that the division had dared to move on the project after he had vetoed it that he tore the radio out of the instrument panel and tossed it out the window. Lear told the story a bit differently to *Flying* magazine: "When I came here from Geneva, one look at the faces of my technical staff told the story. It wasn't good. 'Close but no cigar,' they told me. 'This piece of equipment simply doesn't meet the performance and reliability standards you set.'"

At home again in California, Lear began whipping his team to redesign his aircraft instruments around the transistor. Three Bell Telephone Laboratory scientists — John Bardeen, Walter Brattain, and William Shockley — had just won the 1956 Nobel Prize in physics for their work on transistors, which replaced the old vacuum tubes; the semiconductor integrated circuit, which appeared the following year, made the transistor practical for aircraft instruments. Lear's rantings became legendary throughout the plant as he began shadowing his engineers and criticizing their every drafting stroke, just as he had done on the Learstar. This time his scrutiny was even more intense, for he knew more about electronics than he did about aircraft design.

Recalls Vaughn Hammond, a secretary for Lear during that hectic period: "He did something that I found hard to forgive. He had a very bad habit of dressing people down in front of others, particularly the engineers. It just wasn't fair the way it was done. He was cruel to people. A split personality. Very confident on one side, insecure on the other."

In spite of the emotional harassment, and maybe even because of it, the job got done and the results were spectacular — a transistorized Navcom 100 series of VHF receivers, transmitters, automatic direction finders, and display instruments that private pilots could buy in building-block fashion, to meet their needs and pocketbooks. Individually, the pieces were of the highest quality, light, and relatively cheap; together, they made a major contribution to the safety of private aviation. The Navcom series sold well considering the relatively small number of private pilots in the mid to late 1950s.

Lear also designed and built for the private pilot the ARCON, a life-saving instrument that prevented spiral dives in single-engine aircraft. Although ARCON cost only $1,000 and was technically sound, it failed financially. Private pilots wouldn't buy it because they didn't trust it.

For the commercial airlines, Lear developed Lear Integrated Flight Equipment (LIFE). Built around the new transistorized L-102 autopilot and approach coupler, LIFE displayed for the pilot all the usual attitude, heading, and flight directions on two indicators instead of four, making commercial flying simpler and safer.

To help promote his new lines of instruments, Lear hired King Michael of Rumania, whom he had met in Geneva; and to help sell them, Lloyd Percell, Collins Radio Corporation's golden boy, who in his six years with the company had made impressive sales to every major airline in the country.

King Michael, of the Hohenzollern-Sigmaringen family, had been forced by the Communists to abdicate his throne and leave Rumania in 1947, shortly after the Allied powers placed Eastern Europe under the sphere of Soviet influence. He lived in exile in Athens, where he married Anna of Borbone-Parma, then settled in Geneva, where he scratched out a living as an auto mechanic and part-time pilot of single-engine airplanes. Recognizing the public relations value of having royalty on his staff, Lear had hired King Michael as a pilot and sales representative in Geneva. When he returned to the United States in 1959, Lear sent for Michael, promising to get him a twin-engine airplane certification, then send him back to Geneva to sell Lear airplanes and products and make a fortune. That's what King Michael thought, anyway.

Soon after Michael arrived in Santa Monica, Lear threw a big party to show him off. He asked his policeman friend, Buzz Nanney, to take care of Michael, a tall, gangly, handsome man, naive and unsure of himself. Because the king didn't own anything except a tweed coat with leather patches on the elbows and a pair of gray pants, Nanney spent $600 of Lear's money on clothes for the king.

When he went to pick up Michael for the black-tie party, Nanney found him dressed in his new black pin-striped suit, an old wrinkled short-sleeve shirt, and a frayed string tie. Nanney soon remedied the situation.

Another time, Nanney noticed that King Michael wasn't spending any of the money Lear had put into his expense account. "Why don't you use some of it?" Nanney finally asked.

"I don't know how to write a check," the king said. "I was too embarrassed to ask."

King Michael adjusted reasonably well to the fast pace of Lear's lifestyle and eventually received his twin-engine certification. But, as Bill Lear should have recognized, he was publicity-shy. One morning he was having breakfast at the Huddle, a restaurant-bar across the road from the Lear plant, when a woman recognized him. "You're King Michael, King Michael!" she cried. The king ran out the front door, he was so embarrassed. It came as no surprise to Nanney that when Michael learned that Bill Lear expected him to appear on television and to use his royal name to promote Lear products, he packed his tweed jacket and went back to Switzerland.

Bill Lear's other marketing choice, Lloyd Percell, had received a phone call one day from Lear's office saying that the boss wanted to have lunch with him. Thirty minutes into the meal, Lear had made Percell an irresistible offer, then left the stunned young man sitting at the table.

His first day on the job, Percell told Lear's engineers that if the company wanted to sell LIFE to commercial airlines, Lear would have to repackage all his instruments. The airlines had standard radio rack sizes, he explained, and instrument boxes had to be a standard size before an airline would even look at them. Lear's instruments were too small. The second day on the job, Lear invited Percell to the house for coffee. The lanky young salesman found his boss frying bacon on a grill in the sunroom. "I heard you told some of my engineers that my radios needed to be repackaged," Lear said, on the verge of an eruption. No one had warned Percell about criticizing the old man's work, especially his packaging.

"Yes," Percell admitted. "As I understand it, that's why you hired me. I'm familiar with the needs of the airlines from the engineering and marketing standpoint."

Lear turned purple. "You're fired," he screamed.

Percell backed out of the house. As he slowly drove back to the plant to clean out his desk — not that there was much in it — he tried to figure out what to do next. He couldn't go back to Collins and he didn't have any other job prospects in mind.

"I couldn't blame Bill," Percell recalls. "He had designed [this] great system, half the size of others. He had spent hundreds of thousands to make it small. Then some idiot comes in and says, 'Boy, you're dumb. You have to make it twice that size.' "

When Percell pulled into the parking lot, a group of engineers was waiting for him, shouting congratulations. Pretty morbid, he thought. At Lear, they clap their hands when you get sacked.

"How did you do it?" the engineers asked, pounding him on the back.

"Do what?" Percell was confused. What was so unique about getting fired?

"The old man just phoned," someone explained. "He called us all idiots and told us to redesign the package. He said we got him into trouble by designing it too small."

For the next two years, 1957 to 1959, Percell traveled constantly with Lear throughout the country, selling LIFE to the airline engineers who ultimately requested the purchase orders. "I had an impossible job," he explains. "Bill always interfered and I felt I was losing everything I had gained. He'd call the top of the airline — American, Braniff, United . . . It was very difficult for him to accept the fact that those young engineers could dictate to *him* how to build his equipment. We're talking about a man who did more creatively than all those engineers put together. His mind was working all the time. He scribbled on every bedsheet in every hotel. In the nicest restaurants, he scribbled on the nicest linens."

Percell was quite successful in selling Lear instruments to the smaller airlines. Allegheny, Ozark, and Piedmont, for example, adopted LIFE for their new Fairchilds. Jay Wiggins, the chief operations manager at Ozark, was especially impressed. "I think it was the best system available. It was better than Collins, better than Bendix. Pretty soon they redesigned *their* system around Lear's concept."

But no matter how hard Percell tried, Lear could not penetrate the major U.S. airlines. Braniff bought a few instruments. United had LIFE on sixty of its Caravelles, which came from France already equipped with the system. And when United began buying Douglas DC-8s, Lear felt certain that the company would insist on using his system so that all United carriers would have identical instruments. But Douglas insisted that Lear Incorporated pay for the total cost of getting LIFE certified for the DC-8, a very time-consuming, methodical process. Lear wouldn't pay the several million Douglas was asking.

Lear also thought that the new Boeing 707 would automatically carry LIFE as well. For several years, the Boeing KC-135 tanker (the military version and prototype of the 707) had been using the Lear system for midair refueling of Strategic Air Command bombers. But since the Federal Aviation Administration had nothing to do with the KC-135, it treated the 707 as a new aircraft. Like Douglas, Boeing insisted that Lear Incorporated swallow the total cost of getting LIFE certified for the 707. Once again, the company refused.

Lear's problem convincing the major airlines to adopt his superior equipment was simple. He was trying to penetrate the market two years too late, when most major airlines already had adopted a Bendix or a Collins system with a hangar full of replacements. Furthermore, Lear had not built up a strong network of service centers to install, troubleshoot, and repair his equipment, as the other companies had. Both problems were old ones that had haunted him most of his career.

That Lear had missed the new 707 market was his own fault. Had he not been playing with the Learstar, and stirring up fun and trouble in Europe, he could easily have had the jump on the competition. It still wasn't too late, for the next-generation airplane — the 727 — was already on the drawing board. All Lear had to do was to focus his energy on designing instruments specifically for the new aircraft.

But Lear wasn't interested. Like Ulysses, he kept hearing the Sirens singing from a far island. He found their song, "Build Your Own," irresistible.

20

MOYA WAS HAPPY back home in Pacific Palisades. Bill was closer to her and more dependent on her. She exerted an even more stabilizing influence on his volatile life now than she had as a young bride, sixteen years earlier. How important she was to him, he expressed in a letter written in an airplane en route to Amarillo. "It was so hard to leave you this afternoon and I really shouldn't have," he wrote. "You are so precious to me and I love you so very much even though I have a most unorthodox way of showing it . . ."

It was not easy for Moya to love Bill. One day after an argument about how driven Bill was, Moya poured her frustrations into a letter rather than "whisper them because my throat aches with tears."

She wrote: "Darling, my dearest, I understand my love not being enough. I know you *must* have work to do — tools, men, airplanes. I know it's a hunger that must be satisfied. But I wish you'd learn to mellow, to accept with grace, with good humor, with a healthy philosophy the drawbacks of progress . . . Anyway, I love you. If you think it's not enough. If you think you want more for your money, it's all I've got. Find yourself another girl."

As far as women went, Lear was no different at fifty-five than he had been when he married Moya. His women were still lunchtime talk at the plant, just as they had been back in the Piqua days. Every woman in the office knew he was available if she wanted and could attract him. But he never chased them. One woman in particular called Lear at the office almost every day. In keeping with his promise not to let Moya know about his affairs, he gave her the code name "the General"; she remained his mistress until the end. He succeeded well in hiding her from Moya. One Sunday morning a few years before he died, for example, Moya, Bill, and their son John were having breakfast. When Bill got up from the table, Moya put her hand over John's and said, "Honey, I think I finally have him all to myself." She was so happy. To John's disgust, Bill got on the phone when Moya went to church and cooed to the General.

Like thousands of women in Los Angeles, the General was a model who wanted to be an actress. Five feet three, with dark hair and a stunning, sensuous body, she had a gypsylike quality about her. Lear workers who knew her would never forget her. Lear set her up in an apartment near the airport. He frequently lunched with her, sometimes taking Bill Jr. along if he was in town. After lunch, he'd send his son back to the plant while he "took a little nap." When Lear left on a trip, he'd ask Bill Jr. to entertain the General just as he used to dine and dance with Scarlet A in the Piqua days.

The General had standing orders to be in the car at the end of the Santa Monica runway whenever Lear returned from a trip. He'd radio the hangar he was coming, then someone would call to alert her. She'd listen for him to buzz the airport, his signal that Moya wasn't around. Then she would jump into the Hillman Minx he had bought her and race across the road to the airfield.

Twenty-five years older than the General, Lear jealously guarded her — to a point. He didn't want her sneaking around, dating other men, without his explicit approval. But if he wanted to give her to someone, that was his right. After all, he had placed her on the Lear Incorporated public relations payroll. For example, an old friend to whom Lear owed a favor brought his autopilot into Santa Monica for repairs, "Well," Bill said to him, "what do you want to do while we're fixing it?"

"I'd like a date with [the General]," the pilot said tongue-in-cheek. He thought Lear's mistress was stunning but sensed that Lear was possessive.

Lear grabbed the phone and set up the date.

The personal life of its founder aside, Lear Incorporated was going through another inevitable transition. By 1959, the corporation's sales had reached an all-time high of $87 million. But 90 to 95 percent of these sales were still to the military, and the Pentagon was quickly shifting its emphasis from manned aircraft to missiles. In fact, 90 percent of the Pentagon's research and development money was flowing into the missile program. Lear Incorporated had dug a toehold in unmanned flight immediately after World War II by designing pumps and guidance systems for the Nike-Zeus, Lockheed 7, Boeing Bomarc, JPL Sergeant, McDonnell Green Quail, Martin Matador, Ryan Q-2 and KDA, and the Bendix Talos and the Douglas Thor — none of which interested Bill Lear.

Two things were apparent to Lear executives like Dick Mock and Al Handschumacher. The company had to diversify so it would be less dependent on military contracts, which since the end of the Korean War were becoming scarcer and more competitive; and Lear Incorporated needed new blood pulsing through its executive veins or it would atrophy.

With Mock's support, Handschumacher, then vice president, confronted Lear directly. The company needed new leadership, he said, and some company managers had to be on the Board of Directors. Most important, the new Board had to use the scalpel on unprofitable programs while carefully canvassing the business community for acquisitions to create a proper balance between military and commercial sales.

Reluctant to change the composition of the Board lest he lose control and recognizing that the unprofitable programs were the ones he loved most, Lear balked at Handschumacher's suggestions but invited him to pitch them to the Board itself. It was a clear challenge to a public joust.

When Handschumacher concluded his reasoned presentation to the Board, Lear launched into a persuasive rebuttal. "Now we'll see who controls the company," he told Handschumacher quietly before putting the matter to a vote. The Board rejected each of the vice president's suggestions.

Handschumacher quit and took a job as vice president of the Rheem Manufacturing Company. But Lear wouldn't let him go that easily. He knew Handschumacher was right, and he respected the younger man's advice even if he wouldn't take it. "Now that you're no longer an officer of the company, I want you on my Board," Lear told him. To keep his new board member sweet until he needed him, Lear continued to pay Handschumacher his full vice president's salary on top of what Rheem was paying him. "It was ridiculous," Handschumacher explains. "But that's the way Bill operated."

Lear and the Board decided to look for a new president. Dick Mock had been with the company for nineteen years and its president for eleven. There was little doubt that Mock, more than anyone else, had saved the company from bankruptcy by creating a stable situation that bankers and investors came to respect. Under his guidance, Lear Incorporated had grown steadily in sales and assets without so much as one step backward. Mock had also been Lear's lightning rod and, over the years, had taken a lot of bolts from the chairman of the Board. But Lear and the Board felt that Mock had made his contribution and that it was time to move on. Lear wrote to Mock in appreciation: "Lear Incorporated wouldn't be the company it is today if it had not been for one Dick Mock. This is just my way of saying thanks."

Against the advice of the Board, especially of Handschumacher, Lear appointed as the new president James L. Anast, a former aide to FAA chief Elwood Quesada. It's not clear why. Perhaps because Lear and the FAA in general, and Quesada in particular, had been feuding frequently in the media, Lear thought that the appointment of Quesada's aide would be an olive branch. Anast lasted four months. Lear fired him when he told Lear he couldn't walk through the plant without him, Anast, being present. In an emergency board meeting Lear announced that he had made a mistake, then looked at Handschumacher and said, "Al, now *you're* going to be the president."

Lear gave him two weeks to think it over. When they met to negotiate at the Penn Club in Grand Rapids, Lear asked, "Let's suppose. What would your demands be?"

At forty-one, Handschumacher was a keen, ambitious man, in most ways the direct opposite of Bill Lear. A trained engineer, he was a skilled business manager interested in growth and profit and the challenges that go into achieving them. He was not emotionally attached to any Lear product. It either made money or it didn't; it was good for the image, growth, and stability of the company or it wasn't. Handschumacher believed his major responsibility as president would be to the shareholders, whose investment he was pledged to protect, not to the whims and feelings of the corporation's founder. But, like Lear, he enjoyed power and was not easy to shove around.

Handschumacher knew exactly what he wanted: the company would have to develop an image as an independent corporation, not as an extension of Bill Lear; the corporation had to build its civilian sales to 40 percent even if that meant merging with a larger and stronger company; management had to be simplified; and the Aircraft Radio Division for private pilots would have to face the auction block because, as he later would tell *Business Week*, the instruments were "Mickey Mouse" items.

Lear accepted Handschumacher's terms, not that he intended to implement them. To ease the pain of separation, the company sold the line of small receivers, transmitters, autopilots, gyros, and automatic direction finders to Motorola through Elmer Wavering, who had worked with Bill years before on the car radio. For Lear, it was like burying an old friend who had laughed and cried with him in airport lean-tos and hangars, in lofts and old match factories. As Lloyd Percell put it: "Bill's primary interest was always private and corporate aircraft. He could relate to it. Go out and fly it. Play with the instruments. Sit there on the workbench with them."

Lear promised to give Handschumacher a free hand. All he wanted in return was to go back to Geneva and begin designing an aircraft for business executives. He would use his own funds and, while he was in Europe, sell company products to NATO and the European airlines as well. Naturally, as chairman of the Board, he would continue to receive his full annual salary.

* * *

Thus ended an era (1930–1959) for William Powell Lear during which he had developed an impressive list of instruments for the private pilot. There was the Radioaire in the Glenview airport; the Learoscope in Fred Link's New York loft; the first practical automatic direction finder at the airfield in Mineola; the electromechanical equipment vital to World War II in Piqua; the autopilot and vertical gyro indicator in Grand Rapids; and the LIFE and Navcom 100 series in Santa Monica. With limited resources, the struggle had always been uphill, for private pilots were a small and uncertain market.

Lear's contribution to general aviation during this period was significant. He and his engineers had pioneered generation after generation of instruments. But even more important, Lear almost single-handedly dragged the whole industry forward with him, challenging its concepts, expanding its horizons, forcing it to see his vision and to improve its products — if for no other reason than to compete with him.

As he began the painful process of separating himself from the company he founded — a company that was no longer interested in airplanes and flying, only in products that made money — Lear left behind a generation of engineers like John Schoeppel, Nils Eklund, Vern Benfer, Ken Miller, and Jim Wood, to mention just a few, who would never forget him in spite of their stormy association with him. Schoeppel speaks for most of them when he says: "Bill Lear offered the opportunity for a group of three-hundred-odd technicians to rise above the dull chores of the profession and displace the aircraft instrument leaders of a decade or more from the competitive scene. We beat them one and all . . .

"Under Bill, it was unthinkable to do other than to advance the state of the art. He expected it. It was routine. Once we got over the shock of doing the impossible weekly, it was a great deal of fun . . . Bill stirred men's blood."

Nils Eklund stayed with Lear Incorporated, but most drifted off into other jobs at other companies, finding life at Lear rather ordinary without the old man challenging and driving them.

As for Bill Lear himself, there were many more clouds to fly through. At fifty-seven, he was starting all over again on the biggest risk of his career, and he never looked back. The second move to Geneva was just another in a long string of beginnings.

Part Four

Making History

21

IN THE SPRING OF 1959, Mitsubishi of Tokyo invited Bill and Moya to Japan to talk about a new airplane design rolling around in Bill's mind. Moya was planning to continue around the world alone while Bill returned home. Fourteen-year-old Shanda talked her way into the trip, arguing that her mother would get as far as Bangkok, then be so homesick that she'd fly back to Santa Monica.

In Honolulu, they stayed with "Trader Vic" Bergeron and his girlfriend in a bungalow next to his famous restaurant. Trader Vic invited all the beachboys to a luau in Bill's honor, where they tried to teach Shanda how to surf and, loaded down with leis, how to hula.

In Tokyo, the Mitsubishi engineers treated the Lears to dinner in a geisha house, where Shanda entertained the Japanese with Yum Yum's song from *The Mikado*. With her eyes still swollen from the shots needed for the trip, her black hair and pale face, and dressed in a kimono, she looked Japanese. Everyone at the Imperial Hotel thought Bill had acquired a Japanese mistress.

After his business meetings, Bill kissed his wife and daughter good-bye and returned to the drawing board and the General. Moya and Shanda headed for Geneva to see their new home — via Hong Kong, Saigon, Angkor Wat, Bangkok, New Delhi, Cairo, and Athens. Le Ranch, which had been under construction for three years, had cost a small fortune. All the materials were imported from America because Lear thought "U.S. things were better than European." Nevertheless, he had made up his mind that he wouldn't live there if the house didn't meet his standards. He promised to join Moya and Shanda at the Richemond in Geneva after the Paris Air Show in May. If he liked the house, he'd keep it. If not . . . well, the money be damned.

To the Swiss, Le Ranch was Hollywood under the Alps, totally American and unlike anything they had ever seen. It resembled neither the cold, stately Prevorsier encrusted with history nor the comfortable two-story Swiss homes with their slanted snow roofs. In fact, it was the only ranch-style home in the country. And whereas most Swiss houses sat high on the land, Le Ranch was carved out of the forest, facing the Salève and Jura mountains. Shaped like a horseshoe and covering 27,000 square feet, it had radiant-heated marble floors, a soft-water system, sliding glass window walls, a huge stone fireplace, and high, exposed-beam ceilings. There was a heated outdoor kidney-shaped swimming pool and a flower-banked patio. Its five-acre plot was wooded on two sides and sat right across the road from Geneva's only golf course.

Germaine Stoll was waiting anxiously when Moya and Shanda pulled up to Le Ranch in a taxi. A liaison between the architect, the builder, Swiss customs, and the Geneva banks, she was concerned that after all the time, money, and effort, the unpredictable Lears wouldn't like their new home.

As the cab turned into the driveway and the dream house suddenly appeared from nowhere in all its "elegance and spaciousness," it was love at first sight. Recalls Moya: "It was fabulous. I called Bill. 'Honey,' I said, 'we've got to at least put a fire in the fireplace and turn on the showers. This is the only house we ever built and we've got to live in it for a while.' "

After the Paris Air Show, Bill inspected each room of the house while Moya and Shanda awaited his judgment. He seemed impressed until he discovered only one electrical outlet in each bedroom. "Stupid," he screamed, ready to sell the place to the highest bidder. He later joked to a reporter: "None of the electrical things worked. I called the power company several times. No one would come. Finally, I fixed the furnace myself.

Then the repairman turned up. 'You must be looking for the previous tenants,' I told him. 'They froze to death in here. We bought the place from their estate.' "

Bill stormed out of the house with all three women, especially Germaine, in tears. Moya and Shanda tried to calm him. Except for some minor flaws, they pleaded, the house was wonderful. They wanted to stay. As usual, Moya soothed him into submission, and he sent a telegram to Santa Monica to have all the Lear belongings as well as David and Tina shipped immediately. John would follow after the school year was over.

Once over his first shock, Bill was anxious to try out the swimming pool. Germaine had warned him not to fill it for three days because the paint was still tacky, but Bill couldn't wait. The next day, while Germaine was in town shopping, he opened the spigot and slipped into the pool. Moya and Shanda joined him. As they splashed in the pure mountain water and floated on their backs, gazing at the Jura Mountains, a layer of paint peeled from the wall and drifted toward them like a mat of blue algae. Bill was forced to drain the water and repaint the whole thing.

So began Lear's three-year stay in Geneva. His Swiss associates, employees, and neighbors would never forget him.

The Lears loved to entertain and felt they needed a guest house. Since the Swiss did not have prefabricated housing yet, Bill ordered a $17,000 colonial-style prefab home shipped from the United States and had it erected over a bomb shelter he had dug out a stone's throw from the main house. He had the first prefab home and the first bomb shelter in a home in Switzerland.

For their dinners and parties, the Lears needed a good selection of wine, but neither one knew much about Bacchus. As a Christian Scientist, Moya drank very little, and Bill specialized in Scotch and beer. To stock his wine cellar, therefore, Lear relied on Max, a wine salesman whom he had met in a ski lodge bar.

A frustrated entertainer, Max liked to jump up on a table to sing and tap dance after a few drinks. He was a real ham, simple, funny, sociable, and Bill loved him. Soon after they met at the lodge, Max drove up to Le Ranch. "What kind of wine do you have?" he asked Bill. "Do you want me to check your cellar?"

Lear told him he liked Scotch and didn't have a wine cellar.

"But Bill," Max sang in English with a charming French accent, "with a house like this, you must have French wines." Max began to rattle off the names and years of Bordeaux and Burgundies, whites and reds.

"You're right," Bill said. "Send me some."

"A *tonneau* of each," Max suggested with a flourish.

Several months later, while the Lears were eating dinner, a diesel towing two trailers pulled into Le Ranch. "I wonder what that is," Bill said to Germaine. "Would you go out and see?"

Germaine came back a few minutes later. "Your wine," she said.

Bill, who thought he had ordered only a few cases, was too embarrassed to turn it down, and he told the driver to stack it in the bomb shelter.

"Where do you want to put the rest?" the driver asked after he had unloaded the trucks.

"The rest?" Bill asked. He figured he already had the biggest wine cellar in Geneva.

"Yes, this is only half."

As Max had predicted, the wine was important, for the Lears entertained constantly — the town fathers, business associates from Switzerland, friends from the United States, foreign dignitaries. For Shanda, who had collected a closet full of costumes from the countries she had visited, the dinners were an occasion for ethnic dressing. With Indians and Pakistanis, she'd wear a sari; with Japanese, a kimono. After nine o'clock, she usually ended up playing hostess because Bill and Moya had slipped off to bed without saying goodnight to their guests. Bill was frequently bored with formal parties, and he figured since it was his house, his food, and his wine, he should be able to go to bed with his wife when he felt like it. By ten, the guests would begin noticing that their host and hostess were missing.

"Where are your parents?" they would ask Shanda.

"They went to bed," she'd say. "But don't worry." And the party would go on, with Shanda finally wishing each guest goodnight at the door.

Not all the dinners were stiff and formal. The Lears loved animals, mostly dogs. But David, who was ten, talked Moya into buying him two white finches. Before long they had multiplied into sixteen. Because the cages were so small and it seemed cruel to the youngster to keep them locked up, David let the birds fly loose in his room. Naturally, they left droppings all over the rugs, bedspreads, and walls. The maids complained that every time they went into his bedroom to clean, some of the birds would escape, and they'd have to spend half the day trying to catch them. But Moya couldn't tell her son to lock them up.

One night the Lears were entertaining Igor Sikorsky and his family. Someone opened the door to David's room and the finches got out, swooping into the living room, where the Sikorskys were sipping champagne. By that time David had devised a way to catch the little things. He'd wait until it was dark outside, turn on the vacuum sweeper, and point it at the perching birds, frightening them into flight. Then he'd turn off the lights. The finches would settle quickly on the nearest piece of furniture or on the floor. Then David would toss a jacket or blanket over them before they could take off again.

Bill taught the Sikorskys David's method. He gave each a towel, dragged out the vacuum sweeper, and flipped off the lights. The next hour was spent finch hunting.

Big John loved Le Ranch as much as Moya did. "What a peace haven," he wrote to a friend. "What a snug harbor. What a rainbow's end. What a madhouse! It [is] like Monday morning at Macy's. Two cooks in the kitchen who can't speak anything but Danish. Franco, who . . . is limited to Italian. Ernesto, only French. Anna — worse than Franco. Germaine — 'well!' as Jack Benny mighty say.

"David is up at seven for school at seven. Tina has to be at school at eight . . . Shanda — her diction lesson, rehearsal for the play, her guitar lesson, her French lesson, her Russian lesson, her physics lesson. On the go every minute. Moya — what a precious soul she is. She's the commanding general, the hostess, the arbitrator . . . the interpreter, the housekeeper, the kennel-keeper, emergency chauffeur."

All in all, Le Ranch was a happy place for Tina and David, who went to the nearby public school on their bikes or by limousine. Shanda attended La Chatlainie, a boarding school. Sometimes Moya and Bill were home when she returned on weekends, sometimes not. Shanda especially enjoyed the "long quiet talks" in the car when Moya was around to drive her back to school. Always present was Germaine, who took the children on outings, to their music lessons, to concerts.

Moya continued to love Le Ranch even though Bill wouldn't buy her a Swiss washing machine, which she needed badly. She had a large ranch house with a heated swimming pool and a bomb shelter stocked with wine, a Cessna and a Learstar, a black limousine and a chauffeur — but no Swiss washing machine because it was too expensive.

Of course, Bill had his women in Geneva just as he had in Santa Monica and New York and Chicago. At the head of the list was the General, whom he had brought to Europe, stashing her away like a squirrel burying a nut, sometimes in Paris or Geneva or Munich (where Lear International had a factory), but mostly in Rome.

Lear kept her on a short leash without much money so she couldn't roam around Europe without him or fly back to Santa Monica if he wasn't attentive enough. Once he got into a terrible row with her in Rome. He had dropped by her hotel unannounced one evening only to learn that she had gone out to dinner with a movie producer. He waited up for her in the lobby until one o'clock, when she walked through the door on the arm of a handsome Italian. Fuming and jealous, he left her in Rome with a rather large hotel bill and little cash and went home to Moya. The General called Bill Jr. in tears, begging for a $500 loan to help her pay her bills and airfare home. Lear forgave her on his next trip to the United States and brought her back to Europe when he returned.

Then there was Marie (not her real name), a dark-skinned West Indian who ended up at most of the Lear parties and who had smitten Bill with her beauty, grace, and sensuality, as she had an impressive list of European men. Dressed in a long pink evening gown and petite even in high heels, her black hair spilling over a gold collar and her fiery eyes searching out conquests — both men and women — Marie could stop a party just by walking into the room. Marie eventually fell out of Lear's favor.

June Shields watched the games of musical beds from her vantage point as a Lear secretary. Even though he was as pudgy as ever and was almost sixty, women still chased Bill. "He had enough money to have some power," she explains. "And women like power. He was self-confident, nice looking, well groomed. And he had enough time. He really enjoyed what he was doing and made people around him enjoy it too. And that is appealing to women. I'm sure women felt very feminine around him. But he never let Moya doubt that he loved her and needed her. He cherished her."

The Geneva years were not especially happy for John Lear, who felt more at home flying than he did at Le Ranch or Le Rosey, his boarding school. He had made his first flight when he was fourteen, but he had to wait until he was sixteen for a student's license to fly solo. Once he got it, he decided he wanted to be a commercial pilot. When he announced his goal in his father's office, Bill called in the industrial psychologist he had hired to help resolve company tension. "I want you to talk to John," he said. "I'm going to leave the room for about thirty minutes. See if you can get things sorted out."

"What seems to be the problem?" the psychologist asked John.

"There's no problem," John said. "I just was talking to my dad about what I want to do, and I want to be a commercial pilot. Dad wants me to be a painter or a doctor or a lawyer or something, where flying is a hobby. He said I can have my own airplane. But I don't want my own airplane. I want to fly for a living."

"Well, I think those are pretty normal drives."

John and the psychologist continued to chat until Bill came back.

"Well, have you got things worked out?" Bill asked. "What did you decide?"

"John is going to be an airline pilot," the psychologist said. "I think he has a healthy outlook on life."

"Well, you dumb sonofabitch," Bill yelled. "You both get out of here. Now!"

By the time he was seventeen, John had his private pilot's license with ratings to fly twin-engine aircraft and on instruments, and he had become the youngest pilot in Switzerland to earn an acrobatic rating, the coveted Vol de Virtuosité.

As soon as John turned eighteen (the legal age for flying as a commercial pilot) in December 1960, Al Handschumacher hired him as a Lear International public relations representative and pilot. John flew mostly as copilot with Bob Richardson in the company's twin Cessna, Learstar, and Beech. Because of his lack of experience, John tended to be more of a daredevil than Richardson, who had been flying for years.

On June 24, 1961, two days before his father's fifty-ninth birthday, John took off from Geneva's Cointrin Airport in a little yellow Bucker Jungmann 131 single-engine biplane, which he had rented from the Aero Club. It was in the Jungmann that John did his acrobatic flying, and he had to talk fast to convince the Aero Club dispatcher to rent him the plane for the trip north along the western shore of Lake Geneva to Bern, where he had to run an errand. The club had recently lost a Bucker, and it was difficult to replace the beautiful little trainer.

The weather was unusually clear and crisp, and John could see the peak of Mont Blanc, bald and white in the distance. He flew over Nyon, Rolle and Le Rosey, and Lausanne, then descended over the Rochers de Naye peaks at the north end of the lake and landed in Bern. Two hours later, he was on his way back to Geneva.

As he flew back over Le Rosey, the "school for kings" where he had spent the winter trimester of college the previous year, John decided to put on a show for his former school chums even though the Swiss Federal Air Office permitted aerobatics only over Cointrin Airport for periods of thirty minutes, assuming official air traffic was light. But, like his father, John didn't take federal regulations seriously at that point in his life. Besides, he couldn't resist showing off to his friends.

From time to time, John had made low, noisy passes over the Le Rosey dormitory in the Cessna. The roar of the engine and the tilt of the wings were his calling card. On this clear June afternoon, the whine of the Bucker drew students to the windows, as he knew it would. Wes Holden, Bill Holden's son, took pictures as John began the stunt routine that had qualified him for his aerobatic rating.

He climbed to 3,000 feet, did a roll to the right, then a roll to the left. He looped into a hammerhead to the right, then one to the left. As a finale, he began a three-turn spin at what he thought was 1,000 feet, allowing for the usual 200-foot clearance for his pullout at the bottom. It would be a spectacular finish because it would look as if the Bucker was heading for a crash. Then, at 200 feet, after the third turn, he would pull out, skimming the earth and shooting back up into the sky.

Like a flying cowboy, John shouted "Wahoooo" at the students hanging out of the dormitory windows below and began his first turn. It looked good. But in his exuberance, John misread his altimeter and misjudged the height at which he had started the spin.

During the second spiral, as his nose pointed to the ground, he thought, "Gosh, I sure look low . . ."

As he entered his third turn, it began to dawn on him that he'd never be able to pull out of the dive without scraping the ground.

Halfway through the last turn, a barn he spotted out of the corner of his eye seemed to be just fifty feet closer to the ground than he was. But he still hoped to pull out of the whirling dervish with only a sheared landing gear. As he completed the last turn and began pulling back the stick to force the yellow bird into the sky, waiting for the landing gear to scrape the soft soil, he was thinking of a cock-and-bull story that would explain to the Aero Club how he had managed to shear the gear.

A blink of the eye later, the Bucker slammed into a wheat field at a 30-degree angle. Before he passed out, John sensed an enormous weight threatening to snap his back, and he felt his face smash into the instrument panel between the altimeter and the airspeed indicator.

As he hit the ground, cushioned somewhat by the wheat, both straps of the shoulder harness broke and the Bucker ground to a halt after plowing forward only six feet. Afraid that the trainer would catch on fire and explode, the students pulled John from the wreck. An ambulance sped him to the nearby clinic in Rolle, where doctors performed a tracheotomy because his larynx had been crushed by the edge of the instrument panel. Then they strapped him into another ambulance bound for Hôpital Cantonal in Geneva.

John spent five hours on the operating table while a team of doctors did the best they could to pin him back together. He had broken both sides of his jaw and lost his four front teeth. His face was a mess. The metal rods of the rudder pedals had crushed both heelbones, joints, and ankles. Both legs were broken in three places. His neck had been crushed by part of the instrument panel, injuring his larynx. But miraculously he was still alive.

When he woke up in intensive care, his arms and legs strapped so he couldn't move, tubes and hoses coming out of everywhere, windows barred like a prison, John thought: "They put me in a loony bin, and they're not going to give me a chance to explain."

The wife of the headmaster of Le Rosey called Moya immediately after the accident. The Lears were throwing a large party that day in honor of the town fathers. News of the crash spread quickly among the guests, who filled the house and spilled into the gardens, where music was blaring over the speakers Bill had mounted in the woods. Shattered and in shock, Moya and Bill immediately rushed to the hospital, but Bill never went back again. He was angry at John for making a fool of himself and humiliated that his son had cracked up a rented airplane while putting on an illegal show to impress some friends. As far as Bill was concerned, the accident was just one more fence between him and his son. He believed that he had tried his best to be a good father to John, but that John had not done his part. It seemed to Bill that no matter what he said or did around the boy, it was never the right thing, and he couldn't figure out why. The fences just kept getting higher.

The problem had begun back in Santa Monica when Bill had a room built over the garage so that his eleven-year-old son could have his own little place. Hoping to get the boy interested in electronics, Bill put a ham radio without an antenna on his son's desk, intending to hook up the antenna later. "Now, John," he warned without a word of explanation, "don't ever turn this transmitter on."

After staring at the radio for two weeks, John couldn't fight the temptation any longer. He squeezed the microphone. "CQ . . . CQ," he called. Within minutes, the transmitter started smoking because the antenna was not loaded. Afraid of what his father might do, the boy asked John Ray, a radio man who worked for Lear, if he would fix it without telling his dad.

"Well," Bill began innocently when the family gathered for dinner at the "round table" one evening, "it looks like somebody blew up the ham radio." John tried to deny it, but Bill began flaying the boy in front of Moya and Shanda. "God, how can you be so stupid!" he yelled. "Anybody knows you have to load the antenna first."

By the time John was twelve, he could barely speak in front of his father, like Bill Jr. before him. He began withdrawing and found meals at the round table agonizing. His father would start out as sweet as rock candy, then begin to needle him about some small fault or mistake. Soon Bill would turn nastier until John was in tears, too frightened and humiliated to answer. That made Bill angrier and more contemptuous.

After the family returned from its first stay in Switzerland, in 1956, John spent tenth grade at University High School in Los Angeles and liked it. It was a benchmark, for he had never before completed one full year in the same school, and he was looking forward to joining his friends the following year. About three days before school began, John came home to a note from Moya pinned to his door. "John darling," it said, "please pack your things. We decided to send you to boarding school at Chadwick." The school was in Rolling Hills, just down the road from the Lear home.

John could never remember being so unhappy. He pleaded with Moya and begged his father to change their minds. "Dad and I feel you didn't get good enough grades and you were in with an undesirable element," Moya told him. "It's better for you at Chadwick, and we're going to send both you and Shanda there."

John did everything he could to cause a problem at Chadwick short of getting himself expelled. To get even with his father, he went out for football because his father detested the game; he made the junior varsity and won a letter. Then he told Moya that the letter was the greatest thing that had ever happened to him and asked her to make sure his father came to the sports banquet. Moya usually had to send a "stand-in," like Stan

Brown, because Bill was "out making your future secure." This time, however, Bill came to the banquet and John secretly enjoyed watching him "squirm."

After one last high school prank at Chadwick, Moya finally pulled John out. He enrolled in Santa Monica High and, when the family moved to Geneva, spent the summer at Le Ranch, returning in the fall to finish high school. He lived at the family home in Pacific Palisades with Kim, a Korean houseboy Moya had hired to look after things.

One day Bill flew in from Geneva unannounced and caught John wearing a ducktail haircut. Bill cracked his son so hard that he went sprawling onto the rug, sending up a geyser of the popcorn he was carrying. "Don't you ever let me see you wearing a haircut like that!" he warned. Then he asked his policeman friend, Buzz Nanney, to try to talk some sense into the boy. Anyone who wears a ducktail, Bill reasoned, must be getting into other big trouble as well. Nanney found John in the garage, working on the Model A he had bought with money he had earned working at the Santa Monica Freight Salvage Depot as a stockboy. Bill had leased a car for John on his sixteenth birthday, but the boy had wanted his own wheels. Bill couldn't understand why his son preferred a Model A that barely ran to a new Chevy with a service warranty, and when he caught John painting Playboy bunnies on the hubcaps, he threatened to send him to a psychiatrist.

"Why don't you try to understand your father?" Nanney asked. "He's really trying to help you. He doesn't want you to have all this long hair."

John faced the policeman with his feet apart, as if ready to draw from the hip. "I want to grow up to be *John* Lear," he said. "Not Bill Lear's son."

The crash in the wheat field outside Rolle was, for Bill Lear, just one more example of his son's selfishness and how he couldn't do anything right. "Dad was angry," Shanda recalls. "He thought it was a stupid thing. The guests were amazed that Dad wasn't sitting by his son in the hospital, but could be home, playing the great host. They felt it was a very cruel thing to do. Even today they speak of that. It left a lasting image of Dad's heartlessness to his own children."

Making no excuses and quite mortified, John took full blame for the accident. But Bill couldn't bring himself to face his son a second time. He resorted to several long, scathing letters around the same basic theme: John had brought shame on the Lear name; whatever pain he was suffering, he had brought on himself; he, Bill Lear, would tolerate no more of John's selfishness and stupidity; he would give John six months to heal, then buy him a ticket back to the United States, where he'd be on his own as he claimed he wanted to be; he was finished with trying to help John and, as far as he was concerned, he'd be pleased not to hear from him again. Moya tried to intervene, arguing that Bill should go easy on John; yes, he had made a mistake, but no, he shouldn't have to pay for it forever. But Bill was adamant.

John felt so guilty about the accident (Bill had to buy another Bucker for the Aero Club for $750) that he came to believe he deserved his father's treatment, and he withdrew even further from his family.

Caught between father and son, Moya struck a compromise. Publicly, she stood in silence, taking neither side. Privately, she worked on both of them, urging them to thaw the ice that kept them apart and to show the love she knew they felt for each other.

Bill became just as mercurial with John as he was with his engineers, one moment tongue-lashing, the next enticing. A year after the accident, when John was in college in Los Angeles, Bill wrote a glowing letter: "Dear John: If you had made me a present of the FAA certificate on my airplane, and an order for 300, *and* Fort Knox, you couldn't have pleased me any more than with the wonderful, wonderful letter I got from a wonderful son of whom I am more than ever proud."

22

SUD-AVIATION LIKED the Lear autopilot on its Caravelle so much that it asked Lear to adapt his automatic approach coupler to the Caravelle for use inside France. Like most European airlines, Air France had to cancel hundreds of flights each winter because of low visibility, and it was finding it difficult to compete with the dependable and ubiquitous French railway system. Lear, Dick Mock, and Kenneth Kramer, a Lear engineer, spent months at Sud-Aviation's main plant in Toulouse, redesigning the blind landing system. After two hundred pilotless test landings, Sud-Aviation made its first commercial blind landing at Orly Airport in Paris with sixteen passengers aboard its twin-engine jet airliner. It was, as the *New York Times* phrased it, "a perfect landing . . . with the pilot's hands off the controls . . . in the face of gusty crosswinds." It was also the first commercial blind landing in the world.

Both Lear and Mock had been advocating blind landings for passenger airplanes for several years, arguing that they were safer than piloted landings and should become an FAA requirement. But it took the FAA ten years to allow blind landings in the United States. Meanwhile, there were no Caravelle accidents anywhere in the world attributed to the Lear automatic flight control system.

For his contribution to aircraft safety, the French awarded Bill Lear the Silver Medal of Paris in October 1960; soon after that, the Swedish Aeronautical Society honored him with the bronze Thulin Medal. Although the silver medal was only second place (not highly regarded by the French) and the Swedish bronze was a third, Lear was pleased because he recognized the public relations value of the awards in the United States.

Busy designing his new executive aircraft in Geneva during 1960 and 1961, Lear also had his fingers in all kinds of other projects, trying to make a quick, easy profit. First, there were prefabricated homes. Lear was working on a deal with the National Homes Corporation to export its prefab models to Europe. He lined up potential sales representatives in Italy, Germany, and France. He plied the media with information. He gave tours of his own prefab guest house at Le Ranch, and he threw parties. But he did not understand the European skepticism toward American mass production, which sacrifices individuality for economy. Nothing ever came of the prefab scheme, nor of the electric toothbrush and the electronic sauna, which collected and measured the amount of perspiration lost. There were other schemes as well — gold mines, oil wells, silver and coal mines, land deals in Alaska — but none of them distracted Lear from his dream of a corporate airplane that would make the world stand up and take notice. The other projects were purely moneymaking ventures. The airplane was serious business.

The earliest designs of what would become the Lear Jet dated back to 1959 and were based on the Marvel, a novel airplane designed and built for the U.S. Army by an engineering team at Mississippi State University headed by Dr. August Raspet. The Marvel was a turboprop of molded fiber glass with a single engine mounted aft in a cigarlike nacelle near the propeller, which sat inside a huge six-foot ring on the tail. The six-seater looked like a cross between a Cessna and a spaceship.

Lear liked the Marvel because he had been thinking about a pusher airplane for a long time. Douglas had designed one during World War II, but it never went into production after the war. A Douglas hulk had been sitting on the field at the Santa Monica airport for years, and Lear used to see it every day. Dr. Raspet had managed to lick one of the major problems with pushers (a long shaft from the engine to the propeller) by placing the engine in the tail close to the prop. With a new engine (Allison T-63) designed by the Army–Mississippi State team and flying at a maximum speed of 350 miles an hour, the Marvel was touted as the most efficient subsonic airplane ever built.

Lear called Dr. Raspet three times in April 1959 with the specifications for a pressurized five-place corporate airplane and asked for his recommendations. Dr. Raspet suggested a twin-engine turboprop pusher with the propeller inside a six-foot ring and with the engines (Allison 252) mounted on the tail next to it.

He told Lear that this modified Marvel would have a cruising speed of 344 miles an hour at 25,000 feet and a range of 1,520 miles. Lear's artist, Ted Grohs, did a sketch of the Raspet-Lear concept, calling it the Lear Pusher Turboprop Airplane.

But Lear's design soon evolved into what Grohs called Lear Model 59-3 — Eight Place Executive Airplane Twin Turbofan. With two turbojet engines mounted in the rear next to the T-tail, it looked radically different from the Marvel but quite similar to the Lear Fan, which Lear and his engineers would design fifteen years later.

In the summer of 1959, Lear began negotiating with Mitsubishi, the prime production contractor for the Lockheed F-104 jet fighter. "It is my intention to underwrite the engineering and prototyping," he explained, "and then sell the design." Lear asked Mitsubishi to bid on developing the prototype with him, which he would call the Lear-Mitsubishi Executive Transport Aircraft. He would then bid out the tooling and the larger pieces in Europe, he explained (he had already talked to British, French, and Swedish companies), and the airplanes would be assembled in the United States.

Mitsubishi was interested, but it insisted on a small production contract to support the cost of developing the prototype. The company did not want to end up with a stack of blueprints in an empty bag as Lear had so often done. Lear toyed with the company for almost a year, then dropped it when his oldest son came up with a better idea.

Bill Jr. had fallen in love with a new Swiss fighter-bomber, the P-16. It was a precisely tooled, tough little bird, with a wing that came close to what Lear had in mind for his executive airplane. The P-16 was designed by Dr. Hans Studer and built by Flug-und-Fahrzeugwerke Altenrhein (FFA), but the company was having a problem. It had built four P-16s in the hope of selling them to the Swiss Air Force, but it lost two of them in Lake Constance. The Swiss began calling the fighter "the Swiss submarine." Convinced that the airplane was basically sound, Dr. Caroni, the owner of FFA, asked Bill Jr. to test-fly it.

Bill Jr. took the fighter up five times and found it "incredible." After interviewing the test pilots who had bailed out over the lake, he concluded that there was nothing structurally wrong with the P-16. The accidents, he told Dr. Caroni, were due to mechanical failures and inexperienced test pilots, who had panicked instead of relying on the fighter's back-up systems.

But no one had confidence in the fighter anymore, and it never went into production. Disappointed, Bill Jr. pointed out the aircraft to his father, who was so impressed with it — the wing, in particular — that he tossed all his sketches aside and hired Hans Studer to help him convert the P-16 into a hot-rod corporate jet. Lear would later say: "People thought, 'How could anything that came out of Switzerland be any good?' But it was the best damned ground-attack airplane in the world. The trouble was a lack of systems know-how. They had a hydraulic system on the thing that wasn't pressurized, and as soon as they got to altitude, they had foam instead of hydraulic fluid."

Back home in Santa Monica, Lear was in hot water with his Board of Directors. *Newsweek* happened to mention that Lear Incorporated was building an airplane in Switzerland, generating "a shower of inquiries." Richard ("Dick") Millar, chairman of the Board's finance committee, dashed a letter off to Lear: "I don't have to tell you that psychologically the air frame industry is unattractive to the average investor at this time. I can't prove it, but the report that Lear Incorporated was building an airplane probably cost us around a point in the price of the stock . . . You may find it advisable to keep the Lear name out of the airplane project entirely. This has nothing to do with the merit of the project, of which I think highly."

Lear took his friend's advice. He created a new company, the Swiss American Aviation Corporation, called his new airplane the SAAC-23, and moved his headquarters clear across the country to St. Gallen, next to the FFA factory in Altenrhein. By mid 1961, the basic design of the SAAC-23 was completed. It wouldn't be the first small jet aircraft aimed at the American businessman. The Lockheed JetStar and the North American Sabreliner were already on the market, and the Jet Commander was on the drawing boards. (The French had the Morane Saulnier, which Beechcraft was licensed to manufacture in the United States; the Swedes, the SAAB 185; the Israelis, the B-101c; and the British, the De Havilland Jet Dragon.) Lear didn't think much of the JetStar or the Sabreliner, which had been designed to ferry Pentagon brass and carried a Pentagon price tag. "Royal barges," he called them.

Lear's SAAC-23 would be unique in that it would be designed specifically for businessmen and promised to match or excel its two American competitors in every major category — 500 mph cruising speed, 600 mph maximum speed, 2,000-mile range, 6,000 feet rate of climb, 45,000 feet maximum operating altitude, and a $500,000 price tag. Lear reasoned: "With businessmen flying at 500 mph or 600 mph in 707s and DC-8s, you've got to give him a business airplane, a private airplane that doesn't lope along at 178 mph."

Lear's plane departed from traditional design and engineering theories as well. It would be a pilot's airplane. Lear had begun with a list of deficiencies in most private airplanes, then designed them out of his. He axed the popular walk-around cabin ("If you want to take a walk, go to Central Park") and the high ceiling ("You can't stand up in a Cadillac, either"), and he added a ground heating and cooling system ("Ridiculous for an executive to arrive at the airport in his air-conditioned $5,000 automobile and get into a $500,000 airplane that, until it became airborne, has all the comfort of a sauna bath"). But he rejected elaborate cabin furnishings and flushed the executive bathroom from his design ("A restroom is an admission you're spending too much time getting where you want to go").

Lear also scoffed at the idea that a jet airplane had to be so complex that "even a doctor of engineering could hardly interpret" all the instruments on the panel. On the other hand, he refused to compromise on safety, promising fail-safe dual electrical systems and separate fuel lines for each engine. The cockpit would be large with armchair-type seats as comfortable as passenger seats, and the pilot would be able to scan the sky for 270 degrees through huge, distinctive cockpit windows. There would be no overhead switches or trim controls to distract the pilot. Passenger seats would fold down like those in a station wagon for extra cargo, and each passenger would have picture-window vision.

There was no precedent for the way in which he intended to manufacture the airplane, either. FFA would do the tooling in Altenrhein as well as make the wings and wing-tip tanks; Heinkel of Germany, the fuselage and tail; Thommen of Switzerland, the hydraulic items and undercarriage; and Saurer of Switzerland, the auxiliary power turbines. Alcoa would supply the sheet metal; GE, the CJ-610-2B jet engines; Goodrich, the brakes; and Lear Incorporated, the navigation instruments. FFA would assemble the prototype in Altenrhein and build the first few airplanes.

To the amusement of his critics, Lear estimated that he could sell more than six hundred SAAC-23s. "Industry [is moving] away from metropolitan centers," he reasoned. "Thus firms that are not on the main [air] lines must rely on their own fleets of executive aircraft to get the bosses and salesmen around the country."

The SAAC-23 caused a great stir of excitement in Switzerland, for if Lear could deliver on his promises and projections, his corporate jet would become the most competitive plane in the annals of executive aircraft. The Swiss Federal Air Office was so pleased that Lear had decided to build his plane in Switzerland that it not only promised to speed up Swiss certification but also to cooperate with the FAA in the United States so that both countries could certify the aircraft at the same time. Furthermore, the Swiss people themselves were in love with flying. Hundreds would picnic on the hillside near the Zürich airport on weekends just to see the planes take off and land.

While Lear was in Geneva figuring out how to design, test, and build his new aircraft, Al Handschumacher was trying to make Lear Incorporated look good on Wall Street. To analyze the company's image problems, he hired the public relations firm of Ruder and Finn. Their frank report outlined what many Lear executives had been thinking for years but had never dared to say, at least to Bill Lear:

Wall Street analysts were suspicious of both Lear the man and Lear the company. "No one doubts that he is an inventive genius," Ruder and Finn reported, "but some said he was not a good businessman . . . an egomaniac . . . an eccentric scientific genius. Everyone is glad to hear that he has removed himself from the day-to-day management of the company."

Ruder and Finn went on to quote typical Wall Street comments about Bill Lear: "His actions seem like fun, but they don't necessarily give the stock a good reputation . . . He is a glamour boy — all that running around that he does. In short, he's a playboy . . . He makes rash statements and then doesn't understand why Wall Street doesn't think his company is as respectable as some of the other corporations with which it is competing . . . Some of us who have known Lear over the years feel it would be a great thing if they kept Bill Lear out of the management picture."

The image of Lear Incorporated in the business community, the report went on, is one of corporate instability. What other company would play musical chairs with its presidents? Said one analyst: "We don't know who's managing the company." And under Bill Lear, the company did not seem to have goals or a philosophy. "I'm confused," another analyst told Ruder and Finn. Said yet another, "I've heard nothing good and nothing bad about Lear Incorporated."

In sum, most Wall Street analysts viewed Lear Incorporated as "just another of 5,000" electronics firms, not as a pioneer in aviation instruments.

But the aviation reporters interviewed by Ruder and Finn disagreed with Wall Street. Explained one: "Bill is fabulous. The guy is a genius. He's not dependent on conventions of life to make an impression. Because of this, some of the Ivy League boys on Wall Street don't like him."

What Lear Incorporated has to do, Ruder and Finn recommended, is to create a dynamic picture of its present management, especially Handschumacher, around whom the whole public relations effort should pivot. Bill Lear's move to Geneva, the firm predicted, should go a long way in helping the company develop an image independent of William Powell Lear, whose personality has been a public relations "liability" in the past.

Ruder and Finn concluded in part: "Al Handschumacher has taken over the reins of the company as a professional manager. One gets the feeling that he knows how to run the company and that he is proceeding in an orderly way. Furthermore, and extremely important, one feels that he has a good working relationship with Bill Lear which gives him a free hand in the management of the company. But this relationship, it seemed to us, has not been worked out in such a way as to make it clear what the spiritual fountainhead of the company is today or, more specifically, where or who it is."

Ruder and Finn bared a raw nerve. Lear had never thought of his company as "just another" electronics firm; he didn't mind Handschumacher running the company, but he didn't want the world to know it; and he resented being considered a public relations liability. Not suspecting that his president might know a corporate trick or two, Lear began undermining Handschumacher's authority and dropping selective hints that he was going to fire him, knowing full well that Handschumacher would get the message.

He did. Explains Handschumacher: "We had a problem because he was shooting his mouth off. People were calling me up, saying, 'What in the hell is going on between you and Bill?' It was a real battle of wits."

Handschumacher met Lear head-on. As far as appearances were concerned, Handschumacher stressed in a meeting in New York, they would have to show a united front. Otherwise, Wall Street would continue to be jittery and Lear stock would continue to fluctuate. When Lear agreed, Handschumacher arranged for interviews with *Business Week.*

Lear bluffed. In an article called "Plane Gear Maker Tries Dual Management," *Business Week* noted that Lear "is perfectly happy with the way Handschumacher is running the company, and how he has shaped up management. Lear was most pleased by Handschumacher's thoroughness and his courage." It went on to quote Lear as saying, "He has amassed a stable, young management, and you can't throw a curve at them."

How right he was. Having settled the day-to-day running of the company, Handschumacher went after Lear himself. Lear had been playing an old game, which had worked well in the past. He'd begin working on something like the Learstar and get the company committed before it knew what was happening, "sucking" everyone in, as one associate put it. But Handschumacher, who had worked with Lear for twenty years, knew the game well. Determined to force Lear out of the company for everyone's sake, Handschumacher let Lear have enough rope to hang himself on his new corporate jet.

Lear had understood that the airplane was to be his private project. The corporation had agreed to allow him to spend as much of his time on it as he wanted and even use office space and secretarial help, but it had never agreed to pay for its design, development, and manufacture. When Lear began to order equipment and charge it to the company, as Handschumacher predicted he would do, Handschumacher closed one eye. When Lear began pestering Nils Eklund, who headed the corporation's Solid State Physics Laboratory in Santa Monica, to conduct tests for him and to make some designs, he closed the other eye.

Then, when Handschumacher thought Lear had "sucked" himself so deeply into his own project that there was no turning back, he pinched the pipeline with the full support of the Board of Directors. The jet airplane was a private project, he reminded Lear. The company would not allow Lear to pull engineers like Eklund off their government work on missiles to help him with his airplane, nor would it continue to pay for and ship equipment and parts to Geneva. Handschumacher even insisted that Lear repay the company for some of the things he had already purchased with company money.

When Lear began running out of cash, Handschumacher gladly helped him get loans. With each step forward, the noose got tighter. By the time it became perfectly clear to Lear that the Board would never back down and embrace the corporate jet project, no matter how good it looked on paper and no matter how much personal money he had put into it, Lear was hooked. True, there were sentimental supporters on the Board, but Handschumacher strongly opposed them. To him, it wasn't a question of whether Lear could sell a corporate jet. He knew it would take millions to design, certify, and manufacture any new aircraft. And Lear had a habit of underestimating the cost of nearly everything he developed. Furthermore, Lear Incorporated, now grossing $90 million a year, did not have a staff of engineers capable of designing and building airplanes. To hire engineers and gear up to make airplanes would send a shudder from Santa Monica all the way to Wall Street and could even kill the company. Finally, the new airplane would be in direct competition with some of Lear Incorporated's best customers.

When it came to the bottom line, even Lear's supporters on the Board turned against the project. As Handschumacher put it: "Just because *he* created it was no good reason for the company to build it."

There was still another problem. Lear had agreed with Handschumacher and the Board that the company not only had to balance military and nonmilitary sales, but it also had either to acquire other companies or merge. But every time Dick Mock, the chairman of the acquisitions committee, thought he had a possible merger, Lear would blow the deal. When Mock had brought Curtiss-Wright to the point of serious negotiation, for example, Lear simply told the company that if the smaller Lear Incorporated was to merge with the larger Curtiss-Wright, he would have to be chairman of the Board or he wouldn't deal. Curtiss-Wright laughed. So did Studebaker.

"It was almost as if Bill unknowingly broke it up," recalls Handschumacher, who was determined to get Lear to sell his stock if he wouldn't agree to a merger in which he had to be a small frog in a big pond. "He would not come through and make it, or let it, happen . . . God, I wanted to do anything to get him out. I had three years of really developing the company. I was very proud of my work and very happy."

Dick Millar, an investment banker with William R. Staats and Company as well as the chairman of Lear's finance committee, was the one who finally convinced Lear to sell his shares in the company. Lear had invited Millar to join the Board. Although he had served on a great many corporate boards, Millar had not been prepared for what he found on Lear's. "Bill didn't do anything the way anybody else did," Millar explains. "He would free-wheel. In many ways it was refreshing, sometimes it was frustrating, but there was always a sparkle. After a while, I was never surprised at anything he did."

For one thing, when Millar (who had been discreetly "shoveled off" other boards for opposing the chairman) stood up to him, Lear would discuss Millar's point of view without trying to silence him during or after the meetings. For another, Lear was involved in the nitty-gritty problems of the company when chairmen were not supposed to be. During one board meeting, for example, when he was preoccupied with a sticky design problem, Lear called a short recess so he could check on his engineers. He invited the board members to join him. Only Millar and several others went along.

"What's the problem?" Lear asked a group of ten engineers gathered around a drawing board. They explained. "Did you ever think of this?" Lear made a change on the sketch.

Millar was impressed. "I wished you could have seen the expression on those faces," he recalls. "My God, in a matter of minutes he caught the problem, asked the right question, and gave the answer. All those high-priced engineers had been banging their heads against the wall."

Because they respected each other, Lear and Millar became good friends, and Lear would phone him from all over the world at two or three in the morning. "Want to hear a good one?" Lear would ask. Then he'd rattle off a dirty joke.

Although Millar believed that the corporate jet idea was sound for Lear, he was also convinced it would be a "backbreaker" for Lear Incorporated because Bill Lear had "grossly" underestimated the time and cost of the airplane. So when the Siegler Corporation, a Staats client, expressed an interest in merging with Lear, Millar encouraged Bill to sell his stock to Siegler as the first step toward a corporate merger. With the money he got from the sale, Millar argued, Lear could finance his jet, and there wouldn't be a Board of Directors "looking over his shoulder." Lear agreed.

Like Lear, John Brooks, chairman of the Siegler Corporation, had worked his way to the top, beginning as an office boy for Commonwealth Edison, then moving on to become secretary to Commander McDonald at Zenith and vice president for sales at EKCO Products. In 1954, Brooks became president of Siegler, which had annual sales of $6.5 million. Eight years later, the corporation was selling $100 million worth of equipment a year. According to *Business Week*, the Lear-Siegler merger would be "a perfect fit." Both companies were in electronics, each had sales of around $100 million a year, they were not competitors. Approximately 90 percent of Lear's business was with the military, compared to 40 percent of Siegler's. Each needed the other to grow; wedded, they would be second in sales in the electronics business, behind Litton Industries. The only problem was that

John Brooks didn't like Bill Lear and wouldn't agree to having him show his face as a consultant, member of the Board, or in any other way.

When the S.S. *France* docked in New York on February 8, 1962, after its stormy maiden voyage with Bill and Moya aboard, Al Handschumacher and Dick Millar were waiting. Millar took one look at Lear and knew there was trouble. "Bill was in a very bad humor," he recalls. "Being locked up on a ship for that length of time did nothing but irritate the living daylights out of him."

Lear told Millar that he had changed his mind. He wouldn't sell, even though everything had been set up. John Brooks and a team of Siegler negotiators were waiting at the Carlton House and the Lear team was in another hotel. Lear's shares and those in the trust funds for Bill Jr., Patti, and Charlene amounted to 27 percent of the corporation's stock. If Lear would not sell to Siegler, Handschumacher doubted that the rest of the shareholders would approve a merger.

Soothing his friend as best he could, Millar persuaded Lear at least to attend the meeting, set up for five o'clock that afternoon. Whether Lear was bluffing or nervous, no one could tell.

During the meeting, Lear became more of an antagonist than a negotiator. Attorneys and messengers for both sides worked all evening, with Lear saying yes to one proposal, then changing his mind, then demanding something else. At the heart of the negotiation were the use of Lear's name and his relationship to the new company. At three in the morning, Lear signed the deal.

He sold his 470,000 shares of Lear Incorporated for $22 each, or $10.3 million, and another 100,000 shares in the trust funds for $2.2 million. (The three trusts now had net worths of approximately $850,000 each.) Lear could call his new airplane the Lear Jet. And, as a "sweetener so he couldn't refuse the deal," Lear would serve as a Lear-Siegler consultant for twelve years at $140,000 a year. In return, he agreed not to develop or sell competitive products, and Lear-Siegler could continue to use "Lear" on its products.

Once he signed the deal, Lear was happy. Handschumacher was pleased, too. "As soon as he signed those papers," he explains, "he was out, out, out! I had had it up to here."

For the next several months, Handschumacher began cutting all Lear's threads to his former company, and there were dozens — real estate, cars, and airplanes that Lear had bought with his own money, then leased back to the company at a profit. After the shareholders approved the merger a few months later, Handschumacher became president and chief executive officer of Lear-Siegler. William Powell Lear's name did not appear in the annual report for 1962, and neither Handschumacher nor Brooks, the chairman of the Board, ever asked Lear's advice on company matters. And after a small group of shareholders contested the merger after the fact, a court declared the consulting contract between Lear and Lear-Siegler null and void.

To Al Handschumacher, the merger was not an attempt to get even with Bill Lear; he neither bore a grudge against him nor lost his respect for the man as an individualist and creative force. "Bill will go down in the history of aviation for a combination of creative products which he brought to a new performance level," he says. "It wouldn't have been done without him."

23

IN 1962, BILL LEAR HIRED Buzz Nanney as general manager of his Swiss American Aviation Corporation. With Americans, British, French, and Swiss working side by side, with subcontracting to factories in Germany and Switzerland, with cultural differences and diverse work styles, with language problems and unfamiliar customs, SAAC was up to its blueprints in confusion.

Nanney had met Lear in 1952, when he was a West Los Angeles police detective. They soon became good friends and Lear hired him as a security consultant for Lear Incorporated. What Nanney loved most about Lear was his lack of inhibition.

One time, Bill wanted to try out a new 30-30 rifle that someone had given him even though it was late at night.

"You can't shoot it in Santa Monica," Nanney warned him.

"We can shoot it out over the ocean," Lear said.

"Bill, I don't think I'd do that," Nanney told him.

Bill pointed the rifle toward Hawaii and fired two or three shots. The echo traveled up the dark canyons and lights started popping on like fireflies. Nanney rushed to the patrol car and called the dispatcher.

"You getting complaints about shooting out in Santa Monica?" he asked.

"My God," the dispatcher said, "the phone won't stop."

"I'll take care of it. I'm in the area."

Another time, Lear threw a party for his Board of Directors at his home in Pacific Palisades. Bill asked an actor friend, Vince Barnett, to pose as a disgruntled Hungarian stockholder. Drink in hand and with a convincing Hungarian accent, Barnett mingled with the guests, loudly criticizing the stupidity of Lear Incorporated. The directors called Lear aside and asked him to do something. The Hungarian was embarrassing them.

Lear caught up with Barnett at the pool. "You sonofabitch," he yelled. "You can't talk like that about my company!"

While the directors watched, white-faced, Lear knocked Barnett into the pool. The guests froze. After Barnett climbed out of the water, Lear introduced the actor and everyone had a good laugh.

Nanney liked that fun-loving side of Lear so much that when Bill asked him to come to Switzerland after he retired from the police department, Nanney jumped at the opportunity. He was just forty-two years old, and Bill made the job sound exciting. Besides giving him a decent salary, Lear offered to pay for Nanney's flying lessons and his trip to Europe, and he promised to pick him up in Frankfurt, inviting him and his wife to stay in the guest house at Le Ranch until they could find a place of their own.

Lear also promised that the SAAC-23 would be flying by April 1962, but when Nanney arrived in January, all he saw were drawings and a peck of problems. Not only was Lear snarled in yards of communication and management red tape, but most of the thirty workers Lear had hired from England, France, and Germany did not have work permits, and the police were threatening to send them home.

Lear faced similar problems with Heinkel in West Germany.

He'd fly into Spier for a meeting. The wooden floors shone like mirrors; there wasn't a blotch of grease on the machines; women in white jackets served beer at the coffee break; lunch with cigars, beer, and wine took two hours; and Lear had to hear everything twice — once in German, then translated into English, or vice versa. Lear was getting the feeling that although labor was cheaper in Europe than in the United States, he might not be getting as much for his dollar. He hated meetings and bureaucracies in any country, and felt he was not on top of things if he couldn't scream at his engineers and machinists in a language they both understood.

To make things worse, Lear hired Gordon Israel as a consulting engineer, and Israel did not get along with Dr. Hans Studer, as anyone but Lear would have predicted. Lear had kept in touch with Israel after the company had sold Learstar to the Pacific Airmotive Corporation, which had then hired Israel as a consultant. When Lear saw Israel sometime later at a party in the home of Jimmy Doolittle, the World War II hero, he had shown the engineer Dr. Studer's drawings of the SAAC-23. Israel had told Lear that the plane "looked way out of balance" and that the center of gravity was too far aft. It turned out that Israel was right, and Lear invited him to come to St. Gallen for two months.

The problem began when Israel stepped off the airplane drunk. One crazy American was enough for Dr. Studer and his staff, who "thought Bill was absolutely out of his mind." One day they would be working with a design for a turboprop pusher that had already cost the American close to $1 million; the next day they would be starting over, designing the SAAC-23 around General Electric's CJ-610 engine, which the U.S. government had released for use in general aviation. Now they had a drunken consultant.

The problem grew more complicated as two months stretched into nineteen, with Israel thinking and acting as if *he* was chief engineer. "Bill had a problem identifying duties and responsibilities," Nanney explains. "All his organizational charts looked like an octopus."

The problem became almost impossible when Studer and Israel tried to work together. Although Dr. Studer could speak English well, his approach to aircraft design and engineering was theoretical; that of Israel, a high school graduate, was practical. Studer refused to come to work as long as Israel was there. Nanney negotiated a temporary cease-fire by keeping Studer on the payroll and letting Israel do the work.

The problem became insoluble when Lear took off for the United States in mid 1962 to raise money for his airplane, leaving Nanney in charge, and hired Henry Waring, a former Cessna designer from Wichita, to be his chief engineer. Now SAAC-23 had three chief engineers.

Lear had known Hank Waring from the Wright Field days of World War II, when Waring was a test pilot for the B-17 bomber, the C-46 cargo plane, and the P-47 and P-38 fighters. After the war, Waring joined North American as an aerodynamic engineer on the F-82 and F-86 jets, which carried the Lear autopilot and approach coupler. Then Waring went to Cessna as chief engineer and test pilot for the company's Military Aircraft Division, where he developed the T-37 and L-19 trainers and the 310 and 320 twin-engine business airplanes.

Waring brought along a team of ten Americans to Switzerland, most of whom had worked with him at Cessna. One of them was Don Grommesh, who, like Lear and Waring, was convinced that the market was ripe for a corporate jet and who had been disappointed when Cessna decided not to build one. The conservative company had been hoping that the U.S. Navy would give it a no-risk contract to develop a prototype personnel carrier that it could then sell to the Navy on a plane-by-plane basis as well as to corporations, just as Lockhead and North American had done with the JetStar and Sabreliner. "You'll be back in six months when Lear goes broke," warned Grommesh's bosses at Cessna.

To Waring and Grommesh, the SAAC-23 looked like a disaster. By the time they arrived, the outline of the plane was finished and the airframe structure fairly well set. But none of the systems that made the airplane fly — fuel, guidance, hydraulic, electric — had been designed and no one seemed to be working on them. The tooling appeared to be developing in fits and starts, without a plan. The wing was nearly done and had a fair amount of detail, but the tooling for the fuselage was only partly completed. No one seemed to be in charge.

When he wasn't out with a hangover, Israel had the engineers running in circles. It wasn't that he couldn't design when he was drunk. In the evenings, he sat with a bottle at a table in the Valhall Hotel, right around the corner from SAAC's offices, and sketched for most of the night — or at least until the bottle was empty. Then he had a messenger deliver the drawings to the factory, but he wouldn't show up in person to parcel out the work. Not knowing quite what to do, the engineers sat around waiting for him.

To make the situation worse, the Swiss began to resent the Americans, whom they thought Lear had imported to take over *their* project. They wouldn't give Waring or Grommesh copies of their reports because they feared the Americans were going to criticize them.

Waring concluded that he was wasting his time and Lear's money. "Look, Buzz," he told Nanney after he had been in Altenrhein for a few weeks, "I can't get a handle on this program. I keep wondering why it's here in Switzerland. There's no way we can get the airplane certified here. We can't manufacture it here. The only sensible thing to do is move the project to Wichita."

In an attempt to tighten the reins, Nanney worked on Gordon Israel, whom he had known for years. Once, when Gordon had plowed into six parked cars in Santa Monica, Nanney had pulled a few strings to get him a simple six-month probation for driving under the influence. Nanney recognized that, as brilliant as he was, Israel was not what Lear needed in Switzerland, especially if the old man wasn't around to control the ship.

"Gordon," Nanney warned, "I want you here at eight o'clock in the morning, and I want you to give instructions to all these people. I'm not an engineer. I have to have you here."

Gordon came in at three o'clock the next afternoon and sat in his office, refusing to talk to anyone. Nanney lowered the boom. "Gordon," he said, "I'm really sad but I have to do this. You're fired. You lied to the old man. He thought you had quit drinking. You were drunk when you arrived here, and you've been drunk ever since. I'm sorry because you're a brilliant man."

With only two chief engineers instead of three, Nanney asked Waring to list all the reasons that Lear should move to Wichita, "the World Capital of Aviation." Then he wrote Lear a long letter, arguing that if he didn't bail out of Switzerland soon, there would be no airplane. The project was a financial sieve: the Swiss were coming in at eight, taking a relaxed lunch hour, leaving at four, and not showing up on weekends; and the draftsmen made meticulous ink drawings and read trade journals and newspapers while the ink was drying; engineers waited days, sometimes weeks, for the drawings of parts that they needed to be tooled within fifteen minutes; and after seeing the first drawings, the engineers would say, "No, it's not right. Go back and do it again."

Lear called Nanney as soon as the letter caught up with him. "Is it really that bad?" he asked.

"Yes."

Lear moved so quickly that he surprised everyone, even Buzz Nanney. He began searching for a new home for his jet, boiling his choices down to three — Grand Rapids, Dayton, and Wichita. He invited representatives from each city to attend a press conference in June 1962, during the annual Reading (Pennsylvania) Air Show, when he would announce the winner.

It was high drama. Wanting the revenue and employment that the Lear Jet promised, each city courted Bill Lear. The Wichita Chamber of Commerce even coaxed Boeing and Cessna to cosign a telegram to Lear, saying, "We invite you to join us in Wichita, the air capital, in making the finest aircraft in the world."

For the press conference, Lear commandeered a big tent and kept the three cities is suspense until the very last minute, when he announced to the world that he had chosen Wichita. Recalls Carl Bell, then mayor of the city, "It was Lear Academy Awards. We wondered if he was for real. Aero Commander had a full-size mockup of the Jet Commander it was building. Bill's small mockup of Lear Jet was not impressive."

Weeks before the air show, of course, Lear had already selected Wichita, where 65 percent of the world's airplanes were being built and where rows of aerospace plants and enormous grain elevators broke the flat monotony of the Kansas prairie. Lear had calculated that the per pound cost of airframe was cheaper there than in any other city in the United States. Furthermore, Wichita had offered him a deal he could not refuse. With employment in its aerospace industry down from 48,000 in 1957 to 29,000, the city was so anxious to have Lear Jet that it offered to raise $1.2 million in industrial revenue bonds for a Lear Aero Spaceway, to be built on a sixty-four-acre cornfield on the northern edge of the airport. The complex would include a 100,000-square-foot building with an open manufacturing area larger than a football field, where ten Lear Jets could be assembled at one time, and a half-mile-long taxiway linking the new Lear Jet Corporation to Municipal Airport.

When the Swiss got the word that Lear was pulling out, they were stunned. By and large, they liked and believed in him. And those who knew him thought they had him figured out: an eccentric who could fire people with enthusiasm; a genius driven by the need to give birth to his ideas at all cost — family, friends, business; a visionary, conscious and confident of his place in history; an entrepreneur, blessed with a gift to generate both ideas and money and burdened with "la folie de grandeur"; a self-made man, generous with the money of Lear Incorporated but stingy with his own; a lovable ugly American who did not understand European culture and didn't want to. The Swiss knew all this, but Lear had still surprised them.

Workers thought they had firm contracts; Caroni, the owner of FFA, thought he had a gentleman's agreement to do all the tooling and prototyping; the Swiss Federal Air Office, which had been most cooperative, thought it was making history; and the mayor of Bernex, near Le Ranch, thought he was getting a new swimming pool for the town's children. Lear had promised to pay half if the town would pay the rest.

Nanney began mopping up the mess just as Bill Jr. had done in 1956. There were hundreds of workers whom he had to convince to sign severance contracts, 500 tons of equipment to pack and ship to Wichita (9,300 individual jigs, tools, and dies), and Caroni to appease.

Lear and Caroni had never signed a contract because neither had trusted the other. When Lear decided to close the hangar door without discussion or warning, leaving him with angry workers and a thousand jobs half done, Caroni was not about to give Lear the tools and dies for nothing. Fernand Matile, who had worked for Lear in Switzerland in 1956, negotiated each item and issue with Caroni. But after he had verbally agreed on the terms, Caroni, who was an attorney, refused to sign the contract.

Nanney forced Caroni's hand. "You have a problem and Lear has a problem, but I don't. I can just go away," Nanney threatened. "The day you two couldn't sign a contract is the day you shouldn't have gone into business with each other."

Caroni finally agreed to the settlement and signed the contract. Lear called Nanney at six in the morning the day after he received the agreement. "Hire ten of the best attorneys in Europe," he screamed, "and sue the sonofabitch for every hour, every week, and every month of delay."

Nanney, who had worked hard to get Lear off so lightly, thought Caroni had been more than fair and reasonable. "Bill, I'll tell you something," he said. "You sign every one of these goddamn papers and you send me $50,000, and do it now, or you can come over here and figure this problem out yourself. I've had it. This is going to die in the courts over here, and your plane is never going to be built."

"All right, you sonofabitch," Lear conceded, "but I'm going to hold you responsible."

Without even consulting Moya, who was traveling around Europe with her father, Lear bought the ten-acre Wichita estate of Arthur Kinkaid, a banker. "I bought you the most beautiful house you ever saw," he told Moya over the phone when he finally tracked her down in Yugoslavia. "Furnished!"

Like the Swiss, Moya was stunned. She loved Le Ranch, and she had had no inkling that Bill was even thinking of moving back to the States.

"Oh no! Not again!" she cried. "And of all places . . . Wichita, Kansas."

24

In AUGUST 1962, just one month after he decided to leave Switzerland, Lear broke ground for the Lear Aero Spaceway. He opened temporary offices at seven-thirty on Labor Day morning and locked them at nine-thirty that night. That's the way it would be for the next two years. No foolish holidays, long lei-surely lunches, or punching in and out on the stroke of the hour. On January 7, 1963, six months after the bulldozers took their first bite of cornfield, Lear and seventy-five employees moved into the new building. He promised to have the first Lear Jet in the air by June.

The city of Wichita, whose future rode on the roller coaster of the aviation business, watched Lear with amusement, awe, and skepticism. He was the new kid on the block, the outsider in a town of conservative aircraft executives, and he wasn't playing by their rules. Smirking on the sidelines, they were convinced that it would take an experienced aeronautical designer ten years and $100 million in capital to design, build, certify, and manufacture a business jet. As Lear later joked: "The bankers all went around to my competitors [asking], 'Can he make a jet?' And they'd say, 'Well, he doesn't know anything about aviation. He's not really an accredited aeronautical engineer. He doesn't have over ten million dollars . . . He probably won't be able to do it.'

"And of course the bankers were just rushing to me to make loans. One of them looked at me and he said, 'If you can tell me which one of my eyes is glass, why, I'll make you the loan.' And I said, 'I think it's your right eye.' And he said, 'What made you think so?' And I said, 'I finally detected a gleam of human kind-ness in it.'"

The only way Lear could stretch the $12 million he had set aside to design, fly, and certify the Lear Jet was to skip an impor-tant production step. Airplane manufacturers usually build a prototype craft first, fly it, and modify the design according to flight-test results, then begin crafting the expensive tools, dies, and jigs needed for mass production. Lear was so confident that his jet wouldn't have to be drastically modified after its first flight that he moved right into production tooling. He fully in-tended to sell Lear Jet #1. If he was wrong and major design changes had to be made between the first flight and certifica-tion, he'd be too broke to retool. "With this approach," he once confessed, "you're either very right or very wrong." And every-one from the bankers to the Lear workers to the executives at Beech, Boeing, and Cessna, watching from a wing's distance, knew it.

To make the project riskier still, few aviation and bank executives were convinced that corporations would buy business jets; most believed that the corporate market could not absorb more than a thousand airplanes of any kind during the next ten years. Cessna, for example, had done a marketing survey and concluded that the business aircraft market would not change radically; therefore, conventional piston-driven planes would remain the preference of the businessman. After its own survey, Beech concluded that the market called for a compromise between a jet and a piston-engine craft. In response, it launched into the turboprop. The only company to leap into the business jet market with Lear was Aero Commander. Neither Lear nor Aero Commander considered the JetStar and Sabreliner real competition because of their $1 million–plus price tag.

Lear dismissed his critics with his own brand of logic. "They don't ask the right questions," he told a reporter. "The trick is to discern a market before there is any proof that one exists. If you had said in 1925 that we would build nine million automobiles a year by 1965, some statistician would have pointed out that they would fill up every road in the United States and, lined up end to end, would go across the country eleven times. Surveys are no good. I make my surveys in my mind."

Lear's team understood the race. All he had to do was to turn them loose, give them leadership and direction, and pray that his money would hold out. If they couldn't be first and best — Aero Commander was further along than Lear and was promising the same performance for the same price — then they could at least be best.

Typically, Bill Lear began haunting the hangar, his dog Jet nipping at his heels. He looked over shoulders, challenged sketches, barked orders, called engineers "idiots," and let everyone know that the Lear Jet was *his* airplane, that since he was paying for it, he had the right to make *all* changes. To those engineers tasting Lear management for the first time and thinking that more work was getting done when Lear was out of town than when he was around, the hangar seemed chaotic: everyone running in different directions, smoke and sparks, things done one way on Monday and another on Tuesday, capricious changes. Contemptuous of engineers and their traditions, the old man always poked his chubby fingers into aerodynamic matters he didn't understand, wasting their time and his money.

It was the systems engineers, especially electrical, who bore the brunt of Lear's curiosity and demand for perfection. A connector rod in the control system was a case in point. Lear thought he had spotted a simpler way to connect a rod to give the ailerons better action. In most companies, such a new idea would first go to engineering for evaluation and, once approved, to a draftsman for careful drawings. Then a machinist would tool a prototype, which engineering would test, modify, and resketch. The new piece would go into production at long last.

Not at the Lear plant. There, Lear walked to the hangar corner where the rods were being made, collared a production worker, and modified the part with a few strokes of his pencil, explaining how he wanted the new system put together. "Call me when you have it finished," he ordered.

Test pilot Hank Beaird, who watched Lear work in Altenrhein and Wichita, put it this way: "The skeptics never realized how talented Bill was. If he decided he was going to do something, it didn't matter whether he knew anything about it or not. He'd find out. And it didn't take him very long. He could pick brains and get what he needed better than any man I ever knew."

What the handful of shocked engineers — who would later say that the Lear Jet was a stroke of hit-or-miss luck — didn't understand was that Lear was driven by a vision of beauty and simplicity in which every part sang harmony. ("You never have to repair or replace what you leave out of the design.") It was a vision in which the Lear Jet flew, looked, and felt good to pilot and passenger alike. And although it seemed as if the Lear Jet was jumping backward and sideways at the same time, in fact it was being driven forward in crooked lines by the man and his vision. His presence was everywhere. "Could five hundred men have painted the Sistine Chapel?" he would ask modestly when engineers questioned his tight control.

Part of Lear's vision was a business jet that weighed less than 12,500 pounds. Lear had calculated that the jet would fly one mile farther per gallon for every three pounds he could shave off it. A lighter plane would also fly faster, a critical marketing factor, and would cost less to land and park on the field or in a hangar, for fees are calculated by weight class. And, most important, keeping the aircraft under 12,500 pounds meant that it could be certified by the FAA under category three of its regulations, where specifications were simpler and certification faster. Lear was in a race not only with his bank account, but with Aero Commander as well.

As he passed his engineers and the workbenches, Lear would scan the drawing boards or heft a part to judge its weight. "How much?" he'd ask the engineer or machinist.

"Three grandmothers."

"Get rid of one," Lear would order.

"Grandmother" had been coined one day when an engineer trying to get Lear's approval on a design pleaded that the part weighed only four pounds. "Don't you know," Lear barked, "that I'd sell my grandmother to save just *one* pound?" The name had stuck.

The aerodynamic structure of the Lear Jet — wing, fuselage, empennage (tail assembly) — was not innovative, for Hank Waring, Don Grommesh, and others knew that Lear did not have the money to experiment with radical designs. The most he could expect to do was to push the state of the art forward by creating graceful aerodynamic lines. But within the basic structure, there was room for innovative features.

For example, Lear insisted on a door that opened out rather than in. In pressurized airplanes before the Lear Jet, doors plugged into the airframe from the inside and opened inward so that the cabin pressure could not blow them out. Lear had his engineers design a door that swung out and up, saving cabin space and 150 pounds while creating a natural umbrella for passengers. ("Don't tell me it can't be done!")

Lear and his engineers also worked hard to scale the furnishings so that the cabin looked and felt roomier than it actually was. They designed comfortable chairs that swiveled 180 degrees and slid along a track so that they could be placed anywhere or removed easily to create more cargo space. And he insisted that the baggage area itself be large, even if it meant taking feet from the cabin, because he felt that storage would be important to Lear Jet owners and their wives.

Recognizing that pilots would have a major say in which airplane a corporation should buy, Lear wanted not only a ship that flew beautifully, but a cockpit that was comfortable for pilots. He had his engineers design the same kind of chairs that the passengers had, using his own abundant bottom as the model. He designed a readable and practical instrument panel with no overhead controls, like most jets had. And he demanded a window that gave the pilot a 270-degree view, eliminating the claustrophobic feeling of most cockpits.

The windshield became his pride and joy once he found a Plexiglas company that could build one strong and light enough to satisfy him. He used to keep a three-foot-square piece of the material on a stand in his office. When he wanted to impress visitors, he'd either jump on it or drop a cannonball on it, catching the ball as it bounced back up.

After the pockmarked sample windshield had been abused for months, Fred Waring stopped in for a visit. Lear dropped the cannonball on the glass a few times. "Here, you try it," he told the musician.

"I'm a jinx, Bill," Waring objected. "Everything I've touched in the past couple of weeks has gone wrong."

When Lear insisted, Waring let loose, and the windshield shattered into a hundred pieces. Not embarrassed, Lear got on the phone and began chewing out the manufacturer.

Lear made his most important design contributions to the electronic and avionic systems on the Lear Jet. He hired Samuel Auld, who held six electronic patents with six more pending, to head the Electronics Division. Under Lear's leadership and Auld's direction, the Electronics Division created a whole line of integrated avionic instruments, from remote attitudinal and directional gyros, built around World War II surplus gyroscopes, to the lightest-weight jet autopilot ever made to electronic nose wheel steering.

As he had on the autopilot and Learstar programs, Lear ruled the hangar more through fear than incentive. But when he railed at stupidity and foot-dragging, it was a stage performance more often than not. He frequently "beat on the table, ranted, and raved" during engineering meetings, only to turn away from his red-faced staff and wink at a guest whom he had invited for the show. Recalls Beaird, who often saw Lear use his temper to get what he wanted: "Bill was a ham actor. The best."

But in spite of Lear's bursts of temper and his rigid control, spirit among the workers was incredibly high. Lear's own enthusiasm and confidence, the risk and the game, welded four hundred workers into a team. Fathers brought their children out to the hangar to show them the new airplane. Engineers gathered after work at the Diamond Club in the Diamond Inn and discussed the new ship. Lear would open a bottle late at night and have a nightcap with his boys. His eccentricity ("All geniuses are supposed to be eccentric. So I am"), his rolled-up-sleeves approach to management, and the way he thumbed his nose at the rest of the aviation community became legendary, helping to create an identity and esprit de corps that spilled over onto the Lear Jet itself.

The anonymous *Lear Jet Coloring Book,* "dedicated to the premise that everyone enjoys a good laugh . . . even when it's on himself," became a symbol of the Lear team effort:

"This is Buzz Nanney. Color him all black. His clothes are all black because he has been putting out fires in the back of the plant.

"This is Bob Hagan. He's our new test pilot. Bob is looking forward to the first flight. Color him brave.

"This is the first aircraft. We're all very proud of it. Color it too heavy.

"This is our founder 'chunky' Bill. Right now he's cooking the steaks he invented. Color them rare . . . Color Bill: angry, genius, unpredictable, kind, dynamic, genius, generous, raging, intelligent, genius, happy, ridiculous, friendly, genius, mad, inquisitive, absurd, bothersome, and genius . . ."

Lear loved it all. "What do you do when you've got it made, and you're over sixty years old?" he once asked before the first flight. "I figured it out. I could spend a thousand dollars a day until I was a hundred — and I'd just begin to nibble into the principal. But one way to condemn me to the most awful suffering would be to say 'Lear, you have to go sit on the beach.' Some men enjoy golf, others sports cars. For me, the best of life is the exercise of ingenuity — in design, in finance, in flying, in business. That is exactly what I'm doing here in Wichita."

25

MOST LEAR WORKERS followed the race to the first flight as closely as an Olympic marathon, for the airplane was, in a sense, their jet as well. As John Schoeppel said of the autopilot engineers: Lear had lifted them out of the boredom of mundane work, given them a chance to excel, to trounce the competition that had been turning out airplanes for decades, and to create what the painter and sculptor Harry Jackson would call "a work of art."

The tension and excitement in the Lear plant by day, and in the Diamond Club at night, was almost palpable as Lear drove the team toward the first flight. Ed Chandler, a Lear sales manager, recalls: "It was worth ten thousand dollars a year just to watch the action. You hated to go home at night because you would be scared to death you'd miss something."

- February 2, 1963. Assembly of Lear Jet #1 begins.
- April 23. Workers start sealing "wet" wings (where the fuel is stored), taking special care in molding the skin covering to prevent leaks.
- May 10. The Lear Jet radio station goes on the air, with one transceiver in the plant and one in Lear's station wagon.
- May 24. A life-size mockup of the Lear Jet is sent to the Aviation Writers Association convention in Dallas.
- June 7. The first fuselage leaves its jig. Engineers discover that the thrust of the GE engines exceeds expectations and the tail is redesigned.
- August 2. The forward and aft parts of the fuselage are mated.
- August 16. The wings and fuselage are mated and the door hinges pass the fatigue test (100,000 tests at 8.85 pounds per square inch, 21,000 tests at 11.8 psi) to determine if they can withstand pressurization of the cabin.
- September 15. Lear Jet #1 rolls out of the hangar, months behind the Aero Commander business jet; even though it's Sunday, three hundred Lear workers come to watch.

* * *

The only major change before the first flight was the redesign of the tail. The Lear Jet, which was designed for a maximum speed of 0.8 Mach (550 mph), was to have a horizontal tail in the form of a cross. But early tests showed that the ship would fly at 0.85 Mach (646 mph) or faster. Engineers argued that to keep the horizontal stabilizer (the short arm of the cross) level with the wing, as Gordon Israel had designed it, would be to invite vibrations that could cause metal fatigue and cracking. They recommended that Lear agree either to redesign the stabilizer high on the tail like a T or to cut back the thrust of the engines.

Lear fought the change at first, even though he wanted a hot rod, for it would be expensive and would delay the first flight for six to eight weeks. He told Grommesh, "That would be like taking seven new Cadillacs and driving them over a cliff."

"How would you like the stabilizer to break off during flight one day?" Grommesh answered.

Lear agreed to the change. "I had nightmares for weeks," he told Grommesh later. "I kept seeing that stabilizer breaking off in the air."

When the new tail was completed after forty days of around-the-clock work in shifts, the lines of the airplane looked cleaner and more streamlined than ever. "That," Lear said when they peeled away the scaffolding, "is the best-looking piece of tail I ever saw."

The mating of the new tail to the fuselage was symbolic of the magic Lear spun. Up to that point, the Lear Jet was a dream woven from sketches and drawings, mockups and models, bits and pieces, a wing here, a door there. But when tail wedded fuselage in a hangar ceremony, it was an emotional experience. Moya remembers it clearly: "We just stood there and wept. Everyone who came into the hangar that morning just couldn't believe how beautiful that was."

The first flight was scheduled for ten in the morning on October 6. As it stood in the sunlight, cloud white with a gleaming red stripe, Lear Jet 801-L was breathtaking. The ship was not a hangar-dweller. Its lines, power, and beauty could only be defined by open space and the sky.

To engineers like Hank Waring and Don Grommesh, the first flight meant something different from what it did for Moya, Nanney, and the assembly-line workers. They had never doubted the jet would fly, for it had gone through so many tests that there was no way it wouldn't lift its nose and run for the sky. They recognized, however, the public relations value of the first flight. For most people, the Lear Jet was just a "paper airplane" until it flew. To the engineers the big questions were: How well would it fly? Would it handle easily? How would it respond to the controls? Did the systems work well together? How many major changes would they have to make before the FAA could certify it? They would wait for the evaluation of the test pilots, who would know whether it was a winner or a loser.

To Lear, who was so convinced that his bird would fly that he had wanted to be his own test pilot, the first flight meant that and more. Wichita was littered with airplanes that never flew off the drawing boards. It would never take Bill Lear seriously until his plane was actually climbing into the clouds over the city. And until Wichita took him and his baby jet seriously, Lear would never be able to raise money to mass-produce it. One major setback could snap his fragile financial spine.

As Lear Jet #1 rolled down the runway and broke into a practice taxi, the nose wheel didn't castor when the pilot applied the brakes. The first flight was scrapped. Engineers worked through the night until midafternoon on October 7 to solve the problem. By that time, everyone was jittery but the engineers and pilots, who had expected last-minute delays.

Just after three, the Lear Jet crawled down the tarmac to Municipal Airport's runway 14, where it made a slow-speed run to the end. Everything checked out. The pilot turned the plane around and made a high-speed run of 70 knots (80 mph) on runway 32. Perfect. He brought the plane back to the hangar for its final fueling.

Lear's engineers and pilots had talked the old man out of test-flying the jet himself. The first flight could be dangerous, argued Hank Beaird, who had test-flown F-105s and F-84Hs as the chief experimental pilot at Republic Aviation. Even though the design and construction of the Lear Jet were sound and there was no reason to believe the bird wouldn't be a commercial success someday, something could always go wrong. And if #1 went down with Lear strapped in the seat, there would never be a #2.

Lear resigned himself to watching Beaird and Bob Hagan take his baby up. Like Beaird, Hagan held an engineering degree and, since 1953, had been Cessna's chief of flight testing for the T-37, 310, and 320, which Hank Waring had designed. Hagan would take the plane up, Beaird would bring it down.

At five-forty, Hagan pointed Lear Jet 801-L toward runway 19, where more than a thousand people waited. It was already dusk, and the sky had blushed for the occasion. If they had waited another half hour, the tower would have canceled the flight. Lear was sitting in the cab of a pickup with a transceiver, microphone in hand. Eight technicians were crowded into the back of a truck just in case something went wrong. Moya, Tina, and David stood nearby. "It was the most exciting, wonderful moment of my entire life," Moya wrote Shanda. "Daddy was sopping wet with excitement . . . He had a heavy cold and it disappeared very suddenly!"

Hagan did another slow taxi, then a fast one. Lear pushed the button on the microphone. "That bird looks like it wants to fly," he told Beaird, who was handling communication. "Let her go."

The Cessna chase plane, piloted by Jim Kirkpatrick and John Lear, was already circling the airfield, waiting for 801-L to blast off. Hagan let it go. It ate up 1,700 feet of runway and, at a speed of 103 mph, lifted its nose. June Shields, who had been up until three that morning typing press releases and fact sheets, was near Bill and Moya, her heart hammering. "I'm standing there, almost part of the boss," she recalls, "watching him, watching the airplane. I hear him say to Hank on the radio, 'By gosh, it's up! It's up! You've got it up!' Pretty soon I hear Hank sounding elated. He just sounds like he is on a high, he's so pleased up there. There is this feeling of joy. It is like having a perfect baby born. After all this time, the kid is finally there and you count his toes, just a remarkable thing."

After takeoff, Hagan made a performance climb at 170 knots (195 mph) to 3,000 feet over the north end of the runway, then reduced speed to look over the nose, continuing the climb to 5,000 feet, where the chase plane checked to see if the landing gear was in place and if fuel was leaking. Kirkpatrick gave the go-ahead from the Cessna. Beaird retracted the gear, causing the plane to nose up slightly, then to nose back down when it locked. The engine noise was surprisingly low.

Hagan continued to climb to 10,000 feet, making turns to check the aileron response. The plane obeyed well. He pushed the rudder, allowing the ship to oscillate from side to side. Directional stability was excellent. With gear up and gear down, 801-L felt solid, steady, easy to control.

Increasing his speed to 115 knots (132 mph), Hagan lowered the flaps and landing gear. There was almost no jerky trim change — a remarkable design feat. With the flaps down and speed brakes extended as if Hagan were trying to land at 10,000 feet, the Lear Jet began to fall out of the sky. The speed brakes worked so well that Hagan had to maintain a steep dive angle to hold the speed at 125 knots (144 mph).

Beaird took over, increasing the speed to 250 knots (287 mph) for the descent. The jet had been up and out of sight for nearly thirty minutes.

As soon as the radio stations announced that the Lear Jet had taken off, people began coming out to watch it land. One mile of the shoulder of Highway 42 stretching along the airport was bumper to bumper with cars. The tension was thick as eyes scanned the darkening sky for the first glimpse of a white needle piercing the clouds.

Then they saw it, a speck tinged in orange. The crowd let out a cheer. And long before Beaird brought the bird down to 500 feet for a pass across the airfield, a victory lap, they waved and applauded.

Beaird led the jet back up to its assigned altitude and entered the downwind leg for landing. The speed brakes slowed the ship to 175 knots (201 mph). The deceleration was rapid and smooth. At 125 knots, he extended the gear, making a perfect, graceful landing at 90 knots.

There wasn't a dry eye among the Lear workers. Moya hung on to Tina and sobbed. "Our hearts and our blood and everything else was spread out over the runway that day in Wichita," she remembers.

Only Bill showed no emotion at all. As 801-L rolled to a halt, he pulled out his Lear Jet door key and joked to Nanney, who was weeping, "You didn't think I'd let those truckers jump out and leave that airplane up in the air, did you?"

Hagan summarized the flight in glowing terms. "The airplane performed better on its first flight than any first flight that Hank or I have ever made," he wrote. "There were no unusual noises and the noise level was very low for a plane that is yet without insulation. There will undoubtedly be changes as we get further into the test program, but I think I can safely say that the Lear Jet Corporation has itself one hell of an airplane."

Hank Beaird agreed. "The airplane accelerates faster on takeoff than any airplane I have flown to date, including the jet- and turboprop-powered YF-84H."

There was a party that night at the Diamond Club. Perhaps more than most, Buzz Nanney was on a high, for he had never been convinced the Lear Jet would fly.

"Wasn't that an exciting thing?" he bubbled to Lear.

"Not to me," Lear said.

"What do you mean?" Nanney had been expecting a lecture on how Bill Lear had just made history again.

"I've already flown that airplane so many times in my sleep, I knew it would fly," Lear said. "I had no doubt about it."

After a few more drinks, Nanney got mad at the old man for refusing to admit that his heart was pounding and there was a tear in his blue eye.

Lear poured his congratulations into a brief note to his staff: "My sincere thanks and appreciation to each and every one of you for your unstinted day and night effort. This first flight puts us on 'first base.' Now we will make it a 'homer' by completing certification and delivering aircraft by April next."

The official party for more than six hundred employees and their guests was held a week later at the Cotillion Ballroom. Introduced by Wee Georgie Wood, a British comedian and friend of Ole Olsen, nine-year-old Tina sang "My Pa" and "Hello Mudda, Hello Fadduh"; Moya and Nanney led a sing-along; and John did his Jack Benny impersonation on a squeaky violin.

"They said I would never build the plane," Lear told the press. "Well, I did. They said my plane would never fly. Well, it did. They say we won't succeed. Well, we *will*."

26

THE GAMBLE paid off. During the next nine months, although the Lear Jet was riddled with minor flaws and problems, Lear had to make no major modifications. All he had to do was prove to the FAA that his plane was airworthy before Aero Commander. That would not be easy, for Jet Commander had beaten him to its first flight by almost eight months.

By the end of January 1964, Hank Beaird had logged more than fifty flight tests in Lear Jet #1. During one flight, he pushed the plane to 0.905 Mach (699 mph), making the Lear Jet the fastest business plane ever flown. But during landings, Beaird noticed that the jet had a tendency to stall when it shouldn't. He studied his hands on the final approach and noted that he was frequently correcting the airplane when it should almost have been flying itself. Although he had easily adapted to the personality of the Lear Jet, could he expect less experienced pilots to do the same? After conferring with other Lear Jet test pilots who had observed the same stall characteristics, Beaird recommended to Lear that he redesign the leading edge of the wing.

"I'm not going to," Lear told him.

"You really have to," Beaird said.

"It costs too much. I've already got the tooling set up for the leading edge."

"I'm not going to argue with you," Beaird said. "It's your airplane. If you want a second-class plane —"

Lear grabbed Beaird by the coat. "What do you mean, second class?"

"Well," Beaird said, "it would just be a hot rod that doesn't fly too well."

Beaird, Lear, and his engineers modified the leading edge. To save time and money, Bill hired an auto body repairman for less than $100 to reshape the wing with body putty. The plane almost flew itself.

If modifying the Lear Jet after the first flight was no problem, meeting FAA regulations was. The agency had inherited from the Civil Aeronautics Board a long list of rules filled with over-lapping specifications and outdated requirements. For years, the CAB had been adding regulations without taking the time to catalogue them, and the job of pruning the deadwood had fallen into the lap of its successor, the FAA, which was established in 1958. By 1964, the job had not yet been completed.

To complicate matters, the Lear Jet was the first jet to request certification in category three (under 12,500 pounds), which had no regulations yet. The FAA had rules for piston-driven planes in category three and for jets in category four (over 12,500 pounds). Once again, Bill Lear found himself in uncharted waters. Just as he had forced the manufacturers of navigation instruments to run to keep up with him, he was now pushing the FAA with his jet.

"It just boggled everyone's mind," recalls Stanley Green, an FAA engineer and attorney who helped to draw up a list of "special conditions" for the certification of the Lear Jet. "Everyone at the FAA was adding regulations. The FAA had zero to no knowledge. All its knowledge came from airline experience."

Even after the rules had been made reasonable, the certification process still threatened to become interminable. The whole airplane had to be tested, piece by piece, in the hangar. Stress and fatigue tests on the frame, pressurization tests on the cabin. Evaluations of the electrical, hydraulic, navigation, and utility systems. Then the plane itself had to be flight-tested with an FAA pilot to make sure it performed well and that its systems worked individually and together in flight. FAA pilots had to check takeoff and landing, response time, vibration and stall characteristics, how fast and how slow the airplane could fly safely. Based on the flight tests, the FAA inspectors and pilots had to prepare a list of the Lear Jet's limitations so that pilots would know its maximum speed, weight and fuel requirements, and landing field lengths. Finally, maintenance manuals had to be prepared and approved as well as pilot training and rating procedures. Anything could go wrong anywhere.

And it did. Lear engineers and FAA inspectors caught a host of flaws and problems. To name a few: de-icing, pressurization, fuel additives, weight, temperature control, nose wheel steering, warning lights, lightning strike protection, and oil temperature gauges. For months on end, FAA inspectors lived in the hangar, and Lear hounded them as if they were his own people. When he felt they were nitpicking, he would complain to their bosses in Washington. During one phone call early in June 1964, he told an FAA official in Washington that he was "personally very disgusted with the impractical way" the inspectors were handling the Lear Jet. If he did not get his certification by June 20, he threatened, he would close the factory and "take the matter to the highest authority possible."

It wasn't all bluff. Lear was close to broke. By April 1964, six months after the first flight but before certification, Lear had taken orders for twenty-one airplanes. By May, he had spent the $10,000 deposit he had collected on each and had exhausted his bank credit against future deliveries. Bob Graf helped save the day. An airplane distributor who had fallen in love with the Lear Jet the moment he set eyes on it, Graf became a Lear Jet distributor even though there were no airplanes to deliver. Recognizing that the plane could die in the hangar before proving its worth in the marketplace, Graf put the squeeze on several other distributors. Together they collected orders for another thirty-one Lear Jets. With $310,000 in cash and a string of new orders, Lear got enough bank credit to buy several more months, but not enough to see him through certification.

Under financial pressure, Lear and his engineers found ways to test the jet's components to the satisfaction of the FAA inspectors without expensive equipment. For example, to test the Lear Jet's nose wheel steering, Lear had mechanics weld a huge angle iron with a platform on it to the front bumper of his new Oldsmobile station wagon. He weighted the platform with sacks of sand to simulate the weight of the airplane, attached the nose wheel to the front of the angle iron, and connected it to the steering mechanism of the car. Then he drove it down the runway at speeds up to 110 miles an hour, testing for shimmy.

Clay Lacy watched the testing and problem solving with fascination. Lacy had met Bill at the Lear Incorporated factory in Santa Monica in the late 1950s while shopping for a new transistorized autopilot. Rather than ask a salesman to show him one, Lear took him up in the Twin Beech for a demonstration. They flew to Los Angeles International to test the autopilot and approach coupler on the airport's instrument landing system. After a dozen approaches, Lear gave the wheel to Lacy while he heated up a soldering iron to make circuit adjustments. "He really understands and makes these things," Lacy thought to himself. He bought one.

In mid 1964, a potential Lear Jet customer asked Lacy to check the plane out for him. A United Airlines pilot at the time, Lacy liked what he saw in Wichita. When Beaird took him up for a Lear Jet ride, he liked what he felt even more. "A great little bird," Lacy told Lear. "But it still has a lot of problems." Lear hired him at $100 a day when he wasn't flying for United to help improve the bird. Lacy found Lear open to suggestions. "Bill would take anybody's ideas if they worked," Lacy explains. "After two or three weeks, they became *his* ideas. But that never bothered me. He was not a guy that had to personally reinvent the wheel."

Lacy loved to sit in meetings when Lear engineers proposed solutions to such problems as moisture collecting in the hydraulic cylinders. Lear listened carefully to each proposal. By the time the last engineer was finished, he had selected the idea he wanted to try. Recalls Lacy: "Everyone else would just throw his paper in the trash because that was it. Bill always took the big bite. If something didn't work the first time, he'd take a couple of stabs at trying to modify it. And if that didn't work, he'd chuck it and say, 'Let's start over!'"

Lacy was amazed at how well the Lear system worked. "They turned that thing from a shell that flew pretty well to an airplane with systems that were working well," he explains. "They solved more problems than I could have ever dreamed."

Lear's big break during the FAA inspection came on June 4, 1964. On her way to the plant, Moya saw smoke curling up from a muddy cornfield two miles southeast of Municipal's runway 19. She turned on the radio only to hear that Lear Jet #1 had crashed and burned. She rushed to the plant to get the full story.

It was a test flight with FAA pilot Donald Keubler in the left seat and Lear Jet test pilot James Kirkpatrick in the right. The flight was number one hundred sixty-seven for Lear Jet #1. Keubler was evaluating the airplane's performance on one engine, and after several successful runs, he made a mistake. He forgot to retract the wing spoilers, which destroy lift, after one landing. When he took off, he couldn't keep the airplane in the air and had to set it down easily in a cornfield. He and Kirkpatrick climbed out of the plane, which barely had a scratch. Unfortunately, the landing broke a fuel line and the plane caught on fire. By the time firemen got the flames under control, there was nothing left but a charred airframe and a pile of ashes.

As soon as Lear learned that no one was injured, he was delighted. He called his staff into his office for a briefing. Word that he was finished was traveling through the aviation industry like a brushfire. "Okay," Lear said with a grin, "we've just sold our first Lear Jet." The insurance money could not have come at a better time. Furthermore, Bill had Lear Jet #2, which his friend Justin Dart had bought for cash, sitting in the hangar. Lear used the FAA's embarrassment to extend the flight-test program to seven days a week, with two crews making up to seven flights a day.

The Reading Air Show was in progress and, as Lear told his staff, "we're going to be there." But first, Lear Jet #2 had to be fitted with instruments and ground-tested. Lear drove his team furiously and they made the deadline.

Moya described to her son David the Lear Jet's flight into the Reading airport: "I'll never forget flying to the Reading Air Show and watching them just drop their tools as they saw this beautiful airplane steaming up the ramp. The first Lear Jet anybody's ever seen. That was such a thrill because they all knew we would never make it. No one thought we would. Except me and your dad and a few others."

The Lear Jet, Model 23, received its type certification on July 31, 1964, seven weeks after the first plane crashed and four months before the Jet Commander was certified. From its first flight to certification had taken only ten months, a new record. It was the birth of a new civil aircraft, the first American jet designed primarily for business executives to be government approved. Stanley Green gives Lear full credit. "He drove me and the whole FAA right up the wall," he explains. "He was intolerant of waste or delay."

The certification party at the Diamond Inn was "sheer exuberance," as Moya put it. While Bill was skinny-dipping in the motel pool, a Lear worker swiped his shorts. The next morning, they waved from the company flagpole. Painted on them in big red letters was FAA CERTIFICATION.

For Bill Lear, the flagpole caper was symbolic. Throughout the tense months of inspection, with one crisis tripping over another, he had taken out his frustration with the FAA by calling it "the carbuncle on the ass of aviation."

By the time Najeeb Halaby formally gave Bill Lear the FAA certification, Lear was broke. He had spent the $11 million he had allocated for the development of the Lear Jet and had borrowed all he could, using as collateral Le Ranch, his home in Wichita as well as new homes in Greece and Palm Springs, and Moya's Rubens paintings. Lear had no choice but to go public again. It was the only way he could raise the $6 million he needed to start mass-producing and selling his airplane. On July 30, 1964, the day before certification, Lear applied to the Securities and Exchange Commission for permission to offer Lear Jet common stock to the public.

Naturally, it would take months for Lear to find an underwriter and for the SEC to complete both its investigation of the Lear Jet Corporation and its paperwork. To tide him over, Lear asked all his managers and key personnel to accept a temporary salary cut. He promised not only to pay them back, but to give them stock options as well. Most agreed. They believed in Lear Jet; they had sweat, worry, tears, and a year of Saturdays in it; and they believed in Bill Lear.

They weren't disappointed. Lear Jet became publicly owned on November 30, 1964, when Lear sold 550,000 shares for $10 each through Van Alstyne, Noel and Company. Lear retained a 60 percent ownership and remained the president and chairman of the Board. He bragged that he had firm orders for sixty-three airplanes, worth $30 million. (Aero Commander had yet to sell a single Jet Commander.) Lear saved $2.5 million of the sale price as working capital and spent the rest: $1.5 million to reduce his debts, $1 million for tooling and manufacturing equipment, and half a million to double his floor space. Keeping his promise, he paid all back salaries and gave those who had supported him generous stock options.

Lear was flying. He divided the country into six sales regions, with a Lear Jet distributor in each. Bill Jr., whom the old man had fired as vice president of Lear International during a heated argument and who now co-owned the Executive Aviation Corporation in Geneva, became Lear Jet's exclusive distributor in Europe, Africa, and the Near and Middle East. Distributors paid $50,000 each for the franchise and got a 5 percent discount on every Lear Jet they ordered. Sales contracts called for a $50,000 deposit on signing a purchase order for a jet; $100,000 when the plane went into production; $125,000 on the mating of the wing and fuselage; and the rest of the $550,000 upon delivery.

Always brimming with ideas, Lear had another moneymaking project up his sleeve. Early in 1963, before the Lear Jet made its first flight, Shanda had picked up her father at the Santa Monica airport in a Lincoln Continental that she had borrowed from the son of Earl Muntz, a former used car dealer and inventor. Attached to the dashboard was Muntz's new four-track car stereo tape player. Shanda knew her father would be interested in the Muntz Auto-Stereo because of his early work on car radios and wire recorders.

Not only was he interested, he immediately sensed a great market potential, as Muntz obviously had. Not one to wait for something to happen, Lear asked Shanda to drive him to see Earl Muntz. When he left the inventor a few hours later, Lear was sole Midwest distributor for the Muntz Auto-Stereo. And when Lear landed his Learstar in Wichita, it was filled with Muntz add-on tape players.

Lear and his chief electronics engineer, Sam Auld, began tearing the players apart to see how they worked. Soon they saw ways to improve them. Auld collected a development team (Richard Kraus, James Paysen, Klaus Kindt, Christa Kindt, Sylvester Breit) and began working on the four-track late at night, after spending the day designing and testing Lear Jet avionics equipment, especially the autopilot. "A lot of times, just the two of us would be there until maybe two o'clock in the morning," Auld recalls. "Some nights we were there all night. And a lot of times, when we needed a part modified, Bill would actually go back into the machine shop and take the part with him and chuck it out on the lathe."

At first, Lear and Auld just tried to iron out the bugs in Muntz's recorder, as Lear had done with the Lockheed Lodestar; but the more they modified the instrument, the more changes they felt they needed. One day they simply said: "We'll start from scratch and make one the way it ought to be." The first major change was the motor that drove the tape across the head at an uneven rate, creating musical chords and notes that were far from pure. Feeling more than hearing the interruption in the music, Lear assigned Auld and his team to design a motor that would not oscillate. With the help of Alan Shire, they tooled an inside-out beltless motor with direct drive and low speed for better quality and longer life.

Next, Lear became dissatisfied with the dinner plate size of the cartridge that guided the tape through the player. It was not only too large but was so complicated that the tape tended to bunch up and snarl like Lear's old wire recorder. Lear designed a unique cartridge that soon became standard in the industry.

Finally, Lear began thinking of ways to get two hours of music on the tape instead of Muntz's one. He had two choices: keep four tracks and slow the motor speed to 1¾ inches per second, or use eight tracks at the usual 3¾ inches per second. Since the tape available in the early 1960s did not have good fidelity at slower speeds, Lear decided to go to eight tracks. He consulted Alexander M. Pontitoff, the founder of Ampex and the father of magnetic tape recording. "I tried to put eight tracks on a quarter-inch tape," Pontitoff told Lear, according to Auld. "You can't do it. Just can't squeeze that much information on it." That was all Bill Lear needed to hear.

Lear knew he had a great idea. Late at night, the plant would be dark except for the light in the laboratory, where Lear and Auld would try one thing after another until they had eight tracks on the tape and playing beautifully. "With Lear Jet going on *and* the eight-track," Auld recalls, "Bill was in seventh heaven."

When they finished the eight-track in the fall of 1964, they had a new machine: a smaller, simpler, and more efficient brushless motor; a more rugged spool with fewer parts, hence cheaper to manufacture; an endless tape cartridge that the user would never have to rewind or flip while driving; two hours of music that would begin as soon as a cartridge was slipped into the player; a combined radio and tape player built into the dashboard, not stuck on as an appendage; and fourteen new patents, some of them with Sam Auld.

Lear took the prototype of the Lear Stereo Eight to General Motors and Ford, hoping they would offer it as an option on new cars. Both sent a few new cars to Wichita so that Auld and his team could install demonstration models for their auto executives to test-drive. Auld even put one in Henry Ford's Lincoln Continental — four speakers and a player that produced near-flawless music, custom-crafted to fit the dash. It was a typical Lear prototype, smart-looking and close to perfect.

Ford cautiously agreed to offer the Lear Stereo Eight on some of its 1966 models. Lear's old friend at Motorola, Elmer Wavering, helped put the deal together. Lear wanted to build his own machines, then sell them to Ford, but he didn't have a factory yet. Wavering worked out a compromise: Motorola would make the units for Ford and pay Lear a royalty on each set sold; RCA would tape music from its library and distribute the eight-track cassettes nationally; and Lear Jet would manufacture the plastic cartridges.

In April 1965, five months after Lear had gone public, Lear Jet, RCA, and Ford announced their deal. RCA promised to offer everything from the Beatles to Beethoven in the fall, and Ford promised to offer the Lear Stereo Eight in its Lincoln Continental, Ford Galaxie LTD, and Thunderbird. For Bill Lear, the announcement was two firsts rolled in one — the first to introduce stereo tapes into a new car market and the first to offer the eight-track.

It was a good start, but too limited for Bill Lear, who knew he had a superb product that could not fail. The question was: At the risk of losing great potential sales, should he wait for the eight-track market to develop, then produce players and cartridges to meet it? Or should he anticipate the market and immediately begin mass production, running the risk of carrying a huge inventory until the idea caught on?

Bill Lear anticipated. In February 1965, he leased a 54,000-

square-foot warehouse in Detroit from Motorola and leaped into production. "We had no market," recalls Ken Miller, who ran the operation. "But Bill wanted to hit with great impact. We soon had a hundred thousand players and no orders. We went from a dead start to high production."

But Lear was confident. "Tape playback in automobiles is going to be the next big thing," he said. "I'm going to be in the position of a man with a boat full of life jackets following a ship he knows is going to sink. He won't have any trouble selling them."

William Powell Lear was on a roll. By June 1965, he had firm orders for more than 100 Lear Jets ($60 million) and was projecting sales of 120 per year for the next ten years. A Lear Jet purchased by Harold Quandt flew the 5,577 miles from Wichita to Frankfurt, West Germany, in 10 hours, 11 minutes, averaging 540 miles an hour. It was Lear Jet's first foreign sale and first transoceanic flight. Another Lear Jet set three world speed records on a round-trip flight from Los Angeles to New York (10 hours, 27 minutes) with seven passengers aboard.

Lear plunged forward. Just after Lear Jet stock peaked at $83 a share (he had offered it at $10 a year earlier), Lear announced a new Lear Jet, Model 24, a slightly heavier version of Model 23, to be certified in the air transport category so he could say that the FAA had tested his baby jet as rigorously as a Boeing 707. And he unveiled the Lear Liner, Model 40, destined for an "untapped market."

The Lear Liner, which would sell for $1.5 million, would hold a maximum of twenty-eight passengers and would fill the gap between the small executive jet and commercial airliners like the DC-9, which ferried forty to fifty passengers. It could also be designed to tote a larger number of corporate executives in a roomier cabin than a Lear Jet Model 24. Lear announced that the Model 40 would cruise at 508 miles an hour at a comfortable 45,000 feet and have a transcontinental range of 3,200 miles with fifteen passengers aboard. Lear promised to have the Lear Liner in the air in eighteen months and first delivery in two years.

As if the Lear Liner and Lear Jet Model 24 were not enough, Lear announced in mid November that he was designing a twin-engine, single-propeller pusher aircraft that would sell for $75,000 and be ready in three years. A spinoff of his early SAAC-23 designs, the Lear Single-Twin would hold five to six passengers, cruise at 25,000 feet at 350 to 400 miles an hour, and be built by a new company financed by Lear's own money. To raise the capital, Lear offered 100,000 shares of his own Lear Jet stock in the over-the-counter market, hoping to get $68.20 per share (the mean of "bid" and "asked"), or $6,473,000.

At sixty-three, Lear was flying.

27

BILL AND MOYA WERE happy. The Lear Jet years were the most fulfilling and exciting period of their lives. Moya shared Bill's dream, and because Bill was at the plant most of the time, he was home most of the time too. There was little of the globe-trotting — the compulsive trips to Santa Monica and Grand Rapids, Rome and Munich, the sudden flights to test some new piece of equipment — that had marked the earlier years.

Moya got involved in community affairs, in the Wichita Art Association and the Kansas Historical Society, among others. And Bill played out the role of eccentric genius. He appeared at formal parties in shirtsleeves and old sweaters, sometimes two days early or a week late, his hosts never knowing if he'd be coming alone, with Moya, or with three or four other people who happened to be in his home or office at the time. He was incessantly on the phone and even had one installed in his executive bathroom so he could give the people he was talking to "a chance to hear him tinkle. Half of Wichita thought he was crazy." Stories about him and Lear Jet soon grew into legends in the tightly knit aviation community.

Bill once had a dental appointment in Kansas City, one story went, and wanted to fly there in a Lear Jet. "Which one is ready?" he asked Hank Beaird.

Beaird pointed to two company planes parked outside the hangar.

"I'm not interested in those," Lear said. "Whose is that red and white one?"

"That belongs to Carrol Meyer," Beaird said. Meyer was the chief pilot for Winship Air Service of Anchorage, Alaska.

"Take it!" Lear said. As far as he was concerned, every Lear Jet belonged to him no matter who had bought it.

They roared off in Meyer's jet, and when they returned three hours later, there stood Carrol Meyer in the middle of the ramp, fists on his hips. "Who the hell swiped my airplane?" he shouted.

Lear stepped out of the jet and smiled. "Well, Carrol," he said, "one of the reasons you brought your plane back here was to get the autopilot tuned, wasn't it?"

"You bet."

"Well, I invented that autopilot, and I like to test them myself to make sure they're tuned just right."

Lear and Meyer walked into the customer service building arm in arm.

Another time, Bill sent five Lear Jets and five former fighter pilots to the Reading Air Show. (It was one of the few times Lear himself stayed home.) The finale was the flyby, when the airplanes showed their grace and guts to the pilots and business executives shopping for new aircraft. The FAA rules for the flyby were strict — no formations, only 20-degree banks, no skimming the runway, no rolls.

Just like the Blue Angels, the five Lear Jets came streaking in for the approach in military formation. "Foul," the competition cried.

As they screamed over the airfield, they began to peel off, one at a time, at a 40-degree bank. "Foul," the competition cried.

While the other four Lear Jets disappeared into the clouds, the lead plane zipped back and skimmed the runway at about ten feet, screeching by at 400 miles an hour, then climbing at 80 degrees to the clouds, where it rolled and rolled again. "Foul," the competition cried.

Lear Jet salesmen rushed to the phone to tell Lear what had happened, expecting him to cuss out his pilots. "Wonderful,"

Lear shouted. "Wonderful! Send me the bill for the fines."

Another time, a third story went, Clyde Martin, a Potlatch Forest pilot, convinced company executives to buy a Lear Jet. Martin waited and waited for delivery. "Go down to Wichita," the company finally told him, "and sit there until you get that jet."

Martin registered at the Diamond Inn. Bored with reading magazines and pacing in the Lear hangar, he started giving tours of the plant to visitors. By that time everyone knew Clyde Martin except Bill Lear.

One day, Lear was inspecting the plant with Buzz Nanney and spotted Martin. "Nanney, you see that guy over there?" he asked. "He doesn't do a damn thing but read magazines and walk around the plant. Fire the sonofabitch!"

"That's Potlatch Forest's pilot, Bill," Nanney said. "He's waiting for delivery on his airplane."

"Well, in that case," Lear said, "invite him into the office and I'll buy him a drink."

Bill was never satisfied with his Lear Jet windshield and always found new ways to see how tough it was. One day he told Nanney, "Get me a whole arsenal of guns."

Nanney called the sheriff while Lear set up the windshield in a two-by-four frame on the west side of the Lear Jet ramp. A police officer soon pulled up with a trunk full of guns. The officer selected a .38 and fired at the thick Plexiglas. It didn't break. "What a windshield!" Lear said with great pride.

The officer tried a .45. "Boy, what a windshield," Lear said when it didn't crack.

Next, the officer shot a .44. The windshield held up. "What a windshield," Lear said.

Peeking into the trunk of the car, Lear saw a strange-looking shotgun. "What's that?" he asked Nanney.

"A riot gun with a magnum load."

"I want to shoot it," Lear said.

"It'll knock you on your ass," Nanney said. "Let the officer shoot it."

He did and the windshield blew all to hell.

Lear smiled. "Boy, what a gun!" he said.

The stories kept coming out of Wichita and were repeated

over and over again wherever Lear Jets flew and pilots met. Bill loved it all. But if he and Moya were happy in Kansas, not everyone in the family was. Shanda, for one, was miserable. A long list of hurts over the years came to a head in Wichita and drove her back to Geneva.

When Shanda was little she hardly saw her father, who always seemed to be somewhere else. She would wait eagerly at the airport with Moya and Littlejohn for her father's plane to land because for days her mother had been telling her that Daddy was coming home. But after a big hug and kiss, it would be as if he had never returned. He'd run off to the office, to the General, or someplace else. Whenever they did sit at the round table to eat together, she simply listened to her father lecture. The most she felt welcome to do was ask questions.

One early bruise still ached. She had wanted a horse so badly that she talked and dreamed about nothing else. One day her father came home and told her that he had one. "It's in the garage," he said.

Shanda ran out to the garage, expecting to see a horse in a trailer. When there wasn't any, she opened the car door and found a hobbyhorse on the back seat. She burst into tears.

As she grew older, Shanda welcomed the "stability and sanctuary of boarding school," where she could study in peace because she was determined to get an education. "Dad would always remind us that he never found school necessary," she recalls. "He never pushed us to go to school and to get good grades. I don't remember him ever reading a report card and encouraging us. He felt that since he was a genius, his children should also be geniuses. If our teachers were strict or demanding, the solution was always to leave school. Never were we encouraged to stick it out." By the time she moved to Wichita at the age of eighteen, Shanda had lived in sixteen homes and boarding schools.

Shanda found Wichita especially painful. As a young woman with musical talent, she resented her father's lack of interest in her future career and his attempts to marry her off to a Lear Jet engineer, certain that he only wanted a son-in-law he could use as free labor. But even more than her father's insensitivity, Shanda came to resent her younger sister, Tina.

Having seen more of her father in her ten years than Shanda and John had in their combined thirty-seven, Tina neither feared nor resented her father as they did. As a result, where they were cool and aloof, she was warm and affectionate with him, sitting in his lap and hugging and kissing him, and he responded in kind. It became obvious even to visitors that, as Moya put it, "he absolutely worshiped Tina." He could not resist making comparisons — Tina is sweeter than Shanda, smarter, more talented, more beautiful — abusing his older daughter the way Gertrude had abused him. Like her father at eighteen, Shanda became convinced that the only way she could preserve her identity was to leave home. In 1964, she moved back to Le Ranch. "You were never encouraged to do anything," she says, explaining her flight. "So you sat around and paid court to Dad. Dad was the center of attention. You had to sit there and listen to his old jokes, to his stories on politics, or get out. There was no other way. And I chose to get out."

By contrast, Wichita was quite happy for Tina. Also a budding musician, she loved to perform for guests, and Bill was especially proud of her even though he rarely sat in the room while she played the piano and sang. (She could never figure out why. Sometimes she thought that he couldn't cope with her being the center of attention; sometimes, that he couldn't bear her occasional sour notes during a difficult classical piece.) No matter what time of night people would drop by, he'd awaken her over the protests of Moya and ask her to play. Most of the time she was delighted to do it — especially the night Danny Kaye was there.

One cloud in Tina's sky were her schoolmates, who heard their parents talking about that upstart Bill Lear. "They just hated me," Tina recalls. "I must have been blowing my dad's horn, so I was asking for it in some way. But I remember that it was not happy. They made fun of my father. They would say: 'Your dad thinks he knows everything. He doesn't know anything.' They would make fun of what the Lear Jet was going to look like. Make fun of me because I lived in a big house."

Another cloud was Bill's dog, Jet. Everywhere he went, Jet would go too. The dog loved Bill so much that he wouldn't go to sleep at night until Bill spread the shirt he had been wearing on a chair for him. One day, while Bill and Moya were away, Tina left the screen door open. Jet got out and was run over by a car. When he heard the news, Bill was so sad he stayed away for three days, and when he finally came home, he wouldn't talk to Tina, afraid he might say something that would hurt her.

Wichita wasn't an especially happy place for David, either. Like John, he stood in awe of his father and withdrew, preferring to stay out of his way rather than to endure the question, "Why don't you use your brain for something other than a knot to keep your backbone from slipping?" Like his half-sister, Patti, he learned about his father's women the most direct way. One day he came home from school to see his father and another man sitting in the living room, each with his arm around a young woman. His father didn't seem embarrassed, so the boy didn't think much of it. But as he walked out of the room, David heard the other man ask his father, "Do you think he'll say anything?" A couple of years later, David picked up the phone to make a call and overheard his father and a woman — probably the General — describe in anatomical detail what they would do to each other the next time they met. In a state of partial shock, the teenager called Patti, who calmed him down.

As a teenager, David liked to spend Friday nights camping out in the hangar with some of his buddies. They drove the forklifts around and peeled rubber on anything that moved. One Friday night, David found a new use for the Xerox machine. He copied both sides of a $1 bill, cut them to size, and glued them into play money. Then he shoved the bill into the changemaker in the cafeteria. Four quarters trickled out. David had a little business going. He kept a small stack of the play money in June Shields's file cabinet, under *B* for bills.

When the vending machine employees found the play money, they complained to Buzz Nanney, who called in the Secret Service to hunt down the counterfeiters. One day after school, David answered the doorbell. A man in a trenchcoat was standing there and flashed his badge. "Are you David Lear?" he asked. "I'd like to ask you some questions."

When he heard how his son beat the coin changer, Bill Lear was delighted. "If he can do that when he's only fourteen," he told Nanney, "imagine how good he'll be when he grows up."

It was in Wichita that Bill bought flying lessons for David. Before David thought he was ready to solo, his instructor, Ray

Starr, had him solo. And before David thought he was ready to solo cross-country, Starr had him make the trip alone. David got lost. Starr had forgotten to tell his student that to pick up the navigation beacon, he had to be 5,000 to 10,000 feet up. David was cruising along at 2,500. Like the old airmail pilots, he spotted a water tower and swooped down until he could read the name of the town painted on it.

When Shanda moved back to Switzerland, David asked to go along. With no parental guidance, he had a good time and his grades at the tough Ecole Bénédict, where all the courses were taught in French, began to take a dive. Bill and Moya ordered him home. They met him in Chicago and drove him off to Culver Military Academy in Indiana, where, like his half brother, Bill Jr., before him, he "almost died" of homesickness. For years after he left Culver, David had nightmares about being sent back.

Bill Lear knew he wasn't a good father but could never figure out why. For most of his life, he had, as Tina put it, "moments of terrible grief and remorse about his failings as a father." He'd watch a television show or a movie about fathers and children and start to cry, telling anyone who would listen — Moya, the children, guests — that he was a bad parent. One day, he called Shanda, Tina, and David into the master bedroom in Wichita, put his arms around them, and started weeping. He asked their forgiveness for being a "lousy" father and said he was not "worthy of their love and affection." Hugging him, they protested, saying he was a good father and they loved him. Soon, they were all crying — Bill, Moya, Shanda, David, and Tina.

28

IT DIDN'T TAKE LONG before Lear Jets began cracking up. Most of the accidents were the result of pilot error because companies were checking out their pilots too fast. "Hell, you can fly this," they would say. "It's not hard." But Lear Jet Model 23 was a hot rod, and not everyone could handle a red-hot jet; it was the kind of plane you had to keep ahead of because by the time you reacted, it was almost too late.

Pilot error or not, the safety of the Lear Jet became a topic of conversation all over the country. Says Landis Carr, who worked with Lear on Learstar: "You were almost in an argument in any hangar around the country if you brought up the subject."

The first fatal accident, on October 21, 1965, hurt Bill Lear and Lear Jet the most. It was his own test pilot who died and the cause of the accident was never clear. It happened just as Lear was dreaming about Lear Jet Model 24, the Lear Liner, and the Lear Single-Twin pusher.

Even though Lear Jet N804LJ was in test-flight status and should not have been carrying passengers, it left Wichita at three-ten in the afternoon to fly William Sipprell, a Lear Jet vice president, to a meeting in Detroit. Glen David, a former Air Force pilot with 2,777 hours of flight time (of which 641 were on the Lear Jet), sat in the left seat; Lawrence Bangiola, a former Navy pilot and flight instructor, sat in the right seat. The airplane, owned by Lear Jet distributor Robert Graf, was in Wichita to have its electrical system rewired. Since the Lear Jet service department was understaffed at the time, the airplane was rewired without the usual quality control.

After the wiring was completed, a Lear Jet test pilot spotted smoke coming from the bulkhead just forward of the pilot's seat during his routine preflight test. Noting that some wires had diagonal burn marks on them, he sent N804LJ back to the ramp for more repairs. After mechanics rewired again, the test pilot took the plane up for a two-hour spin, during which he noted "twenty discrepancies on the aircraft." The pilot brought the plane down, planning to test-fly it again later, but Glen David offered to "fly the next flight" himself.

David's trip to Detroit's Metropolitan Airport was about as perfect as it could be. He landed and parked N804LJ at the Executive Aircraft Ramp at 5:38 P.M., supervised the refueling with 495 gallons of Aeroshell turbine fuel 640, then reviewed weather conditions with the U.S. Weather Bureau meteorologist. David expressed some concern about the cloud build-ups he had observed over Indiana on the flight down.

Satisfied that probable turbulence would be only "moderate," David filed his flight plan — direct to Carleton, Michigan, direct Lafayette, Indiana, direct Springfield, Illinois, direct Butler, Kansas, direct to Wichita at 41,000 in an estimated nonstop flight of 2:40 hours on 3:30 hours of fuel. All quite normal.

At 7:25 P.M., Glen David got his clearance from the tower, ". . . turn left after departure, three zero zero, cleared for takeoff." It was raining lightly and freezing levcl was 9,200 feet. At 7:29, David told air traffic control he was passing 18,000 feet. Two minutes later he reported that he was at 25,000 feet and asked to be cleared for 41,000 "as soon as possible." The radar showed he was twenty-five nautical miles east-northeast of Jackson, Michigan.

Air traffic controller James Lutsch was tracking David. "I placed a radar marker on the aircraft target and followed it for about ten miles to the southwest when the aircraft started a sharp turn to the right," Lutsch reported later. "As the aircraft passed through a northerly heading, the beacon target disappeared from the radar. I immediately turned up the normal radar gain, but never saw the aircraft on radar again."

When it hit the ground in a near-vertical dive at a high rate of speed, N804LJ dug a crater 8 feet deep, 45 feet long, and 15 feet wide. Its parts were strewn half a mile.

Bill Lear talked to everyone he could about the accident, thought and rethought the design of the airplane, but couldn't figure out what had happened. Clay Lacy, who had been urging him to add a third gyro as a back-up in case the airplane lost its electrical power, was convinced that Glen David had experienced an electrical failure and, without gyro horizon instruments during nighttime turbulence, had lost control of his airplane (as Bill Lear once had done in a Learstar over the Rockies). But Lear could not be persuaded that his fail-safe electrical system had failed. (The National Transportation Safety Board later ruled *probable* cause as loss of control "resulting from AC electrical power failure under night, turbulent conditions.")

Three weeks later, on November 14, John Lear was ferrying passengers back and forth between Burbank and Palm Springs in a twin-engine Aero Commander owned by the Paul Kelly Flying Service, a subsidiary of the Flying Tiger Line. (Bob Prescott, the president of Flying Tiger, had been one of the original Flying Tiger pilots under General Claire Chennault.) When John landed in Burbank at three-thirty in the afternoon, Paul Kelly, who had been flying a Lear Jet that day, told him there was one more pickup in Palm Springs, where the World Air Congress had held a show earlier in the day. "Why don't you go take the jet and do it?" Kelly said.

The Palm Springs airport sat in a ten-mile-wide desert valley surrounded on three sides by the San Gorgonio Mountains to the north, the Chocolate Mountains to the east, and the San Jacinto Mountains to the west. The airport had no permanent tower, but the FAA had set up a temporary one to handle the traffic for the air show on visual flight rules (VFR) because instrument landings and takeoffs were impossible there. Instrument flight rule (IFR) instructions after takeoff came from the FAA tower in nearby Thermal, California.

John was not keen about flying back to Palm Springs for another load. The weather was getting bad down there, he told Kelly, and there was a stack of little planes flying in circles under the clouds, waiting for clearance from Thermal. "I'd rather not go," he said.

"What's the matter? You chicken?" Kelly asked.

"It just doesn't seem safe, but I'll go as your copilot," John offered. He loved to fly Lear Jets, and even though he considered Paul Kelly "extremely marginal" as a Lear Jet pilot, he couldn't resist the temptation to ride in the right seat, bad weather and heavy traffic or not.

Paul Kelly said no, taking as his copilot David Faulkner, who had "minimal" flying experience and who was not a qualified Lear Jet or instrument pilot.

Kelly landed in Palm Springs at 4:45 and was ready for takeoff at 5:17 because his Lear Jet didn't need refueling for the fifty-minute flight back to Burbank. He was in such a hurry that he declined a weather briefing, even though it was dark and rainy, with a 5,000-foot ceiling and patches of clouds scattered at lower altitudes.

Clay Lacy watched Kelly take off in N243F with six passengers, one of whom was Peter Prescott, the only son of Bob Prescott. When he saw Kelly "clean up the airplane like he was doing four hundred miles an hour," Lacy tuned in his radio and heard Thermal tell Kelly to stand by for his clearance to climb through the clouds. Lacy was more than curious. He knew John Lear worked for Paul Kelly and thought John might be flying the jet. "I don't know what his hurry is," Lacy told a friend. "He's only going twelve miles and he has an hour to get there."

Lacy, who was a Lear Jet distributor, had spent most of the day at the World Air Congress with Bill Lear, who had flown in from Wichita in a company Lear Jet. Early that afternoon, Lear had gotten a phone call from the factory, and as he took the call in Lacy's trailer, his face turned grim and his jaw jutted out as it did when he was spoiling for a fight. "Get a screwdriver," he told Lacy when he hung up. "Follow me."

They walked over to Lacy's Lear Jet demonstrator parked nearby.

"That's the sonofabitch that did it!" Lear said.

"Did what?" Lacy asked. Lear was pointing to an oxygen valve. The hangar had just told him that the valve on a plane being repaired had caught fire and exploded.

"Caused the airplane to crash in Michigan," Lear said. He was clutching at every straw to explain how Glen David had gone down. Lear had then jumped into his jet and had flown back to Wichita, convinced he had solved the riddle.

Although he was as anxious to get back to Los Angeles as Paul Kelly, Lacy wasn't about to take off in nasty weather only to fly circles for an hour until he got his clearance. Frank Sinatra was circling up there in his Lear Jet and so was Arthur Godfrey. "Let's don't get up in this mess," Lacy had told one of his passengers just after Kelly took off. He went out for dinner instead.

Kelly flew a mile and a half southeast of the airport toward the Indio Hills and began a left turn. The terrain below him was dark and filled with cloud shadows. With rain pelting the windshield and visual clues from the ground hard to interpret, Kelly found himself one very busy pilot. He had to watch his instruments to make sure he had the correct pitch and bank. He had to scan the sky for the other half-dozen airplanes circling and waiting for clearance from Thermal. And he had to read the terrain under and in front of him. He couldn't rely on his inexperienced copilot for much help, either.

John Lear was relaxing at home when Ann Prescott called. It was after seven o'clock. Had he seen her son, Peter? "He was supposed to be back at Burbank at six-thirty or seven," she said.

"No. Let me do some checking," John told her.

John called all the airports around Los Angeles only to find out that Kelly had not landed anywhere yet. Then he called Thermal.

"I don't want to alarm you, Mr. Lear," a controller said, "but there's been a report of a crash in the Chocolate Mountains."

After dinner, Clay Lacy also called Thermal for a weather and traffic report. Recognizing him as a Lear Jet pilot, the controller asked Lacy if he had seen N243F take off. Lacy told him he had.

"Are you sure?"

"I'm sure. I heard him call Thermal and you tell him to stand by."

"That's what I was afraid of," the controller said. "We haven't heard from him since. The sheriff reported an explosion of fire through the mountains north of here."

Lacy checked around to make sure John hadn't been flying with Kelly, then called Bill Lear, who had just walked into the house. "I've got some bad news," he said. "But the first thing I want to tell you is that John is not involved . . . It looks like N243F went down in Palm Springs."

Lear began to cry over the phone and in between sobs kept saying, "What could be happening? What could be happening?"

"Well, Bill," Lacy said, "I don't think anything happened. The weather's bad here. I saw the guy take off. I just think he tried to stay underneath, and he was out there in the dark and going very fast."

The next morning, John, Clay Lacy, Al Paulson, and Jack Conroy drove as close as they could to the crash, then climbed the canyon for three hours. They went over a ledge and stood there, looking down into a bowl. Kelly had hit it, nose down, at a 60-degree angle. The sight was not pretty. The biggest piece left was the tail, and even though the coroner had already picked up whatever he could find, there were still pieces of bodies scattered around. John stumbled through the wreckage in total shock, looking for clues to explain what had happened. He had never seen a crash before, and he would never forget this one.

Before the day was out, investigators from the National Safety Transportation Board arrived by helicopter, and John volunteered to help them reconstruct the accident. For two weeks he diagrammed, marked, and tagged pieces of the airplane. (The NSTB later ruled as probable cause "spatial disorientation of the pilot, resulting in a loss of control.")

On December 10, a month after Kelly crashed, Lear wrote a letter to all Lear Jet owners saying that evidence indicated that "complete electric power failure" was not the cause of either accident. It is clear, he said, that the Glen David problem began in the cockpit. At first it was thought that the windshield blew out. It is now believed that the oxygen valve may have caused an explosion when it was turned on at a high altitude. The valve, Lear hastened to point out, was certified by the FAA and was not built by Lear Jet. Lear went on to warn his customers to turn the oxygen system on before takeoff rather than during flight, at least until the valve was modified. "We now offer a new and completely independent artificial gyro horizon powered by its own battery," Lear added. "We strongly recommend this self-contained back-up system."

A month later, Harold Quandt's Lear Jet crashed in Zürich, killing the copilot. It was pilot error. Four months later, another Lear Jet crashed in Lake Michigan. Pilot error, but no fatalities. Then, on April 23, Lear Jet N235R mysteriously crashed in Clarendon, Texas. The accident rocked Bill Lear.

Lear Jet N235R belonged to the Rexall Drug and Chemical Company, whose president, Justin Dart, was a close friend of Bill Lear. The plane had passed its hundred-hour inspection just three days earlier, and its pilot, William Majowski, was flying with FAA inspector James Sweep during a routine flight check, for type rating. Both men were experienced pilots.

Majowski and Sweep took off from Amarillo en route to Fort Worth, a short hop away, at 12:26 in the afternoon. It was raining. Nine minutes later, the plane disappeared from the air controller's screen. It had been flying in clouds at approximately 33,000 feet and experiencing moderate to severe turbulence. Like Glen David's Lear Jet, Majowski's just seemed to fall out of the sky. (The NSTB would later rule probable cause as electrical failure, or "loss of control of the aircraft, in turbulent, instrument conditions, which could have been caused by a failure of both gyro horizons.")

With three fatal accidents and five landing "mishaps," Lear Jet stock fell by nearly one fourth. The impact on sales was impossible to predict. Bill Lear continued his frantic search for clues, still refusing to admit that electrical failure just *might* be the problem. Three weeks after the crash in Clarendon, investigators discovered a defect in the pin that bound a hinge on the plane's horizontal stabilizer, which controlled vertical movement. Even though there was no proof that the pin caused the Clarendon and Jackson crashes, Lear requested all Lear Jet owners to ground their 110 planes until his mechanics could fix the pin. "Where airplanes are concerned," he told the press, "if there's a doubt, there is *no* doubt. You ground them. I fly my own family in my airplanes, and most of my customers are friends of mine. I couldn't sleep the rest of my life if someone was killed in one of my airplanes when I could have prevented it."

The day after this announcement the FAA praised Lear for his courage, then ordered the planes grounded. Lear lashed out at the FAA. "It was just a me-too action of bureaucrats who didn't want to get caught with jam on their faces," he fumed. "I didn't need that. I'll ground it again if necessary."

Lear Jets stayed grounded for two days, then took to the air again, while Lear stock gained about half of what it had lost. Predictably, Lear's competitors claimed he had voluntarily grounded the planes because he had gotten wind that the FAA was going to order them out of the air the next day anyway. Maybe he did. Regardless, Lear never believed the pin was the problem, and he continued to search for the real cause of the Jackson and Clarendon accidents, convinced they were related.

One day when Lear was discussing the accidents with Clay Lacy and Gordon Israel in Lacy's office in Van Nuys, Lacy said he knew of a United Airlines DC-7 that had had a problem during a flight from Fresno to Los Angeles after midnight in heavy rain. The ship had just broken out of the overcast at 2,000 feet to prepare for landing when it began rolling and yawing about

40 degrees. The pilot, who was fighting the violent shudder, ordered a member of the reserve flight crew to organize evacuation procedures in case he was lucky enough to get the ship down. Once he had the plane under control, he asked the tower to divert him to Mather Air Force Base, near Sacramento, where the runway was wider and longer and the emergency equipment better. Then he shot a few practice approaches before he dared lower the landing gear. Afraid to slow the ship down and risk another convulsion, he came in at a fast 160 knots. When it hit the runway, the DC-7 spun to the right and skidded to the end of the tarmac. It took investigators a long time to find the source of the problem. Although the DC-7 had a drain hole in the rudder, workers had covered it with a skin of aluminum. Water had accumulated inside, and the extra weight caused the airplane to shudder violently.

It was raining in both Detroit and Amarillo before David and Majowski had taken off, wasn't it? Lacy reasoned. Both pilots had reached the same high freezing altitude before they lost control, hadn't they? And even though the Lear Jet had drain holes in the rudder, some ground water could have frozen inside before it had a chance to drip out, couldn't it? The extra weight would create an imbalance, causing a flutter at a very high speed, wouldn't it?

There was a minute of complete silence. Israel was the first to speak. "You know, Bill," he said, "Clay's got a pretty good theory there."

"Grab your coat," Lear told Israel. "We're going to Wichita."

As Israel turned Lacy's idea over in his mind, he spun a theory of his own that was even more plausible. Maybe the Lear Jet was sucking water into the rudder as it flew, not while it was sitting on the ground during a storm, and maybe the water got trapped inside, then froze. Israel rigged up a spray — five tubes attached to the leading edge of the stabilizer and a hose connecting the tubes to a can of dye check, a red fluid used to spot cracks in aluminum. At 23,000 feet, Israel uncorked the dye; it ran through the hose, out the tubes, and into the air. When he checked the inside of the rudder after landing, sure enough, it was coated red.

Lear was elated. To test Israel's theory even further, he attached two-ounce weights, the approximate weight of the ice that would have accumulated inside the rudder, to the back of the elevators. Then he and FAA test pilot Ron Puckett took the jet up once more. At 550 miles an hour, the plane began to vibrate so badly that, like the pilot of the DC-7, Puckett could barely hold on to the wheel.

The problem was simple enough to understand. The pressure inside the elevator was lower than the pressure outside, making it physically impossible for the water trapped inside to flow out. The solution was just as simple. Israel designed a small aerodynamic scupper (drain) that would make the inside pressure greater than the outside and allow the water to drip out. Lear replaced every Lear Jet elevator, certain that he had found and solved the problem. "It wasn't like he was 90 percent convinced," recalls Sam Auld. "It was like he was 110 percent convinced."

To the National Safety Transportation Board, the problem was not quite so simple. It asked seventy-three Lear Jet owners-pilots about the airplane's electrical system. One out of three who answered the questionnaire said they had had problems with their inverters, which converted the direct current of the batteries into the alternating current needed to run the gyros; half said they had experienced difficulties with the gyros themselves. One of the owners with gyro problems was Lear's friend Justin Dart, who had lost a pilot and a jet in the Clarendon crash. Israel had heard Dart tell Lear that he had had to replace several gyros in his two Lear Jets and that if Lear didn't do something about getting better ones, he'd push his remaining Lear Jet into the Pacific.

The FAA took no chances. It issued a directive ordering Lear Jet to install a third gyro with an independent power source on all old and new planes. Although twenty-five Lear Jets would be "written off" in the United States during the next thirteen years, the NSTB would never again rule electrical failure as probable cause. And with new elevators, better oxygen valves, and a back-up electrical system, it was impossible to sort out what had caused the Jackson and Clarendon crashes. John Lear and Clay Lacy still believe it was electrical failure; Sam Auld and

Hank Beaird are convinced it wasn't; and Don Grommesh won't even hazard a guess since the Lear Jet Model 23 systems were so interrelated.

To his dying day, Lear was convinced that he had solved the mystery. "Again I went over the plane," he wrote nine years later. "For some reason I was drawn to the plane's elevators . . . I studied them carefully, noting the usual drain holes in them. Something tugged at me. Could those drain holes have something to do with it? . . .

"I knew I had the answer to the problem."

29

WHEN LEAR HEARD that his good friend Arthur Godfrey was going to fly around the world in a Jet Commander, making it the first business jet to do so, he was more than miffed. His new Lear Jet Model 24 had just been certified but had yet to prove itself; the Rexall Drug Company Lear Jet Model 23 had just crashed in Clarendon; and Lear Jet sales were down. With the "ole redhead" piloting it, the Jet Commander was bound to make news. A Lear ARCON single-axis autopilot had once saved Godfrey's life, and Lear figured that the comedian, not known for his generosity, owed him one.

The Lear Jet and Jet Commander were fierce competitors, though the latter was slower, heavier, and more expensive. Aero Commander, which manufactured it, had started a friendly but intense ad war early in 1965, a year before the proposed around-the-world flight. One ad featured a Jet Commander in a hangar at night with a craftsman working on it. The caption read: "We don't shell them out like peas in a pod."

Lear, who always liked a street fight, took out a two-page ad that featured a photograph of green Lear Jets lined up in the hangar. The caption read: "Just like peas . . . And every one perfect."

Anxious to prove that his new Lear Jet Model 24 was a safe, fast, tough little bird vastly superior to the Jet Commander, Lear called Godfrey. They were friends, he said. How could Arthur do that to him? Godfrey explained that Aero Commander had offered to let him use the jet free for one year if he made the flight. It was a deal he couldn't turn down.

Lear stewed for an hour, then called in Hank Beaird. "How long will it take you to set up for around the world?" Lear asked. "I want to whip Arthur's ass."

Beaird said he could be ready in a week if Lear could get all the necessary clearances from the National Aeronautic Association (the U.S. representative of the Fédération Aéronautique Internationale in Paris), which supervised all U.S. attempts to establish or break world records. Scheduling was no easy task, for once Beaird had mapped his course, he would have to get clearance from each airport where he planned to land, arrange for refueling, secure permission to fly through the various national air spaces along the way; the National Aeronautic Association would have to arrange for official timers and observers. Beaird would have to do all this before the Jet Commander, which had a head start, could complete its paperwork and get ready.

Beaird told Bill Lear that he wanted John as one of his two other pilots. John was good on Lear Jets, and Beaird knew that the young man would eat his heart out forever if he couldn't fly the first Lear Jet to attempt to circle the globe. But the old man's chin scar turned pink and he cursed a red streak. He and John were still at odds, no matter how many reconciliations they had had since John's accident, four years earlier.

When John returned to the United States at the end of 1962, a few months after his crash, he was torn between a career in flying or art. To please his father, who thought professional pilots were one step above cab drivers, John enrolled in the Art Center College in Los Angeles to study industrial design. The old man was the happiest father in the world and sent John $5,000 for tuition and living expenses, but John lost the money in a stock investment. When he told his father, Bill responded in a highly emotional and stinging letter.

"From now on and up until you have really come to your senses," he said, "I don't want your friendship anymore. You take advantage of every kindness I show you. *Stupid!* Yes, John, stupid. And here's how stupid you are . . . From now on you're on your own and you can expect no more from me or your mother . . . I am going to spend my time trying to perfect ways and means of preventing you from ever getting any more from me or mine either by intent or accident. I'm sorry, John, because you could have had so much if you had just been smart and not smart aleck. There's a world of difference. As far as you're concerned, the difference would have been approximately two and a half million."

At the heart of the letter was Bill's still smoldering anger at the crash. "You hurt yourself with the freedom I provided you by giving you airplane time in Geneva," he continued. "You used your opportunity to darn near kill yourself and brought dishonor upon yourself by violating the Swiss laws, the Aero Club rules, etc. But you couldn't help selfishly strutting in the air. A big showoff. You won no respect, a lot of expenses, a great deal of pain, and still you came out of the whole thing not even any smarter. No, John, I guess you'll just have to admit it. You're dumb."

In the end, Bill said he'd send his son $150 a week to help him through school, but no more. If a real emergency developed, he hastened to add, he would do what he could to help out.

To hurt his son even more, Lear wrote to John's girlfriend in Geneva, saying that he had cut his son out of his will and placed him on a limited income. John has no pride, he told her, almost as if he were trying to break them up, no honor, no sense of responsibility. Explaining how John had asked him for her airfare to Los Angeles, Lear wrote that if he paid for her trip, he, not John, would be the one to sleep with her. In conclusion, he warned her that if John was the kind of boy she wanted, then, God bless her, she should have him.

Uncertain whether his father had actually mailed the letter or was bluffing, John did the predictable thing. In December 1962, after finishing his second semester at design school, he scraped together $300 and bought a ticket on a nonscheduled airline for Geneva. He also made a mistake. He invited his girlfriend to Le

Ranch. When his father found out, he was furious. He too did the predictable thing. He ordered John out of the master bedroom, out of Le Ranch, out of the country, and home for Christmas.

When John refused, the old man sent Buzz Nanney to Le Ranch. "Put handcuffs on him," Lear said, "and send him back to Wichita."

Nanney paid John a visit. "I'll tell you what's going to happen," he threatened John, who had just turned twenty. "I have a ticket for you to Wichita. Now, you're going to have to get [your girlfriend] out of the house. If you don't, all I have to do is call the police and tell them to cancel her work permit for moral turpitude because you're underage. You'll be evicted from Switzerland and you'll never be able to come back again."

"What time does the balloon go up?" John asked.

"Eleven o'clock. I'll meet you at the airport." Nanney figured that if he gave John the ticket, he'd cash it in and run.

Like father, like son. John called his girlfriend, told her to take a cab to the road behind Le Ranch, and to wait. John climbed through the window and skipped off to Paris.

When John didn't show at the airport, Nanney drove out to Le Ranch and found the bedroom door locked and the window open. He called Lear and told him his son was gone. "Cut off all the bank accounts, close everything," the old man shouted. "Let the sonofabitch starve."

When the dust had settled after a few months, Lear asked Nanney what to do.

"Bill, you keep letting this wall build up between you and John," Nanney advised. "It's been going on for years and years. Why don't you be a little magnanimous and say, 'John, okay, let's let bygones be bygones.' Then give him a job."

Against his better judgment, John started working in the Lear Jet public relations department, where he wrote and edited the company's biweekly newsletter, *Charge!* He quit when his father would not allow him to get checked out in a Lear Jet and found a job flying chartered airplanes. Soon, he was one of the youngest pilots in the country to earn an FAA air transport rating for jets.

When Moya learned that a Lear Jet was going to go around

the world without her son John, she began to work on Bill, telling him he was being stubborn and unreasonable. "Why are you doing this?" she argued privately. "John's a fine pilot, a very fine pilot. He and Hank can make a perfect team." Bill gave in to please her.

It was billed as a dogfight. The Lear Jet versus the Jet Commander, even though the two airplanes would be in different record-setting categories because the Lear Jet was 6,000 to 8,000 pounds lighter than its opponent. But to the aircraft industry on the sidelines, it was still a competition. Would they make it? And if they did, which was faster? It was two "biz" jets, each trying to prove it was better, tougher, smarter, and had more endurance than the other. It was Bill Lear versus Arthur Godfrey.

The Lear Jet pilots were straining to take off. They adopted as their motto, "Lie, Cheat, Steal." They had needed smallpox, typhus, yellow fever, and cholera shots. Robert R. ("Rick") King, the third Lear Jet pilot, had lied by forging his yellow fever shot record because there wasn't time to get one and wait for the results. And John had cheated by taking all four shots on the same day.

Then they stole Arthur Godfrey's thunder. When the Lear Jet took off from Wichita at 5:13 P.M. on May 26, 1966 (just a week after Lear had heard about the Godfrey–Jet Commander deal), the "ole redhead" and his team (Dick Merrill, Karl Keller, Fred Austin, and Jerry Germyn) were still racing around for permits and adding fuel tanks to their ship. Therefore, if the Lear Jet finished the flight, it would be the first business jet to fly around the world. Its times between cities and its overall time from takeoff to landing back in Wichita would automatically become world records in the 13,227-to-17,636-pound category.

To be first and to set a string of automatic records, however, was not enough. Bill Lear wanted to be the fastest ever. That meant flying faster than 62 hours, 27 minutes, and 35 seconds, the record set by a Boeing 707 six months earlier, flying at an average speed of 420.66 miles an hour. To beat that time, N427LJ would have to fly flawlessly and its crew would have to refuel — seventeen times — faster than it takes to order and eat a Big Mac. Even so, it would be next to impossible to beat the 707 because it had a longer range and, therefore, required fewer fuel stops.

Besides John Lear and Rick King (a former Air Force pilot), Hank Beaird took along the aviation writer John Zimmerman as an unofficial flight observer. The Lear Jet carried a Collins high-frequency transceiver, and Collins was taping the whole trip from its factory in Cedar Rapids, Iowa. Bill Lear had a patch into the system so he could telephone the airplane from his office. The plane carried no extra fuel tanks. What flew was exactly what the Lear customer bought — an important point in Lear's strategy to rebuild the image of the Lear Jet.

Beaird drove, John rode shotgun, King transmitted a blow-by-blow to Bill Lear, and Zimmerman was chief steward. They were all excited. Not only were they out to set records, which they hoped would last a long, long time, but they were pushing a Lear Jet as no one had ever pushed it before.

They cruised at 41,000 feet, dodging a few thunderstorms. When they landed at Bradley Field in Windsor Locks, Connecticut, a Lear fast-act refueling team was waiting. So was the press. Unaware that the Lear Jet had already taken off, Aero Commander had just announced at the Aviation Space Writers meeting that its Jet Commander was going to be the first business jet around the world. "Tell them good luck," the Lear crew told the press before they jumped back into their business jet for Newfoundland.

John piloted the second leg to St. John's. It was midnight and pitch black up at 41,000 feet. Hank told jokes, but the others were so tense, no one really laughed.

King took the third leg to Santa Maria, in the Azores. When they landed in the morning, the mayor and town dignitaries were waiting. "Are you Arthur Godfrey?" one of them asked John.

By that time, the Lear team had a system to beat the clock. Zimmerman took their passports through customs; Beaird filed the flight plan and checked the weather; John and King refueled the bird. Off they went to Barcelona. John was the pilot, and Beaird rolled pictures with his new movie camera, as he would during the whole trip when he wasn't sleeping. "Where's Arthur Godfrey?" airport workers asked when they landed. "You got an Esso card? . . . How fast does this go?"

John also flew the next leg, from Barcelona to Istanbul. By this time, the crew had learned not to talk on the radio with the old man, who was becoming impatient, meddling, and demanding. Dealing with him took so much energy that they ignored him, as Clyde Pangborn used to do when test-flying the Learstar back in the early 1950s. Somewhere over Albania on this leg, Danny Kaye, now a Lear Jet vice president, phoned from Lear's office to say what a great day it was for the company.

Clay Lacy had introduced Lear to Danny Kaye, an aviation buff who was thinking of buying a Lear Jet. Lear and Kaye had hit it off from the start, and Danny liked the Lear Jet so much that he became a partner in a Lear Jet distributorship. When the planes began crashing, Lear had called him in tears late one night, saying that he had to do something to restore confidence in his airplane. Kaye had come up with the idea of flying across the country in a Lear Jet, stopping along the way to visit children in hospitals — something he intended to do with or without a Lear Jet. Recognizing good promotion when he saw it, Lear had jumped at the idea, eventually offering Kaye a vice presidency.

There were no problems in Istanbul, Teheran, or Karachi, and the crew dined on water, crackers, and candy bars. It was when they took off from Karachi for Colombo, Ceylon, that the fun started. The way the crow flew would take them across India. But they didn't have permission to fly over India (they hadn't been able to cut through the bureaucracy in time) and had been told that if they tried, they would be shot down without warning. To skirt the country, however, would be to lose time. They decided, what the hell. You couldn't set a world record without taking some chances.

Bombay got on the air. "427LJ, could you give us your position?" the tower asked.

"Rog . . . stand by one."

They charted their exact position, then — "Lie, Cheat, Steal" — they drew a perpendicular line to a point about thirty miles off the coast and radioed Bombay the false position.

Fuel became a problem on this leg. Beaird was in the left seat and John in the right. John had calculated their fuel consumption four times. Not sure they'd have enough to stretch, he developed a contingency plan to land at another airport. If they did, they would lose time. Beaird decided to go for Colombo.

When they had 750 pounds of fuel left (enough for forty minutes of flying at very high altitude), John saw the shoreline and a thunderstorm coming right at them. He called the Colombo tower, declaring a state of emergency. Beaird descended to 500 feet under the storm and skimmed the lush jungle all the way to the airport. When N427LJ landed, it had just 100 pounds of fuel left, enough for about ten minutes in the air.

From Colombo to Singapore was going to be tricky because the 1,703-statute-mile run was just beyond the range of the airplane, at least as far as the engineers were concerned. Beaird had hoped to push it and, with favorable flying conditions, felt he could make it. But the weather was bad and the headwinds were 100 knots. Even Beaird recognized that if he took off under those conditions, they'd "have to swim" the last hundred miles.

The four men sat in the BOAC lounge, cursing their luck (up to Colombo, they were ahead of the Boeing 707's time) and waiting for a break in the weather. Maybe a tailwind. It was hot and muggy, and everyone was beat. After about three hours — most other refueling stops had taken between thirty and sixty minutes — John came up with an idea.

The tip tanks of the Lear Jet left space for fuel expansion, in accordance with FAA regulations. John removed the inspection plate, which prevented tank-topping, and was thereby able to pour in several extra gallons. Then, to save fuel, the crew towed N427LJ onto the runway. They still weren't certain they had enough to make it to Singapore, but they decided to go for it. The team roared down the runway shouting, "Lie, cheat, steal!"

John charted the coordinates and estimated fuel consumption. When they cut across Diamond Point in northern Sumatra, they were twenty-eight minutes behind schedule because of the headwinds. As they zoomed down the Straits of Malacca, an hour from Singapore, they had just 1,000 pounds of fuel, clearly not enough to make it. Beaird decided to push it anyway. Estimates could always be wrong.

Half an hour before touchdown, they made contact with the Singapore tower. They passed over Kuala Lumpur, then Malacca; they had only 400 pounds of fuel and a flashing red fuel light. They started their descent early because of thunderstorms; only 300 pounds. John studied the maps so he could tell

Beaird exactly where they were and where he could crash-land. Beaird throttled back and John, thinking one of the engines had died, jerked his head up from the maps so fast he hit the cabin roof. Everyone began to laugh, and it snapped the tension.

Breaking through the clouds, they saw Singapore Bay below them, but the airport lay thirty miles ahead. They were down to 250 pounds. All four men crowded into the cockpit. Beaird seemed cool as he rolled pictures of the approach. Still twenty-five miles to go; only 150 pounds of fuel and a red light gone crazy. No one could see the airport yet.

They radioed the tower. Only ninety seconds of fuel left, they said, and they still couldn't see the airport. The tower began giving them a radar steer to the end of the runway.

Beaird chickened out. "First flat place," he announced, "we're going in."

Just as he said that, John caught the white gleam of the airport, Peya Lebar, in the distance. "I've got the airport in sight," he shouted. "I think we can make it."

They declared an emergency. Beaird throttled back, and they glided onto the runway and coasted up into the ramp with less than 50 pounds of fuel in the tank, enough for three minutes in the air.

They rode the long leg across the South China Sea to Manila against headwinds and through a typhoon. On the flight from Manila to Osaka, they started having trouble with radio frequencies, so they stopped trying to report their position. Somewhere close to Okinawa, John woke up to a light flooding the cockpit. He looked out the window and saw nothing but brilliant white.

"Jesus, what's that?" he asked.

"Searchlight," Beaird said.

The light moved away, and John saw an F-102 fighter peel away. When they had failed to check in, the U.S. Air Force base in Okinawa had sent up a couple of jets to make sure the blip on its radar screen was N427LJ and that it was okay.

The leg from Osaka to Chitose, in northern Japan, was one of the shortest on the trip, but the news there was not good. On the next leg, their longest, to Shemya in the Aleutians, they would have to buck slight headwinds and face poor landing visibility — 100 feet and one-quarter mile. There was no alternate airport. If the weather was bad when they arrived, they might have to crash-land someplace.

They decided to make the first third of the flight and then check Shemya's weather once again. The three pilots would then vote either to go for it or to turn back.

After an hour and a half in the air, Shemya's tower reported no change in the weather. "That settles that," John said. "I vote to return."

"Me, too," King said.

Beaird was in the left seat. What the hell! You couldn't break world records if you didn't take a few chances. "You just lost your voting privileges," he announced. "I'm going to chance it. Let's go."

While they were thinking about swimming the last hundred miles to Shemya, King came into the cockpit. "We got company," he said.

John looked out the window and saw a Russian MiG-17 pulling alongside, the pilot and his wing rockets clearly visible. N427LJ was northeast of the Kuril Islands and clearly outside Soviet airspace. But airspace rules were not popular in the Kremlin.

The MiG kept shadowing them from a distance of about a hundred yards. They tried to contact it to say "Keep cool. We're just flying for the hell of it. No guns, no rockets, no bombs. Just crackers and Hershey bars." But there was no response.

King got nervous and tried to raise Collins Radio to tell it they were being shadowed. If they went down, he wanted the world to know why. But they were still having problems with their radio, and no one answered. After looking at each other through Plexiglas at 41,000 feet for a long six minutes, Zimmerman raised his camera with a telephoto lens for a couple of candids. The MiG dove away.

Beaird approached Shemya on instruments, broke out of the fog at 300 feet, visibility three quarters of a mile, and headed for the airport, where an honor guard was standing at attention in the Alaskan freeze.

"Where's Arthur Godfrey?" the commanding officer asked when they piled out of the plane. They explained. "Well, I can't bring out the honor guard a second time when the Jet Commander comes," the C.O. said.

Grinning from ear to ear, the Lear Jet crew agreed. Beaird

and King inspected the honor guard to the clicks of a military photographer ordered to catch the historic moment.

Anchorage, Seattle, Van Nuys, Wichita. Reporters were waiting in Anchorage, a huge hot breakfast in Seattle, Danny Kaye with photographers in Van Nuys. Twenty-two minutes later, they were on the home stretch, three hours and eight minutes behind the time set by the Boeing 707 even though their average speed was 37 miles an hour faster. The five and a half hours they had sat on the ground in Colombo had robbed them of the title "Fastest Time Ever."

As they approached Municipal Airport, they began calculating their bonuses. Lear had promised them $1 each for every minute under 69 hours up to 60 minutes and $5 for every minute thereafter. They screamed past the Wichita tower to have their time officially recorded — 65 hours, 39 minutes total elapsed time; 50 hours, 19 minutes flight time.

More than two thousand waving and cheering people lined the airfield, including the mayor of Wichita, John Stevens, and the governor of Kansas, William Avery. Moya stood by with leis. The Lear Jet had established eighteen world records. As it turned out, Arthur Godfrey and his Jet Commander left a week later and took seven hours and ten minutes longer to make the trip.

"Boy, the old man must really be happy," Beaird said as he brought N427LJ in. "He let everybody off work."

When they stepped out of the plane after 22,993 miles of flying, Bill Lear was grinning and holding three bundles of $666 in singles, tied with red ribbon. And just to prove that Lear Jets were safe, tough birds, he ordered his mechanics to refuel N427LJ, then sent it on a business trip to Detroit.

30

IT HAD BEEN a perfect trip. The Lear Jet had used no extra oil, and the General Electric twin engines had "purred like kittens" all the way. Everyone was hopeful, as Bill Jr. put it in a telegram to the flight crew, that the around-the-world flight "will really put us over" the financial hump.

From the Lear public relations office poured a steady stream of photographs of famous people standing next to Lear Jets — former Vice President Richard Nixon, Steve Lawrence and Eydie Gormé, Joe E. Brown, Madame Chiang Kai-shek, Senator and Mrs. John McClellan, singer Roger Miller, the Smothers Brothers, ABC-TV anchormen Peter Jennings and Howard K. Smith, and of course Danny Kaye and Bob Cummings. But nothing seemed to help Lear Jet crawl out of the hole Lear and the economy had dug for it.

December 1965 (six months before the big flight) had been Lear Jet's biggest month, with fourteen deliveries, making the year's total eighty new airplanes. But the 1966 recession hit Lear Jet hard. Money was tight, interest rates were high, and the IRS had suspended the 7 percent investment tax credit that amounted to $50,000 for a new Lear Jet. By the middle of 1966, after Lear Jet's lifetime sales had hit 120, nothing moved in spite of the hoopla surrounding the airplane's record-setting flight. Soon there were eight Lear Jets sitting on the ramp, lonely and unsold, $5 million worth of time and aluminum. And it was no consolation to Bill Lear that other companies, from North American to Aero Commander, were caught in the same squeeze and that, recession or no, he was still outselling them.

Like the other aircraft companies, Lear Jet could have weathered the recession — confidence in the plane was fully restored — if Bill Lear had not moved in so many directions so fast in the hope of making more money and carving a new Lear kingdom. Individually, the moves were wise and sound; as a group, they turned out to be a millstone.

In February 1966, Lear expanded the Wichita plant for the third time and increased his work force to 2,400, anticipating continued high sales of Model 24 and future production of the Lear Liner.

In May 1966, Lear bought 97 percent interest in the Brantly Helicopter Corporation of Frederick, Oklahoma, one of the leading manufacturers of choppers for the civilian market. When Lear bought it, Brantly was making five machines a month — a two-seater (B2B) and a four- or five-seater (305). Expecting to increase production to twenty a month, Lear and his engineers immediately began designing a new turbine-powered model.

By the middle of 1966, the design of the Lear Liner Model 40 was complete and construction of the prototype was planned for the fall. Lear had already signed a $1 million purchase agreement with Rolls-Royce for its Spey-25 engines for the twin-engine Liner.

In July 1966, Lear broke ground for a one-story, 50,000-square-foot building on a 106-acre plot adjacent to Kent County Airport in Grand Rapids. The building was the new home of the Lear Jet Avionics Division, which had moved from Wichita six months earlier and currently was operating out of a leased building. Besides supplying Lear Jet with fifteen devices from autopilots to hydraulic systems, the Avionics Division was cracking the general aviation market with instruments such as the autopilot and the back-up gyro, and it had hopes of landing fat military development contracts as well. Lear had expanded the division from 150 workers to 500 while projecting $4 million in sales during the next year.

Also in July of that year, Lear Jet Stereo Division was taking off in Detroit. The division had more than 450 employees, and it was turning out 1,000 players a day and 700,000 cartridges a month. Bill Lear had just sealed a licensing agreement with RCA-Canada and was working on the European, Latin American, and Far Eastern markets as well. He had a deal with Chrysler to offer add-on units through Chrysler dealers; he was selling home players through Capitol Records; he had set up a string of 5,000 distributors across the country; and he had talked Sears into featuring his Stereo Eight in its Christmas catalogue. Lear was projecting the production of 10,000 players a day by the end of the year and 2 million cartridges a month.

In August 1966, a new Lear Jet, Model 25, made its first flight. It was slightly larger than Model 24. Lear announced certification for the spring of 1967 and production very soon thereafter.

In September 1966, the shareholders ratified a Board of Directors' decision to change the name of the company from Lear Jet to Lear Jet Industries, which would more clearly reflect the growth of the company. It also ratified a board decision to move its corporate headquarters to Los Angeles and to set up a sales office in New York and a research and development center in Los Angeles.

By the end of 1966, the whole empire had begun to crash. In 1965, Lear Jet had reported $54.3 million in sales and a profit of $4.2 million. In 1966, sales were cut in half, resulting in a $12 million net operating loss. Lear had spent $1.7 million in developing the Lear Liner but had no money to push it into production. Brantly Helicopter had lost another $1.8 million in reorganizing and development costs. And Lear Stereo reported a $5.7 million loss due to production, sales, and quality control problems. Never had a Lear company been in worse shape.

In reality, the problem didn't just happen. Like a slow paralysis, it crept up on Lear while he was building new empires and having fun. He had relied on his management team to keep him informed, but some people were so afraid he'd kill the messenger that they hid the truth. Others told him the truth, but only indirectly, through reports, memos, and letters. A few like William Webster, Lear Jet's vice president of finances, Buzz Nanney, whom Lear routinely fired twice a day, and Fran Jabara, Lear's financial consultant, who had negotiated the Lear industrial bond issue with the City of Wichita, told him the brutal truth. But Bill Lear didn't want to listen.

When Nanney returned from the Hanover Air Show early in 1966, just before the around-the-world-flight, he was depressed. After listening and talking to buyers and sellers alike, he had become convinced that the fast-hitting slump in aircraft sales was universal and that it would be around for a long time. But Lear was still trying to push ten airplanes a month out the hangar door even though the marketing department couldn't sell them.

Nanney leveled with Lear. "You know, you've opened new offices out in California," he said. "Very expensive. And you've opened offices in New York and you've got the office in Geneva. I would cut everything back and wait and see what happens. I just don't believe that we're going to have that fruitful a year and we're in bad trouble."

Listening to Nanney up to a point, Lear cut back 10 percent. But he was determined to take the gamble; there had to be a bottom in sight. Convinced he could weather the storm, he hired Theodore A. Bruinsma, executive vice president of the

Packard-Bell Electronics Corporation, as president of Lear Jet Industries and, in September 1966, moved to his new headquarters in Century City, where he could crack the whip over the entire Lear empire.

Nanney and his wife, Ursula, were taking a vacation in Colorado Springs at the end of the year when Lear finally realized how much trouble he was in. Fran Jabara had called him and read him the riot act. Lear had sold only three jets during September, October, and November. December hadn't been much better. Lear phoned Nanney on New Year's Day; it was one of those "Rome is burning and you're on vacation" calls.

Nanney returned to Wichita, and when he walked into Lear's office, the old man "looked like death drawn over." He hadn't slept, and the full impact of the financial crisis had hit him. "What do you think we ought to do?" he asked.

"I think you can charge ahead with great courage because you've made all the mistakes already," Nanney said. "There aren't any left."

Lear worked out a plan. He had few choices. He fired Ted Bruinsma and a raft of managers, whom he blamed for not being honest with him; he laid off half of his people; then he bypassed his Lear Jet dealers and began selling airplanes directly to customers just to meet the payroll and bills, which came to more than $500,000 a week. In the end, Kenneth Johnson saved the day.

Johnson, an officer of the Kansas State Bank in Wichita, believed in Lear Jet and Bill Lear. Nanney would run in to see Johnson at the end of the week, begging for a half-million-dollar loan until early the following week, when Lear expected to get paid $650,000 for an airplane it had just sold or hoped to sell. Anything to keep Lear Jet floating. Sometimes the sale didn't come through, and when Nanney went back for another half million the next week, Johnson would say, "Buzz, what am I going to do? We're just a little bank."

Nanney would "promise everything that was holy" and Johnson would come through again. Personally, Bill Lear was ready to pour in every single penny of his own money to keep the company going. He knew he had three great products — the Lear Jet, the Lear Stereo Eight, and Lear Avionics — and he was willing to go down with his ship, not that he ever believed it would really sink. He spent a few million of his own money and, once again, put up his and Moya's Rubens paintings and their home as collateral on a loan before Fran Jabara talked him out of spending any more cash. When it heard how Bill Lear was trying to go it alone, Rolls-Royce dropped all claims against Lear Jet Industries for the $1 million purchase order Lear had signed for jet engines for the Lear Liner. The sporting thing to do, Rolls executives said.

Although things were beginning to improve by April 1967 after the delivery of nine airplanes in January, February, and March, and although it looked as if Lear Jet Industries was turning the corner, the company was still teetering on the edge of bankruptcy. It needed to deliver three planes a month just to meet operating expenses, six a month to see daylight. The market just wasn't there yet, even though everyone could glimpse it coming. Only a huge infusion of cash could save the company. It was Lear's old friend Justin Dart who finally convinced him to sell.

It was no secret in the aviation industry that Lear had a superior product but couldn't weather the storm, and that the longer Bill Lear held out, the cheaper Lear Jet Industries would become. Lear gave the order to send feelers out to both Cessna and Beech. Cessna declined to consider Lear because it was developing its own business jet. Beech's president, Frank Hedrick, who saw red every time he heard the name Lear, was insulted at the suggestion, even though Beech did not have a business jet and could have bought a winner without having to pay development costs. The animosity between Hedrick and Lear dated back to World War II when Beech was buying components from Lear Incorporated, which was usually late on delivery. Hedrick and Lear would engage in a verbal war, with Lear saying that ever since Walter Beech had died, the company hadn't come up with one fresh idea. The animosity got so bad that Hedrick wouldn't allow any of his executives to set foot in a Lear Jet.

Olive Ann Beech, who had taken over the direction of the company after her husband's death, supported Hedrick. Although she got along well with Moya (they had taken a trip around the world together), she couldn't stand Bill, who liked her even less. (A few years earlier, Lear had been thinking about buying a large piece of beachfront property in Sardinia. He used to joke that he was going to name the beach Olive Ann Beech and then piss on it every morning.) So when she heard about the informal offer to buy Lear Jet, Olive Ann scoffed at the proposal and reportedly said: "I do not propose to pull Bill Lear's chestnuts out of the fire."

Most analysts recognized at the time that the marriage of Beech to Lear Jet would have been beautiful and practical, but when Beech showed no enthusiasm, Gates Rubber made an offer.

Charles C. Gates, the forty-four-year-old president of Gates Rubber ($260 million in annual sales), had just bought Combs Aircraft from Harry Combs, a Lear Jet distributor. Knowing that Gates Rubber was diversifying quickly into transportation and agriculture, Combs told Charlie Gates that Lear Jet was in trouble and that the company would be a good buy. Gates approached Lear through Dick Millar, Lear's old friend at William Staats.

At first Gates asked to buy only the marketing rights to Lear Jet for $6 million up front. But Nanney talked Lear out of the deal, and rightly so, for $6 million would never pull Lear Jet over the hump. The only way out was for Lear to sell his 1.2 million shares of common stock to Gates. Lear Jet stock was hovering around $20 a share on the New York Stock Exchange, quite a drop from its high of $82.50 in 1965, but a lot better than the $8.50 it had been going for in 1966. When Lear declined to sell the marketing rights, Gates expressed an interest in buying Lear out.

Bill and Moya went to their home in Palm Springs to think about the offer. The more Bill pondered it, the more depressed he got. He had recently told a reporter: "There is nothing I'd rather be doing than exactly what I'm doing right now. If someone offered me $160 million for my company . . . with the provision that I would have to retire, I'd spit in his eye. For me, the best of life is the exercise of ingenuity — in design, in finance, in flying, in business. And that's what I'm doing."

When Bill threatened suicide, Moya phoned Justin Dart, who also had a home in Palm Springs.

Justin Dart, a pilot since the 1930s, had known Lear since the old Learstar days. Also a self-made man, he understood both the agony of defeat and what made Lear tick. He had had such great confidence in Lear and his Lear Jet that he bought one for cold cash before the airplane was certified. And even though it was his Rexall Drug Company Lear Jet that had crashed in Clarendon, Texas, he had never stopped believing in Lear and his airplane.

"I think you have two choices," Dart said after Lear had outlined his problem during a golf game at the El Dorado Country Club. "Either you can accept this offer or you can go out in the backyard and blow your brains out. You can no longer swing this alone."

Dart never doubted that Lear Jet would continue to be successful once the recession bottomed out and the company tightened its belt. But, as he later told David Lear, "Bill was essentially broke. No question about it."

When Bill returned home after talking with Dart, it looked as if the golf game had drained the life right out of him. He lay motionless on the bed and stared at the ceiling. Moya thought he had had a stroke. "What's wrong?" she asked.

"Justin told me that I should sell the company to Gates," he said. Tears began to stream down his face as he told Moya he didn't want to live anymore. Moya held him in her arms and they cried together.

Tears or no tears, Lear bit the bullet. When Bill and Moya returned to Wichita early in April, Lear told Charlie Gates he was ready to sell. The night before the negotiation, Lear paced in the bedroom and dictated the terms of the sale to Moya, who typed them out. "I want *this*," he'd say. "I want *that*."

Moya was proud of Bill that night. "I just mopped up my tears," she said later, "because I thought, 'Here he is with his back up against the wall and he wants the whole world wrapped up in a blue ribbon. He'll never get it.' "

The next morning, Moya and Bill held hands as they drove to the plant. "Well," Bill told her before he left to sell his baby, "I'm going to go in and make a deal with these bastards . . . We had a lot of fun anyway."

Lear gave his terms to his attorney, Carl Bell, a former mayor of Wichita, and told him and his other negotiator, Fran Jabara: "I won't take a nickel less. I have three divisions. Each of those is worth what I want for all three."

What Lear wanted was $11.89 for each share of his common stock, which amounted to just over $21 million; $3.5 million for his debentures, to be sold at a future date; and an option to continue working for the new company for five years, which option either he or Gates could cancel.

Lear walked into the conference room, where negotiators for both sides were waiting, and said, "Everybody knows what my terms are. I've got other things to do." He walked out of the room and came back only once — dragging Edgar Bergen and Charlie McCarthy in to meet the boys. The Gates people weren't sure what to make of the frivolity.

The negotiators began to feel each other out and by midafternoon had reached a predictable impasse when the Gates team made a counteroffer to test Lear's will. Lear turned it down flatly. It was a calculated risk on his part because he knew that several Lear Jet vendors had threatened lawsuits, and if all of them actually filed in court, Lear Jet Industries would be forced by law to declare bankruptcy.

Dick Millar called Moya from his office in Los Angeles, where he was following the negotiations. "Is Bill all right?" he asked.

"Yes. Why?"

"Well, he wants to turn the deal down," Millar said.

"If he doesn't want to do it," Moya advised, "don't try to force him. I gotta live with him."

Soon after Millar's call, Lear phoned Moya. "Put the fire on for steaks," he said. "I'll be home in a little bit. Gonna turn the deal down."

"Okay, honey," she said. "Come on. We'll work it out somehow."

When it became clear that Lear wasn't going to budge, Gates's team began conceding, at which point it became obvious to Lear's team just how badly Charles Gates wanted Lear Jet. His negotiators would ask for a disclosure that wasn't listed on the audited financial records before them, and Lear's negotiators would stall. Gates's team would back down without pressing.

By ten o'clock that evening, the agreement had been negotiated, drafted, and accepted by Charles Gates and Bill Lear.
Sales negotiations at that level normally take days or weeks, but
the Gates–Lear Jet deal went through in fourteen hours. Lear
got exactly what he had asked for.

At sixty-four, Bill Lear was a multimillionaire once again, but
he didn't realize how deeply the sale of Lear Jet would affect his
and Moya's life.

Under the management of Charles Gates, Gates Learjet
would turn the corner and prosper. By the time Lear died, in
1978, the company had sold even more business jets than Lear
had predicted when he first announced the airplane. And the
Lear Stereo Eight also weathered the storm, eventually becoming a steady profitmaker.

Bill Lear had to either retire or start over.

Part Five

Risking It All

31

"WHAT THE HELL do I do now?" Lear asked Buzz Nanney on June 26, 1967, his sixty-fifth birthday and two months after he had sold Lear Jet. "Life is slipping away."

"Bill, I feel awfully sorry for you," Nanney told him. "You got your pockets full of money. You have the world in your lap. With that fertile mind, you'll find something."

But he didn't. At least not right away.

Besides buying a home in Reno, the Lears had recently bought the Beverly Hills estate of Leonard Firestone in the wooded hills above Sunset Boulevard, complete with tennis courts, swimming pool, and guest house. They also owned homes in Geneva, Greece, Wichita, Laguna Beach, and Palm Springs.

But Lear was not happy in Beverly Hills. With nothing to do, he soon became a caged lion. He was up, he was down. He played the organ, he took a nap. He read the paper, he made a sandwich. He ate candy and more candy. He drove Moya "up the walls."

That summer Lear joined the rest of the family at Le Ranch, relaxing and flying around Europe. When he returned to the States in the fall, a parcel of land at Stead, Nevada, ten miles north of downtown Reno, caught his eye. The huge chunk of high desert, covered with sage and little else, would become the home of his new empire and the backbone of his estate.

The Army Air Forces had built the Reno Army Air Force

Base during World War II. It sat in the Lemmon Valley surrounded by the foothills of the Sierra Nevadas — Mount Peterson, Fred's Mountain, Granite Hills, and 8,000-foot-high
Peavine Mountain. After the war, the Strategic Air Command
used the base for survival training before turning it over to the
Nevada Air Guard. When Air Guardsman Crofton Stead was
killed in a plane crash, the state renamed the base.

Late in 1964, the federal government notified the city of Reno
that it was going to close Stead and offered to sell the base to
Reno for a nominal fee. The City Council appointed a committee to make recommendations for the airport, the buildings,
and the two thousand acres of desert around them. The land
was valuable to the extent that whoever owned it could secure
water rights from the state under Nevada's rigid water laws,
which made the state water engineer "God in the valley."

The committee recommended that the city break up Stead:
keep and operate the airport as a public airstrip, turn over the
school buildings to the county and to the University of Nevada,
and sell the land and other buildings for an industrial park. For
a year and a half, Reno searched for someone with enough
imagination and money to do something with the land. In
stepped William Powell Lear, with $21 million to spend.

Lear met with members of the Reno City Council in the fall of
1967, telling them how he would build an industrial park with
small businesses that wouldn't consume a lot of water, shopping
malls, private residences, and a lake. How he would revitalize
the airport with a new Lear hangar, an aircraft service and design center, and a flight school. How he would bring in the
railroad, develop roads through the desert, and dig wells. How
he would open a titanium processing plant, Titanium West.
Lear offered to buy the land for cash if the city would promise
to help him get water rights for 4.25 million gallons a day, which
he had calculated he would need to develop the land properly.

The council wasn't convinced that Lear would actually deliver what he had promised, but it believed he would try. And
with no other serious offers, it sold him 2,081 acres for $1.35 mil-
lion. Lear put down $135,000 and agreed to pay the remainder
in full as soon as the city arranged the sale with the federal government. As a condition of the sale, Lear would have to present

a master plan to the City Council and would have to pour $2.5 million into land development to show he was serious.

In December 1967, Bill slipped and broke his ankle. Cemented into a hip-length cast, he had orders to stay off his foot for six weeks. Typically, he was furious. "I broke my goddamn ankle," he'd shout, "and they have me in a cast clear up to my hips."

Later in December, when Moya left for Geneva to attend Shanda's wedding, Bill was unable to go along. When Clay Lacy stopped by a week later to discuss sketches for a pusher airplane he found Lear trying to cut his cast off with a saw. "Bob Cummings gave me some calcium pills," Lear told Lacy. "I can feel my leg is okay."

When he couldn't do it himself or talk his chauffeur into doing it for him, Lear shopped around until he found a doctor willing to replace the hip-length cast with a knee-high one. Once again, the doctor told Lear to stay off his foot for six weeks.

But Bill Lear knew better. A few weeks into the new cast, he went to a fund raiser for Richard Nixon, where he danced with Pat Nixon. A few days later, he was back in the hospital. To repair the damage, the doctors rebroke the unhealed ankle and pinned the bones. Lear became the terror of the hospital, as if to prove he was still in command. At home and confined to bed, Bill was miserable. Taking no chances this time, Moya asked her cousin Louise Gosage, a nurse, to babysit for Bill.

At first Lear slept a lot. Then he started demanding pain pills. Louise would carefully dole out the Darvons, but he'd want more. "Bill, you just had one," she'd tell him. "I don't care, goddamn it!" he'd shout. "I want another pill."

"All right," Louise said finally, trying a little psychology. "You can have all the pills you want. If you want to cloud up that brilliant mind of yours, go ahead and do it." Lear never took another pill as long as Louise was there.

After Louise left, early in 1968, Lear's depression grew more severe. He had been having a minor problem with nosebleeds for years. But suddenly they became worse and brought with them maddening headaches. "Dad is not at all well," Moya wrote Shanda. "He got a very heavy cold — then a severe nosebleed which went on day and night for a week. It was finally cauterized Friday and we thought it was over . . . Last night it started again and Dad is so despondent he really doesn't want to live anymore. I've sent up the alarm to all his associates to get him involved in engineering because he feels that his purpose in life is over . . . When he gave up the idea of being with you for your wedding, it sort of marked the beginning of giving up."

One Sunday morning after church, Moya and her mother had planned to stop for ice cream, but Moya had a premonition. Rushing straight home, she pulled up in front of the house in time to catch Bill slipping out the front door with a little suitcase.

"Where do you think you're going?" she scolded.

"Just out," Bill said.

"You turn around and go right back to your room!" she ordered.

Moya put Bill into his pajamas and told him "to quit acting like a baby." When she went downstairs, she found a note addressed to her on the table. He couldn't live like this anymore, the note said. He was going to rent an airplane and fly over the Pacific until he ran out of gas.

Lear later joked about that suicide threat: "The only plane available that night was a Lear Jet. And I wasn't about to waste one."

By early February, Bill seemed to perk up. But one Saturday night, his headache became unbearable and blood started dripping through the packing in his nose. The headache was so bad that Bill threatened to pull out the cotton to relieve the pressure. Moya rushed him to St. John's Hospital in Santa Monica, where Dr. Richard Barton was waiting. When he removed the packing, blood spurted all over the operating room. It was obvious that Lear had ruptured a blood vessel and that there wasn't much time to find it. He was losing blood so fast, he needed transfusions. Taking a calculated guess, Dr. Barton removed Lear's right eye, found a burst vessel, tied it, and replaced the eye.

While Lear was recovering in Beverly Hills, Joe Latimore, the city manager of Reno, went to see Lear's administrative assistant, Buzz Nanney, in his Reno office. The city had been waiting patiently for Lear to pay the more than $1 million he owed for the land at Stead. Latimore said he was sorry about Lear's health problem, but without $100,000 good faith money, he didn't think he could hold the council any longer and Lear would lose the deal.

"I'll see what I can do," Nanney said. "Bill is doped up and he can't talk, and Moya doesn't know much about the business."

Nanney called one of Lear's banker friends. "You know," he argued, "this is probably the most profitable thing that Bill has ever gone into. He's under sedatives. I can't find anyone who will bounce a hundred thousand dollars to secure this thing by Monday."

"Nanney, what are you asking me to do?" the banker said.

"Draw the money out of his account and send it to me."

"For Christ's sake, we can go to jail for that," the banker objected.

"Just send me a cashier's check."

"Buzz," the banker said, "I'll do it. I don't know why, but I'll do it."

Propped up in bed in his home in Beverly Hills a week later, Lear presented Latimore with a check for $1,118,604 to become Reno's biggest landlord.

32

His health problems aside, it was inevitable that the loose consulting relationship that Lear had negotiated as part of the sale of Lear Jet Industries would come undone. When it did, Lear was bitter. It wasn't that Charles Gates didn't respect Bill Lear's expertise or hadn't really intended to ask his advice. The two men simply could not get along, and none of the people who knew both of them were surprised. Their management approach, leadership style, and business philosophy were totally different. Gates thought Lear was trying to run the new company; Lear thought Gates was sitting too close to the corporate ledgers to see anything.

As a Gates Learjet (as Gates called the plane) consultant and a member of the Board, Bill felt like a divorced father with visiting rights. "The janitor has more to say than I do," he complained. "At least he can decide where he's going to sweep."

Isolated from the Lear Jet and unable to sit still either before his health problems had begun or while he was recuperating, Lear played with his money for a while. He took Buzz Nanney on a trip to Alaska, and while Nanney went salmon fishing, Bill explored a slice of wilderness that was up for sale and climbed through a few gold mines. Back in the lower forty-eight, he began looking into oil wells. He bought a jeep with a drill on the back and went out into the desert to explore for uranium. But he soon gave up. Nothing really caught his fancy; everything he did was just an attempt to keep busy.

Exactly how Bill Lear stumbled into steam in the spring of 1968 while recovering from his operation, no one is quite sure. More than likely, it was a combination of several factors: Lear's long-standing interest in auto engines; his boredom and tireless curiosity; the romance of the steam dreamers like the Stanley brothers and Abner Doble; the national emphasis on clean air; the urge to prove that the Lear Jet was not a stroke of "luck," as some critics were saying; the Williams twins; and, most important, the fact that under the terms of his sales agreement with Gates, he couldn't build or design airplanes for five years.

Ever since the late 1950s, Lear had been seriously interested in alternatives to the internal combustion engine in automobiles. After he bought a home in Reno, he used to visit Harrah's Automobile Collection of more than a thousand antique, vintage, classic, and special interest cars. Lear and Bill Harrah, who owned casinos in Reno and Lake Tahoe, soon became buddies, and Harrah would allow Lear to puff around the parking lot in his classy Doble Steamer, which had cost $9,900 in the 1920s before Abner Doble went bankrupt on it. Lear may have been sixty-six, but he was still a boy at heart, filled with a sense of wonder and curiosity.

Calvin and Charles Williams, twins from Ambler, Pennsylvania, a small town north of Philadelphia, who had begun working on a steam power system in 1934, piqued Lear's curiosity further. In the spring of 1968, they drove their steam car to Washington, D.C., where they treated an endless stream of politicians to rides around the capital. Their car was powered by a Rankine cycle engine — water heated by kerosene produces steam, which drives a turbine or pistons, which, in turn, drive the shaft that moves the car.

The Williams brothers went bankrupt, but not before Bill Lear had heard about them. Hooked on steam, Lear asked Sam Auld, who was still working for Gates Learjet, to find the twins and tell them Bill Lear was flying in for a visit. That proved to be no easy task, for the Williamses were so broke they didn't have a telephone. Auld finally called the local sheriff and set up an appointment to talk to the brothers on a county phone.

Lear was impressed with the Williams Steamer to a point. The twins had licked some of the problems that had stumped the Stanleys and Doble, but their car was still too impractical to compete with Detroit. If Bill Lear were to try a Lear steamer, he would apply the latest in space age technology to an old idea. He decided to go ahead. It was as if he had purchased a new lease on life.

Lear's steam goals were far from modest. Detroit had only a few years left to meet the first emission standards ever imposed on the auto industry. Lear was not sure Detroit *could* comply or that if it did, the pollution problem would go away. And he was convinced that the nation was serious about cleaning up its air at almost any cost. If he could do what no one else had been able to — come up with a practical steam engine — he would revolutionize industrial society and earn an undisputed place in history. "I want to be the man who eradicated air pollution," Lear said modestly. "Wouldn't that be something?" An inveterate gambler who understood risks and odds, Lear hastened to add that he "could possibly lose all my money. Steam may not be the answer."

Lear's plan was to spend $1 million on experimental research and $9 million on initial tooling for the steam engines he would make and sell to the manufacturers of cars, buses, trucks, boats, and helicopters. Lear expected no help from Detroit, recognizing, as Henry Ford had emphasized earlier that year, that the auto industry had billions invested in the conventional car. "They are not only in love with the internal combustion engine," Lear explained in a speech, "but they are stuck with it. And as a result, there's not much going to be done about it."

Lear's problems in developing a practical steam engine (Rankine cycle) were far from simple. They were the same problems that had made the Stanley, Doble, and Williams steamers impractical: how to make the engine light and small enough to fit under the hood of a car; how to make it "get a head of steam" quickly; how to keep the liquid that produced the steam from evaporating as well as freezing in the winter; how to make the engine as cheaply and get as many miles per gallon as Detroit; how to design it so simply that it would be at least as easy to repair as the internal combustion engine.

Even if he was able to apply the best creative engineering to steam, Lear still would have to make one of two scientific breakthroughs: either create an alloy that could withstand tremendous heat without metal fatigue, yet still be cheap enough to be practical; or find a safe fluid that would vaporize at low temperatures and not freeze in below-zero winters, yet still be cheap enough to be practical.

When he quietly began work on his steam car in the summer of 1968, Lear set his priorities clearly. First, he wanted a nonpolluting engine; second, a fuel-economizing one. If he could achieve his first objective, with time and better engineering the second would follow.

As his chief engineer, Lear hired Hugh Carson, who had worked for him off and on over the years. Like all steam tinkerers and scientists before them, Lear and Carson were stumped at first by a number of basic questions. Should they design a turbine engine or a piston engine to be driven by steam? Should they create the steam from water or from an organic fluid that would not require the huge boiler and condenser that water did? If an organic fluid, which one? Lear and Carson were getting nowhere until Ken Wallis stepped in.

Wallis was an English engineer who had built Andy Granatelli's gas turbine racer in 1967. Even though Granatelli had lost the Indianapolis 500 that year, racing fans and drivers alike thought the engine was sensational. In 1968, Wallis built a pair of turbo cars for Carroll Shelby, but Shelby and Wallis withdrew them from competition just before the final inspection. There were allegations that the racers were "cheaters," illegal under the rules.

Wallis walked into Lear's office in August 1968, asking for a $39,000 loan for a forty-foot yacht that he intended to use for ocean research. Wallis had a bit of Lear in him. He was a smooth talker, bubbled with enthusiasm, radiated confidence, and spoke with dazzling engineering knowledge. "I liked him so much," said Lear, who knew about Wallis's problem in Indianapolis, "that I bought him the yacht and made him my chief engineer as well."

With Wallis in charge, Lear changed his strategy. He still wanted to design and build a steam engine that he could manufacture and sell. But to draw attention to it, he asked Wallis to build a steam racer that he would enter in the Indy 500 with one of the best drivers in the country behind the wheel. His plan was to qualify just ahead of the fastest piston-driven engine on the track, then open her up during the race itself, leaving the field eating the dust behind him. He'd beat the other cars so badly before the eyes of the whole world that millions would rush out to order a passenger car fired by a Lear steam engine. Then he would give the purse to the second-place car, winning even more publicity for his generosity. Why couldn't he win? Hadn't the Stanley Rocket, reaching the unheard-of speed of 127.6 miles an hour, beaten a Ford Model K in a thirty-mile touring race in 1906? If Stanley could do it, why not Lear?

Lear made his announcement soon after he hired Wallis: "I am going to build a steam-powered passenger car. And to publicize it, I am going to build a steam race car. With it, I expect to win the 500."

The response was electrifying. Lear got more than four thousand résumés in the mail from engineers all over the world who wanted to join his new corporation, Lear Motors, in Stead. Letters from well-wishers, cranks, and kooks poured in. He got orders for two hundred cars, many of them accompanied by down payments.

Lear put bulldozers to work at Stead, pushing aside sagebrush and tumbleweed and sand for a racetrack that would ring an artificial lake, to be called Lear Lake. The plans called for a two-and-a-half-mile blacktop with the same banks, straights, and pits as the Indianapolis Speedway. He announced that he would start practicing on the track on March 1, 1969, in preparation for the Memorial Day race. He floated a rumor that former 500 winner Parnelli Jones might drive the car. And he cut through the top of the Indy 500 bureaucracy by going directly to Tony Hulman, who owned the Speedway, to make sure the Lear Racer wouldn't be disqualified because it was different. Hulman welcomed the idea.

Lear walked even farther out on the limb in early 1969 by announcing that he would be producing five hundred to a thousand steam engines a day within eighteen months. And he stated his performance projections. His steam engine would fire up in 16 seconds at 40 degrees below zero; take off from a standstill like a cork from a bottle of Dom Pérignon; burn anything from kerosene to camel dung; and not freeze or need its fluid replaced for ten years because his fluid, Learium, contained a top-secret formula.

To Lear it was a game. He not only understood that his steam engine might never meet his projections, he also knew he might never even come up with a good steam engine. Basking in the hot media lights, however, he was having fun with his money, and if he had to eat crow someday, he would do it and move on to something else.

Overnight, the deserted Air Force base at Stead became alive with 133 engineers and craftsmen. While Wallis was working on the steam racer (without much help from Lear), Bill began digging wells, improving roads, and haggling for water rights for the industrial park, which he called Leareno. By March 1969, however, there was neither a track to test the steam racer on nor a steam racer to test. Wallis had been working on a Delta prototype engine in which the steam drove six pistons (which formed a triangle, hence the name Delta) that moved the crankshafts that pushed the car. The Delta didn't work, so Wallis began working on a Delta II.

Losing his patience and confidence in Wallis, Lear leaked a story that he wouldn't be going to the 1969 Indy after all, not because he wasn't ready, but because his motor didn't need the promotion. He was thinking of entering it in the 1970 Indy. Then he put Hugh Carson back to work on his original plan for a steam turbine for passenger cars.

In June, Wallis installed his Delta II in the sleek race car body that he had designed and that Lear had shown off during the International Automobile Show in the New York Coliseum earlier that year. Wallis gave the car the gun. Delta II exploded . . . and so did Bill Lear. He had just lost $4 million. He fired Wallis. Then he fired Carson, who had had nothing to do with the Delta. Then he fired half his engineering staff in anger and frustration.

At the root of Lear's frustration was the acute awareness that, at sixty-seven, he was growing older and he wasn't sure how much time he had left. After muddling along for a few weeks, he repented and rehired Hugh Carson, telling him to charge ahead on the steam turbine engine. He set up a second team of engineers to work on a string of other projects like a versatile brushless motor, a new autopilot, and an alternator for the Lear Jet. Explains Lear engineer Don Wildermuth: "There were six or seven things going on at once, all due Wednesday and undercapitalized. Lear was a guy with a new idea every day and we'd chase off in a different direction. He never exercised the discipline to see them through. He robbed yesterday to feed today. The steam project was consuming too much money and Lear saw the other projects as get-rich-quick schemes."

By late fall of 1969, Lear was ready to give up on his steam engine. After a year and a half of searching, he had not discovered the critical fluid he needed. He and his team had tried more than a hundred combinations. Nanney recalls one experiment: "Bill hired a chemist from a university, and he came out here and set up a laboratory to make heavy water. And it took hours and hours to get a drop. We needed gallons. So then Bill went to all of the chemical companies. They tried to tell him that this or that fluid would do it. Christ, he ended up actually making Teflon one time and it plugged up the radiator."

Like the steam enthusiasts before him, Lear had to rely on water. To fool the media, he called it Learium, his top-secret formula.

Because he had to use water (mixed with oil to prevent corrosion), Lear faced two problems. If he used a large vapor generator and a large condenser, he would have a difficult time fitting his engine under the hood of a car. And if he heated water to a very high temperature so he could use smaller vapor generators and condensers, he would blow holes in the coils through which the steam passed. Nothing worked.

Lear was getting more discouraged and poorer by the day. Besides designing, building, and testing several steam turbine engines, he and his engineers tried to convert the slant-six piston engine inside a new Dodge Polaris into a steam engine. Lear hoped to sell it to the California Highway Patrol, which wanted to experiment with a steam-powered pursuit car. But each conversion Lear Motors made was too heavy, too bulky, and too expensive to be practical.

After having built and tested about ten engines at a cost of $6 million, Lear began eating crow. In a speech before the Society of Automotive Engineers in Detroit, Lear said proudly and with no apologies: "A steam engine will never be mass-produced because it's too costly to build. It would be impossible to maintain, and for larger cars, the condenser would be too big to fit . . . You couldn't find a garage mechanic who could repair one . . . I told the federal government this, much to their chagrin. They thought the steam car was the answer to the pollution problem and I was the savior. I let them down."

Despite his apparent pessimism, Lear continued to work on steam. It's not clear whether he really meant what he had told the SAE, if he was just venting his growing frustration, or if he was trying to buy a few months of peace and quiet. Nevertheless, he joked about his failure. "I've never had so much fun with my clothes on," he bragged to a reporter.

Moya stood behind Bill during those maddening months of steam as she always had, with pride and encouragement. She wrote to Shanda in March 1970: "This morning Dad was going to call the press, pull the plug, and retire. He's tired and despondent! But retiring wouldn't help." Moya went on to explain how she went to the plant and called the engineers into Bill's office and how they talked him out of tossing in the sponge. "It's 4:30," she wrote. "He's behaving like Dad — and the air is beginning to sparkle."

Lear's bouts with depression early in 1970 were part of a two-year pattern that had begun with his broken ankle and nosebleeds. Soon after the steam project got under way, Lear began leaving the plant promptly at five and stopping at the Holiday

Bar for some Scotch and a game of craps before going home. No more haunting the hangar as he did in the Lear Jet days or bending over boards and screaming at engineers as he did during Learstar; no more testing late at night and leaving squawk sheets for the morning autopilot crew as he did in Grand Rapids. For one thing, he was worried about losing his stamina and mental agility. For another, on anything that was not aeronautic or electronic, he was out of his element. Although he was keen about solving air pollution, Lear was not terribly interested in the engineering challenges of the steam engine itself. And having given so much responsibility to Ken Wallis and Hugh Carson, he felt like a stranger on his own project.

Concerned for Bill's very life, Moya had asked Wallis to involve her husband more in the everyday specifics of the steam racer. Wallis did, and Bill's enthusiasm rose — until the failures started. Tina remembers them well: "He always cried when he was despondent, and he got despondent a lot because it was never going right. It was too big. He was exhausted . . . He loved Wagner [who] would move him to tears. I grew immune to his suicide threats. He would disappear with a gun and leave notes. And I'd say to myself, 'He's just playing around. It's such a dirty thing to do. Why doesn't he just shut up about it and go on and do it?' But I never knew whether that would be the *one* time when he'd do it."

Despite the fits of depression — he was taking a lot of Valium at the time — Lear did not give up. In June 1970, he signed a contract with the State of California to develop a steam-driven passenger bus, to be tested in San Francisco. The California Steam Bus Project was the brainchild of the State Assembly, which had decided to quit talking about improving the air and start doing it. The state squeezed $2.3 million in grants from the U.S. Department of Transportation, allowing it to hire three companies to build steam buses for experimental use in San Francisco, Los Angeles, and San Diego.

The steam engine was more practical for buses than for cars because of their size. Lear had thought about working on a steam bus before a car, but buses didn't grab the nation's imagination as much as racers or cars, so he hadn't placed the Lear Steam Bus high on his list.

With only two years to get a bus ready for use by the San Francisco Municipal Railway (Muni), Lear divided his engineers into a steam bus team and a steam car team. Overnight he turned "tiger" and became the old Bill Lear again. "It was seven-thirty to seven-thirty or eight every night," recalls Delos Hood, who worked first on the car, then on the bus.

Things finally began to click. In September 1970, three months after he signed the contract with California, Lear pulled a thirty-pound, single-wheel steam turbine out of his hat. "It's the answer to smog," he announced. He went on to say that his steam turbine engine would be noiseless, vibrationless, have just one moving part, and cost about $30 to mass-produce (it had cost him $7 million so far).

Edward Cole, the president of General Motors, gave Lear a new fifty-passenger bus and a Chevrolet Monte Carlo in which to test his new turbine, and Lear loved to joke about GM's contribution to his steam project. "Eddie," he told Cole, "when I come up with the answers that'll be embarrassing to you, you can say: 'He couldn't have done it if I hadn't given him a bus and a car.' "

33

IN JANUARY 1972, Bill Lear began testing the steam bus, which he had to deliver by August 1. Driving the bus around the hangar and around the Stead airport was a boost to the whole Lear team, even though the turbine engine was still plagued by complex problems. The condenser froze in the cold high desert temperatures because Lear's mystery fluid, Learium #3, was only water. ("It mixes well with Scotch," Lear joked with his engineers. "De-Learium," quipped his critics.) The bus was emitting too much carbon monoxide because Lear hadn't yet found a way to burn the fuel completely before it was vented as exhaust. The steam turbine was consuming one-third more fuel than a diesel bus, in part because the turbine spun at a constant speed, burning the same amount of fuel at 10 miles an hour as it did at 60. And the boiler kept blowing holes from heat fatigue. But the Lear Steam Bus was running.

On February 11, Lear Motors unveiled its bus, a silver fifty-passenger GM Coach with a sign on the front: STEAM IS BEAUTI-FUL. "Come to Leareno," said the invitations to politicians and reporters all over the world, "to witness a historic event."

From a stage in the Lear Motors hangar, master of ceremonies Art Linkletter tossed a string of one-liners to the two hundred reporters and dignitaries who had come to congratulate Lear or to satisfy their curiosity.

Lear promised to build a thousand steam turbines by the end of the year for $150 each. And he said he planned to drive his steam car right into Washington, D.C.

The attraction of the day was a ride on the Lear Steam Bus, driven by Del Hood, its project director. Hood was close to exhaustion. The turbine had blown a boiler the night before, and he had been up until three in the morning fixing it. He knew it could blow another one at any time. As he drove load after load of reporters around Stead, almost afraid to breathe, he felt the bus getting more and more sluggish. After one jerky run with a growling engine, Hood opened his window and motioned to Lear to come over. A photographer was snapping pictures. "I don't think I should drive this anymore," Hood told Lear quietly. "It's tired."

Speaking through smiling teeth as the camera recorded the conference, Lear said just as quietly, "Park the fucking thing over by the hangar."

For the most part the day was a success, even though reporters remained respectfully unconvinced by their "jerky" ride. Patrick Bedard, who wrote a scorching column in *Car and Driver,* was the disrespectful exception. After detailing Lear's record of unfulfilled promises, Bedard described his ride on the Lear Steam Bus: "The cooling fans . . . make almost as much noise as a normal diesel. And commuters accustomed to city buses would not have approved of its jerky ride. There was much racing of the engine and dropping the transmission into gear. Each time, the accompanying lurch sent a TV cameraman, who was trying to record the historic moment from just behind the driver's ear, down to his knees as though he had been kicked. What it felt like was a normal piston engine with the choke stuck . . . ''

After a feverish race against the clock, the Lear Vapor Turbine Powered Coach began service in San Francisco on August 12, 1972, running the Embarcadero Route from the Southern Pacific Terminal to Fisherman's Wharf. Del Hood and his team stood by with wrenches and blowtorches to tune the engine each night. The coach ran perfectly the first two days, but had to be withdrawn between August 9 and 11 to replace the boiler and adjust the burner, which was allowing too much exhaust to escape. From August 11 to 25, the last day of official service, it carried up to ninety-eight passengers without a problem. As a further test, Muni officials simulated the weight of fifteen passengers and sent the bus up and down San Francisco's steepest hills. The bus climbed well. To prove just how tough the Lear Steam Bus was, Hood drove it home over the Sierra Nevadas to Reno.

Of the three coaches in the California Steam Bus Project — one in Los Angeles, made by William M. Brobeck and Associates, and the other in San Diego, made by Steam Power Systems — the Lear Steam Bus performed the best, with the most number of days in service and the fewest breakdowns.

Lear had predicted that his initial steam turbine, "the answer to smog," would be twice as clean as the 1976 clean air standards required. It was. Tests conducted by the California Steam Bus Project showed that the Lear turbine coach emitted nearly the same amount of carbon monoxide as a Muni diesel bus, but seven times fewer of the more deadly hydrocarbons and nitrogen oxides. Its fuel economy, however, was predictably poor — 2.2 miles per gallon (kerosene) at 30 miles an hour compared to between 7 and 12 miles per gallon for a standard diesel.

The California Steam Bus Project pronounced the experiment an unqualified success. With adequate funding and progressive engineering, it reported, the steam engine will be ready for general use in less than a decade.

Elated by his success, Lear took his bus to Washington in the fall of 1972. The Nixon administration and the politicians on Capitol Hill seemed interested, but not enough to promise the

$30 million he said he needed to develop a production prototype. Instead, the Environmental Protection Agency tossed him a bone — a $900,000 grant to build a laboratory version of the Rankine cycle engine for cars that would meet the 1976 emission standards, get at least 8.5 miles per gallon, and reach 65 percent of full power within 45 seconds after startup at room temperature.

Back in Reno, Lear turned his full attention to the steam car, which engineers like Hood and Wildermuth had been saying would never be practical. The converted Monte Carlo made its first run up and down the shop floor on January 23, 1973, a year after the steam bus had greeted the press. On its fifth day of testing, engineers Karl Budde and Randy Carlson drove the steam car up into the Sierra Nevadas, over the Donner Pass, down the freeway past Sacramento, and into San Francisco, where it broke down.

That May, testifying before a Senate subcommittee on the environment, Lear tried a bluff. "I have been forced to make a most distasteful decision," he announced. "Within thirty days, I will cease all development of the Lear steam auto-propulsion system. After spending fifteen million dollars, it is my decision that I cannot go on alone."

But Lear didn't give up on the steam car and Washington did not offer him $30 million. Lear had always seen General Motors as his trump card. It had followed the steam project, had given him at least $200,000 in equipment, had offered him advice, and had hinted at a possible financial deal. Early in November 1973, he sent his bus to the GM Research Laboratories in Dearborn, Michigan, for evaluation on the dynamometer. The results were similar to those of the California Steam Bus Project, but on the city bus schedule test, the Lear bus averaged only 0.85 miles per gallon.

General Motors decided it did not want to buy either the rights to Lear's steam turbine engine or the research he had conducted. And the Department of Transportation told the California Assembly that it would no longer fund the California Steam Bus Project.

Lear was devastated. All he had to show for $15 million was an imperfect steam turbine engine that no one wanted to buy, a room full of research data, and a $900,000 grant from the EPA. Seventy-one years old, discouraged, and not sure what to do next, Lear became moody and depressed.

When Moya suffered a mild heart attack from all the pressure and tension, Lear became really frightened. The morning after he forced her into a hospital (medical attention conflicted with her Christian Science beliefs), Bill went into his office and closed the door, which he rarely did. Concerned when he didn't start bellowing, his secretary Dorothy Olson peeked in. Tears were streaming down his face. A wet handkerchief lay on his desk and he held a fresh one in his hand. Olson put her arms around him. "Mr. Lear," she said, "Moya's going to be all right."

34

LONG BEFORE HER heart attack, it became clear to Moya that Bill needed help in running Lear Motors. He tired more easily; the steam project was more complex than he had anticipated; the smaller projects he had spawned needed more attention; and Bill was running out of money. He was planning to sell his Lear Jet Model 24 for cash and keep only the larger Model 25. Moya talked Bill into hiring John as his pilot, hoping to bring Bill the support he needed and to give father and son a chance to bury the hatchet.

John took the job. He had always thought that his father's legendary flying exploits were more legend than skill. And he took a dim view of how his father kept bending FAA rules, which, as a professional pilot and flight instructor, he had come to respect. But once he began flying with his father, John was shocked to see how slow the old man's reflexes had become.

On one trip with Moya in the back, Bill tried to land in San Francisco, where he had to bring the plane through the fog on instruments because his Lear autopilot wasn't working. As he flew over the outer marker, he missed the glide slope radio beam and started to descend too late.

"Let's go around, Dad," John suggested. Bill was too high to make a safe landing in a Lear Jet.

"No, no, no, we're just over the outer marker," Bill objected. Another pass would mean a thirty-minute delay with the heavy air traffic that morning.

"When the weather is this low," John cautioned, "there's no margin of error down there."

Bill agreed. During the second approach, he couldn't hold the jet steady without the autopilot. The plane began rocking back and forth, taking bigger and bigger bites. Realizing his father was in trouble, John prepared to take over. Bill broke through the fog at 200 feet in a 45-degree bank, heading for San Francisco Bay. John caught sight of the runway strobe light out of the corner of his eye. His father had missed it completely. With no time to explain, John grabbed the controls, recovered the airplane, and completed the landing.

Bill and Moya stepped out of the plane without saying a word, as if such near misses happened every day. Another time, John and Bill took off from Detroit for Stead. As they zoomed into Utah, John cautioned his father, "Dad, let's land at Salt Lake and get some fuel." There was barely enough to get them to Stead, where the weather was bad.

"No, we'll make it," Bill said.

They started their descent over the mountains into Stead with 500 pounds (they should have been in the hangar with 500 pounds). The Reno weather was zero, zero, and the tower took them as low as it could on radar. At 150 feet, Bill finally broke through the fog and saw a row of lights. "There it is," he said with relief. "There it is." Putting the gear and flaps down, Bill approached for a landing. John checked his compass.

"Oh Christ, where are we?" Bill moaned when the runway turned out to be the railway tracks.

"Just turn to the right," John said. "I think I see the airport."

After he landed, Bill played the usual game with his hangar crew. Cutting his engines, he glided straight for the hangar door. God help the crew if the doors weren't open, and God help Lear if the electrical system or the brakes took a few minutes' rest.

The more he flew with his father, the more concerned John became — not just for the old man, but for Moya and his own daughters, who sometimes flew with their grandfather when John was not aboard. "I was a blithering idiot after those flights," John recalls. "And the whole time I was up there, flying safety pilot for him, it was like that. Each flight was a disaster."

John began working on sharpening his father's Lear Jet flying skills. Bill did not have an FAA rating to fly the Model 25. Whenever he filed his flight plan, he would list John, who had the rating, as pilot. Then Bill would sit in the left seat. Not happy with the deception, John suggested that his father apply for a rating, which involved taking an oral test in Wichita to prove that he understood the mechanics of the airplane and then, if he passed, a flight check. "Set it up," Bill told his son.

Every time John arranged for the exam, however, Bill would squirm out, saying he was too busy. John finally pinned his father down to a test on April 13, 1971, to be given by FAA inspector Lew Axford, who had agreed to administer the examination in Reno.

"Your check ride is tomorrow," John reminded his father on April 12. "Do you want to go out this afternoon and do a little practicing?"

"Too busy," Bill said. "Put it off for two weeks."

"Lew's already here," John said. Bill was angry but didn't say a word. "He knew I got him," John recalls. "And boy, was he pissed."

The next morning, Axford explained to Lear that he'd give an oral first, then have Lear take him up for a check ride. "I'd like you to work up a weight and balance for the flight," Axford said.

"You know what I always say, Lew," Lear quipped. "If you can get the door closed, you can go."

"Well, Bill," Axford said, "that's not the way we're going to do it."

After a half hour, Axford walked out of Lear's office. "John," the inspector said, "he failed."

John leveled with Axford. "Look, Lew, the old man's dangerous. I'm not always going to be around to watch him. But he doesn't think he's dangerous. For the sake of his family, I would appreciate it if you'd give him the check ride."

"Well, as long as I'm here, I'll do it," Axford agreed.

John went to his father's office. "You didn't do so well on the oral," he said. "But Lew's going to give you a check ride anyway, then I'm going to work with you on the paper stuff."

Lear took off with Axford and landed twenty minutes later. The old man stepped out of the Model 25, his face red and puffy. Axford called John aside. "John," he said, "that was the worst flying I've ever seen in my life."

Buzz Nanney was waiting for John in the hangar the next morning. "I guess you know you're not working here anymore," Nanney said.

"I figured that."

John returned to Los Angeles. But hoping to establish at least a fragile cease-fire, Moya and John's wife, Marilee, encouraged him to go back to Reno to prepare his father for another oral exam and flight check. After taking his father up for a ride, John wrote a pointed critique that angered Bill, who scribbled sarcastic remarks all over the report and sent it back to John.

Upset that his father was making a joke of a serious matter, John asked for a conference. Without telling him, Bill put a tape recorder in a drawer and hid the microphone under some papers on his desk. He planned to play the tape later to Moya so she could hear for herself what a good father he was and what a bad son John was. John discovered the microphone early in the conference, which quickly turned into a verbal brawl, with John shouting "Bullshit" at his father and Bill threatening to disinherit him for not showing respect.

As soon as his son left for Los Angeles, Bill put in a letter what he had found difficult to say face to face. "The going has been hard all my life but I've tried to make it look easy," he wrote John. "The going is especially hard now, and I need your help. There is a pretty good future here if you'll try to find it. And I'll help as much as I can. Mom mentions some old letters I've written. Tear 'em up and forget them. Harboring is a losing game."

That letter wasn't the end of the fight. Still worried that his father might kill himself, and maybe Moya or his daughters as well, John asked the FAA to revoke his father's pilot's license for medical reasons. He was certain that a family doctor had once told him that his father had had a "little trouble with his ticker," and he knew his father "took a lot of pills." Although he knew his father would be sputtering mad, John had no idea how vindictively the old man would punch back.

After reviewing Lear's medical history, the FAA notified John that his father had passed his Model 25 type rating (with help from Clay Lacy, who thought Lear flew reasonably well) and that "he is medically qualified" to fly. Bill, in turn, reported John to the FAA, requesting that his son be grounded. In his letter to the FAA, he accused his son of flying under the influence, having legs too weak to move the pedals due to his injuries in the Geneva crash, and being a flying risk because of psychological problems. The FAA office in Los Angeles called John in for an evaluation. They told him they thought Bill Lear's letter was nothing more than a family feud, but that since they had investigated the father, they had to examine the son. After interviewing John for several hours, the FAA panel gave him a clean bill of health.

But Bill was so angry with John for trying to get his pilot's license revoked that he wouldn't take his own advice, "harboring is a losing game." During an interview for a *Playboy* profile, Lear described how he had beaten up John so badly over a disrespectful remark that he thought he had "killed" his son. The story was not true and, for John at least, was just one more example of his father "bullshitting." John decided to take a job in Cambodia as an airline pilot.

Since Bill couldn't turn to his older son for help either — after being fired the second time, Bill Jr. had wisely decided never to work for the old man again — he turned to Shanda's Italian husband, Gian Carlo Bertelli. Lear had glimpsed his talents in June 1972, when he and Moya flew to Rome to hunt for steam car investors. Gian Carlo had impressed Lear immensely. He held a doctorate in European literature and institutions and had studied at Columbia University in New York on a Fulbright fellowship. In 1972, he was executive vice president of the European division of Hill and Knowlton, a public relations firm based in New York.

In a series of letters between June 1972 and October 1973, Moya wrote Shanda how "desperately" Bill needed "Gian Carlo's young steady hand." Although he was not eager to work for his father-in-law, to please Shanda, Gian Carlo wrote Bill that he could arrange for a leave from Hill and Knowlton for two or three years. Like Bill Jr. before him, Bertelli tried to find out what lay behind that vague invitation to "come to Reno."

Lear answered a few weeks later. "I want you here as my right hand," he said bluntly and with characteristic optimism. "Actually to take over the corporation when I decide to run off with some other woman or kick the bucket. In the meantime, assist me in helping this company grow into a multimillion-dollar affair . . . I am sure it will take $50 million to do the first phase of our production plans [develop prototypes] and another $50 million to get our products to market. Financial houses are beginning to show a great deal of interest in our company, and I feel sure of the proper amount of money when the time comes."

The arrival of the Bertellis at River House, the Lears' home on the Truckee River in Verdi, in December 1973 was a great comfort to Moya. She was, as she wrote Patti, "enormously relieved to know Dad would have somebody to lean on — because I was afraid your dad was finally going to throw in the towel." The oil embargo had begun three months earlier; Lear did not have the $50 million he had told Gian Carlo he expected; and investment bankers were no longer interested in Lear Motors.

Just as Gian Carlo was getting his introduction to Reno and to the three Lear companies — Lear Motors (the steam car, steam bus, steam minibus, steam boat engine, brushless motor, battery recharger), Leareno Development (the Stead real estate), and Lear Avia (the autopilot, helicopter muffler, yaw damper, sound suppressor, and a "superwing" for a jet), Lear was rushed to St. Mary's Hospital with severe abdominal pain. Doctors discovered that he had swallowed a toothpick, which had punctured the wall of his stomach. While Lear was recovering in the hospital, Bertelli, armed with power of attorney (which he never used), began to study Lear's business. What he found was far worse than he had anticipated.

The account books were chaotic; there was no money to support the thirty Lear projects on the drawing board or on the workbench, few of which seemed to have any immediate commercial potential; and there wasn't enough money to meet the weekly payroll. Furthermore, Lear had surrounded himself with two types of people — honest engineers who told it like it was, and freeloaders who managed to hang on by deception and flattery.

Bertelli began to chip away on problem number one, the steam engine, which, by Lear's counting, had cost nearly $15 million so far. To get his own feel for its market potential, he called Ed Cole at General Motors and Giovanni Savonuzzi at Fiat, saying Lear Motors needed a final answer. Did they or didn't they want rights to the steam turbine? Would they or wouldn't they help Lear? Both said no. Next, Bertelli called Lear's old business advisers Justin Dart and Dick Millar. Both said that Lear should pull the plug on steam. If that news wasn't dismal enough, the EPA announced publicly that it was withdrawing Lear's contract because Lear Motors had failed to meet its specifications. That meant Lear owed the EPA $900,000.

Bertelli negotiated with the EPA, whom he found reasonable but understandably defensive. For four years, Lear had ridiculed the agency before reporters, during congressional hearings, in letters to congressmen, and to President Nixon himself. Lear never tired of calling the EPA administrators "professorial nincompoops," labeling one in particular a "little bastard." Patti had sent him a BULLSHIT rubber stamp, and he used it freely to answer EPA letters.

Bertelli reasoned with the EPA, which finally agreed to let Lear keep the $900,000 as partial payment for the valuable research data he had collected. Then, in May 1974, after six months of watching and studying, Bertelli wrote Bill and Moya a brief, clear, and hard-hitting analysis of their problem. The Lear companies, he pointed out, were suffering from four "diseases": difficulty in making transitions from development into production; too many projects; a lack of consistency and continuity; and a dearth of realistic planning data.

Bertelli offered a plan of action as well: cut or sell any project that is losing money; focus on a few short-term products close to completion; after reviewing all long-term projects with sound market research data, select two or three for development, cut the payroll accordingly, and look for financing. Bertelli pointed out that the Lear companies had less than $1 million in liquid cash to work with. Other than that, they had a hangar, flight school with helicopters, a Lear Jet, and some salable inventory that, altogether, was worth between $2.5 and $3 million. Not very much. But the Lear companies still had Bill Lear and his name.

Lear responded by searching for money to bolster his crumbling empire. He went to Venezuela and Taiwan to find men with "loads of money to invest," but he came home with empty pockets. He met with Saudi princes and the shah of Iran, who sent a team of men "in dark green Yves Saint Laurent suits" to check out Stead. And when the money didn't follow their return to Iran, he still wouldn't give up his steam engine.

Next, Lear got involved in what he called "an unbelievable refining process which will derive gold, silver and platinum out of the waste of mines . . . just sitting there since the mines were established." He invited the astronaut Edgar Mitchell to River House to pore over geological survey maps, then to scan the desert and mountains in a helicopter, looking under rock and sand for the pot of gold that would save the steam turbine. Nothing worked, but Lear couldn't let go, not while he thought there was still one more chance to pull the project through.

While Lear was looking for a miracle, Bertelli was asking local bankers to loan Lear money for specific projects. After studying product proposals, they said that Lear's age was a handicap and demanded a guarantee of continuity in management. Lear would not hear of it. He didn't want to have anything to do with men of such "provincial" views, he told his son-in-law. Then he appointed Bertelli president of both Lear Motors and Leareno Development while he himself remained president of Lear Avia, where he could concentrate on airplanes and flying. It was the best and most important decision he had made in five years. He knew that was where he really belonged, with his autopilot and "superwing," and he was beginning to sense he should never have left.

35

LIKE MOST LEAR PRESIDENTS before him, Gian Carlo Bertelli was hardly more than an executive vice president. Lear turned over to him such administrative details as settling the twenty lawsuits pending against the Lear companies and searching for prospective buyers for the Leareno land, for which the water rights had not yet been completely secured. Lear also allowed Bertelli to pluck off a handful of projects clinging to the corporate vine and to cut the payroll accordingly. One of the people Bertelli chopped was a $600-a-month secretary who never came to work. But not for long. Bertelli got a phone call from June Shields, who told him that the woman was the General and he had better give her back her job.

Together with Preston Hale and James Sweger, a consultant who had helped Lear buy Stead, Bertelli helped negotiate two important land deals. He worked out an agreement with the Western Pacific Railroad to build a spur from the main line into the industrial park at Stead at its own expense ($1 million) in exchange for a right-of-way and a twenty-three-acre yard. The tracks would make Leareno more attractive to industry. And Bertelli helped negotiate a $1 million option with J. C. Penney for 197 acres on which the company planned to build a 2.2 million-square-foot catalogue distribution center. If it exercised its option, J. C. Penney would not only bring jobs to Stead, but could well attract other, non–water-consuming businesses to the industrial park.

Even though Bertelli did not have the authority he needed to do what he (and others) believed was necessary to rebuild the Lear companies, his personal relationship with his father-in-law was good. They were both creative and shared a great sense of humor. They drove to work together each morning at seven and returned together in the evening for dinner at the round table. Since Bill's eyesight was getting bad and he liked to ride the center line, Gian Carlo did most of the driving. They shared the same office in the plant and went to parties together.

Lear loved to spend weekends at the Bohemian Grove, deep in a redwood forest sixty-eight miles from the Golden Gate Bridge. The grove was owned by the exclusive Bohemian Club, founded in San Francisco in 1872 by a dozen newspapermen who liked to talk but didn't like the noise and smoke of the city's bars. By 1960, the club owned nearly three thousand acres of giant redwoods, among which nestled 128 separate camps for its members. Lear was frequently a guest and he loved the storytelling, the fun-loving spirit, and the boyish games of the all-male club.

During a 1974 August weekend, after plenty of champagne, Lear was walking down some steep outdoor steps arm in arm with Harry Jackson, the sculptor who had married Tina, "singing and clowning," when he pitched forward and fell on his head. The club's doctors kept him quiet and under observation for two days before they let him up to romp. Soon after he went home, Lear began showing signs of what appeared to be creeping senility.

Fifteen minutes after lunch, he could no longer remember what he had eaten. He forgot the names of his closest associates. He would give instructions to his engineers one day, and the next, having forgotten what he had said, would give another set. (Some engineers used the memory lapse to work on whatever pleased them.) He also began to lurch slightly when he walked, as if off balance. Most frightening, the memory lapses and stumbling would come and go unannounced, like a headache. Then Lear would be fine for days and weeks on end.

Lear, of course, was aware that something was happening to him. He didn't know what but suspected it was old age. One day an employee showed him an article about pyramids that suggested, tongue in cheek, that because of their symmetrical design, pyramids had the power to prolong life, improve concentration, and stimulate insight. Not giving a damn what anyone might think, Lear had a carpenter build a small pyramid in his office; he put a chair inside. Then he sat in his pyramid for a while each day, meditating. To some Lear managers, the pyramid incident only confirmed that the old man was slipping; to others, it seemed like a typical Bill Lear antic — try anything once, no matter how stupid it might seem to others.

It was at home at River House, however, that Lear showed how deeply he was rocked by his walking and memory problems. He became depressed, began drinking more and taking Valium again, and repeatedly threatened suicide.

One time, after a few drinks with Harry Jackson, who was visiting, Lear went into the bedroom to get one of several loaded pistols he kept stashed around the house. He walked back into the living room with a .38 Special. Jackson could see the brass of the bullets in the chamber as Lear walked around the room, waving the gun and putting on a show. Moya stood in the hallway peeking through a crack in the door. Jackson, who was sitting nearby, could see her eyes. They were wide, like a scared animal's.

Lear sat on the couch across from Jackson. He placed the gun against his right temple and leaned forward. "Harry," he said loud enough for Moya to hear, "just put a little pressure on the trigger finger. I want to end it all."

Jackson considered Lear an authentic genius with incredible imagination, drive, and savvy. Underneath Bill's hard veneer, he sensed a man who wanted to love but didn't know how. And he understood Lear's mood swings, which could change in the blink of an eye.

"Bill," Jackson said, "you're going to have to do your own killing."

"Come on, Harry! Just a little pressure."

"You're going to make an awful mess," Jackson warned. "Brains all over the wall and that beautiful couch. Have you ever seen brains spattered all over an interior?"

Lear gave Jackson a look that said, "You dirty sonofabitch, you called my bluff."

"Why not go down by the river and shoot your brains out there," Jackson said without emotion. "It'll be cleaner." He watched Lear closely, unsure of what Bill would do next. Pull the trigger. Aim the gun at him. Shoot a hole in the ceiling as he had done one day in his office.

Lear set the pistol on the table, its barrel pointing at Jackson. The artist slowly spun the .38 away from him and Lear and waited. Bill calmed down. The crisis had passed.

Like Tina before her, Shanda frequently heard her father threatening to shoot himself, but she saw it more as a "game" than as a serious problem. "One time, he left an empty bottle of Valium in the bathroom next to a half-empty bottle of Scotch on purpose, and went to bed. So we called a doctor."

Another time, Bill disappeared with his gun after an argument. Moya, Shanda, and Gian Carlo searched everywhere but couldn't find him. The next morning he appeared, as Shanda describes it, "laughing like a child who had played a really good trick on his mommie so that she would be sorry she had been so mean."

Another time, to punish the family for an alleged injury, he disappeared for three days to see the General. (Shanda had learned about her from Lear employees who used to wait in the car outside the General's home.) When Lear returned after his three-day tryst, no one dared ask for an explanation.

Lear's resentment toward his son-in-law began to show in December 1974, after J. C. Penney had decided to buy the land in Stead. Up to then, Lear and Bertelli had gotten along reasonably well, even though it was apparent that Gian Carlo's management style was radically different from Lear's. Bertelli was soft-spoken, organized, and consistent. He was more aloof from the employees than Lear, not inclined to empty a bottle of Scotch with the boys after a long day, not interested in engineering details or aviation, and not capable of turning out a part on a metal lathe or soldering a circuit. Although he appreciated the rolled-up-sleeves approach to management, Bertelli did not think it was the only way to run a company.

When the Penney people came to River House on December 30 to sign the purchase contract, Elsie Christensen, the Lears' cook and housekeeper, had a magnificent breakfast spread on the round table for them. Lear had to listen as the Penney people praised Bertelli over their eggs and coffee, telling him how lucky he was to have such a capable, persistent son-in-law working for him. In recognition of Bertelli's work, they suggested that Gian Carlo witness their signatures. After the guests had left, Lear began "raging," then went to his bedroom.

In May 1975, Lear talked to Dr. William Sweet, a professor of neurosurgery at Harvard, whom he met at the San Francisco Hilton. Lear asked for a private consultation. When he finished explaining his walking and memory problems, Dr. Sweet told him that he was probably suffering from hydrocephalus (water on the brain), caused by his fall in the Bohemian Grove, but that he couldn't be certain until Lear had had a CAT scan. If Lear did have hydrocephalus, Dr. Sweet explained, the problem could be cured by a relatively simple and safe brain operation. He offered to give Lear the test in Boston or to arrange for one in San Francisco or Reno. Lear put him off.

When Lear told the family — Moya, Shanda, and Gian Carlo — what Dr. Sweet had said, Gian Carlo called the doctor for an explanation. Dr. Sweet told him that since Lear suffered from memory loss and temporary confusion, there was the risk that in a moment of depression he would sign papers jeopardizing his business.

If Bertelli had been in a tough spot before, he was in an impossible one now. Noting how Bertelli locked his office desk and gave no one a key, some Lear employees convinced the old man that Bertelli was hiding business matters from him and was trying to get him declared mentally incompetent.

One Sunday morning, Lear called Maxine Zimmerman, one of his secretaries, and told her to come to the office with a locksmith. Lear took them to Bertelli's desk and told the smith to pick the lock. When Bertelli came into the office on Monday morning to find that his desk had been broken into and searched, he was furious. "Honesty cannot be found in a drawer," he wrote Lear. Realizing that the bond of trust between him and his father-in-law had been shattered, Bertelli gradually stopped going to the office. He had come to Reno to help his father-in-law as a favor to Shanda and without pay. He felt it was time to leave and return to writing and producing films. Given the personalities of the two men, the crushing financial problems of the Lear companies, and the power struggle between employees who were forced to take sides, the break was inevitable. The relationship between Lear and Bertelli remained cordial but strained.

Lear later said that his relationship with his son-in-law had crumbled because someone had told him that Bertelli had called him "senile" and said that he, Gian Carlo, would save the Lear empire. He accused Bertelli of spending all his liquid cash on expensive brochures and projects in spite of the note he had written Bertelli in September 1974: "Shoot the works, it's okay — Everything! Love, Bill." In reality, most of the cash flowed into Lear Avia, over which Bertelli had no control.

Moya did everything she could to help Bill cope with his physical problems, his business ups and downs, and his depression. For his seventy-third birthday, Moya planned a special surprise party to perk up his sagging spirits. Each year, Bill would tell Moya and Dorothy Olson, "Goddamn it, I don't want a birthday party and I mean it." They'd give him one anyway. In 1975, he told

Moya that under no circumstances should she throw a party for him on June 26. Moya gave him her solemn promise, then planned the party for Saturday, June 28.

Moya began preparing in May. June Shields and Alice Rand, former Lear secretaries who lived in Los Angeles, drew up the guest list. Shields would call Olson to say who was coming and, if the person owned a Lear Jet, its registration number. Olson would then make hotel reservations and reserve parking spots at the Reno airport, where the planes would wait until the coast was clear at Stead. The week before the party, Olson was spending up to six hours a day on the phone, speaking in code whenever her boss was nearby, and Moya was shadowing her husband and screening his calls, praying he wouldn't smell a celebration in the wind. He didn't, but three days before the party, he charged out of his office shouting to Olson, who was making a call, "If I catch you on that goddamn phone one more time, you're fired."

On Thursday, his birthday, Olson gave Lear a little spice cake with a candle on it for lunch. He was clearly disappointed.

Saturday presented a problem. How could they keep Lear off the ramp at Stead, while twenty-five Lear Jets lined up like so many scrubbed children, and out of the hangar, which Lear employees had polished and decorated, until midnight? Moya had asked John Heiser, an old friend, to keep Bill busy until three o'clock. Heiser took Lear out to a gold mine and then to lunch.

Back at the hangar in Stead, 250 guests, including Nevada's Governor Mike O'Callaghan, Representative Jim Santini of Nevada, and Representative James Corman of California, Patti's husband, waited. Over the closed hangar door hung a huge banner, LEAR JETTERS. At the center rear of the hangar stood a stage shaped like a Conestoga wagon facing rows of folding chairs and tables filled with food and drinks.

Lear didn't suspect a thing. But as Saturday wore on, he kept bugging Heiser. "Goddamn it, I've got to get over to the plant." By the time Heiser turned off Stead Boulevard and down the road leading to the airport, Lear was restless. As they neared the hangar with a string of Lear Jets gleaming in the afternoon sun, he still didn't catch on. "I hope all these sonofabitches came in for repairs," he said.

Moya was waiting under the banner, and when the car stopped, the hangar doors opened and the guests spilled out, shouting "Happy birthday!" Bill was so overwhelmed, he pulled out his handkerchief and turned away from his family and friends to dry his eyes.

J. Sheldon ("Torch") Lewis, to whom Lear had sold his first commercial autopilot almost twenty years earlier, introduced Lear from the Conestoga: "Most people in Mr. Lear's station in life, being as controversial as he is, have managed to make a lot of enemies. But few have ever succeeded in alienating all thirty-seven thousand people in the Federal Aviation Administration as Mr. Lear has."

After the laughs turned to chuckles, Lear took the microphone to a standing ovation. He had just learned that the National Business Aircraft Association had selected him Man of the Year, and the emotion at this point in his life was just too much. "He started to say something but couldn't," David Lear recalls. "He broke into tears and he wasn't acting."

They showed *By the Seat of His Pants,* a documentary film about Lear's life narrated by Lloyd Bridges. "It was great," Lear told the press, "but only PG."

In September 1975, Lear finally blew the whistle on the steam engine, which, by his calculation, had cost him $17 million, and he did it with a Lear flourish. He had been trying without success to get a government contract to develop the electric fly-wheel minicar, and he was, for all practical purposes, stone broke. He telexed his friend and supporter Senator Barry Goldwater to complain how desperately he needed government contracts and sent a copy of the telex to other friends in Washington, including President Gerald Ford. "If we weren't to the point of desperation, Moya and I would never bother you," he telexed the White House in a cover note.

Lear felt bitter toward the Nixon administration, which President Ford had just inherited. He had given Richard Nixon a $200,000 campaign contribution in 1967. He and Moya had joined the Nixons for a small dinner party in San Clemente. (Moya was somewhat embarrassed because Bill had insisted on wearing his brass WPL western belt buckle with his tuxedo.) The men ate in one dining room and their wives in another.

Lear had asked for a job in Washington if Nixon won. What Lear wanted to be was secretary of Transportation; what the White House finally offered him was chief of the Forest Service, which he considered an insult. And even though the White House hadn't helped him get contracts and grants — in fact, Secretary of Transportation John Volpe had thrown "water on Lear's steam" — Lear never lost faith in Richard Nixon or the Republican party.

When it became obvious that Washington would not pull a rabbit out of the national treasury, Lear finally allowed the steam engine to die with dignity. Instead of blaming Detroit or Washington for his failure to develop a practical steam turbine for cars, he placed the blame on himself, saying that if he had read a physics book, he would have known it couldn't be done.

At seventy-three, Lear was tired and sick. But although he didn't have much cash to invest in business, he was far from poor. River House, which was paid for, was worth several million; Moya's paintings and jewels, the cars, and investments in bonds, stock, oil wells, and mines were worth another million. And then there were the approximately twenty-five hundred acres at Stead, including a hangar and some buildings. Lear could have retired in comfort, but he wouldn't. A new project had fired his imagination. A new airplane that he believed had great commercial possibilities and that he had begun working on in 1974, when the steam project seemed dead and his five-year noncompetition agreement with Gates Learjet had expired. In fact, it was *because* Lear had something else to turn to that he was able to scratch the steam program. It was just like old times. Lear had let go of the autopilot when the Learstar caught his fancy, and he gave it up for the vision of the younger, more beautiful Lear Jet. Now he was itching to change partners again. "Let's get back to what we know," he told Moya. "Building airplanes."

Actually, Learstar 600 began as a "superwing" based on the research being conducted at NASA and Boeing and in other laboratories around the country. The radical, thicker wing would provide less drag, assure longer range, give better fuel mileage, and allow slower landing speeds. Lear planned to design and manufacture a "superwing" specifically for Lear Jets, then retrofit the airplanes for a fee. But after talking to aircraft executives and business jet owners, Lear decided it was time for a new-generation jet aircraft, something unique and special, an airplane that would meet market needs ten to fifteen years into the future, the child of a superwing mated to the latest turbofan engine. A ship no one could beat.

Having been burned by fuel economy over his steam engine, Lear was acutely aware of the need for an airplane that got more miles per gallon even if it flew a little slower. Most aircraft manufacturers, he noted, had not been planning for the day when gas would cost one to two dollars a gallon.

Lear brought his ideas to the aerodynamic engineer Larry Heuberger. Together they came up with a preliminary design of a turbofan with graceful aerodynamic lines and three applications: as a fourteen-passenger executive airplane that could fly 4,000 statute miles (transcontinental and transoceanic) at 45,000 feet and cruise at 600 miles an hour; as a cargo plane; or as a thirty-passenger commuter that could make five hundred-mile commuter flights without refueling. Lear's stiffest competition was Grumman's Gulfstream II, a ten-to-nineteen-place business jet with the same range and speed Lear was projecting for the Learstar 600 but that cost twice as much, weighed twice as much, and burned twice as much fuel.

To be more technical, Lear was proposing an airplane designed around his own version of the supercritical wing, with its higher lift, and the new Lycoming ALF 502D turbofan engine, with its high bypass ratio. Together, the new wing and the turbofan would make a lighter aircraft, which could store more fuel in the thicker wing, thus increasing its range, and which could fly as slow as 88 knots (or 101 mph), allowing it to use airports with runways too short for most jets. If anyone had seen the commercial value of the marriage before Lear, no one had proposed it.

During 1975, Lear made the rounds with his design package to banks, investment brokers, and airplane manufacturers like Gates Learjet, Beech, and Cessna. Everyone turned him down. As Sam Auld put it: "The aircraft companies reject anything stamped NIH — not invented here."

By November 1975, Lear was sick enough to decide finally to

see Dr. Sweet for the CAT scan he had suggested more than a year earlier. The test, which Sweet gave Lear at the Massachusetts General Hospital in Boston, confirmed the specialist's suspicion. Lear did indeed have water on the brain.

Cerebrospinal fluid normally flows out of the two cavelike lateral ventricles of the brain, where it is made with clocklike precision, over the surface of the brain, down the spinal cord, and into the bloodstream, where it is absorbed. In Lear's case, the scar tissue that formed after his fall in the Bohemian Grove was trapping the cerebrospinal fluid in his lateral ventricles. The pool of water was exerting pressure on the brain, which, in turn, caused his ataxic walk, memory lapses, and temporary confusion. If the hydrocephalus was not corrected, it could cause permanent brain damage. Dr. Sweet offered to perform a shunt operation to relieve the pressure, but Lear was too frightened to have any doctor, even one as well qualified as Bill Sweet, toy with his brain. If he left the water alone, maybe it would just dry up and go away.

36

IN APRIL 1976, Canadair Limited of Montreal bought an option on the Learstar 600 for $375,000, and its engineers began studying Lear's design concept and performance projections — cost, speed, range, fuel consumption — while its sales staff tested the market. Founded in the 1920s and bought in 1952 by what would become the General Dynamics Corporation, Canadair became the property of the Canadian government in January 1976 in the hopes that the company would revitalize the Canadian aerospace industry. Fortunately for Lear, Canadair was looking for a centerpiece project. Carl Ally, Lear's longtime associate in New York, introduced Lear to Canadair and negotiated the option agreement.

To Lear, the deal sounded sweet. Although he would have

preferred to follow in the footsteps of the Lear Jet — design, build a prototype, fly, certify, and manufacture — he didn't have the nest egg he had in the early 1960s. Instead, Lear settled for an option agreement that would give him, like the author of a book, advances against future royalties on the Learstars that Canadair would build: $1.5 million upon exercising the option; $3 million upon the Learstar 600's certification; and $2.4 million twelve months later. That amounted to $7.2 million before a single airplane was sold. Canadair also retained an option to rent Lear Avia's hangar and offices in Stead to develop, certify, and demonstrate the Learstar 600, which it would manufacture in Montreal, and to use Lear's name and reputation to promote the airplane.

With the obligation to serve as a consultant until the prototype was finished, Lear signed the agreement in New York and held a press conference afterward. It was an important moment, a Bill Lear comeback after he failed to deliver on the steam engine. He was standing once again where he liked to be, on the stage, announcing the third-generation business jet.

Driven by the smell of success and memories of the happy. Lear Jet days, Lear wasted no time. If Canadair exercised its option, Lear would rise out of the ashes of bankruptcy like an aged phoenix. His credibility, tarnished by the unfulfilled promises of the steam turbine, would be restored. And if he lived to see the Learstar 600 certified, he'd have $7 million in his pocket, not counting the steady stream of royalties for Moya after his death. Filled with a new sense of hope and excitement, he hired Sam Auld, whom he trusted implicitly, as executive vice president and chief operating officer of Lear Avia and Leareno. Auld would run the business while Lear worked on the Learstar.

When he arrived at Stead in April 1976, shortly after the option agreement had been signed, Auld found a Nevada ghost town. The hangar, where four hundred people had once worked at a feverish pace, was empty and up for sale. Desks stood side by side, some covered with blueprints and reports but with no one to read them. "The place looked haunted," Auld recalls.

Auld immediately began to raise more capital to keep Lear Avia flying until Canadair exercised its option. He sold the last remaining helicopter and a couple of training airplanes for approximately $300,000. Lear did not object as he had when Bertelli had tried to sell them just twelve months before. Then Auld hacked off half a dozen programs that were siphoning capital: a helicopter firefighting service, a flight training school, an aviation repair service, the Lear battery charger, the helicopter muffler business, and the jet noise suppressor. Lear did not object. All but the Lear battery charger were Lear Avia projects that Lear had shielded from Bertelli's streamlining program. Next, Auld sold Lear Motors to Del Hood and Don Wildermuth for less than $200,000. Lear did not object. With the Learstar 600 on the drawing board and an enthusiastic prospective buyer, there was no longer a need to be surrounded by the last vestiges of a dream gone bad.

As his chief engineer, Lear hired Richard Tracy, who held a doctorate in aeronautics from the California Institute of Technology and who had worked in airframe design and structural analysis at Douglas and North American before doing experimental design work for his own company, Flightcraft. A social as well as professional friend since 1968, Lear had consulted Tracy several times while developing the Learstar 600 concept, then hired him for one day as a consultant after the Canadair option.

Tracy was impressed with the Learstar 600 to a point. He thought the concept was "brilliant — a seemingly effortless marriage of what's technically available to the needs of the market." But he thought Lear's design package was "superficial" and his performance projections about as optimistic as he could make them without lying. Still, the new plane excited Tracy.

It was like the old days. Tracy had come to Reno as a consultant for one day and stayed for years as chief engineer, enticed by the confidence, commitment, and excitement of Lear himself. Following the old man's lead, Tracy collected a team of engineers and began shaping Lear's concepts into a preliminary design, beautiful and simple, one that would perform as Lear had promised.

While Auld was putting Lear's financial house in order and Tracy was working on the preliminary design, Lear went to Montreal as a Canadair consultant, fully determined to stay there as long as necessary to guide the Learstar 600 through the prototype stage. Although Canadair president Fred Kearns had all but promised Lear "design responsibility with only [Kearns] as the final authority," it became immediately apparent to Lear that Canadair itself did not share Kearns's enthusiasm for his leadership. The problem was simple and predictable. Canadair had bought the design, the research, and the authority to do whatever it wanted with the Learstar 600. But Lear considered the design his; he wanted no changes unless they were his or unless he "perceived them to be his," as Canadair's chief engineer, Harry Halton, phrased it; and he insisted on riding herd over Canadair's engineers. Lear returned to Reno "keenly disappointed," as he later told Kearns. The battle lines were taking shape.

The first salvo came over the size of the cabin. Lear had specified a fuselage with an 88-inch diameter. For both engineering and marketing reasons, Canadair insisted on at least six feet of cabin headroom. After recalculating Lear's figures, Canadair engineers specified a 106-inch diameter. "Let's face it," James Taylor, a Canadair consultant and the architect of its promotion program, told *Business Week*. "This plane meets a need. Corporate executives don't want to sit in the prenatal position in an executive mailing tube for long periods of time."

What Taylor and Canadair didn't realize when they began playing with Lear's design and criticizing it in public was that they were stirring the lion in Lear. Although he was seventy-four, his roar was still mighty, and he was, as Tracy put it, "livid with rage." Lear chose the National Business Aircraft Association convention in Denver that September to take on Canadair, even though the company had not yet exercised its option. He told the media that Canadair had "departed significantly" from his design and had destroyed the "fineness ratio" of his airplane. To increase the size of the cabin would mean changing the size of the wing, Lear stressed, which would destroy the beautifully clean aerodynamic line of the airplane, make it heavier, cut the range to the point that it might no longer be transoceanic (a major selling point), and slow it down. Lear dubbed Canadair's version of his Learstar 600 "Fat Albert."

Forbes reported: "The Canadians are now calling the shots, leaving Bill Lear in an unaccustomed position of relative powerlessness and, like Shakespeare's King Lear, raging against his fate."

In spite of the tongue lashing, Canadair sealed its Learstar option in November. Harry Halton was convinced that Lear was miffed at the change in cabin size merely because Canadair, not Bill Lear, had suggested it. To buy peace, Halton proposed a compromise. There would be a competition. Lear and his team would redesign the airplane around the 106-inch cabin and the Canadair team would do the same. The two teams would meet to evaluate the designs, and Kearns would pick the winner. Confident that he would come up with the better airplane, Lear swallowed the bait. His problem with the wider cabin disappeared overnight. Admits Halton: "It was a bit of a subterfuge to keep Bill quiet."

The Lear-Canadair engineering meetings were held late in January 1977 and ended in a shambles. Neither team could agree on the interpretation of the test data relating to the projected speed of the wider Learstar 600. There were shouts and threats, allegations of falsified data, and a complete breakdown in communication. Understandably, Fred Kearns chose the Canadair design. Recalls Tracy: "It was a bitter pill for me, our team, and Bill Lear."

Wanting to leave the door cracked, however, Kearns invited Lear to submit another design. To fund it, Canadair would advance Lear Avia $50,000 a month against future Learstar 600 royalties. Lear seemed pacified. "I think you are right that the present arrangement has been difficult for both of us owing to the differences in our methods and those of our organizations," he wrote to Kearns. "In this light, I accept your proposition that my organization develop, prototype, flight test, and certify an airplane of my design."

With that sugarplum dancing in his head, Lear decided it was time to have his hydrocephalus corrected even if that meant allowing a neurosurgeon to drill into the Lear brain. He put Tracy to work on a new design, the Allegro, and made an appointment to see Dr. Lewis Levy.

Lear had met Dr. Levy during a party early in 1977. Introducing himself to the Reno neurosurgeon, Lear went straight to the point. "I'm losing my mind," he said. "I've seen doctors in Boston and San Francisco. I'm told I need a shunt."

Lear described his problems. He had become so adept at covering his condition that Richard Tracy, for example, did not spot it. Tracy noted that Lear slipped into dark moods, sometimes for hours, but he did not notice any weaving or memory lapses. He found Lear's evaluations and decisions clear, but his eyesight poor.

"Well, if you're demented," Dr. Levy told Lear after hearing him out, "then I would like to have known you when you weren't."

Dr. Levy suggested an examination and another CAT scan. After taking Lear's medical history, giving him a physical (he was in very good health), and studying the test results, Levy confirmed Dr. Sweet's original diagnosis of water on the brain. Lear was exhibiting two of the three classic symptoms of normal pressure hydrocephalus — an ataxic walk and impaired memory with some personality change. Although Lear said he did not suffer the third symptom, urinary incontinence, the shadows on his CAT scan clearly showed cerebrospinal fluid trapped in his lateral ventricles.

To test Lear's mental agility, Dr. Levy began to explain Pascal's law as applied to water on the brain. As he got into the theory, he asked Lear if he knew the law. Lear gave the surgeon a precise lecture on hydraulics, barely stopping for a breath. Satisfied that Lear did not have dementia, Levy told him that the brain pressure he was experiencing was "nominal" and probably could be corrected with a shunt. Lear agreed to have Levy insert one.

In February, Levy performed the shunt operation, which he had done about four hundred times before. He drilled a hole in the back of Lear's skull and inserted a flexible plastic tube, the thickness of a ballpoint pen refill, into the right ventricle, where the fluid was dammed by the scar tissue on the surface of Lear's brain. Then he threaded the tube under the skin of Lear's scalp, along his neck, and into his jugular vein. Levy continued to push the tube through the vein into the right atrium of the heart, using X rays to guide him.

During the hour-and-a-half operation, Dr. Levy made only two incisions — one in the scalp and one into the vein. Although the operation was major and not without risk, it did not interfere with either the respiratory or digestive systems, and it caused minimal postoperative pain. As a result, Lear could get out of bed and eat as soon as he woke up.

Lear recovered so well that at four o'clock in the morning after the operation, he was on the WATS line he had ordered on his hospital phone, calling the East Coast, where it was already seven. Within days, the walls of his room were covered with sketches and designs for the Allegro. At Lear's insistence, Auld and Tracy visited him daily to discuss plans and progress and to get instructions and decisions. Except for "flaming Agnes," his red-headed day nurse who hovered over him and brushed off his passes with aplomb, it was almost as if Lear had never been in surgery.

After recovering from the shunt, Lear stayed in St. Mary's to have a cataract removed, hoping to improve his failing vision. While the eye was healing, Dr. Levy noticed that his patient was getting lethargic, one indication that the shunt might be malfunctioning. Early in March, the surgeon performed a second operation to check the shunt; he concluded that the segment going into Lear's heart was too short, so he lengthened it. Lear recovered well and soon was back at Stead, bullying the Allegro into shape.

By the end of March, however, the same symptoms returned. "His judgments became poor," recalls Rodney Schapel, a Lear aerodynamic engineer. "He'd come into my office and be completely rational and go over every little detail. Then it would be like he didn't know what he was doing."

Suspecting a malfunctioning valve on the end of the shunt, Dr. Levy performed a third operation. As he tugged on the tube leading to the heart, trying to pull it through the jugular so he could examine the shunt valve, he felt resistance. But where and by what? Tense and tentative, Levy pulled a little harder. The tube came out.

Close to the top, near the valve, Dr. Levy found a knot that was blocking the flow of the fluid into the heart. All he had to do was untie it and reinsert the tube. The shunt worked beautifully after that, and a later CAT scan showed that, for all practical purposes, Lear was cured of hydrocephalus. His walk returned to normal, and gone were the memory losses and confusion.

Once Bill was resting comfortably and out of danger, Moya left for Italy to rest, but not before asking Maxine Zimmerman to stand guard in Bill's hospital room. Telling Auld, Tracy, and Schapel they were not welcome, Zimmerman rationed Lear's phone calls. She'd dial, then hand him the receiver. He liked to talk to the General, and he'd moan and tell her that he was certain he was dying. Zimmerman had to smile because it was such an obvious and unashamed play for sympathy.

Soon after Lear returned to work, the final Allegro design was ready. Lear and his team had submitted a series of preliminary Allegro sketches and design concepts to Canadair that the company neither rejected nor accepted. Although engineers like Tracy and Schapel were beginning to suspect that Canadair was trying to buy the old man off, the thought never crossed Lear's mind. It should have. Instead of being radically different from the Learstar, the Allegro was a further refinement of Lear's original design and, as such, was in direct competition with Canadair's version of the Learstar 600. Lear was hoping that Canadair would either scrap its own design in favor of his or manufacture both airplanes.

The Allegro was a sleek ship that purported to be not only lighter and faster than the Learstar 600 but more elegant and more fuel efficient as well. Except for its airframe, most of the Allegro — leading edges, ailerons, flaps, spoilers, dorsal fin, engine cover, rudder, and elevator — was made of advanced composites, a material tougher and lighter than aluminum.

Advanced composites is a carbon or graphite cloth one thirteen-thousandths of an inch thick. Stretched over a frame in layers, it is impregnated with an epoxy resin such as Fiberite. When the "skin" hardens, it looks and feels like black steel. Unlike aluminum, which is 40 percent heavier, advanced composites does not need rivets to fasten it to the airframe.

When he first proposed using advanced composites on the Allegro, Tracy had found Lear well informed but opposed to the idea. However, recognizing that Lear was "always open and pushing the state of the art," Tracy and Schapel brought experts to Stead to talk about advanced composites in aviation, from rockets to spaceships to pieces of Boeing bombers. They showed Lear parts made from composites so he could heft them and see for himself how many "grandmothers" the graphite material would save. They argued that composites had greater durability and was potentially cheaper.

Lear soon changed his mind. And when he saw the final Allegro drawings, he got so excited he called Kearns immediately. "Fred, wait until you see my latest airplane," he bubbled. Almost in the same breath, Lear told the media how the Allegro was better than the Learstar 600, the original design of which Canadair had dared to change. Canadair marketing executives complained to Kearns that customers were getting confused. What was Canadair building, anyway? A Learstar 600 or an Allegro? And who was Lear working for? Himself or Canadair?

Kearns was forced to tell Lear in no uncertain terms that the company was not interested in the Allegro or in any other design that would compete with the Learstar 600. Then, because the company no longer needed Lear's image to "penetrate the market," it changed the name Learstar 600 to Challenger 600.

After Kearns rejected the Allegro, it became obvious to everyone, including Lear, that Canadair had merely wanted to keep Bill busy while it forged ahead with the Challenger 600. Fifty thousand dollars a month against future royalties was a small price to pay for peace and quiet.

Rod Schapel, for one, was ready to quit. He had joined Lear at the invitation of Tracy because the Learstar 600 sounded like fun, a real engineering challenge that had an excellent chance to get off the drawing board and into the air, where every aerodynamic engineer wants to see a design fly. And in its early discussions with Lear, Canadair had talked about using Lear's whole team to bring the airplane through certification. In the light of the latest rejection, however, it was clear that the Learstar was in Montreal and there it would stay.

The more Tracy and Schapel talked about Lear Avia and the old man, who was angry, hurt, and discouraged, the clearer it became that Lear needed another airplane to work on. As Tracy explained to Schapel: "Bill's going to die if he doesn't get one last shot." They decided to see if they could come up with a design concept that would grab the old man.

Ever since 1954, Lear had been toying with a pusher airplane with two turbo engines and a single propeller mounted on the tail. Early in 1976, Lear had asked Tracy: "How much fuel and how long would it take to fly an airplane with six to eight passengers from Los Angeles to New York at 400 miles an hour, at 41,000 feet, in a twin-engine propeller-driven pusher?" Tracy made the calculations. With two 500-horsepower gas turbines, he told Lear, about twelve statute miles per gallon in six hours. Over the next twelve months, Lear and Tracy would chat about the pusher every couple of weeks.

Although pusher airplanes had been around for a long time, none ever became commercially successful. There was the top-secret Douglas XB-42 medium attack bomber, which made its first flight in June 1944. The war ended before it could be mass-produced. There was also the unsuccessful five-person Douglas Cloudster, introduced in January 1947. Great Britain had the Planet Satellite, a four-passenger plane built in 1949. But after flying the second prototype, its designers gave up.

Tracy suggested to Schapel that he make up some preliminary sketches. The plan was to present Lear with a drawing of his own pusher idea designed around the latest advances in engine and material technology. Schapel worked on the design at home, bringing it to the office only on Saturdays when he needed to use the three-dimensional drawing board. One weekend Lear caught him.

"What are you doing?" he asked Schapel.

"Working on an airplane. It's a prop."

"I don't want to see anything like that around here," Lear said.

Lear was locked into jets, even though he was still interested in the pusher. But Schapel kept working on the design anyway, and Lear again caught him bent over the drawing board the following Saturday.

"I don't want to see that around here," Lear repeated. But he didn't sound convincing. He frequently said no just to see how committed his engineers were to their own ideas.

"This is your new airplane, Bill."

"Bullshit!" Lear said.

Two weeks later, Tracy had to lay off several engineers because the Canadair pipeline was frozen and nothing was flowing into Lear Avia from anywhere else.

"Where's the airplane you've been working on?" Lear asked Schapel soon after the cutback.

"At home."

"Bring it in," Lear said.

Schapel laid out the blueprints and cleaned Lear's glasses. Lear's eyes were so bad that Schapel talked him through the design for an hour, tracing the outline of the airplane and its parts with a black felt-tip pen as he explained the sketch and answered questions.

"That's our next airplane," Lear said. There was no hesitation, no ifs or buts, no maybes.

Neither Tracy nor Schapel recommended that Lear use 100 percent advanced composites for the pusher because the material was still in the experimental stage. True, it was impervious to corrosion. But would it crack eventually? What effect would sun, moisture, and lightning have on an all-composites airplane? And would the FAA certify such a plane if these questions remained unanswered?

Besides, just because advanced composites was 40 percent lighter than aluminum did not mean that an all-composites airplane would be 40 percent lighter than an aluminum one. And if advanced composites didn't make the airplane significantly lighter, why build an entire airplane out of it in the first place? Tracy, in particular, argued that it would be financially risky to design a ship with three unknowns — all-composites, a new Lycoming engine, and a pusher propeller.

Lear stood firm. If his airplane succeeded, he would have two more firsts to add to his string — first all-composites passenger airplane ever built and first pusher passenger airplane ever mass-produced. Lear believed it would be a new-generation ship at least ten years ahead of its time, a gamble worth taking.

By June 1977, the Lear Fan was clearly recognizable on the drawing board. For Bill, it was like a rebirth. He became so excited, Tracy recalls, that he started "flogging everyone." At seventy-five, Bill Lear knew that time was running out on him.

37

THE FALL OF 1977 was hectic. Lear gave a speech to pilots in Denver, then flew to Dallas to talk to LTV executives about buying the Lear Fan. From Dallas he and Moya went to Washington, where he met with congressmen on the Hill. Then up to New York for the *Today* show, with Jessica Savitch. On to Hartford to discuss the Lear Fan engines with Lycoming. Then back to Denver to consult with an engineer before going home for Thanksgiving.

Moya wanted John at River House for Thanksgiving in the worst way because she thought it would be good for Bill. John wasn't interested. The thought of another dinner at the round table with his father did not appeal to him. But when Moya, Dorothy Olson, and his wife, Marilee, ganged up on him, John finally agreed.

Bill couldn't wait to show John the Lear Fan. The plane was what kept him going and, probably, alive. He had told his son David that he thought history would remember him for two things — the Lear Jet and the Lear Fan. When John arrived the evening before Thanksgiving, Bill was waiting to take him to the plant.

John was not impressed with the Lear Fan mockup. He spotted what he thought were a series of engineering flaws — correctable, but still flaws. He thought the pusher's projected performance was overly optimistic, and he didn't think the ship would meet a market need even if it was certified. And that "if" was a big one because the airplane was to be all-composites. In a word, John thought the Lear Fan was a bad idea. Recognizing how important it was to his father and not wanting a fight, John looked at the airplane and listened to Bill explain the drawings, but neither praised nor criticized the project.

Noticing how disappointed Bill seemed after he and John returned from the plant, Marilee began working on her husband.

"Why can't you show some interest in what your father's doing?" she asked.

"It's a farce," John said. "That plane has no more chance of being successful than the man in the moon. I don't want to become involved in it. I don't feel like telling him my ideas on it."

"It's not right to treat him like that," Marilee pressed. "Tomorrow I want you to show some interest. He's upset. Ask him some questions about the airplane."

Bill and John ended up alone at the round table the next morning as if by plan. The moment was so awkward that both father and son found it hard to break the ice.

"How are you going to check the oil?" John finally asked his father, somewhat out of the blue. Bill didn't want the white fuselage of the Lear Fan to have access panels, which would mar its baby-skin appearance. "You'll need a dipstick about five feet long."

"You don't know your ass!" Bill said. Thanksgiving Day or not, the gauntlet was down.

"How are you going to maintain the engines?" John asked. The only way to get at the engines, which were embedded to preserve the clean line of the airplane, was to lift off the top portion of the tail, fan and all.

"We don't need any maintenance," Bill said. "Lycoming is going to certify the engine to forty-five hundred hours before overhaul."

"Yes, but you have to have fifty-hour inspections and hundred-hour inspections and —"

"We don't need any of that," Bill said.

"You can't be thinking right on this thing, Dad," John said. There was no way for either of them to turn back now. "How are you going to take the top off?"

"A crane," Bill said.

"A crane! How many cranes are around an airport that could pull that much weight off?"

"You don't know your ass," Bill said.

John kept jabbing just as his father had done to him fourteen years earlier when *he* was in pain and pinned and wired together in a Geneva hospital. Now it was Bill who needed support, and John was pounding away. "Are you going to have a wind tunnel

test?'' John asked. He still hadn't said one positive thing about
the Lear Fan.

"No."

"Why not?"

"Because we don't need one," Bill said.

John went on to criticize the Lycoming engine as untested and
unsuitable for the Lear Fan and the tail design as poor. He told
his father it was a mistake to use a belt drive in the transmission
because belts were potentially unsafe in the air, and he said that
Lear's promise to build the fan under 6,000 pounds gross weight
was a pipe dream. The word "stupid" flew around the table a
few times, heating tempers even more.

While the argument grew nastier by the minute, Moya and
Marilee stood by, helpless. As often happened in a fight between
Bill and John, the conversation eventually got around to Hal
Herman.

To impress his friends with his cockpit cool, Lear liked to tell
how he and Hal Herman, a veteran Navy pilot and John's first
flight instructor, were flying from Santa Monica to Montreal
one evening in the mid 1950s. Lear was in the left seat, Herman
in the right. Somewhere over the Rockies during moderate turbulence, Lear and Herman smelled smoke. Herman panicked
and shut off the master electrical switch, which shut down the
gyros along with everything else. Even if Herman turned the
juice back on immediately, it would take two full minutes for the
gyros to work again. The Learstar started into a graveyard
spiral. Within seconds, Lear and Herman were in a 90-degree
bank heading down at 6,000 feet per minute. Lear knew they
were dead unless he could make the right decision fast. He
looked over at the white-faced Herman, who was pulling on the
controls. Recognizing that he couldn't count on his copilot even
though he was an experienced flier, Lear grabbed the controls
and guessed which way to turn; it was the right decision.

As a pilot, John had always had problems with that story. One
day, he asked Herman what really had happened up there. Herman's version was quite different from Lear's.

Lear was in the back, cooking hamburgers on an electric grill
without an exhaust. The electrical circuit was not wired properly and soon began smoking. Lear turned off the grill, but the
smoke kept pouring out. He rushed into the cockpit and, with-

out saying anything to Herman, the captain, or to Clyde Cooper, the copilot, reached over to the instrument panel and cut off all the electrical switches. The gyros froze; Herman was without bearings; and the Learstar began a dive. As soon as he realized what had happened, Cooper turned the electrical system back on and cut the *one* circuit that controlled the grill and transceiver. The smoke stopped. Lear was ghostly white. Meanwhile, Herman had to make a fast decision. It would take the gyros two full minutes to start working again. Should he turn to the right or to the left? A wrong move spelled certain death. Herman took a guess and turned right. He managed to level the ship and hold it until the gyros were working again.

John believed Herman's story and always tried to make his father admit that his version was "bullshit." But Bill stuck to his story over the years and that Thanksgiving morning was no exception. The breakfast had turned into what John later called "the Thanksgiving Day massacre" — sarcasm, anger, bitterness, shouting, and Moya siding with Bill, Marilee with John. Marilee wanted peace at all cost. Bill wanted respect from his son. John wanted honesty and nothing less. Moya wanted John to stroke his father and was angry when he wouldn't. "John did it in such a snarling, nasty, critical way," she recalls. "Bill was already in physical trouble, and at Thanksgiving dinner, he was pale and couldn't eat. John just destroyed him."

John left for home the next morning. Every flaw he had seen on the Lear Fan would eventually be corrected after his father's death. The airplane would have access panels to service the engine, a wind tunnel test, a gross weight of more than 7,000 pounds instead of 6,000, a gear drive instead of a belt drive, a different engine, and a new tail.

Soon Lear made four decisions that would influence irrevocably the future of the Lear Fan. After reviewing the quotes he had gotten from outside companies for tooling the prototype (the cheapest was $3 million), Lear decided to have Lear Avia do its own tooling. He told his staff he wanted the Lear Fan in the air by his birthday, June 26.

In the meantime, NASA had released a report cautioning the use of composites made of carbon-graphite fibers. It had discovered that fibers floating in the air, although not a health problem, could play havoc with electrical equipment because carbon-graphite is an excellent conductor. Consequently, if a composites airplane crashed and exploded, it would send millions of fiber particles into the air that, in turn, could cause an electrical blackout. If Lear went forward on the all-composites Lear Fan, and if NASA held firm on its cautious preliminary study, the FAA might not certify the airplane, no matter how well it flew. Lear decided to go ahead anyway. As it happened, NASA later retracted its warning.

Third, Lear had to decide whether to build a production prototype Lear Fan, as he did with the Lear Jet, or a proof-of-concept prototype. In the production prototype, the design is basically frozen at the time of tooling in the hope that no major changes will be made after the first flight. As Lear had pointed out during the Lear Jet days, "With this approach, you're either very right or very wrong." In the proof-of-concept prototype, the design is looser and the tooling is temporary and relatively inexpensive so that the aircraft's systems and aerodynamic principles can be tested before expensive, permanent tooling begins.

Richard Tracy argued strongly for the proof-of-concept prototype because the Lear Fan, he said, had too many unknowns. He suspected that many important changes would have to be made after the early flight tests, and that if Lear rushed into production prototyping, the cost of retooling could break both him and the airplane. Tracy further pointed out that he was reasonably certain that if Lear followed the proof-of-concept prototyping, it would cost only $15 to $20 million to bring the Lear Fan to certification.

Fearing that Tracy would never be able to freeze the design and that change would follow change, Lear bit the bullet and decided on a production prototype. Tracy was so upset at what he thought was a foolish decision that he stomped out of the meeting at which the decision was reached. A few weeks later, Lear fired Tracy as chief engineer, offering him a job as configuration engineer so that he could contribute to the airplane without "managerial worries." (Sam Auld had already fired Rod Schapel, who strongly opposed the inverted Y tail that Lear wanted.) Tracy decided to accept the demotion because he "was in love with the airplane." As his new chief, Lear hired Nicholas Anderson, a Gates Learjet engineer and a Lear Fan consultant.

Finally, with some new development money from Canadair in his pocket, Lear told Auld to hire some engineers. For months he had been shouting at Tracy, "Goddamn it, Dick, get some people in here. Let's get going." But there was no money. Now, in a matter of weeks, Lear had thirty new engineers, a new chief engineer, and a new tooling production manager, William Benjamin. In effect, Lear and Auld had created a brand-new Lear Fan team. It was at just that point, in January 1978, that Lear developed a painful new physical problem.

Lear's back, which had bothered him on and off in 1977, was beginning to cause such excruciating pain that he couldn't even bend over a drawing board anymore. Dr. Levy gave him a myelogram. Bone slippage and degenerative changes in Lear's spinal disks due to age and previous injuries were so severe that the dye in the myelogram could barely pass through the vertebrae.

Lear had two choices. He could risk another major operation, in the hope that his worst disks could be repaired, or he could take painkillers, probably for the rest of his life. Lear didn't like either alternative. On the one hand, he was scared to death of another major operation. In the previous three years, he had had operations to repair a puncture in the stomach, to insert or repair his shunt three times, and to remove a cataract. Each had taken a toll on his system. On the other hand, he didn't want to live on painkillers because he had to keep his mind clear for the Lear Fan. His team needed him at this critical time in the development of the airplane.

Lear compromised. He'd take just enough Percodan to numb the pain when he needed it but not so much as to fog his mind. If that didn't work, he'd risk the operation.

Lear went to Stead during most of January and February and spent the day on the couch in his office, where he met his engineers. His mind was clear and he was as decisive as ever, according to Tracy and Auld, but a spark was missing.

For decades Lear had haunted his hangar, checking each drawing, watching machinists turn out parts, offering suggestions, making floor decisions. Part of his leadership style was to feel each problem in his bones, through osmosis, which led him to good intuitive decisions. And the Lear workers knew that the old man, like God, was everywhere and watching and, on occasion, omnipotent. They could feel his breath on their necks and hear his "sonofabitch" from one end of the hangar to the other. No one had to tell them who was in charge.

But Lear's back problem isolated him from the hangar, from the feel of the new airplane, from his boys. Without his shadow on the fuselage and in the hands of a new staff, not all of whom understood Lear's vision, the Lear Fan began drifting.

On the days when his back was especially bad, he stayed home and held meetings there. When the pain was too great, he stayed in bed with Percodan or Valium. He even tried marijuana once because he heard it didn't have any aftereffects, but it wasn't strong enough. Fighting pain and grogginess, he insisted on being told every new Lear Fan detail. Nothing was too trivial. There was a quiet desperation about him, and though he rarely talked about it, everyone knew that Lear wanted to finish his airplane before he died.

38

To ENSURE THE CONTINUATION of the Lear Fan in case he died before its completion, Lear made a string of closely related business decisions in late 1977 and early 1978. Explains Sam Auld, whom Lear appointed president of Lear Avia in January 1978 as part of his plan for the future, "I did not think that he thought death was imminent, but that it required an orderly handling." To begin with, Lear carefully selected the Lear Avia Board of Directors, which included Moya, Sam Auld, Fran Jabara, and Milton Weilenmann.

Moya, to whom he gave power of attorney and the right to sign company checks, would lend the family name and the Lear presence to the Fan after Bill died. Her faith in the project was as boundless as her confidence in her husband.

Fran Jabara, dean of the School of Business at Wichita State University and Lear's consultant for almost twenty-five years, would bring a broader financial perspective to the Lear Fan to keep it flying straight.

Milton Weilenmann, a Utah restaurateur and real estate developer, would take over the development and sale of the land at Stead. To make Weilenmann work even harder after he was gone, Lear verbally promised him a 2 percent commission, over and above his salary, on all the land sold.

Lear had met Weilenmann in the late 1960s in Salt Lake City, where Lear was to speak at an inventors' conference. The governor had asked Weilenmann, who was director of development for the State of Utah at the time, to meet the Lears at the airport and to take care of them. Weilenmann had tried to convince Lear that Utah was a better home for Lear Motors than Nevada. They became friends quickly, and Lear liked to discuss God, religion, and the deeper meaning of life with the Mormon. At least once, Lear had hired the developer to buy the mineral rights to certain parcels of land in Utah. And while Tina was attending Brigham Young University in Provo, Weilenmann had promised to keep an eye on her.

Sam Auld would be special. In the two years he had been executive vice president of Lear Avia, Auld had become more to Lear than just a right hand. Throughout his illnesses and physical problems, his operations and stints in the hospital or at River House, Lear had grown to depend on Auld to follow through on the Learstar 600 and the Lear Fan. Even more, Lear had begun treating Auld like a son, visiting him in the evenings or on Sunday mornings when Moya was in church, or frequently inviting him and his wife to River House. Lear felt he could count on Auld to be faithful to his vision.

Those four were to be the Lear Fan team after Bill's death.

Next, to generate a steady flow of capital for the Fan, Lear renegotiated (with the help of Auld) his contracts with Canadair. First, Lear declined Canadair's offer for development money for the Lear Fan, which meant that Canadair would no longer have any claim or option on the design. Next, Lear agreed to accept a much smaller royalty on the sale of future Learstars in exchange for $2.3 million a year over the next five years. If the Learstar 600 was not manufactured or if it failed to generate enough royalties to pay back the advance, neither Lear nor his estate would have to repay the first $6 million. (It would have to repay the second $5.5 million.)

In addition, Lear agreed to stop publicly criticizing the Challenger 600, not to design an airplane that weighed more than 18,500 pounds gross takeoff weight, and to bury his Allegro designs.

Further, to ensure the ultimate success of the Challenger so that royalties would continue to flow into Lear Avia after he was gone, Lear signed separate agreements with Auld and Jabara, giving each between 3 and 5 percent of his Canadair Challenger royalties after the first $5 million. The agreement pledged the money to "motivate [them] toward superior contribution and unusual personal involvement in the development of the aircraft for Lear."

Next, as an incentive for his team to stay together and to continue to work hard for the success of the Lear Fan, Lear decided to give stock options for $1 per share. In the fall of 1977, he and Moya began preparing the list, which included bankers, attorneys, accountants, his sons Bill Jr. and David, board members Jabara, Auld, and Weilenmann, engineers, Dorothy Olson, and Lear Avia managers. If the Lear Avia Board of Directors actually approved and issued the options (they would not be legal until it did so) and they were all exercised, Lear would be giving away approximately 60 percent of his company for less than $2,000. Believing in stock options as incentives but not eager to give up the family control of Lear Avia and, consequently, the Lear Fan, Moya objected. Bill lectured her, she would later say, that she didn't have to own half the stock to control the company. He had held less than one third of the common stock of Lear Jet Industries and still ran the show.

Finally, Lear told his attorney, Earl Hill, who would receive and exercise a stock option, that he wanted to rewrite his 1973 will and to set up a trust fund. Hill referred Lear to another attorney, Eli Grubic, a specialist in estate planning. Lear had one conference at River House with Grubic to dictate who his beneficiaries were to be, how he wanted his assets distributed to them, and the terms and intent of the trust agreement. But because there was no urgency, Grubic did not begin drafting the documents immediately.

A few days after meeting with Grubic, Lear decided to have the back operation after all. The pain had become unbearable, forcing him to spend less time in the office and more at River House. Dr. John Saunders, whom Lear had met at the Bohemian Grove, made arrangements for Lear to be admitted to the University of California Hospital in San Francisco. Before entering the hospital, Lear wrote an important two-page letter to Sam Auld that clearly expressed his "purposes and desires so far as Lear Avia and Lear Fan are concerned."

In part, he said: "My agreement with Lear Avia Corporation is intended to make the Canadair advances available to Lear Avia Corporation for the company's development of the new aircraft. After I am gone, it is paramount that the company (Lear Avia Corporation) continue with the project. To do so, it will need the financing and the Canadair advances to make that possible.

"My agreement with Leareno Development . . . is intended to provide a further means of master-planning and marketing the Stead property for sale after my death to enable Leareno to continue the sales of that property. The land development and sales program plus such other funds which may become available should be utilized together with the Canadair advances plus such other funds which may become adaptable in the forming of a total financing package with the Nevada National Bank.

"The Lear Avia stock options I have executed and will continue to execute are designed to diversify the ownership of the company and to provide incentive to my team. Lear Avia is to continue the development and production of the aircraft after death or incapacitation — Sincerely, Bill Lear."

As a final precaution, Lear told Auld to order Grubic to finish the Will and Trust Agreement because he wanted to sign them before his operation, on the morning of March 13. Lear instructed Auld and Weilenmann to wait until Grubic had finished the documents, then hand-carry them to San Francisco. Grubic worked from 5 A.M. on March 11 until 7 P.M. drafting and supervising the typing of the documents. With no time to proof them carefully — Auld was waiting in the office — Grubic stapled the pages together and gave them to Auld, who would later state in a sworn deposition that the first time he read them was on the airplane to San Francisco that evening. Grubic advised Auld to make sure Bill and Moya either read the documents before signing them, or had someone read them aloud, and to see to it that the Lear signatures were witnessed.

For most of his life, Lear had signed checks and letters without bothering to read them. June Shields frequently typed on the top of a Lear letter: "Dictated but not read." Over the previous few years, however, especially after his eyesight began to fail, Lear had fallen into the habit of signing the minutes of board meetings, contracts, and other legal documents without reading them as well, relying on Moya, his attorneys, or executives like Auld to read or explain them to him. Lear had to pay close attention because his hearing was also bad. On the evening of March 12, hours before his surgery, Bill signed both the Will and the Trust Agreement, and Moya the Trust Agreement, without reading them or having either read to them. As Moya recalls the scenario:

"Now Bill, I want to read this to you," Auld advised.

"I don't want to hear it," Bill said. "Does it take care of Mommie?"

"Yes, it does take care of Mommie."

"Does it appoint you and Milt and Fran trustees?"

"Yes, it does that."

"Does it set up a fund for the project?" Bill asked. "Does it protect it?"

"Yes."

"Then I want to sign it."

Moya was more cautious. "Bill, don't you want to have Sam read it to you?" she asked.

"Damn it, let me have it," Bill insisted. "I want to sign it. If I sign it, you sign it!"

"He was tired and he was hurting and so he signed it," Moya explains. "Do you think, at that point, I'm going to say, 'Well, before I sign it, I'm going to read it?' So I never read it, and neither did Bill."

The Will was a simple one-page document that stated that *everything* but Lear's death and funeral expenses was to be placed in "The William P. Lear and Moya Olsen Lear Family Trust Agreement," of which Moya would be executrix.

The fourteen-page Trust Agreement, however, was rather complex. It gave Moya outright the house and everything in it. The rest of the assets would go into a trust fund, half of which would be Moya's. The other half Bill willed to his children, some grandchildren, and to Moya's sister, Joy. Named as trustees were Auld, Jabara, and Weilenmann, whom the Trust Agreement authorized to sell, lease, and improve the Stead land, to loan, borrow, or invest money, and to buy property, enjoining them to "exercise judgment and care . . . which men of prudence, discretion and intelligence exercise in the management of their own affairs."

The Trust Agreement further specifically authorized and empowered the trustees to "continue the design and development of the Lear Fan aircraft, or derivatives or modifications thereof, or any other aircraft, with a view to the successful completion and marketing of such aircraft." To make sure there would be enough money to finish the Fan, the Trust Agreement did not obligate the trustees to distribute a single penny of Bill's half of the trust fund to his beneficiaries "until the goals are completed." And to make sure the trustees did not treat the Lear Fan too cautiously, the document freed them of all liability to Bill's beneficiaries for any losses incurred in developing the airplane.

As a last precaution to discourage Bill's children from trying to block the development of the Lear Fan after his death, the Trust Agreement disinherited any beneficiary who dared to contest it.

In sum, Moya had agreed to use her half of the family assets (except the house and its contents) to develop the Lear Fan. And Bill had pledged his half, including the Canadair advances, for the same purpose. After the Lear Fan was completed or terminated, the trustees could distribute what was left, if anything — half to Moya and half to Bill's beneficiaries.

In his haste to prepare the documents, Eli Grubic made several errors. The division of Bill's assets to his beneficiaries totaled 103 percent. Tina was referred to as Valentina Moya Lear instead of Valentina Moya Lear Jackson; the last name of Moya's sister was misspelled; and Grubic called David Richard Lear just Richard Lear one time.

It was Sunday evening when Auld and Weilenmann brought the Will and Trust Agreement to the hospital. Auld grabbed a phone book and began calling to find a notary public who would come to the hospital to notarize Bill's signature on the Will and the signatures of both Bill and Moya on the Trust Agreement. But as he later said in a sworn deposition, Auld couldn't find one. In the end, Auld and Weilenmann witnessed Bill and Moya's signatures even though they were named as trustees. The next day Auld told Maxine Zimmerman, a Nevada notary, to notarize the signatures made in California the previous day.

When he came to after the operation, Lear was in great spirits. Moya and her cousin Louise wheeled Bill from the recovery room to his own room. When a nurse got him into bed, Bill mumbled something. "Are you in pain, Mr. Lear?" she asked. He mumbled again.

"I can't understand him," the nurse said to Louise.

Leaning close to Bill's mouth, Louise said, "Bill, say it louder."

"Do you know why mice have tiny balls?" he managed to whisper.

"No," Louise said. "Why do mice have tiny balls?"

"Because so few of them know how to dance."

Lear was recovering well from his lumbar surgery and expected to be on his feet in a few weeks, roaming the hangar, back to his Lear Fan. But after making the usual postoperative tests, the doctors discovered that Lear's white blood count was high. At first they weren't worried because it is not uncommon for white cells to multiply after the body has been invaded by major surgery. But instead of going down, the count doubled and tripled.

The hospital called in specialists. Their diagnosis was clear. Lear had acute leukemia, which frequently strikes without any warning. He had only a few months to live.

39

CLAY LACY TOOK Bill Lear home in a Lear Jet. He tried to go to the office every day at first (the boys built a ramp for his wheelchair), but soon he didn't have the energy. Moya showed her bravest face to everyone but her closest friend, Ruthie Brown. She was collecting pills, Moya told Ruthie one afternoon, in tears, and as soon as Bill was gone she was going to join him. Without Bill, life would have no meaning. She couldn't live with the memories and the loneliness. Ruthie hugged her and told her that suicide was not what Bill wanted. He needed her to carry on after he was gone. Ruthie made Moya promise not to do anything foolish.

In front of Bill, Moya never gave up hope, for she didn't want to burden him with her own despair. She smiled, read to him from James Herriot's *All Things Bright and Beautiful,* and even got around to asking him a question that had troubled her for thirty-six years. When they were first married, Bill had asked her to lay out every evening his clothes for the next day, just as his other wives had. Moya never missed a day. As the years went by, she began to wonder about Ethel, Madeline, and Margaret. "Did they really lay out your clothes?" she asked him one day. He smiled that half smile of his. When she could no longer be around Bill without breaking down, Moya went to Europe to visit her daughters and to build her spirits for the days ahead.

Some days, Bill spent most of his time in bed. Other days, he would meet with his engineers in the family room, dressed up in shirt, tie, and red sweater and sitting in his wheelchair. He did not want his key personnel, except Sam Auld, to see him in bed when he was his weakest. But no matter how poor he felt, he still insisted on a swim in the heated pool just feet from the patio at the edge of the Truckee River. He made everyone skinny-dip with him — Moya, Ruthie, his nurse Jane Crooks, Dorothy Olson. He'd tell them not to worry because he couldn't see with his glasses off anyway. He'd have to feel who it was. He'd lean on whoever was there as he walked from the patio door to the pool-side, then allow himself to be helped into the water, where he'd swim three laps. Recalls Ruth Brown, "I used to watch him and think, 'How could he? What guts! He's just not going to give in.' And that's the way it was."

The approach of death did not rob Lear of his sense of humor. One day Dorothy Olson came by to discuss business matters with the "ornery old sweetie," as the secretaries called him. When she got up to leave, he said, "Turn around!"

She did, and he chuckled. "That's the skinniest ass I've ever seen."

"Mr. Lear!" she said. "You could have gone all day without saying that."

"When you get back to the plant," he said, "don't let me hear you telling everyone that you worked it off for *me*."

Lear still continued to demand progress reports on the Lear Fan and still made all final decisions. The last important one concerned the tail. The results of the wind tunnel tests showed that the Y tail (the original design) was superior to the inverted V (which Rod Schapel had opposed to the point of being fired). After reviewing the data and watching a videotape of three toy, remote-controlled replicas, each with a different tail, Lear chose the original Y.

No one talked to Lear much about death. He knew he was dying and so did everyone else. What was there to say? There were a few exceptions, like Buzz Nanney. For Christmas, Lear had given the Nanneys a black schnauzer pup, whom they named Charlie. Moya called the Nanneys to say it would give Bill great pleasure to see them and Charlie once again.

Moya and Ursula chatted in the family room while Bill and Buzz visited in the bedroom.

"Are you afraid of dying?" Nanney asked. He knew Lear well enough to be direct.

"No," Lear said. "It's been a long life."

"Ten years ago you said you hoped you had ten years left."

"Yes, I know," Lear said. "But there's still so much I would like to do."

"You'll always have so much to do," Nanney said. "I think you've generated enough enthusiasm so that things will still go on after you've passed away."

Toward the end of April, six weeks after the back operation, Lear was feeling much better and wanted to go to the plant to inspect the progress on the Lear Fan. The press was waiting. Once inside, Lear refused his wheelchair, and when Moya called Maxine Zimmerman to his side so he could lean on them as he walked to his old office, he pushed them both away. "I don't want your help," he said. "I can walk by myself."

Lear straightened up and began strutting as if he had just returned from a long vacation. He toured the hangar to see, as Zimmerman put it, "how his boys were doing." With some difficulty, he negotiated the steep stairs that led to the full-scale plywood mockup of the Lear Fan. But when he sat in the pilot's seat he was like a kid again, playing with the controls of a toy plane. He put on such a good show that some of the workers really thought Lear had pulled off another miracle.

Sitting behind his desk with a scale model of the Lear Fan on top, Lear gave his last interview. He told a reporter that he was an iconoclast smashing aviation tradition with his Lear Fan, which was flying backward to the Wright brothers only to zoom into the future as the most advanced airplane in the history of flying. "When you're an iconoclast," he said, "you have to be there in the front."

A few days later, on April 29, Lear told his chauffeur and pilot Gunnar Christensen that he wanted to take up the Cessna 340. Even though he was getting weaker by the day and his reflexes were very slow, Lear needed to sit in the left seat one more time. "The thing that I love to do more than anything else is to fly," Lear had told Merv Griffin a few years earlier. "When I'm really all wrought up and think that there's no end — you know — never find a solution to something, I get in my Lear Jet and go up and do a few rolls. (If the FAA doesn't find out about it.) I get all relaxed and then I can start again. Flying is one of the greatest things you can possibly do."

It took Gunnar half an hour to get Lear out of the car and into the left seat. He felt privileged to be Lear's copilot that day. The ten years he had spent with Lear had been the best of his life. Like many of the men who had worked for the old man, Gunnar had a love-hate relationship with Bill Lear. He couldn't count the times Lear had yelled at him at River House, "Goddamn, get out," only to throw his arms around him the next morning and say, "I love you, Gunnar." Sometimes he'd shake Gunnar's hand after a fight and press a hundred-dollar bill into it. As Gunnar puts it: "When he was nice, boy, he was the nicest guy in the world. When he was mad, I hated him. That was his way. He sure was the greatest."

Gunnar started the engines and taxied out to the runway. Then he gave the controls over to Lear. They both knew it was his last flight. Gunnar wasn't frightened as much as he was worried. He would have to watch Lear's every move and be firm with him. There was no way Lear could fly the Cessna alone. He was almost blind. His reflexes were too slow, and he didn't have much strength left in his arms.

Gunnar checked out the plane, then told Lear it was ready for takeoff. Lear was quick on the throttle. "Mr. Lear," Gunnar cautioned, "let's slow down a little." Lear eased back and they rolled down the runway. Unable to read the instrument panel, Lear was flying by feel, relying on Gunnar to tell him if he was making a mistake. Halfway down the runway, Lear began to ease up on the throttle. Gunnar coaxed him into giving the twin engines more gas. Lear lifted off. The plane wobbled a bit and one wing dipped. Gunnar talked Lear into straightening the ship out.

They climbed to 8,500 feet above Stead, above Reno and the Truckee, above the mountains and the sage-covered desert. "Gunnar, let's make an ILS to Reno," Lear suggested. He wanted to fly by instruments just one more time. He wanted to test the autopilot.

Gunnar was nervous but said okay. He called the approach tower, which confirmed that commercial air traffic was heavy. "I don't think we should land there," Gunnar said. But Lear insisted.

Gunnar guided Lear and the Cessna down to the minimum altitude for the ILS approach but then chickened out. He called the tower for a missed approach and took the controls from Lear. As the plane began climbing again, Lear chewed him out as he had done so often before. "Goddamn it, what the hell did you do that for?" Lear said. He wanted to approach again, but Gunnar wouldn't. "Mr. Lear, p-l-e-a-s-e!" he begged. Lear didn't press him.

At 8,000 feet over Reno, Lear went into a clean, controlled dive. Gunnar watched the instruments. He and Lear were working together now, four hands like two. Gunnar pulled the Cessna out of the dive. Lear did not fight him.

"Let's go home," Gunnar suggested gently. He could see the old man was mad, his jaw sticking out as if he was ready for a fight. But he also seemed very tired and drained, and he nodded yes.

As they flew back to Stead, Lear said he wanted to land the Cessna. Gunnar said no. He was sad to the point of tears because he wanted to give the old man that one last pleasure, but it was too dangerous.

"Gunnar, I will never be able to fly again," Lear said. It was a statement, not a plea. "I can't see."

"Yes you will," Gunnar lied. "Next month you'll be going to L.A. to get your new glasses. You'll be able to fly."

Lear let Gunnar take the controls without a struggle. There were twenty people waiting when they landed. Cameras clicked as Lear got out of the Cessna and into the waiting car.

William Powell Lear died two weeks later, on May 14, 1978. Two days before, he didn't want to go to the hospital for chemotherapy. "I want to go to the plant," he told Moya.

"My darling, why?" she asked.

"I want to beat on my boys."

Bill finally gave in but insisted on wearing his smart Levi suit and his favorite cowboy shirt. Moya sat with him in the hospital room until eleven-thirty at night. When Jane Crooks came to relieve her, Moya looked so tired that the nurse encouraged her to go home and get some rest. She promised to call if Bill, who was sleeping peacefully, took a turn for the worse.

Moya phoned the hospital at two forty-five in the morning. "How is he?" she asked.

"Not well," the nurse said. Moya rushed off to the hospital.

Moments after Moya hung up, Bill began calling, "Mommie! Mommie!"

Crooks took his hand and stroked it just as Moya did. Bill thought it was she. "Finish it, Mommie," he said. "Finish it!"

He died thirty seconds later.

Epilogue

THEY TOOK UP Bill's ashes — Moya, John, David, Shanda, Gunnar — in the Cessna 340 and gave them to the wind over the Pacific. Said one old Lear friend who read about it in the paper, "I ain't going near that ocean for a month. It's going to be so mean and turbulent, it won't be safe."

Lear's friend had a point. Bill Lear's Will and Trust Agreement created turbulence, and his Lear Fan is still debated in aviation and business circles around the world.

Lear had left less than $1 million in cash, oil well investments, and securities. The rest of his estate consisted of approximately 2,300 acres of land in Stead, future royalties from Canadair for the sale of Challengers, and possible future profits from the sale of Lear Fans or the company, Lear Avia, itself.

The Lear heirs were satisfied with the percentages they received in Bill Lear's 1978 will, which were comparable to those in his 1973 will — David (20), Tina (20), Shanda (16), Bill Jr. (10), Pat (6), Moya's sister Joy (10), and Mary Louise (6). But some were not pleased with the stipulation that — with the exception of Mary Louise and Joy — their money, if any, was to be held in trust, and that all they would receive in their lifetime was their share of the interest. John was not completely surprised that his father had disinherited him. His 15 percent went to his children.

To avoid problems in probate court (because Lear's attorney had mistakenly given 103 percent of his assets to his beneficiaries), Joy offered to reduce her inheritance from 10 to 7 percent. The court accepted her offer.

If they had no basic problem with the Will, Lear's children had difficulty accepting the Trust Agreement. When they began asking the trustees questions about both documents, copies of which they first saw weeks after Bill Lear's death, they felt the answers were incomplete and evasive. After discovering almost by accident that the Lear Avia Board of Directors, which included Auld, Jabara, and Weilenmann, had approved stock options that amounted to slightly less than half of the company without notifying them, they became suspicious. These same board members, they learned, had each received 6 percent of Lear Avia and had extended the period during which the options had to be exercised from four months (as their father had wished) to two years. They also noticed what they believed were other technical irregularities surrounding the stock option matter.

Concluding that the trustees were hiding something, some Lear children began doubting the integrity of the trustees and Moya's ability to manage the estate and business. The more they watched the development of the Lear Fan, the more they became convinced that without their father's leadership, the airplane would never fly. And if it did, it wouldn't be certified; and if it was, it wouldn't sell.

Unable to reach a compromise out of court, Tina filed for revocation of probate four months after Lear's death, alleging that her father had not fully understood the "effect" of the documents on Lear Avia and the estate; that under Nevada law Auld and Weilenmann were not competent witnesses to the will because they were "financially interested" in it; and that Auld and Weilenmann had exerted undue influence on her father, whose real intentions were expressed in his 1973 will. She asked the court to block the use of the Canadair advances for the Lear Fan, arguing that "there has been no satisfactory feasibility study done on the Lear Fan project to determine whether or not it is a prudent investment." The court eventually agreed.

Nine months later Shanda sued the trustees personally, alleging poor performance. She further alleged that they were guilty of "massive and flagrant breach of their fiduciary duties . . . fraudulent misrepresentation and concealment." She asked the court to remove Auld, Weilenmann, and Jabara for conflict of interest, pointing out that they were trustees, stockholders, directors, and managers all at the same time.

Privately and publicly, Moya defended Bill Lear's right to spend his money exactly as he wished, dismissing any intimation that he did not know what he was doing when he set up a trust to protect his airplane. She told her daughters that the money in the trust fund was not theirs until their father's wishes had been carried out, which she intended to do out of faith, not coercion. Furthermore, she pointed out, their father had always felt that by giving each of his children (except Mary Louise) between a quarter of a million and a million dollars in cash, real estate, or securities during his lifetime, he had adequately taken care of them.

Four years and more than a half-million dollars in legal fees after Bill Lear's death, Tina, Shanda, Moya, and the trustees settled out of court. Auld and Weilenmann would continue to administer Lear Avia stock (the Lear Fan); new trustees, chosen by Tina and Shanda, would administer the other assets (land and royalties). As the executrix of Bill Lear's will, Moya would not move to have Tina disinherited for challenging the Will as the Trust Agreement specified. And the trustees declined to sue either Shanda or Tina for libel, since the allegations were made in protected court documents.

When the Challenger 600 failed to fly as far without refueling as it had promised, Canadair developed the Challenger 601, a variation of the original design. By the summer of 1985, the company had sold more than 120 Challengers.

After spending $6 million of the Canadair advances, Lear Avia found two backers for the Lear Fan — the Wall Street investment banking firm of Oppenheimer and Company and the British government. The plan of the new company, Lear Fan Limited, was to certify the airplane in Reno and manufacture it in Belfast, Northern Ireland.

The Lear Fan made a flawless first flight on New Year's Day 1981. But when Lear Fan Limited began running low on cash in mid 1982, it sold the plane to a group of mostly Saudi Arabian investors. They formed a third company, Fan Holdings, Inc.

By the spring of 1985, the Lear Fan had consumed an estimated $260 million and had yet to be certified. The Lear family now owned approximately 1 percent of the airplane.

In May 1985, Fan Holdings declared bankruptcy. Whether anyone else will try to certify and manufacture the Lear Fan is uncertain.

By the summer of 1985, Bill Lear's beneficiaries had not received a penny. How much they will eventually get from the sale of real estate and from Canadair royalties, once the taxes, loans, and other bills have been paid and Moya takes her half, is not certain.

**Acknowledgments
Patents
Selected Bibliography
Notes
Index**

Acknowledgments

I wish to thank the Lear family for its cooperation: Bill Lear's former wives, Madeline Lear and Ethel Ellis; and his children, Mary Louise, Bill, Pat, John, Shanda Bertelli, David, and Valentina Jackson. Lear's widow, Moya, who is working on her own book, was cooperative to a point. She opened up the Lear archives for me, allowed me to quote from a dozen letters to or from her husband, and answered all my questions. However, she did not permit me to read or quote from the boxes of her personal materials. Special thanks go to David Lear, who gave me the transcripts of sixteen interviews he conducted not long after his father's death.

Appreciation to the following: James Greenwood, Donald Grommesh, John Lear, Dick Mock, and Michael O'Leary, for reading parts or all of the manuscript for accuracy; Linda Durkee, for insightful editorial comments; James Greenwood, for help and advice in research on the Lear Jet; Jody Graham, for legal advice; Peggy Rawlings, for extensive help in research on Lear's life in Quincy, Illinois; Jayne Hopson, for research in the archives of the First Christian Church of Tulsa.

In no particular order, thanks to the following for their research assistance: Donald Cohen, Chicago Board of Education; Wanda Tyson, National Aeronautic Association; Robert Sanborn, Ford Motor Company; Nicholas Komons, U.S. Department of Transportation; Walter Weinstein, National Bureau of Standards; Thomas Wilgus and Judith Farley, Library of Congress; Charles Shaunnessy and Edward Reese, U.S. National Archives; James Schueler, FAA, Wichita Aircraft Certification Office; Jeralene Green, Environmental Protection Agency; Bonnie Whyte, Urban Mass Transportation Administration; James Hall, John Thurston, C. Edwin Enright, Robert Davenport, and Philip Smith, Federal Bureau of Investigation; Julie Maddocks, RCA; Anne Turner and Robert Walker, Department of the Air Force; Richard Huff, Mary Ann Childs, Madelyn Johnson, and L. Jeffrey Ross, U.S. Department of Justice; John Burke, U.S. Department of State; Harris Wood, Philco International Corporation; Nick Stanislow, Lieutenant Colonel USA (Ret.); Robert Galvin,

Motorola, Inc.; Linda Neglia, Horatio Alger Association of Distinguished Americans, Inc.; Clarence Woodward.

My appreciation to the more than a hundred friends, acquaintances, and colleagues of Bill Lear who were eager to talk. Their names appear in the chapter notes.

I would like especially to thank Dorothy Kaufmann, for transcribing hours of tape-recorded interviews, research on Lear's patents, and poring over old telephone books and newspapers; and my wife, Paula Kaufmann, for her support and understanding during a difficult undertaking.

Patents

Radio Control Device, 82,164 and 82,165, September 30, 1930

Magnetic Interrupter, 1,943,240, January 9, 1934

Radio Apparatus, 1,944,139, January 16, 1934

Magnetic Interrupter, 1,944,940, January 30, 1934

Coupling Device, 1,971,315, August 21, 1934

Potential Changer, 2,032,424, March 3, 1936

Switching and Supporting Device for Electrical Apparatus, 2,103,035, December 21, 1937

Magnetic Interrupter, 2,187,950, January 23, 1940

Remote Control Mechanism, 2,249,836, July 22, 1941

Electromagnetic Clutch, 2,267,114, December 23, 1941

Antenna Reeling System, 2,272,213, February 10, 1942

Antenna Drag Cup, 2,287,257, June 23, 1942

Radio Tuning Mechanism, 2,288,722, July 7, 1942

Motor Positioning System, 2,294,786, September 1, 1942

Radio Azimuth Indicator, 2,296,285, September 22, 1942

Rotatable Loop Antenna, 2,301,418, November 10, 1942

Hand Reel for Antennas, 2,304,184, December 8, 1942

Automatic Radio Direction Indicator, 2,308,521, January 19, 1943

Electronic Control Circuit, 2,308,620, January 19, 1943

Radio Apparatus, 2,309,323, January 26, 1943

Drag Device for Antennas, 2,317,622, April 27, 1943

Directional Radio System, 2,317,922, April 27, 1943

Mechanical Actuator System, 2,319,463, May 18, 1943

Aircraft Navigation Instrument, 2,321,606, June 15, 1943

Radio Navigation System, 2,323,337, July 6, 1943

Quadrantial Error Correction Systems, 2,330,226, September 28, 1943

Quadrantial Compensator, 2,336,361, December 7, 1943

Loop Antenna System, 2,343,306, March 7, 1944

Radio Tuning Mechanism, 2,344,825, March 21, 1944

Selected Bibliography

This bibliography includes books and articles by and about Lear cited in the notes in an abbreviated form. Not included are the sources cited in the notes that are not by or about Bill Lear.

Ashley, Tom. "History in a Hurry." *Flight Magazine,* October 1965.

Bach, Richard. "Lear's Jet." *Flying,* April 1964.

Boesen, Victor. "Make Way for the Lear Steamer." *True,* November 1973.

——. *They Said It Couldn't Be Done: The Incredible Story of Bill Lear.* New York: Doubleday, 1971.

Brown, David A. "Lear Liner Sales to Near 500 in Decade." *Aviation Week,* November 1, 1965.

Bulban, Erwin. "Customer's Reaction Enlarges Lear Liner." *Aviation Week,* May 30, 1966.

"Canadair Sees Big LearStar 600 Market." *Aviation Week and Space Technology,* July 26, 1976.

"Canadair's Gamble on the Learstar 600." *Business Week,* November 15, 1976.

Cheverton, R. E. "The Private Jet." *Town and Country,* January 1977.

Coplen, Leonard, and Robert Johns. "The Tape Cartridge Comes of Age." *Electronics World,* November 1966.

"Damn the Smog: Full Steam Ahead." *Forbes,* February 1, 1971.

Davidson, Bill. "Collier Trophy." *Collier's,* December 23, 1950.

Diehl, Digby. "Q and A: Bill Lear." *Los Angeles Times, West Magazine,* April 23, 1972.

——. *Supertalk.* New York: Doubleday, 1974.

Dwiggins, Don. "A New Era in Executive Jets." *Flying,* April 1960.

——. "Philosophy of the New Lear Program." *Flying,* October 1958.

Einstein, Charles. "Bill Lear and His Amazing Steam Machine." *Los Angeles Times, West Magazine,* February 23, 1969.

"Excelsior for the Sportsman." *Sportsman Pilot,* February 15, 1935.

"The Extraordinary Bill Lear." *FAA Aviation News,* July 1973.

"Flight to Russia." *Time,* July 9, 1956.

Fuska, James A. "Lear Designs Light Plane IFR Equipment." *Aviation Week,* September 15, 1958.

Garrison, Peter. "King Lear." *Flying,* February 1970.

——. "Lear." *Flying,* September 1977.

Gelin, Lazar. "Lear Avia, Inc." *Aeronautical Engineering Review,* November 1942.

Gilmore, C. P. "Hard-Nosed Gambler in the Plane Game." *True,* January 1966.

Harrison, Neil. "Lear Jet." *Flight International,* March 10, 1966.

Hawkes, Russell. "Bill Lear Takes On an Industry." *American Aviation,* December 1963.

"How Lear Handles Gyro Output." *Aviation Week,* January 15, 1951.

"The Incurables." *Forbes,* July 1, 1969.

Jamison, Andrew. "Steam Cars: Jet Tycoon, Others Espouse the Cause." *Science,* January 24, 1969.

"King Lear?" *Forbes,* March 1, 1977.

Klass, Philip. "Lear Aims Dual Autopilots at Civil Jets." *Aviation Week,* October 21, 1957.

———. "Lear Jet Expands Varied Avionics Effort." *Aviation Week*, February 28, 1966.

Larson, George. "Living Legends." *Flying*, December 1976.

"Lear Jet Designing Twin-Engine, Single-Propeller Pusher Aircraft." *Aviation Week*, November 22, 1965.

"Lear Pilots Cessna into Vnukova Airport." *Aviation Week*, July 2, 1956.

"Lear Sees 80,000 Planes by 1960." *Aviation Week*, May 3, 1954.

"Lear-Siegler to Combine Divisions." *Aviation Week*, June 18, 1962.

"Lear's New Spin for Prop Planes." *Business Week*, March 20, 1978.

"Lear Steams Back." *Newsweek*, September 21, 1970.

"Lear Takes the Controls." *Business Week*, March 7, 1964.

Lear, William P. "Aviation Radio: Before, During, and After the War." Speech to the Aviation Writers Association, New York Chapter, March 7, 1945. Reprinted by Lear, Inc.

———. "Early Life." A seventy-five-page transcription of tape-recorded recollections about Lear's childhood and business ventures up to 1944. Undated. Courtesy, John Lear.

———. "Lear Radio Direction Finder." *Aero Digest*, March 1935.

———. "Modern Executive Airplane as a Medium of Transportation." *Skyways*, May 1954.

———. "Moment of Decision." *Guideposts*, November 1975.

———. "Moscow Trip." A tape recording of Lear's 1956 trip to Moscow. Undated. Courtesy, John Lear.

———. "The Reminiscences of William Lear." Aviation Project, Oral History Research Office, Columbia University, 1960. Kenneth Leish, interviewer.

———. "William Powell Lear on Autopilots." *Design News*, November 8, 1971.

Leipold, L. E. *William P. Lear: Designer and Inventor.* Minneapolis: Denison, 1967.

———. YPO address. Undated. Lear archives.

Ludvigsen, Karl. "Lear: The Steam King?" *Motor Trend*, February 1971.

———. "The Wonderful Wizard of Lear." *Signature*, February 1971.

McCarthy, Clint. "The Jet That's Making History." *Private Pilot*, September 1961.

"Matching Up a Perfect Fit in Electronics." *Business Week*, February 24, 1962.

"Mr. Navcom." *Time*, May 4, 1959.

"A New Executive Jet Plane." *Business Week*, November 11, 1961.

Ottum, Bob. "Let There Be Steam." *Sports Illustrated*, February 3, 1969.

Petrakis, Harry. *The Founder's Touch: The Life of Paul Galvin of Motorola.* New York: McGraw-Hill, 1965.

"Plane Gear Maker Tries Dual-Control Management." *Business Week*, December 3, 1960.

"Radio Compass: Fly by It and Listen to Broadcast Music." *Newsweek*, February 16, 1935. Geoffrey Kruesi's letter to the editor, April 20, 1935.

Roberts, Steven. "Bill Lear and His Incredible Steam Machine." *Playboy*, March 1972.

Shalett, Sidney. "Aviation's Stormy Genius." *Saturday Evening Post*, October 13, 1956.

Shaw, David. "What Bill Lear Wants — Bill Lear Invents." *Esquire*, September 1969.

Siegler Corp Buys Lear's Family's Stock, Plans to Acquire Company." *Aviation Week*, February 19, 1962.

"Small Jets for Big Business." *Time*, May 1, 1964.

Smith, Philip. "Bill Lear's $10-Million Gamble." *Weekend Magazine*, January 24, 1970.

Stanfield, Robert. "Lear Jet Model 23: A Fast, Rugged, Flexible Business Tool." *American Aviation*, July 1964.

"Steam Bus Race to Beat Pollution." *Business Week*, February 26, 1972.

"Steam Cars Try to Get Back into the Running." *Business Week*, March 29, 1969.

Wells, Dick. "Lear's Steam Dream: A Reality?" *Motor Trend*, June 1969.

Wood, Robert. "Lear Sticks Out His Chin." *Aviation Week*, May 10, 1954.

Notes

Abbreviations: *Associated Press (AP); Aviation Week (AW); Business Week (BW); Los Angeles Times (LAT); New York Times (NYT); Wall Street Journal (WSJ); Bill Lear, Jr. (BL); David Lear (DL); John Lear (JL); Mary Louise Lear (MLL); Moya Lear (ML); Pat Lear (PL); Shanda Lear Bertelli (SL); Tina Lear Jackson (TL); William P. Lear (WPL).*

Prologue

Interviews: Charles Bell, JL, MLL, PL, TL.
Sources: Cummings, *The Lear Log,* June 1954. That Lear quashed the project is the recollection of JL, who heard it from his father. Lear Jet N802L hung in the National Air and Space Museum from 1976 to 1983. It is currently in storage.

I

Interviews: Ethel Ellis, Clarence Gamble, Madeline Lear, and Peggy Rawlings.
Sources: Philip L. Coupland, "Tribute to the Pilots of the U.S. Air Mail Service," *The Roll Call: Magazine of the Association of Air Mail Pioneers,* 1956. Carroll V. Glines, *The Saga of the Air Mail* (Princeton: Van Nostrand, 1968). Benjamin B. Lipsner, *The Air Mail: Jennies to Jets* (Chicago: Wilcox and Follet, 1950). Ken McGregor, *Saga of the U.S. Air Mail Service: 1918–1927,* ed. Dale Nielson (Air Mail Pioneers Inc., 1962). "Planes of the Air Mail Service," *Roll Call,* 1956. Page Shamberger, *Tracks Across the Sky* (New York: Lippincott, 1964). Dean Smith, "The Sound of Wire," *American Heritage History of Flight* (New York: Simon & Schuster, 1962).

7 Early childhood and experiences at Grant Park, WPL, "Early Life" and "Reminiscences."
7 Englewood High School records show that WPL did not complete the first semester.
10 *WingFoot Express, Chicago Daily News,* July 22, 1919, and *Chicago Tribune,* July 23, 1919.
11 Lear family history, *Ancestry of William Powell Lear* (Salt Lake City: Institute of Family Research, June 23, 1977). Details about Barry, Illinois, Peggy Rawlings.
11 Ethel Ellis recalls Ruby Lear and WPL's grandmother Mary Lear talking about Gertrude walking out and her string of affairs. Both Madeline Lear and Ellis also recall Gertrude's saying what a sinful woman she was when she was younger and how she changed once she got religion.
12 "the most generous": Madeline Lear.
12 "living in sin": Madeline Lear.

3

2

Interviews: Ethel Ellis, Madeline Lear, Peggy Rawlings, Elmer Wavering.
Sources: "Last Will and Testament of William B. Powell." "Chattel Property of William B. Powell," April 21, 1921. *Barry Adage,* March 23, 1921; April 2, 1896; and the 1913 Seventy-Fifth Anniversary Issue. Carl Landrum, *Earliest Days of Local Radio: From Quincy's Past,* May 12, 1968. Shaw, *Esquire,* 1969.
Sources, Early Radio: *QST,* August 1920–June 1922; *Wireless Age,* October 1921–October 1924; *Popular Radio,* January 1926–May 1928; *Radio Age,* May 1922–December 1923. Orrin E. Dunlap, *Dunlap's Radio and Television Almanac* (New York: Harper and Brothers, 1951); *The Radio Manual* (Boston: Houghton Mifflin, 1924); *Radio's 100 Men of Science* (New York: Harper and Brothers, 1944); Sidney Gernsback, *Sidney Gernsback's Radio Encyclopedia* (New York: Gernsback, 1927). Archer L. Gleason, *History of Radio to 1926,* (New York: American Historical Society, 1938).

14 WPL told people that he ran away from home when he was sixteen and lied about his age to get into the Navy. His naval records show he joined on September 14, 1920, when he was eighteen years old.

14 WPL claimed he was a wireless instructor. His last rating on his military record was AS-E (Apprentice Seaman Electrician). According to a Navy spokesperson, Jill Merrill, there was a radio school at Great Lakes in 1920–1921 and "E" could be construed to cover "radio instructor."

14 "to charge off": WPL, "Early Life."

15 WPL's interview with Reed, "Early Life."

17 Ad, November 20, 1922, under Radio Equipment.

18 The WPL stories, Leipold, 1967.

19 Yente: WPL, "Early Life."

20 WPL with barnstormer and Lincoln Beachey, "Reminiscences." Nutwood Park, *Dubuque Times Journal,* July 13, 14, 16, and 21, 1912.

3

Interviews: Ethel Ellis, Jayne Hopson, Madeline Lear, Louise Van Antwerp, Elmer Wavering.
Sources: Minutes of the board meetings of the First Christian Church of Tulsa, 1923–1926. "Petition for Separate Maintenance — Ethel Lear vs. William P. Lear," District Court of Tulsa, No. D-260, April 20, 1926. Deposition of WPL in "Ethel Ellis et al. vs. William P. Lear," U.S. District Court for Southern District of Ohio, Western Division, No. 111, October 1941, as well as Ethel Ellis's answer to the deposition, undated. *Letters:* Mary Peterson to Ruby Lear, July 8, 1926; WPL to Ethel Lear, undated; WPL to Ethel Lear, 1927; Ruby Lear to Mary Peterson, June 15, 1926; Gertrude Kirmse to Ethel Ellis, January 18, 1927. FBI 1926 documents, case no. 31-15-720-4, "White Slave Traffic Act: W. P. Lear alias William Powell, Madeline Bensen, Victim": Kansas City, Missouri (KCM) 5-29; Dallas 6-5; Oklahoma City (OKC) 6-29; Chicago, 7-1; OKC 7-3; KCM 6-30 and 7-9; OKC 7-12; Buffalo 7-14; KCM 7-27; Buffalo 7-26; KCM 8-6; Buffalo 8-3 and 8-11; OKC 8-14; Buffalo 8-17; Chicago 8-22; Buffalo 8-26, 9-4, 9-20.

23 "I just know": Ellis.

23 "overhaul," "new apparatus," "most powerful": *Christian Standard,* January 10, 1925, p. 366. Minutes of the First Christian Church show that the church bought WLAL on or about December 15, 1924, for $500 and sold it on or around February 15, 1926.

23 WPL's radio show, Wavering.

24 "What about": Ellis.

28 "You don't know": Wavering.

29 "nothing she wanted more" and "Ethel, get some": Ellis.

29 "We have to talk" and following, Ellis.

29–30 Madeline-WPL escapade, FBI documents and Ellis.

30 "gross neglect": Decision of the District Court of Tulsa County in "Ethel Lear vs. William Lear," No. D-260, June 23, 1926. Somewhere during this period WPL got the "clap." It is not clear where, when, and from whom. WPL refers to it in an interview with Diehl, 1974.

31 WPL's indictment, *Tulsa Daily World,* September 1, 1926.

31 "You better not": Madeline Lear.

4

Interviews: Ethel Ellis, Warren Knotts, BL, Madeline Lear, PL, Genevieve Mitchell-McLeod, Elmer Wavering, Ray Yoder.

Sources: FBI documents case 31-15-720-4 for 1927: OKC 2–11 and 2–26; KCM 3–13. *Letter:* Gertrude Kirmse to Ethel Ellis, January 18, 1927. *NYT:* "Chicago Gets First Glimpse of Latest Styles in Radio," June 19, 1927; "Radio Announcing Contest Planned," September 5, 1929; "Cadillac Cars Equipped for Reception," September 18, 1929; "At the Wheel," May 12, 1929; "New Radio for Chrysler Car," October 10, 1929; "Trade Notes and Comment," January 12, 1930; "Wired for Transitone," January 12, 1930; "Radio Automobile Calls for an Ordinance," January 26, 1930; "Sees Auto a Field for Radio Sales," February 11, 1930; "St. Paul Bans Radios in Autos," March 22, 1930; "Automatic Volume Control Developed for Radio on Automobiles," March 30, 1930; "Radio on Motor Cars," September 14, 1930; "Auto Radio Shown with Robots at Fair," September 24, 1930; "Report on Atlantic City Show," June 8, 1930; "Radio Show to Open in Atlantic City," June 2, 1930; "Secrecy Guards New Sets," June 11, 1930; "200 Radio Makers Show New Models," June 2, 1930; "Auto Radio Spurs Business," July 9, 1933. *Philadelphia Inquirer:* "M.A. Head Tells Romance of Radio," June 1, 1930; "Radio Industry Opens Convention," June 1, 1930. *Chicago Daily News:* "Radio Trade Show and Parley Opens," June 12, 1928; "Program Covers Trade Problems," June 12, 1928; "One Million Worth of Devices Seen," June 9, 1928; "Manufacturers Loud in Praise of Results of Exhibit," June 18, 1927; "Radio Show Opens . . . 10,000 Here to Study Exhibits," June 14, 1927; "Dials, Speakers, Condensers and Other Devices Draw Public's Eye," June 17, 1927. Lawrence M. Cockaday, "Just a Dashboard of Reception," *Popular Radio,* June 1927. "Commander McDonald of Zenith," *Fortune,* June 1945. Edgar H. Felix, "What You Should Know About B Power-Supply Devices," *Radio Broadcast,* March 1927. Henry Gibson, "Dynamic Speakers: How They Work," *Popular Radio,* May 1928. Keith Henny, "New Trends in Radio Design for 1929–1930," *Radio Broadcast,* November 1928; "What Happened to Radio in 1929," *Radio Broadcast,* December 1929. Robert Kruse, "Automobile Receiver Design," *Radio Broadcast,* April 1930. "The Latest Radio Valves, *Popular*

Radio, July–August 1927. H. A. McIllvane, "Autobiography of Valves," *Popular Radio,* November 1927. Alice Goldfarb Marquis, "Radio Grows Up," *American Heritage,* August/September 1983. T. A. Phillips, "Market for Battery Set," *Radio Broadcast,* February 1930. Howard Rhodes, "Perfecting the B Socket Power Device," *Radio Broadcast,* May 1927. David Sarnoff, "Radio of Today and Tomorrow," *Wireless Age,* June 1922. French Struther, "The Radio Patent Structure and What It Means," *Radio Broadcast,* November 1926. *What Is Transitone Radio?,* Automobile Radio Corporation, undated.

32 Dismissal of white slavery charges, FBI above.
38 "But they can't": WPL, "Early Life."
41 "It takes no": *NYT,* March 22, 1930.
42 "Did you run": WPL, "Early Life."
45 "How the hell": Petrakis, 1965, page 91.

5 and 6

Interviews: Ethel Ellis, Warren Knotts, BL, Madeline Lear, PL, Fred Link, Ray Yoder.
Sources: *Air Commerce Bulletin,* 1930–1933. S. R. Winters, "Radio Beacons to Aid Air Mail Flyers," *Radio Age,* September 1927. *NYT:* "Radio in Automobile More Popular," March 30, 1934; "Auto Radio Spurs Business," July 9, 1934.

46 WPL photo, unmarked news clip, Lear archives.
46 Flight to Long Island, WPL, "Reminiscences."
48 "happy as hell": Knotts.
52 Lear ad, *Aviation,* February 1933, p. 64.
52 Mallory-WPL, "Early Life." The vibrator concept was apparently the brainchild of Marvin Nulsen, whose name appears on at least one patent, as does Yoder's.
55 North Carolina quotes, Knotts.
56 "I don't want": WPL, "Reminiscences."
57 "What do you expect" and following, Madeline Lear.
59 Motorola car radio story, Wavering and Petrakis, 1965.
60 Lear paid next to no child support between June 1926 and January 1934 according to Ellis's records. Also letters: Ellis to WPL, September 21 and October 2, 1933; January 23, 1934; WPL to Ellis, January 17, 1934.
60 Alice Miller quote, Link.
60 WPL suicide story told to many people, many ways.

7

Interviews: Lazar Gelin, Warren Knotts, Fred Link, Joseph Lorch.
Sources: Old Army Record Group 13, Direction Finder and/or Radio Compass, 413.4 A,B,C, 1925–1940, National Archives. Monte D. Wright, *Most Probable Position: A History of Aerial Navigation to 1941* (Wichita: University of Kansas Press, 1972). "Aeronautic Radio Research," *Air Commerce Bulletin,* May 1, 1931. "The International Air Race," *QST,* November 1933. *NYT* coverage of the 1934 international air race: September 30, October 14, 21, 22, 23, and 28.

63 "What is it": Link.
64–65 WPL and Cunningham, "Early Life." RCA said it has no records of the Lear tuner even though it holds the patent.
67 WPL-Hegenberger-Kruesi, "Early Life."
70 Ingalls letter, June 7, 1934, Old Army Records, A.
71 "We saw nothing": *NYT*, October 21, 1934.
71 "When we saw": *NYT*, October 22, 1934.
72 "On home stretch": Nichols to WPL, October 23, 1934.
72 "I want to express": Nichols to WPL, October 25, 1934.
73 "Radio Compass," *Newsweek*, 1935.
73 *Herald Tribune*, January 22, 1935.
73–74 Rickenbacker, unmarked news clip, Lear archives.
74 Vidal, *Air Commerce Bulletin*, April 15, 1935.
75 "I've always wanted to": *Herald Tribune*, March 17, 1935.

8

Interviews: Lazar Gelin, Warren Knotts, Madeline Lear, Fred Link, Joseph Lorch, Lloyd Percell.
Sources: *Lear Developments*, undated company brochure. *Air Commerce Bulletin*, April 15, 1935. WPL, *Aero Digest*, 1935. "Excelsior," *The Sportsman Pilot*, 1935. Earhart flight to Mexico, *NYT:* March 14, 17; April 19–30; May 1–11 and 29, 1935; *New York Herald Tribune:* March 17, April 20, May 9, 1935.
76 "revolutionary": unmarked April 4, 1935, news clip, Lear archives.
76 Thomis, AP, April 3, 1935.
76 Lear's comments to press, "Radio Compass Inventor Sees New Era in Flying," unmarked news clip, Lear archives.
76 "Howard Ailor used to": WPL, "Aviation Radio," 1945.
77 "appeared on the run": *LAT*, April 20, 1935.
77 "uneventful," "perfect weather": *Herald Tribune*, May 9, 1935.
78 "worked excellently": *NYT*, May 10, 1935.
78 "I wish to be free": *Air Commerce Bulletin*, September 15, 1935.
78 Hughes buying WPL instrument, Link; Hughes not paying for gas, Percell.
79–80 Supporting WPL's story, Old Army Record Group 13, 413. A,B,C, December 20, 1934, to December 14, 1935. Mashbir reports WPL to military, April 3, 1935.
80–81 Signal Corps competition, WPL, "Early Life," also Old Army Record Group 13, 413.4 B: flight test under way, December 4, 1935; new specification, September 23, 1936; two proposals submitted, October 23, 1936; RCA won, February 27 and April 16, 1937.
81 Financial data about Lear Developments here and in rest of this section, SEC, *Lear Incorporated*, No 2-5663, March 1945; and Military Intelligence, "Section I Rating Summary Investigation, Division A, Lear Avia, Inc., Piqua, Ohio," May 12, 1941, U.S. National Archives.
82 "golden sword" and following story, WPL, "Early Life."
83 "The navigation of": Robert Williams to General H. H. Arnold, May 17, 1937, Old Army Record Group 13, 413.4 B.
83 Radio Technical Commission, *Air Commerce Bulletin*, January 15, 1936.

84 Meeting with Russians and dialogue, Gelin. *Maxim Gorky, NYT:* October 10, 23, 25, 1937; and January 21 and April 12, 1938.
85 Background on Bendix, *Dictionary of American Biography,* ed. Allen Johnson (New York: Scribners, 1957). WPL's conflict with Bendix and dialogue, WPL, "Early Life."

9

Interviews: Sam Auld, Ethel Ellis, Lazar Gelin, Ed Gilles, Warren Knotts, Madeline Lear, MLL, PL, Fred Link, Joseph Lorch, George Paddock, John Ray, Nick Stanislow.
Sources: Gelin, *Aeronautical Engineering Review,* 1942. *Learadio: The Pilot's Preference* and *New Learadio ADF-6 Automatic Radio Direction Finder and Receiver,* undated pamphlets, Lear Developments, Inc. H. K. Morgan, *Aircraft Radio and Electrical Equipment* (New York: Pitman, 1939).

90 National Academy of Sciences, report to the U.S. President, November 24, 1939, as well as correspondence, Old Army Record Group 13, 413.4.
90 Defective ADF-6, Auld.
91 RCA story, WPL, "Early Life."

10

Interviews: Stan Brown, Bee Edlund-Burtis, BL, JL, Madeline Lear, Marilee Lear, ML, PL, SL, TL, Sydney Nesbitt. Also, DL interview with ML.

93 I could not find Margaret Radell Lear Sinclair.
93 "He had this": TL.
97 "I've never seen": Edlund-Burtis.
97 "Dad broke up": JL.
98 WPL accident, "Early Life"; *Miami Herald,* January 9, 1941; and AP, January 8, 1941.
99 Olsen to WPL, March 28, 1941.

11

Interviews: Ward Davis, Lazar Gelin, Albert Handschumacher, Joseph Lorch, Howard McLaughlin, Dick Mock, George Paddock, Jay Wiggins.
Sources: *The Learomatic Navigator* (Dayton: Lear Avia, 1940). Memo to WPL from Gelin, "Report on Trip Through Central and South America," December 26, 1944. "Dayton Aircraft Radio Builder Tornado Man of Many Airplanes," *Dayton Daily News,* November 8, 1940. "William Lear Wins Aircraft Award," *Dayton Journal,* November 30, 1940. *Learadio: ADF 8* (Dayton: Lear Avia, Inc., undated).

99–100 WPL struggle with Signal Corps, "Early Life."

101 "critical essential item": Old Army Record Group 13, 413.4. Lt. Col. Allen to R. Kimball, October 20, 1939. Other documents in the group relating to SCR-269 are: Arnold to Smith, January 2, 1939; Brett to chief of Air Corps, August 22, 1939; Contract W-287-SC-25 74, August 30, 1941. Also, George R. Thompson et al., *The Signal Corps: The Test (December 1941 to July 1943)* (Washington D.C.: Department of the Army, 1957), pp. 184–185, 506–507.

101 Sloppy construction, Lorch, Paddock, Ray.

102 "Bill could really": Handschumacher.

103 Hawks award and quotes, *New York Herald Tribune,* December 5, 1940.

104 "*Our* pilots fly" and "That will keep you": Gelin.

105 "quite significant": Richard Marsen memo to T. S. Harris, June 16, 1941.

106 WPL story and dialogue about antenna reels, "Early Life."

109 "You know what, Bill?": McLaughlin. Also flexible shaft story and dialogue.

12

Interviews: Stan Brown, Ethel Ellis, Al Handschumacher, Bill Kabacker, BL, MLL, ML, PL, Howard McLaughlin, Claire Mock, Dick Mock. Also, DL interviews with Stan Brown, ML, and Howard McLaughlin.

110 ML to WPL, December 1941.

112 "was gold": BL.

113 "She fell for it": Claire Mock.

117 Curtiss-Wright and radar stories and dialogue, McLaughlin.

121 Kickback scam is based on nearly 200 pages of FBI documents, "Vern S. Christensen: Fraud Against the Government — no. 46-376." The Justice Department dropped the case without formal charges so that Lear's work on the autopilot would not be delayed. Quotation from: FBI, Cincinnati, Ohio, May 11, 1945.

13

Interviews: Same as Chapter 12.

Sources: Irving B. Holley, *Buying Aircraft: Materiel Procurement for the Army Air Force* (Washington, D.C.: Department of the Army, 1964). *The Learavian,* September 1943, July–August, September, November 1944. *The Lear Log,* January, February, March 1945. *Lear Know-How,* Lear, Inc., February 1945. *Product Survey: Report to Lear Avia,* R. A. Lasley, undated. "Lear, Inc., Demonstrates Use of Wire Recording," *New York Herald Tribune,* April 11, 1945. "Sale by Lear, Inc., Will Be First Made to Public," *NYT,* May 15, 1945. WPL, "Aviation Radio." Lear Incorporated ads, October and December 1944, and December 1945. Internal reports: E. M. Smith, June 5, 1945; Marsen to J. Allwood, undated; Marsen, June 6, 1945.

122–23 WPL-Harris dialogue, McLaughlin.

125 Financial data in this chapter, SEC report, *Lear, Inc.,* undated. Also quote, "Nor can any."

126 Ellis-MLL dialogue, Ellis and MLL.

127 Ellis threat and suit, child support note at end of Chapter 6 as well as following correspondence: Jerome Sinsheimer to Robert Ellis, December 30, 1940; Howard Sams to Sinsheimer, December 10, 1940; Sinsheimer to Sams, December 12, 1940; Samuel Finn to Sinsheimer, June 13, 1941; Ellis to Guy Manatt, June 30, 1941; Ellis to Sinsheimer, August 16, 1941; WPL to MLL, August 23, 1941; Finn to WPL, August 27, 1941; WPL to Finn, August 28, 1941; Ellis to Finn, September 4, 1941; Ellis to Sinsheimer, October 29, 1941; Finn to Ellis, November 25, 1941; Finn to Sinsheimer, January 7, 1942; Ellis to Sinsheimer, January 17 and 27, 1942; Sinsheimer to Ellis, February 24, 1942. Also, sworn affidavit of U.S. Marshal Leslie G. Downey, June 14, 1941, and agreement between Ellis and WPL, January 31, 1942.

127 "insurance policy": Ellis to Sinsheimer, January 17, 1942.

127 "I'm not interested": MLL.

128 "By sliding a": *New York Sun*, March 11, 1945.

128 Favorite postwar projects, Dick Mock.

14

Interviews: Nils Eklund, Al Handschumacher, Bill Kabacker, Al Landes, BL, ML, PL, Kenneth Miller, Claire and Dick Mock. Also, DL interview with ML.

Sources: Annual reports of Lear Incorporated, 1945–1950. *Beauty Speaks for Itself in Lear Home Radios,* brochure, Lear Incorporated, undated. Memo to WPL from Gelin, "Home Radio," December 26, 1944. *NYT:* "RCA Throws Open Patent Doors," January 12, 1946; "$14,000,000 Loan Paid Off," April 6, 1946; "Lear Acquires Another Plant," July 3, 1946; "Radio Speed-Up Plan," November 5, 1946; "New Wire Recorder Displayed in Chicago," January 20, 1947.

134 "Oh, honey": ML.

135 Shaw, *Esquire,* 1969.

136 "royalty": ML.

137 "the most versatile": *NYT,* January 20, 1947.

15 and 16

Interviews: John Adkins, Vernon Benfer, Nils Eklund, Vera Eklund, Al Handschumacher, Bob Hoover, ML, J. S. Torch Lewis, Kenneth Miller, Dick Mock, Bill Schall, John Schoeppel, Gunnar Wennerberg, Jay Wiggins.

Sources: Annual reports of Lear Incorporated, 1945–1951. WPL, "William Powell Lear on Autopilots," *Design News,* November 8, 1971. *F-5 Automatic Pilot* and *The Lear L2 Autopilot: A New Concept in Flying Ease and Safety,* Lear Incorporated, undated. "How Lear Handles Gyro Output," *BW,* 1951. Memos: Marsen to Allwood, May 24, 1945; Marsen and Smith to staff, May 23, 1945; Marsen to Allwood, May 24, 1945; Marsen to WPL, May 22, 1945; Marsen to Eklund, May 24, 1945; *Saturday Evening Post,* 1956. "Automatic Pilot, in Production, Called All-Weather Guide — Cited by Collier Award," *NYT,* December 14, 1950.

140 "A pilot's": WPL, "Reminiscences."

143 "Well, what about": Nils Eklund.

144 "You can stay": Nils Eklund.
144 "How long will": Nils Eklund.
145 "Every time we'd go": WPL, "Reminiscences."
145 "dreamboat": Benfer.
145 "I understand you": Schoeppel.
147, 148 "You watch" and "My God": Nils Eklund.
148 "Nils, would you": Nils Eklund.
149 Schall story and dialogue, Nils Eklund.
150 "For Christ's sake" and following, Nils Eklund.
151 "I'm not going": WPL, "Reminiscences."
153 "they liked Bill": Handschumacher.
·153 "We're going to" and following, Schoeppel.
154 Smith, UPI syndicated story, December 14, 1950. Levine and Knecht quotes, Davidson, *Collier's*, 1950.
157 "rat's nest": Handschumacher.
157 Collier Trophy background: Frederick R. Neely, "The Robert J. Collier Trophy: Its Origin and Its Purpose," as well as "The Winners of the Trophy," *Pegasus*, December 1950.
159 "Nils, without you": Nils Eklund.
159 Horatio Alger background: Ralph Gardner, "The Immortal Spirit of Horatio Alger," *Saturday Evening Post*, May–June 1981; "Horatio Alger Association of Distinguished Americans, Inc.: A Profile," leaflet of the association.
160 "a big downer": ML.
161 "I made a mistake": WPL, "Reminiscences." Hoover confirms WPL's story.
163 "If you're screwing": Dick Mock.

17

Interviews: Vernon Benfer, Ethel Ellis, Vaughn Hammond, BL, DI., MLL, ML, PL, Howard McLaughlin, Kenneth Miller, Dick Mock. Also, DL interviews with Sam Auld, Landis Carr, Gordon Israel.

Sources: Tape-recorded interview of Hal Herman by JL. *The Leareporter,* Lear Cal Division of Lear Incorporated, December 1955. Don Dwiggins, *They Flew the Bendix Race* (New York: Lippincott, 1965). Fred Hunter, "Dick Mock's Ideas Help Lear Grow," *American Aviation,* July 4, 1955. Letters: Ellis to MLL, January 11, 1955; Ruby Lear to MLL, December 17, 1954; MLL to family, February 21, 1955; Ellis to MLL, June 24, 1954; WPL to MLL, January 30, 1955; MLL to family, June 26, 1954; WPL to MLL, March 12, 1956. *NYT:* "New Plane Device Guides Landings," June 13, 1952; "New Private Plane Gets Test," May 13, 1954; "Aviation: Streamlined," September 20, 1953.

165 All quotes in BL story, BL, and BL, "Bill Lear, Jr., and his P-38," *Sport Flying,* August 1972.
169 Israel background, Richard Bach, "Biography of a Hired Gun," *Flying,* April 1967.
171 "One more degree" and "twisted, squirmed": Carr.
171 WPL and Israel fight, Carr.
172 "Goddamn it": BL.
173 "Does the name": ML.
173 Coan, *The Lear Log,* June 1954.
174 "his pride": Carr.

18

Interviews: Al Handschumacher, DL, JL, ML, SL, Dick Mock.
Sources: Gian Carlo Bertelli interview with Fernand Matile and Germaine Stoll for the author. "William P. Lear's Trip to Moscow," *Management Information*, Lear Incorporated, June 26, 1956. "Flight to Russia," *Time*, July 9, 1956. FBI 1956 reports: June 29, July 3, July 6, July 27, August 3, September 4, November 29. Cables of U.S. Embassy Berlin to secretary of state: June 22, 26, 29, 1956. Cables of U.S. Embassy Moscow to secretary of state: June 27 and 28, 1956. Cables of U.S. Embassy Paris to FBI: August 3 and September 4, 1956. *NYT* coverage of Lear and Gen. Nathan Twining: June 23, 27, 29, 30, and July 2, 1956. AP stories: June 22, 26, 27, 28, and July 1, 1956. Report of Gen. Nathan Twining, "Preliminary Report of Visit of the United States Air Force Delegation to the Soviet Union: 23 June–1 July 1956."

176 "Little girl": SL.
176 "Dear Gang": *The Leareporter*, December 1955.
177 Blind Landing Lear story and dialogue, WPL, "Reminiscences."
178 BL story and dialogue, BL.
181 "I have a mission": Handschumacher. All references to an undercover assignment have been excised from FBI and State Department documents for national security reasons.
181 WPL meeting with the Soviet consul and vice-consul as well as dialogue, *The Moscow Story*, Lear Incorporated, 1956. Also quote about Vilna.
183 "none whatsoever": AP, June 28, 1956.
183 "Can it turn?": *The Moscow Story*.
184 Bohlen memo, no. 2939, June 28, 1956.
184 "The United States": AP, June 28, 1956.
185 Moscow analysis, WPL, "Moscow Trip."
186 "The visiting delegations": Twining, "Preliminary Report."

19 and 20

Interviews: Vaughn Hammond, Al Handschumacher, BL, JL, ML, SL, J. Sheldon (Torch) Lewis, Howard McLaughlin, Kenneth Miller, Dick Mock, Buzz Nanney, Lloyd Percell, John Schoeppel, Jay Wiggins.
Sources: Annual reports of Lear Incorporated, 1957–1960. JL taped interview with Hal Herman. *Lear Management Information*, December 15, 1958. *Lear Log*, October and December, 1959. Klass, *AW*, 1957. "Lear Designs Light Plane IFR Equipment," *AW*. *NYT:* "Grand Opening," September 26, 1959; "Motorola Plans to Buy Lear Cal," December 8, 1959. "Lear Inc. Expects 1959 Net Near $2,500,000," *WSJ*, November 11, 1959.

186 Geneva riot, *La Suisse*, November 6, 1956.
187 "absolute pandemonium": BL.
188 "To some on Wall Street": *Lear Incorporated: Public Relations Analysis and Program*, Ruder and Finn Incorporated, August 1960.
189 "bootlegged" and VHF story, Miller.
189 Dwiggins, *Flying*, October 1958.
191 "Why don't you" and other Michael quotes, Nanney. Background on Michael, Osvaldo Pagani, "Inconto con Michele di Romania," *Storia Illustrata*, June 1984.

192 Percell story and dialogue, Percell.
194 WPL to ML and ML to WPL, undated.
195 "Honey, I think": JL.
195 "took a little": BL.
196 "Well, what do" and story, anonymous.
197 "Now we'll see" and following, Handschumacher.
197 WPL to Mock, August 3, 1959.
197 "Al, now *you're*": Handschumacher.

21

Interviews: Nils Eklund, BL, DL, JL, ML, SL, Buzz Nanney, June Shields.
Sources: Gian Carlo Bertelli interview with Fernand Matile. WPL letters to JL: summer 1962, June 29, 1962, June 30, 1962.
204 "U.S. things were": SL.
204 "elegance and spaciousness": ML.
204 "Stupid . . . None of": WPL, "Reminiscences."
205–6 Max story and dialogue, SL.
206 "Where are your": SL.
207 Olsen letter, March 1, 1961.
208 "long quiet talks": SL.
209 All quotes and stories about WPL and JL, JL.
210 Accident details, JL, and JL, "Deadly Mistress," *Air Trails,* winter 1976.
214 "Why don't you": Nanney.
215 WPL's letters to JL have been lost. Summary is JL's.
215 "Dear John": WPL, June 30, 1962.

22

Interviews: Al Handschumacher, Leonce Lancelot-Bassou, BL, DL, JL, SL, Richard Millar, Dick Mock, George Roche.
Sources: WPL, *Skyways,* 1954. Cheverton, *Town and Country,* 1977. Dwiggins, *Flying,* 1960. McCarthy, *Private Pilot,* 1961. "A New Executive Jet Airplane," *BW,* November 11, 1961. Raspet to WPL memo, "Five Place Executive Airplane of Ultra High Performance," April 20, 1959. WPL-Mitsubishi letters: July 8 and October 1, 1959; August 24 and September 16, 1960. *NYT:* "Companies Plan Sales Merger," February 10, 1962; "Siegler Holders Approve Merger," June 1, 1962; "Santa Monica Firm Only Half Year Old Has Big Week," December 12, 1962; "Sixteen on Jet Landed by Beam in Paris," December 19, 1962. "Lear, Siegler Merge Following Tax Ruling," *WSJ,* June 6, 1962. "Lear-Siegler Merger: Made for Each Other," *LAT,* June 10, 1962. Agreement between the Siegler Corporation and WPL, February 8, 1962.
216 "a perfect landing": *NYT,* December 19, 1962.
216 There is a rumor that WPL paid for the Silver Medal.
218 WPL-Mitsubishi, July 8, 1959.
218 "The Swiss submarine": BL.

219 "People thought": WPL, "Reminiscences."

219 Millar to Lear, June 17, 1960.

220 "Royal barges . . . With businessmen" and following short quotes, Cheverton, Dwiggins, and McCarthy, among others.

221 "Industry [is moving]": Dwiggins, 1960.

221-22 Quotes, *Lear Incorporated: Public Relations Analysis and Program*, Ruder and Finn Incorporated, August 1960.

223 "sucking": Handschumacher.

226 "a perfect fit": "Matching Up a Perfect Fit," *BW*, 1962.

227 "sweetener": Handschumacher.

228 Consulting contract null and void, "Agreement Settling and Finally Dropping of These Proceedings," Louise Floethe et al. vs. William P. Lear, Sr., et al. Civil Action #62c 1093 in the U.S. District Court for the Northern District of Illinois, Eastern Division, March 1, 1965.

23

Interviews: Carl Bell, Don Grommesh, Fran Jabara, Harry Jackson, BL, JL, ML, Buzz Nanney. Also, DL interview with Gordon Israel and Gian Carlo Bertelli interview with Fernand Matile.

228-29 Nanney stories and quotes, Nanney.

230 "looked way out": DL with Israel.

230 "thought Bill was": Nanney.

231 "You'll be back": Grommesh.

232 "Look, Buzz" and rest of dialogue, Nanney.

233 Telegram, as recalled by Bell.

235 "You have a" and following, Nanney.

24, 25, and 26

Interviews: Sam Auld, Henry Beaird, Carl Bell, Stanley Green, James Greenwood, Don Grommesh, Fran Jabara, Harry Jackson, Clay Lacy, DL, JL, ML, TL, Kenneth Miller, Buzz Nanney, June Shields, Elmer Wavering. Also, DL interviews with Sam Auld, Ed Chandler, Bob Graf, Gordon Israel, ML, Buzz Nanney.

Sources: FAA records of Lear Jet, 1963–1966. "Agency Reported Pleased at High Performance," *Chicago Tribune*, February 3, 1964. Bach, *Flying*, April 1964. Boesen, 1971. Brown, *AW*, June 1964. *Charge!*, Lear Jet Incorporated magazine, 1963–1965. Cheverton, *Town and Country*, January 1977. Copen and Johns, *Electronics World*, November 1966. "Famous Flyers," *FAA News*, July 1973. "The First Executive Jet: The Lear Jet 23," *Interavia*, #10, 1965. "Go, Man, Go," *Flight Magazine*, June 1964. Hawkes, *American Aviation*, 1963. John Husar, "Bill Lear and the Lear Jet: Where Dreams Become Reality," *Topeka Capital-Journal*, December 1, 1963. "Inventor Rests Hope on Baby Jet," *NYT*, April 26, 1964. Larson, *Flying*, 1976. "Lear 'Goes for Broke' on an Idea," *Wichita Eagle*, November 18, 1963. "Lear Jet," *Flight International*, March 10, 1966. *Lear Jet Corporation*, SEC, S-2 Registration Statement, November 12, 1964. *Lear Jet Corporation: Agreement Among Un-*

derwriters, Van Alstyne, Noel and Co., November 1964. "Lear's Miracle: Jet Is Ok'd in Nine Months," *Chicago Tribune*, August 6, 1964. Robert Serling, *Little Giant: The Story of Gates Learjet*, May 1, 1974. Shaw, *Esquire*, 1969. "Small Jets for Big Business," *Time*, July 1964. Stanfield, *American Aviation*, 1964. "A Stereo System Devised for Cars," *NYT*, April 16, 1965. Ludvigsen, *Signature*, 1971. John Zimmerman, "Lear Plant Is City's Entry into Executive Plane Race," *Wichita Eagle-Beacon*, Sunday magazine, April 7, 1963. Also, *Wichita Eagle* report of first flight, October 8, 1963, and crash, June 5, 1964.

236 "The bankers all": WPL on Merv Griffin show, 1970.

237 "They don't ask": *BW*, March 7, 1964.

238, 239 "Call me when": Gilmore, *True*, 1966. Also, "grandmother."

240 Waring story and quotes, Nanney.

241 Coloring book by JL and Curt Brubaker.

241 "What do you": "Lear Takes Controls," *BW*, 1964.

243 "That would be" and following quotes, Grommesh.

243 "That is the best-looking": Boesen, 1971.

245 ML to SL, undated.

245 "That bird looks": Shields.

247 "The airplane performed": Bob Hagan, "First Flight of the Lear Jet," internal memo, October 9, 1963. Following quote, Hank Beaird, "Highlights from Flight Test Report," internal memo, October 7, 1963.

247 "Wasn't that an exciting" and following, Nanney.

247 "My sincere thanks": *Charge!*, November 1, 1963.

247 "They said I": Gilmore, among others.

248 "I'm not going" and following, Beaird.

250 "personally very disgusted": memo of a phone call from Eichen to Weeks, June 12, 1964, FAA Lear Jet certification records.

251 "He really understands" and following quotes, Lacy.

252 "Okay, we've just" and following quote, Beaird.

257 "Tape playback in": Gilmore.

257 "untapped market": Lear Jet press release, October 12, 1965.

27

Interviews: Hank Beaird, DL, JL, ML, SL, TL, Buzz Nanney.
Sources: Boesen, 1966. Shaw, *Esquire*, 1969.

258 "a chance to hear": Shaw.

259 Meyer story, Beaird; Reading Air Show, Martin, and windshield stories, Nanney.

261 SL stories and quotes, SL; TL stories and quotes, TL; DL stories and quotes, DL.

264 "lousy . . . worthy of": DL.

28

Interviews: Sam Auld, Hank Beaird, Don Grommesh, Clay Lacy, JL, ML. Also, DL interviews with Landis Carr, Bob Graf, and Gordon Israel.
Sources: Aircraft accident reports of the National Transportation Safety Board, Wash-

ington, D.C.: "Lear Jet 23, N235R, Rexall Drug and Chemical Company, Clarendon, Texas, April 23, 1966," issued December 19, 1967; "Lear Jet Corporation, Lear Jet Model 23, N804LJ, Jackson, Michigan, October 21, 1965," issued December 11, 1967; "Paul Kelly Flying Service, Inc., Lear Jet Model 23, N243F, Palm Springs, California," issued June 19, 1967. WPL sworn deposition in *Frances Kelly vs. Lear Jet Corporation, The Flying Tiger Line, Inc., et al.*, No. 897,195, Superior Court of Los Angeles, March 25, 1969. *WSJ:* "Lear Jet Tells Owners to Ground 100 Planes Until Hinge Is Checked," May 11, 1966; "Lear Jet Clears 36 Planes in Check of Hinge; 70 to Go," May 12, 1966; "Lear Jet Tells Owners of 2 Jet Models They Can Resume Flying Craft," May 13, 1966.

265 "twenty discrepancies on" as well as other quotes, NTSB report.
267 "Why don't you" and following quotes, JL.
268 "clean up the" and following WPL quotes, Lacy.
269 "He was supposed" and following, JL.
269 "Are you sure" and following quotes, Lacy.
270 "complete electric power": WPL, "To Our Jet Customers," memo, December 10, 1965.
271 "Where airplanes are" and following WPL quotes, "A Flaw Prompts Aircraft Maker to 'Ground' Customer Planes," *National Observer,* May 16, 1966.
272 "You know, Bill": Lacy.
274 "Again I went over": WPL, "Moment of Decision."

29

Interviews: Hank Beaird, James Greenwood, JL, ML, Buzz Nanney.
Sources: "Around the World in Sixty-Five Hours," Lear Jet Corporation brochure, undated. "Four Set 18 Records in Lear Global Flight," *Wichita Beacon,* May 26, 1966. "Globe-Circling Flights Not All Glamor, Fun," *Miami Herald,* June 12, 1966. Lear Jet Corporation news releases, June 2 and July 8, 1966.

275 "How long will": Beaird.
276 WPL to JL, summer 1962.
277 "Put handcuffs on him" and following, Nanney.
278 "Why are you": ML.
279 All dialogue during the race and most description, JL and JL's unpublished recollections of flight.
284 "Boy, the old man": Beaird.

30

Interviews: Sam Auld, Carl Bell, James Greenwood, Fran Jabara, BL, JL, ML, Dick Millar, Buzz Nanney, William Webster. Also, DL interviews with Justin Dart and ML.
Sources: *Annual Report 1967,* Lear Jet Industries, Inc. Lear Jet Incorporated news releases, July 8, August 18, November 5, 1966. "Notice of Annual Meeting and Proxy Statement," Lear Jet Industries, September 11, 1967. SEC, *Lear Jet Corporation,* Form S-1, November 1, 1965. Ashley, *Flight,* October 1965. Bulban, *AW,* 1966. Brown, *AW,* 1965.

Klass, *AW*, 1966. "Lear Jet Designing Twin-Engine," *AW*, 1965. *NYT:* February 4, May 5, August 19, September 14 and 20, 1966; March 2 and April 25, 1967. *WSJ:* January 4, May 25, September 12, October 11, 12, 31, 1966; April 10 and 11, July 24, 1967.

284 "purred like kittens": John Zimmerman, "Flight Summary," Lear Jet Corporation, undated news release.

287 "You know, you've": Nanney.

288 "Buzz, what am" and following, Nanney.

290 "I do not propose": anonymous.

290 "There is nothing": Gilmore, *True*, 1966.

291 Dart story and quotes, ML to DL.

292 "I won't take": Jabara.

292 "Everybody knows what": Webster.

292 "Is Bill all right" and following, ML to DL.

31

Interviews: Sam Auld, Gunnar Christensen, Nils Eklund, Louise Gosage, Claude Hunter, Clay Lacy, DL, ML, Clarence Thornton, Maxine Zimmerman. Also, DL interviews with ML and Buzz Nanney.

Sources: Shaw, *Esquire*, 1969. "Petition by Leareno Development, Inc., for a Declaratory Order in the Matter of CPC 689, Sub 1, Held by Sierra Pacific Power Company," transcripts of a hearing, October 19, 1976, Reno, Nevada, before the Public Service Commission of Nevada, No. 849.

297 "What the hell": Nanney.

297 "up the walls": ML to DL.

299 "Bob Cummings gave": Lacy.

299 "Bill, you just": Gosage.

299 ML to SL letter, January 22, 1968.

300 "Where do you think": ML.

300 "The only plane": Boesen, 1971, among others.

300–301 Latimore story and dialogue, Nanney.

32 and 33

Interviews: Sam Auld, Delos Hood, Harry Jackson, ML, PL, TL, Buzz Nanney, Dorothy Olson, Donald Wildermuth.

Sources: Boesen, *True*, 1973. *California Steam Bus Project Final Report*, January 1973, NTIS, PB-217 508. "Damn the Smog," *Forbes*, 1971. Diehl, *West*, 1972. Einstein, *West*, 1969. Garrison, *Flying*, 1970. "Is the Gas Turbine the Ultimate Engine?" *Fleet Management News*, January 1971. Jamison, *Science*, 1969. Kimmis Hendrick, "Lear Says Steam Auto Not Antismog Answer," *Christian Science Monitor*, January 28, 1970. "The Incurables," *Forbes*, 1969. "Lear: The Steam King," *Motor Trend*, February 1971. Coleman McCarthy, "A Car with Everything but Full Steam Ahead," *Washington Post*, October 17, 1970. John McDonald, "Father of 540 MPH Jet Favors Ceiling on Car Horse Power," *Chicago Tribune*, March 16, 1970. Roberts, *Playboy*, 1972. Wells, *Motor Trend*, 1969.

302 "The janitor has": Shaw, *Esquire*, 1969.
303 "I want to": Ottum, *Sports Illustrated*, 1969.
303 "They are not only": YPO speech.
305 "I liked him": Ottum, 1969.
305 "I am going": Ottum, 1969.
308 "A steam engine": "Steam Cars Try to Get Back in the Running," *BW*, 1969.
308 "I've never had": Smith, *Weekend Magazine*, 1970.
310 "It's the answer": *LAT*, September 1, 1970.
310 "Eddie, when I": YPO speech.
311 "Come to Leareno": Patrick Bedard, *Car and Driver*, April 1972.
311 Bedard, April 1972.
313 "I have been forced": *Gallery*, November 1973.

34 and 35

Interviews: Sam Auld, Lew Axford, Gian Carlo Bertelli, Gunnar Christensen, John Ehrlichman, Delos Hood, Harry Jackson, DL, JL, ML, PL, SL, TL, Lewis Levy, Torch Lewis, Dorothy Olson, Richard Tracy, Don Wildermuth, Rose Mary Woods. Also, DL interviews with John Saunders and Red Martin.
Sources: "W. Lear's Contract for Steam Run Auto Is Vaporized by EPA," *WSJ*, January 31, 1974.
315 "Let's go around" and rest of JL-WPL stories, JL.
316 WPL test, JL and Axford.
317 JL critique, July 15, 1971.
317 "bullshit" taped conversation between JL and WPL, summer 1971; WPL to JL, July 1971; FAA to JL, November 5, 1971.
318 "desperately," "Gian Carlo's young": ML to SL, October 19 and June 5, 1973.
319 "I want you here": WPL to Bertelli, April 18, 1973. Bertelli to WPL, March 12, 1973.
319 "enormously relieved": ML to PL, February 20, 1975.
320 "professorial nincompoops": Diehl, 1974.
320 "little bastard": *Gallery*, November 1973.
320 Bertelli report, "The Lear Companies," May 15, 1974.
321 "loads of money": Bertelli.
321 "an unbelievable refining": unmarked document, Lear archives.
321 "provincial": Bertelli.
323 "singing and clowning": ML.
324 "Harry, . . . just put": Jackson.
325 "raging" and following, Bertelli.
326 "senile": ML.
326 "Goddamn it, I": Olson. Also, "If I catch" and following.
327, 328 Heiser story, Lewis. Also, WPL introduction.
328 "It was great": *Nevada State Journal*, July 1, 1975.
328 WPL to Goldwater and Ford, September 17, 1974.
328 Nixon campaign contribution, ML; job request, JL; "water on Lear's steam," Ehrlichman. WPL's FBI records show he was considered for a job by the White House.
329 "Let's get back": ML.

36

Interviews: Sam Auld, Harry Halton, Fred Kearns, Ron Pickler, Rodney Schapel, Richard Tracy.
Sources: WPL-Canadair contract, April 2, 1976, February 4, 1977, January 20, 1978, and February 10, 1978. "Memorandum of Understanding," Canadair Ltd. and WPL, June 28 and November 18, 1977. Bulban, *AW*, December, 1974. *Learstar 600* and *Learstar 600 Aircraft Program*, Reno: Lear Companies, undated.

334 "design responsibility with only": WPL to Kearns, February 10, 1977.
334 "keenly disappointed": Kearns.
334 "This plane meets": *BW*, November 1976.
334 "departed significantly," "fineness ratio": *BW*, November 1976.
334 "The Canadians are": *Forbes*, 1977.
335 "I think you": WPL to Kearns, February 10, 1977.
335 "I'm losing my mind": Levy. Also, following.
338 "always open and": Tracy. Also, WPL quote to Kearns.
340 "What are you doing?" and following, Schapel.

37, 38, 39, and Epilogue

Interviews: Sam Auld, Hank Beaird, Charles Bell, Ruth Brown, Gunnar Christensen, Jane Crooks, Louise Gosage, Eli Grubic, Harry Jackson, Clay Lacy, Ann Lear, BL, DL, JL, Marilee Lear, ML, PL, SL, TL, Buzz Nanney, Dorothy Olson, Ron Pickler, Rodney Schapel, Richard Tracy, Maxine Zimmerman. Also, DL interview with Milton Weilenmann.
Sources: "Canadair Challenger Is Flight Tested," *AW*, December 4, 1978. "Canadair Challenger Flies," *Professional Pilot*, December 1978. "Canadair Delivers 100th Challenger, Reorganizes Company," *Professional Pilot*, May 1984. "Configuration Set for Lear Fan 2100," *AW*, December 4, 1978. Jack King, "Business Jet Direct Operating Costs," *Professional Pilot*, November 1978. "The Lady and the Fan," *Guideposts*, March 1982. "Inventor's Widow Carries On Dream of Lear Fan Turboprop," *Tulsa World*, April 24, 1983. "Lear Fan Announces Preliminary Accord to Finance New Plane," *WSJ*, September 1, 1982. "Lear Fan Business Plane Faultless in Maiden Flight," UPI, January 3, 1981. "Lear Fan Closes the Hangar," *Fortune*, July 9, 1984. "Lear Fan Design Changed," *Aviation News*, June 1978. "Lear's Wife Pilots His Company Now," *San Francisco Examiner*, December 10, 1979. J. Mac McClellan, "Lear Fan: Big Bite into the Business Fleet," *Flying*, May 1981. Rush Loving, "The Dramatic Struggle over Bill Lear's Dream Plane," *Fortune*, April 9, 1979. "More Bad News for Belfast," *Time*, June 11, 1984. "Queen Lear," *Time*, July 7, 1980. "Saga in Epoxy," *Time*, November 15, 1982; as well as BL, JL, and Arthur Godfrey letters to the editor, December 20, 1982.

343 WPL-JL dialogue, JL.
344 Herman's story, JL taped interview with Herman.
346 "managerial worries" and following, Tracy.
351 WPL to Auld, March 6, 1978.
354 "Are you in": Gosage.
356 "Turn around!": Olson.

356 "Are you afraid" and following, Nanney.
357 "I don't want": Zimmerman.
357 "When you're an": "A Plastic Plane, Unmistakably Lear," *Washington Post*, April 25, 1978.
357 Gunnar-WPL, story and dialogue, Christensen.
359 "I want to go": ML.
359 "Mommie, Mommie" and following, Crooks.

Index

392

automatic (ADF), 89–91, 92,
99–107 *passim,* 124; SCR–269,
100–102; Learomatic navigator,
102–4, 108, 137; Lear Orienter,
137. *See also* Autopilot;
Radio(s)
Doble, Abner, and Doble
Steamer, 302, 303, 304
Doolittle, Gen. Jimmy, 230
Douglas, Donald, 158
Douglas Aircraft Company, 108,
193, 196, 217, 333, 340

Earhart, Amelia, 52, 57, 74–75,
77–78
Eastern Airlines, 73
Eaton Corporation, 147
Eclipse Aviation, 85
Edlund, Bee, 96
Eisenhower, Dwight D., 182
Eklund, Nils, 142–51 *passim,* 158–
59, 164, 178, 199, 224
Ellis, Bob, 23–24, 92, 126
Ellis, Ethel, *see* Lear, Mrs.
William Powell (first wife)
Ellis, Moses, 23
Entratter, Jack, 114
EPA (Environmental Protection
Agency), 313, 314, 320
Esquire magazine, 2, 135

FAA (Federal Aviation Administration), 197, 216, 267, 277, 281,
316–18 *passim,* 328; Lear breaks
rules of, 3, 259, 357; certification by, 193, 221, 238, 243,
248–52 *passim,* 257, 270, 341,
346; and Lear Jet, 271, 273
Fairchild Aerial Camera Corporation, 80–83 *passim,* 165, 169,
193
Fan Holdings, Inc., 362. *See also*
Lear Fan
Faulkner, David, 267
FBI, 30, 31, 32, 121, 127, 183, 185
Ferris, Dr. Robert, 63, 64, 106

FFA (Swiss firm), 218, 219, 220,
234
Firestone, Leonard, 297
First Christian Church (Tulsa),
23, 29
Fitzsimmons Veterans Hospital
(Denver), 17
"Flaming coffins," 7, 9, 10, 154
Fletcher, Thomas, 35
Flightcraft Company, 333
Flying magazine, 189
Flying Tiger Line, 267
Fokker Aircraft Company, 56,
108
Forbes magazine, 334
Ford, Gerald R., 1, 328
Ford, Henry, 303; and Ford
Motor Company, 256
Ford Trimotor ("Tin Goose"),
48, 56
Fortune magazine, 2
Franklin Institute (Philadelphia), 2

Galvin, Paul, and Galvin Manu-
facturing (later Motorola)
Company, 39–54 *passim,* 59,
60, 66, 87. *See also* Radio(s)
Gates, Charles C., and Gates
Learjet, 290–93 *passim,* 301–2,
303, 329, 330, 346. *See also*
Lear Jet
Gates, Howard, 40
Gelin, Lazar, 84, 91, 93, 104
General Dynamics Corporation,
331
General Electric Company, 59,
100, 230, 242, 284. *See also* "Big
Five"
General Motors Corporation, 41,
256, 310, 313, 320
Germyn, Jerry, 278
Ginsbury, Sylva, 175
Glenn Martin Company, 84. *See
also* Martin, Glenn
Godfrey, Arthur, 268, 274, 275,
277–79, 283, 284